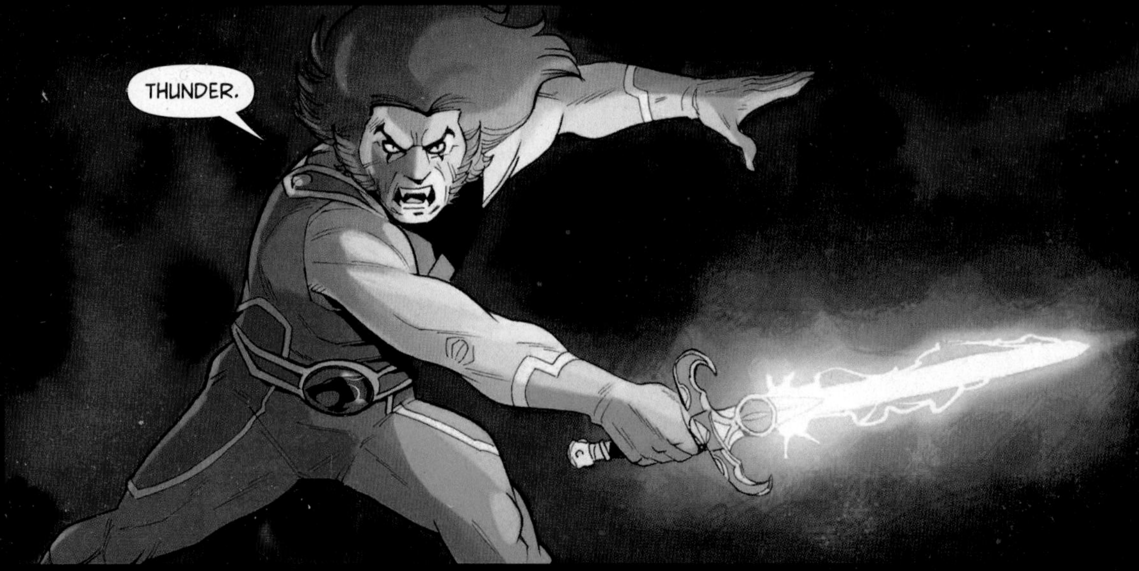
THUNDER.

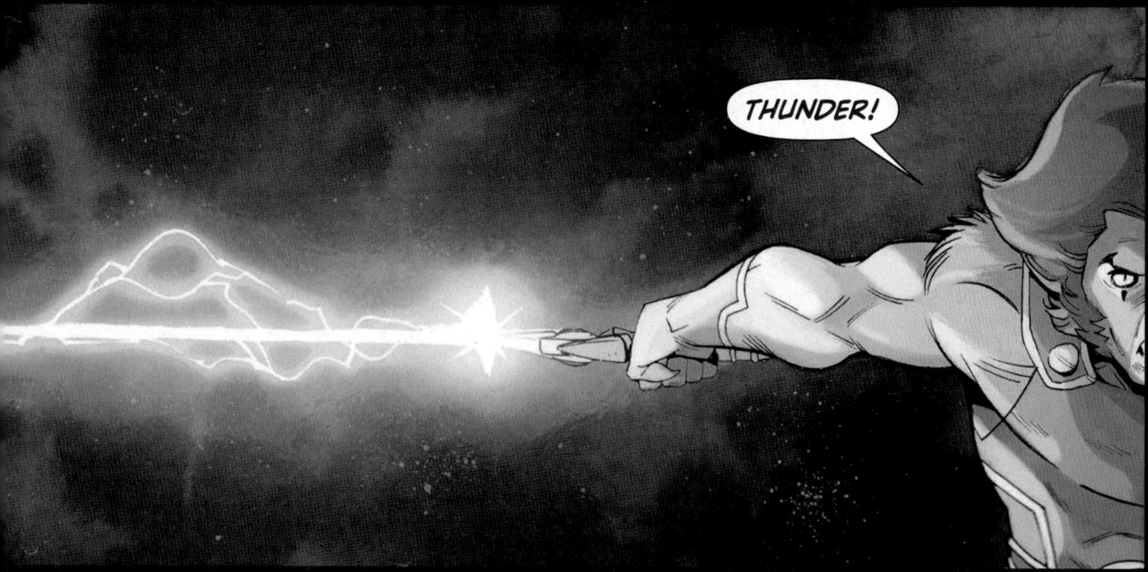
THUNDER!

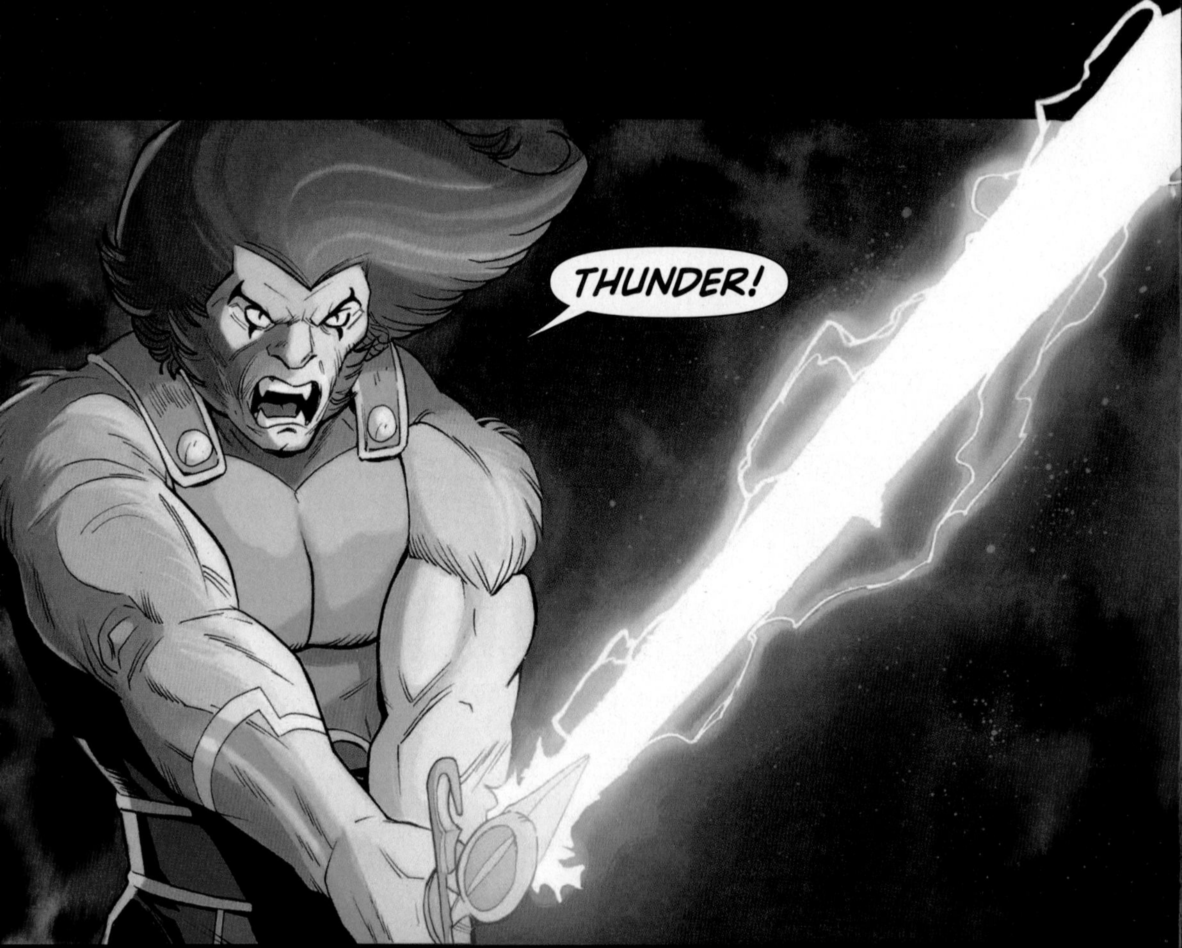
THUNDER!

THUNDERCATS™

OMENS

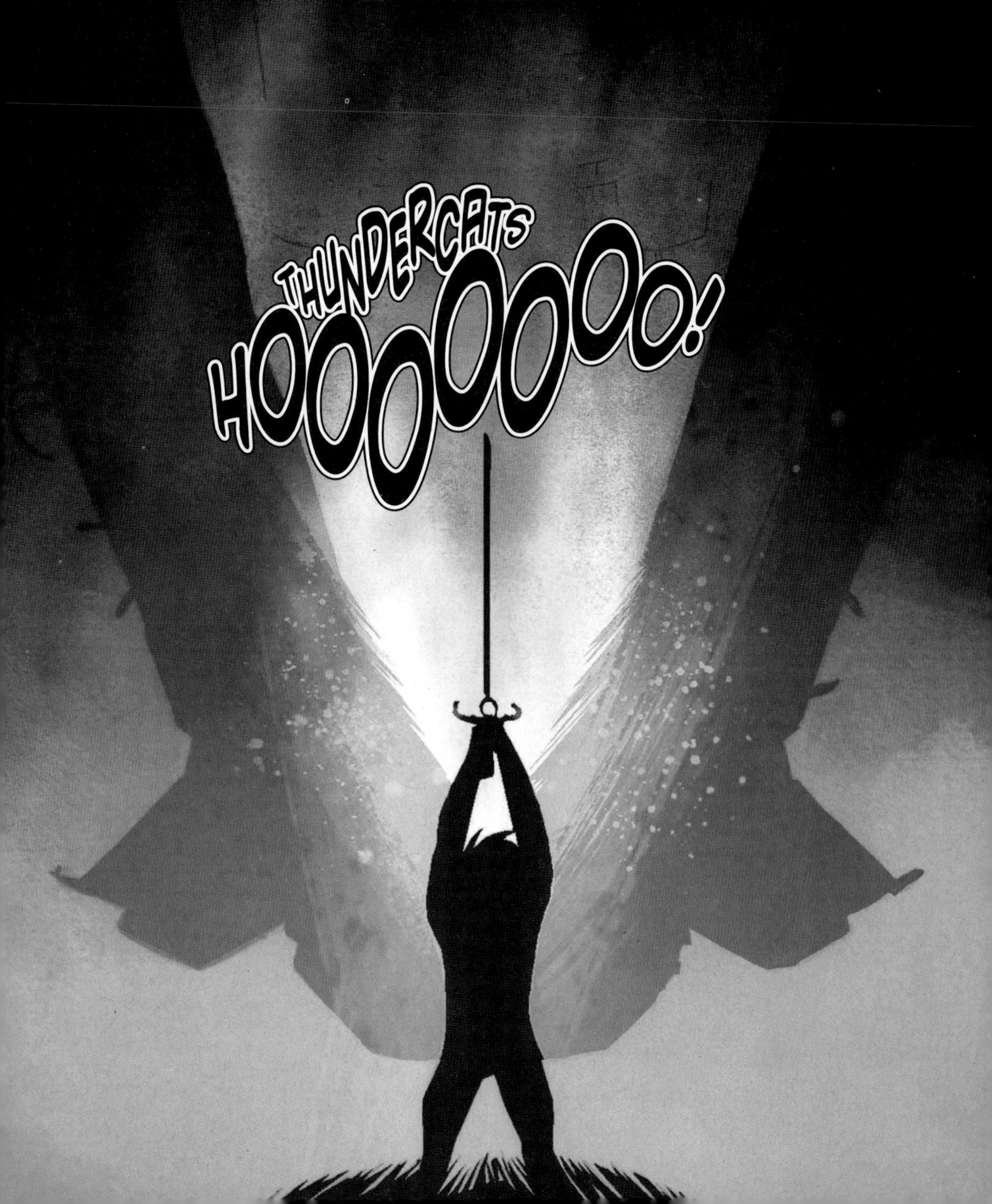
THUNDERCATS HOOOOOOOO!

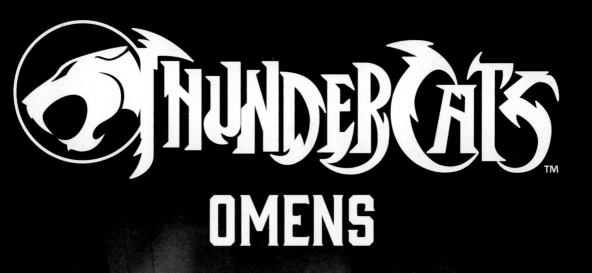

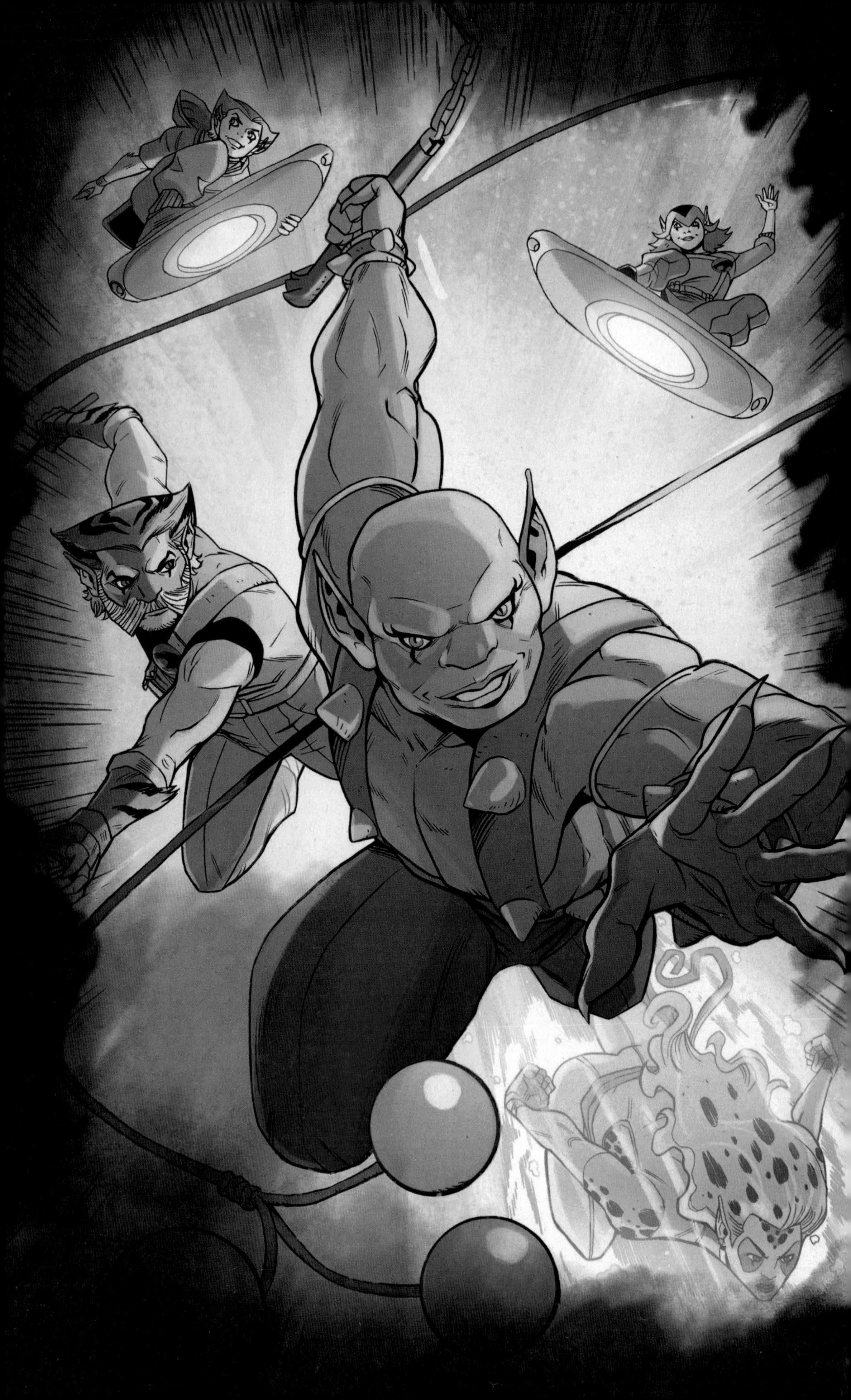

WRITER **DECLAN SHALVEY** [#1-4]

ARTIST **DREW MOSS** [#1-4]

WRITER/ARTIST **STEPHEN MOONEY** [#5]

COLORISTS **CHIARA DI FRANCIA** AND **MARTINA PIGNEDOLI** [#1-4]

COLORIST **MAURO GULMA** [#5]

LETTERER **JEFF ECKLEBERRY**

COLLECTION COVERS BY **DAVID NAKAYAMA**

COLLECTION DESIGN BY **NICK PENTZ**

PACKAGED & EDITED BY **NATE COSBY**

COLLECTION EDITOR **IVAN COHEN**

SPECIAL THANKS TO **JOSH ANDERSON, KURTIS ESTES** AND **BENJAMIN HARPER**

DYNAMITE.

Online at www.dynamite.com
Facebook /dynamitecomics
Instagram /dynamitecomics
Twitter @dynamitecomics

Nick Barrucci, CEO / Publisher
Juan Collado, President / COO
Brandon Dante Primavera, V.P. of IT and Operations

Joe Rybandt, Executive Editor
Matt Idelson, Senior Editor

Alexis Persson, Creative Director
Cathleen Heard, Senior Graphic Designer
Nick Pentz, Graphic Designer
Matthew Michalak, Graphic Designer

Alan Payne, V.P. of Sales and Marketing
Vince Letterio, Director of Direct Market Sales
Rex Wang, Director of Sales and Branding
Vincent Faust, Marketing Coordinator

Jim Kuhoric, Vice President of Product Development
Jay Spence, Director of Product Development
Mariano Nicieza, Director of Research & Development

PAPERBACK ISBN: 978-1-5241-2602-5
HC ISBN: 978-1-5241-2603-2
SPECIAL EDITION ISBN: 978-1-5241-2656-8

First Printing 10 9 8 7 6 5 4 3 2 1

INTRODUCTION

Horns blare as a blood-red screen flashes a roaring black cat head that cracks like a whip and flashes across the screen in a stream of light, striking across the cosmos towards a mysterious planet.

An ethereal voice whispers the word… " *ThunderCats.*"

And I was hooked.

When editor Nate Cosby offered me the unique opportunity to helm a new iteration of ThunderCats, it was exciting from the very start. It is amazing that over three decades after seeing that flash of red strike a silver sword, wielded by a powerful, hulking cat-like hero… that excitement remained just as powerful.

While I'm definitely of the generation that watched the original ThunderCats cartoon (my Lion-O action figure didn't survive his battle with my sister and being thrown down the stairs, but my Mumm-Ra figure in in a box somewhere in my mum's house), I was also just a little too young to remember all the detailed lore of the show. The spark of that infamous title sequence remained though, which is what attracted me to take on this project.

That is what I've wanted to channel into this book; the immortal excitement that the original ThunderCats introduced. And to give new readers a chance to fall for these characters and give original fans something to bring them back home… back to Third Earth.

From the very start, I knew the success of this book would be down to the artist. Drew Moss was the first and last name considered as Nate and I were spit-balling (hair-balling?) ideas of what the book could be. Without compelling visuals, this new incarnation could easily fall apart. While I got to have my fun in that regard in creating a visual identity with the covers, at the end of the day, whoever was going to be drawing these characters, reinterpreting them as well as the iconography of the show… the success would truly rest on them. The incredible work Drew has done on this book is what its success is truly built on, in my opinion. We clicked together immediately, and I hope we get

to develop this story together for as long as possible. Martina Pignedoli's colour work and Jeff Eckleberry's wonderful lettering have also really levelled up the book into the visual feast I was hoping for. Not all projects come together so wonderfully, but I feel so lucky that this book has formed together so beautifully.

What I failed to realise when taking this project on, and that's has become clear to me since, is that there has been a huge demand for new ThunderCats stories, for a fresh take where new and old fans can find a way back. I'm delighted to have been a part in delivering that and am hugely proud to see the joy and enthusiasm this book has been delivering to readers.

That blood-red crackle is flashing once more. Once again, after all this time, the ThunderCats are loose.

Declan Shalvey
Ennis, Ireland,
May, 2024.

ONE

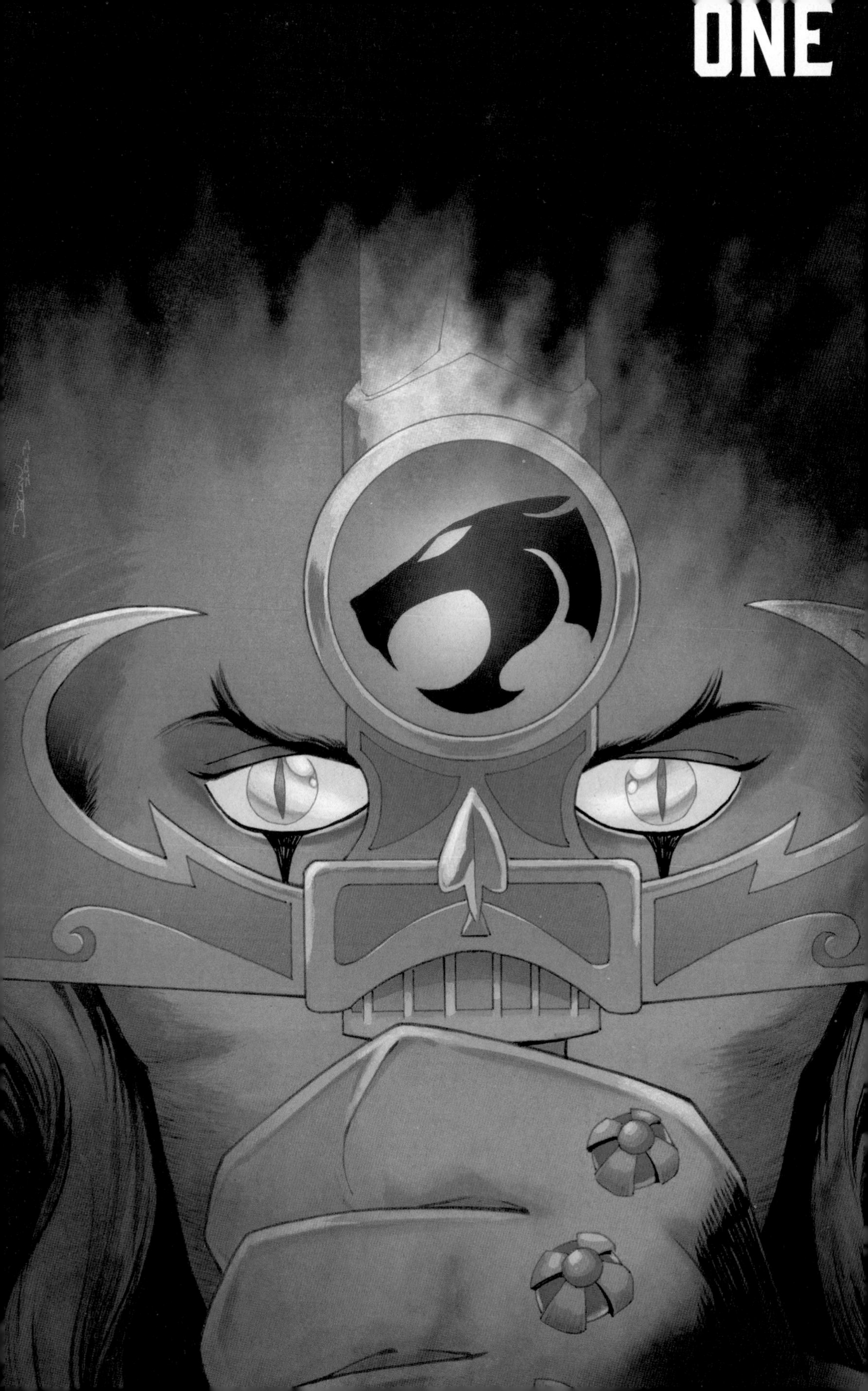

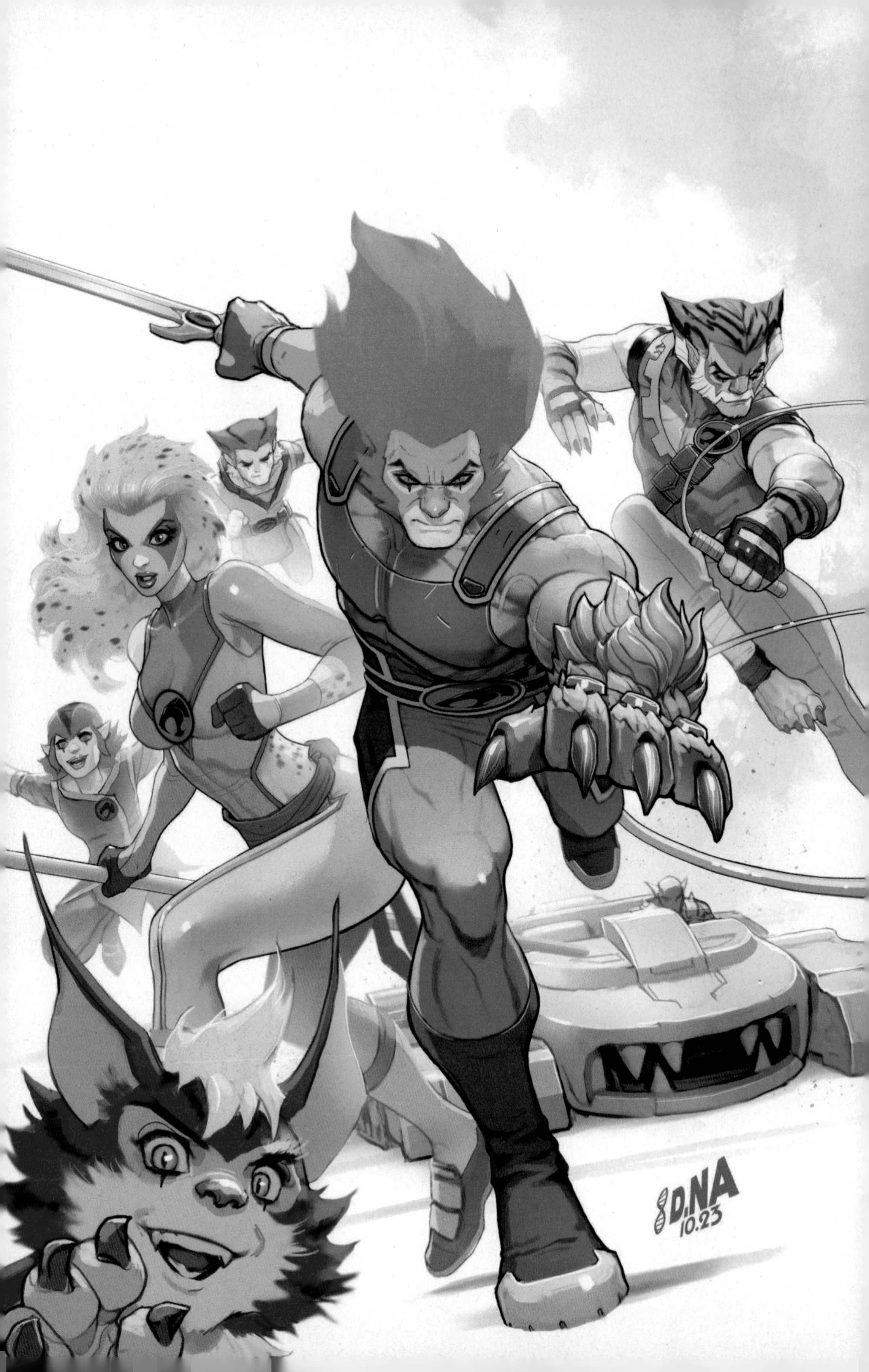
D.NA
10.23

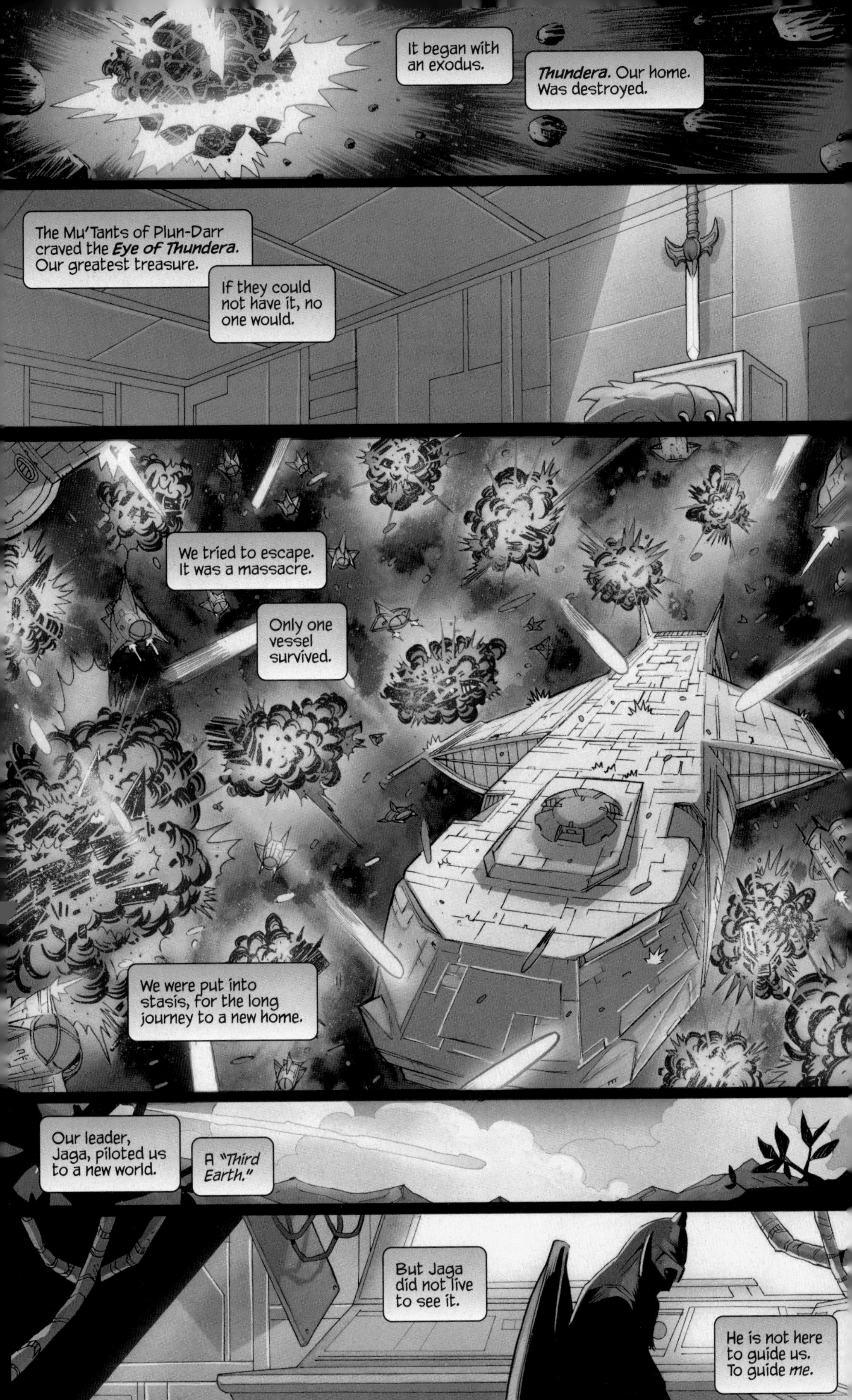

It began with an exodus.
Thundera. Our home. Was destroyed.
The Mu'Tants of Plun-Darr craved the ***Eye of Thundera***. Our greatest treasure.
If they could not have it, no one would.
We tried to escape. It was a massacre.
Only one vessel survived.
We were put into stasis, for the long journey to a new home.
Our leader, Jaga, piloted us to a new world.
A "*Third Earth.*"
But Jaga did not live to see it.
He is not here to guide us. To guide *me*.

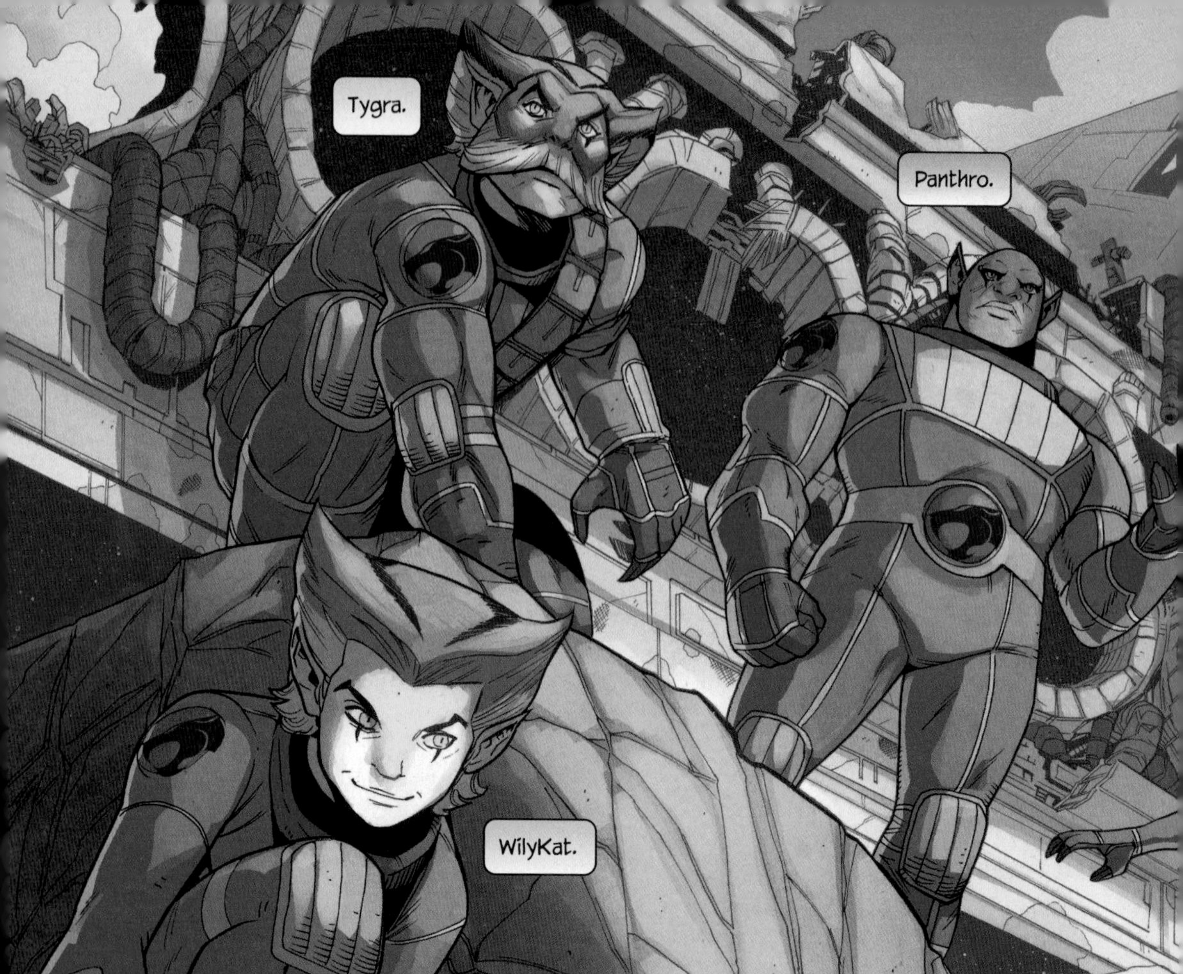
Tygra.
Panthro.
WilyKat.

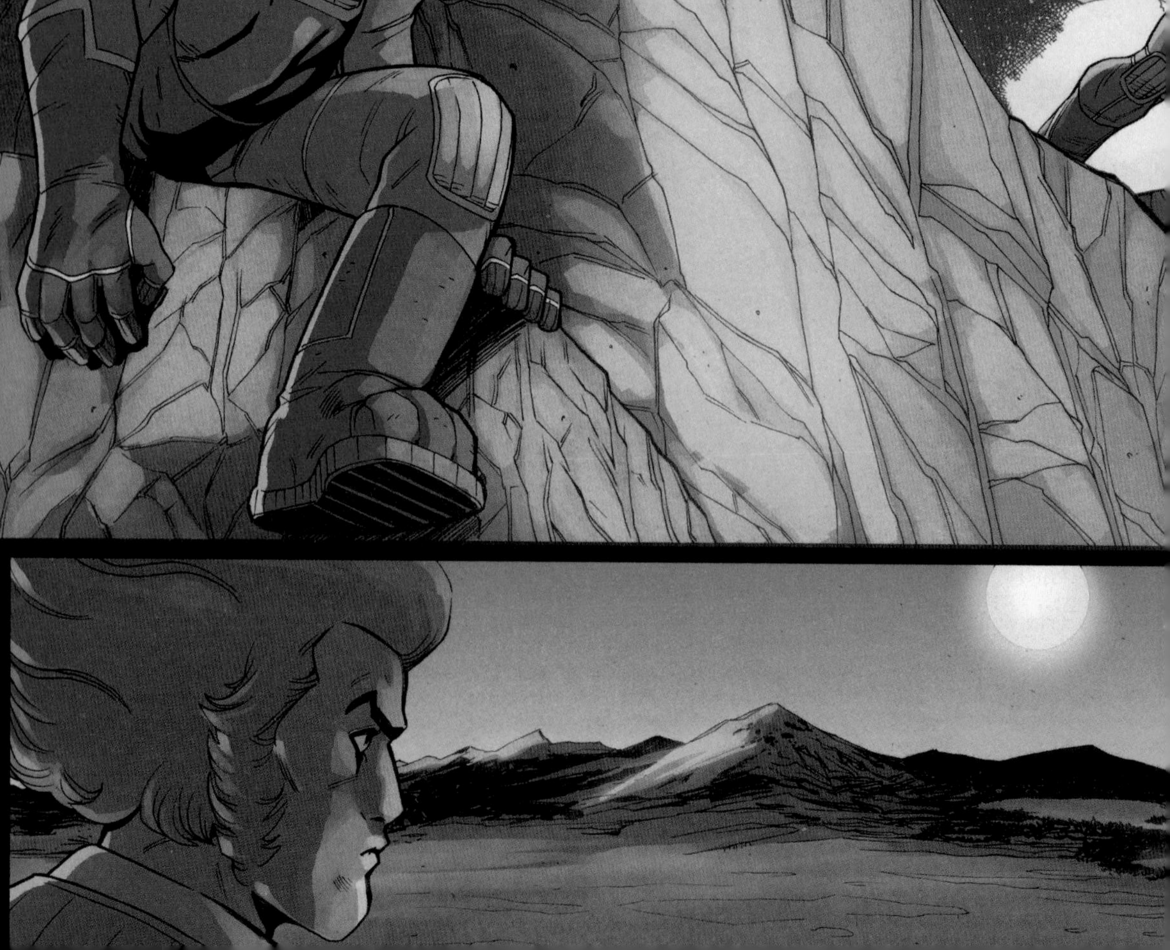

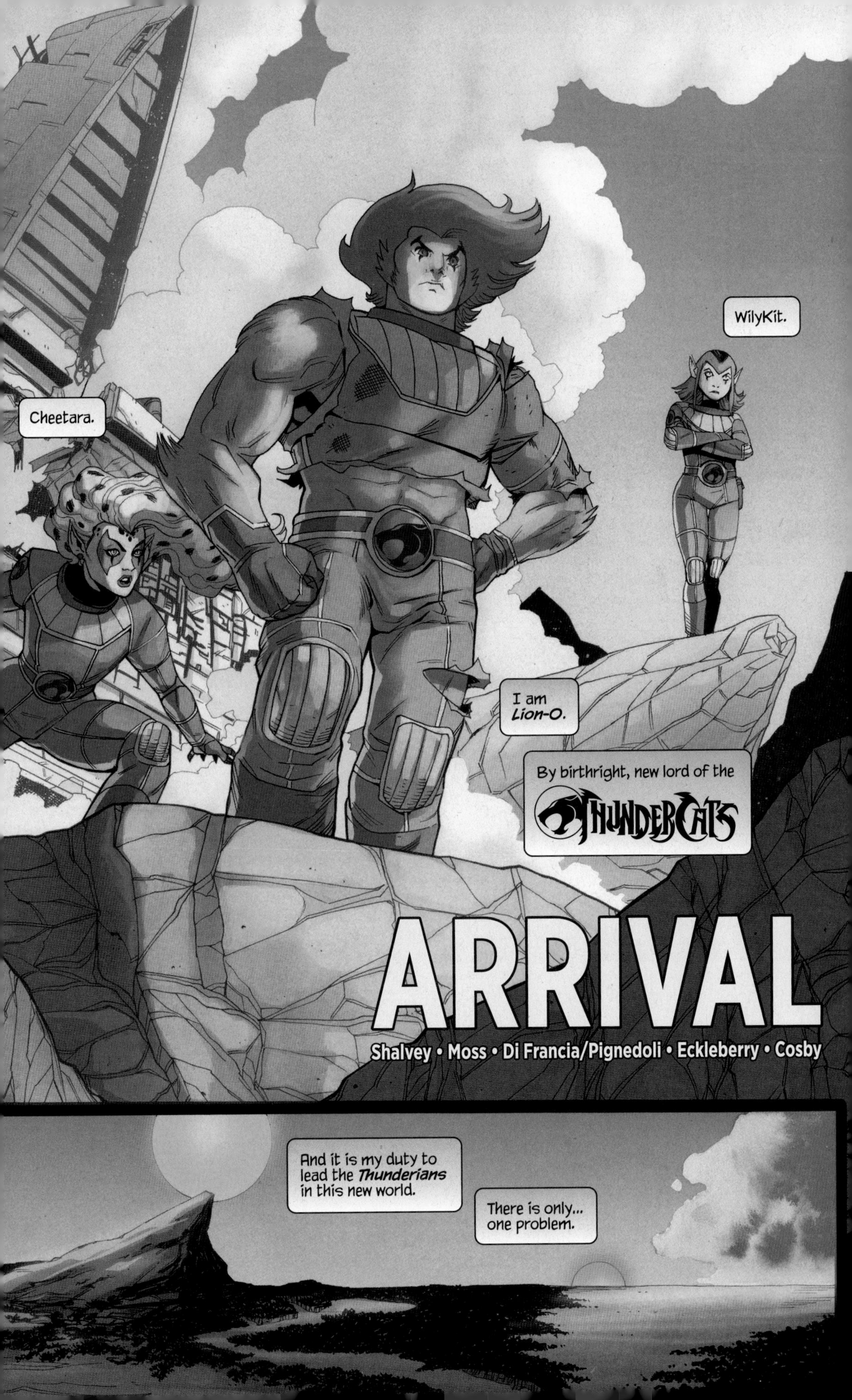
Cheetara.
WilyKit.
I am Lion-O.
By birthright, new lord of the
THUNDERCATS
ARRIVAL
Shalvey • Moss • Di Francia/Pignedoli • Eckleberry • Cosby
And it is my duty to lead the Thunderians in this new world.
There is only... one problem.

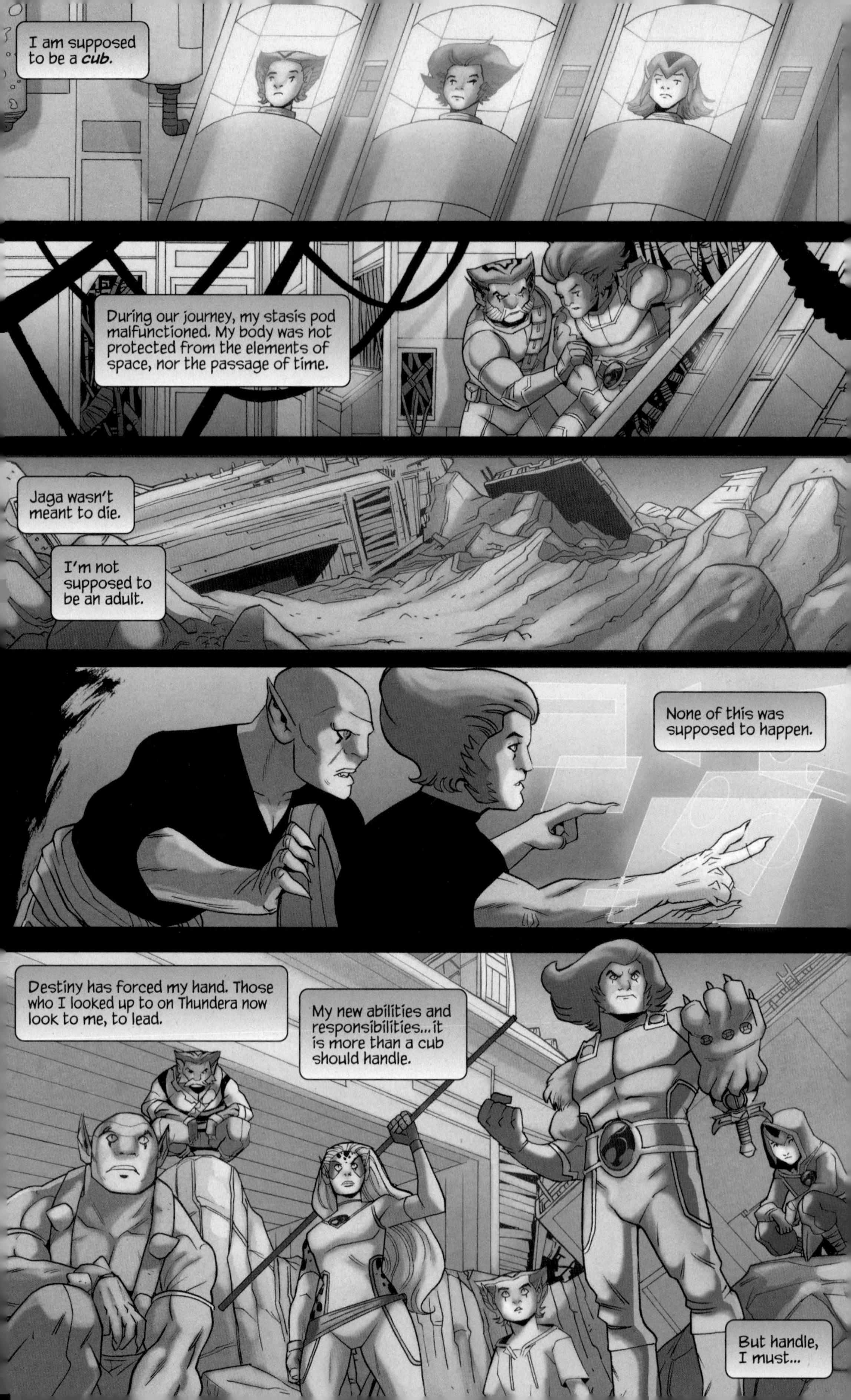
I am supposed to be a *cub.*
During our journey, my stasis pod malfunctioned. My body was not protected from the elements of space, nor the passage of time.
Jaga wasn't meant to die.
I'm not supposed to be an adult.
None of this was supposed to happen.
Destiny has forced my hand. Those who I looked up to on Thundera now look to me, to lead.
My new abilities and responsibilities...it is more than a cub should handle.
But handle, I must...

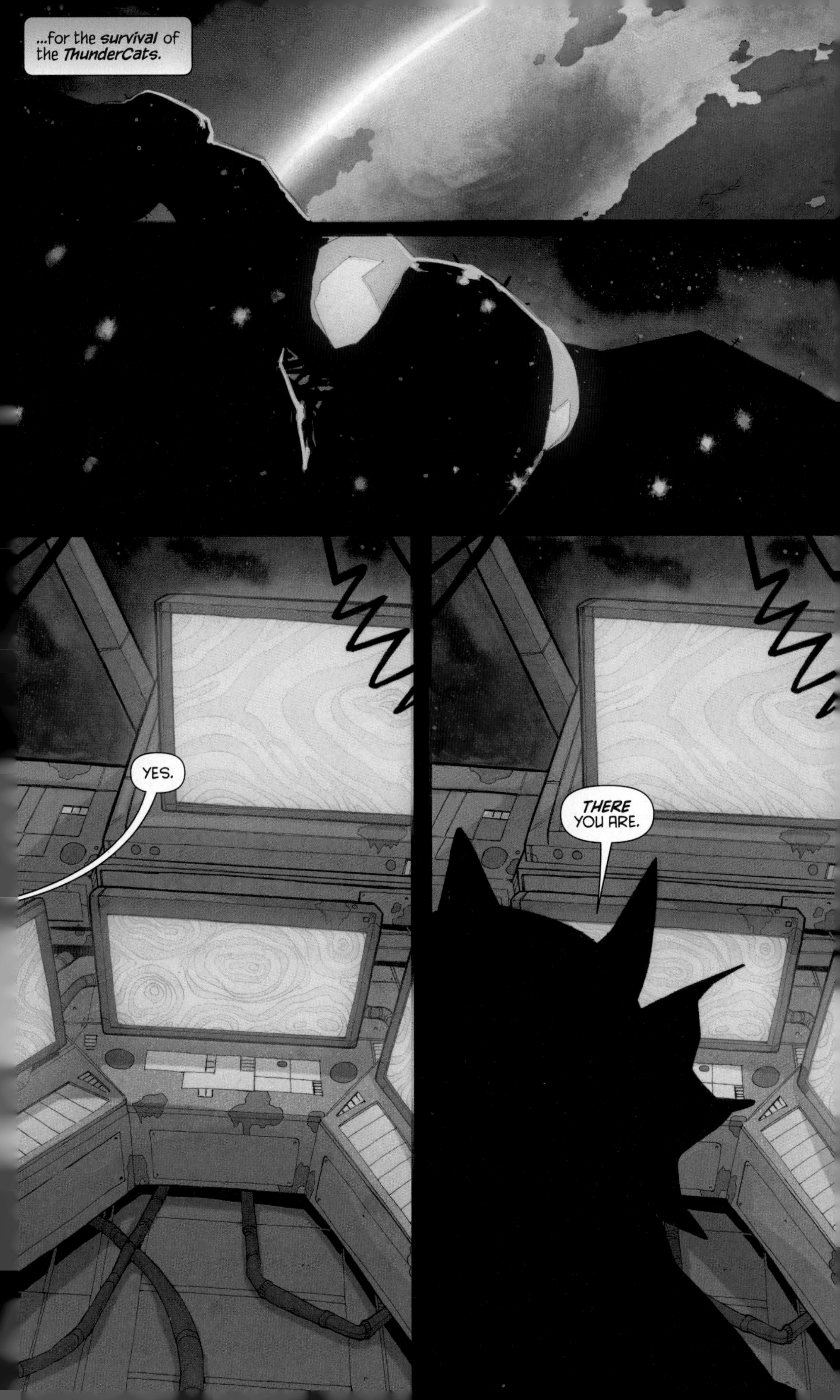
...for the *survival* of the *ThunderCats.*
YES.
THERE YOU ARE.

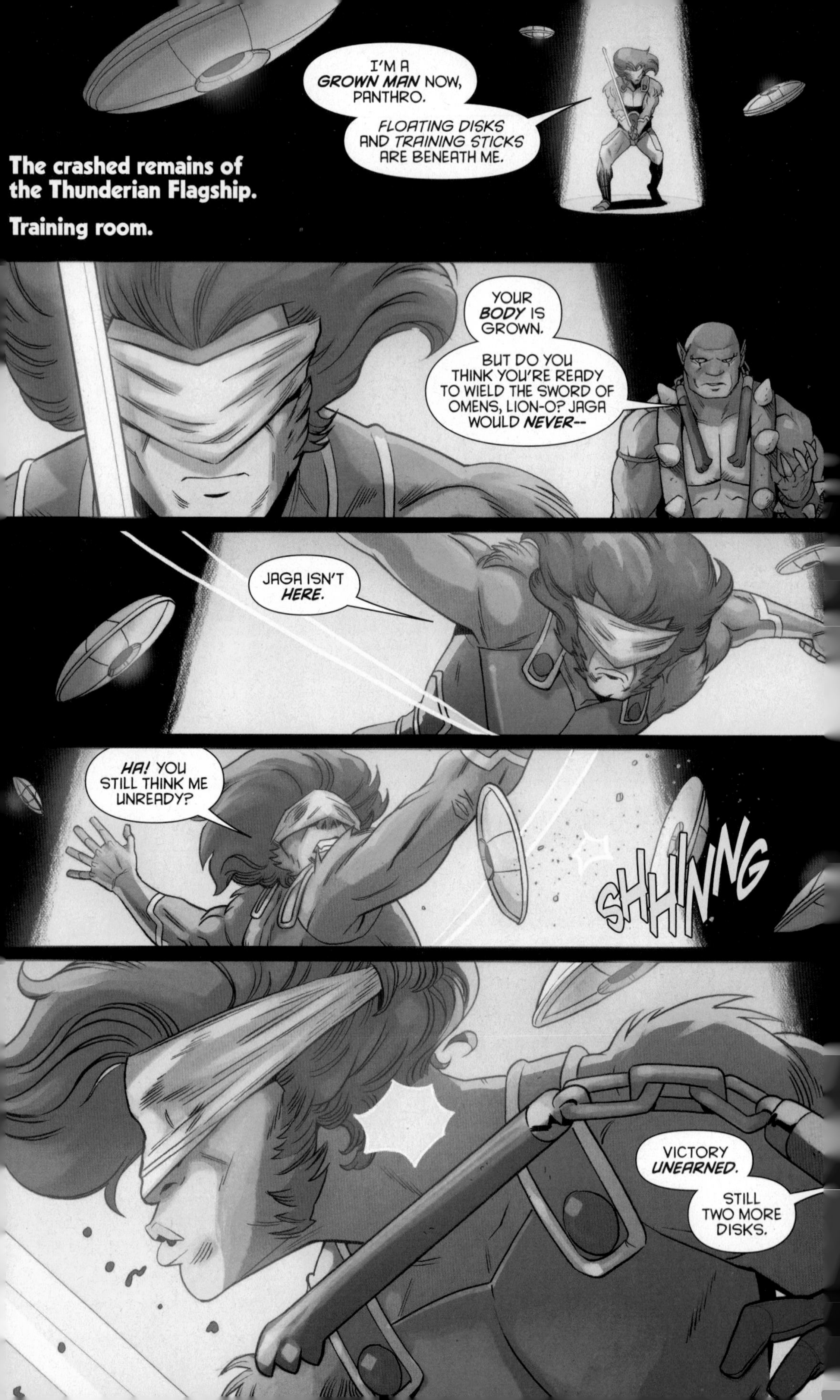
The crashed remains of the Thunderian Flagship.
Training room.
I'M A GROWN MAN NOW, PANTHRO.
FLOATING DISKS AND TRAINING STICKS ARE BENEATH ME.
YOUR BODY IS GROWN.
BUT DO YOU THINK YOU'RE READY TO WIELD THE SWORD OF OMENS, LION-O? JAGA WOULD NEVER--
JAGA ISN'T HERE.
HA! YOU STILL THINK ME UNREADY?
SHHING
VICTORY UNEARNED.
STILL TWO MORE DISKS.

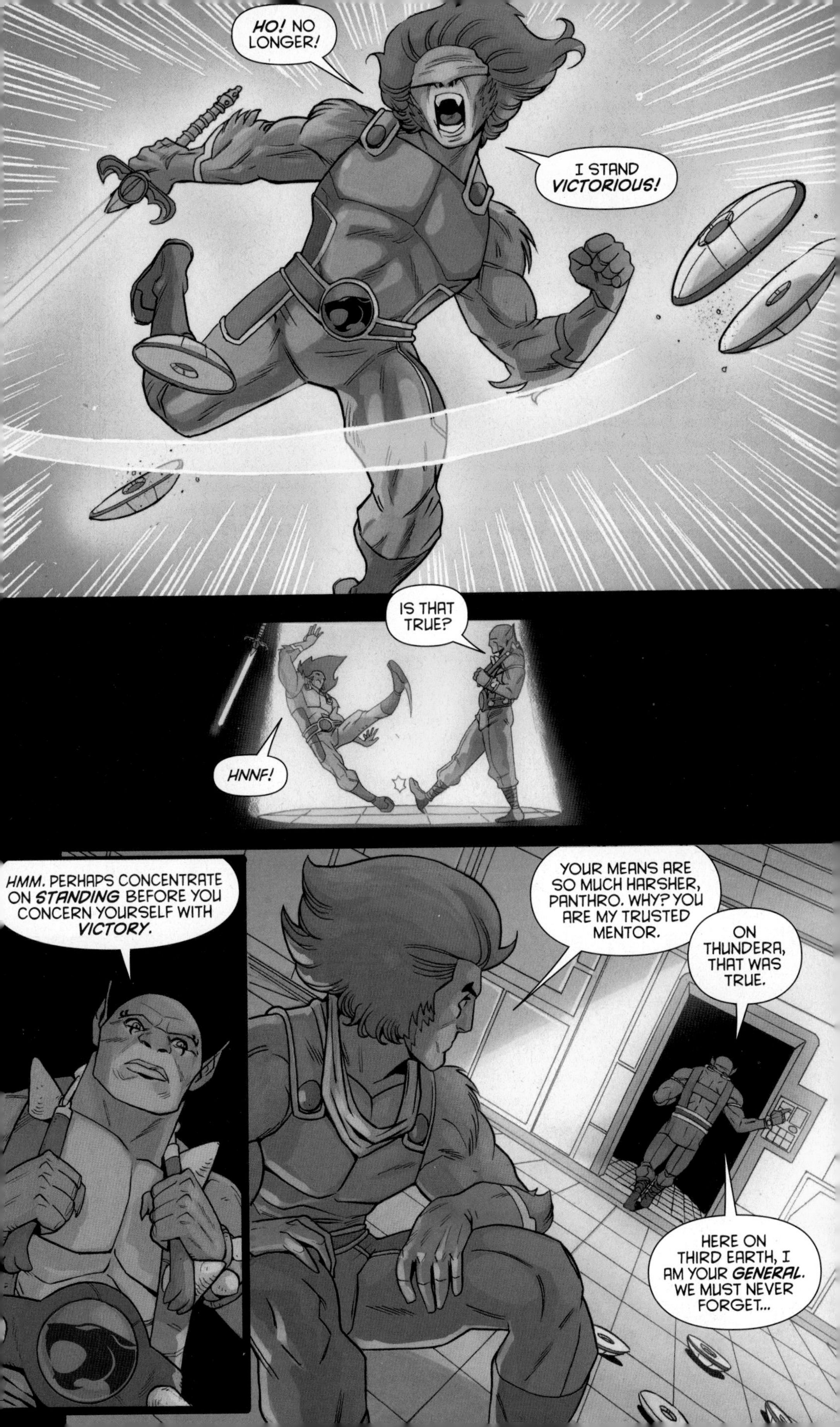

HO! NO LONGER!
I STAND VICTORIOUS!
IS THAT TRUE?
HNNF!
HMM. PERHAPS CONCENTRATE ON STANDING BEFORE YOU CONCERN YOURSELF WITH VICTORY.
YOUR MEANS ARE SO MUCH HARSHER, PANTHRO. WHY? YOU ARE MY TRUSTED MENTOR.
ON THUNDERA, THAT WAS TRUE.
HERE ON THIRD EARTH, I AM YOUR GENERAL. WE MUST NEVER FORGET...

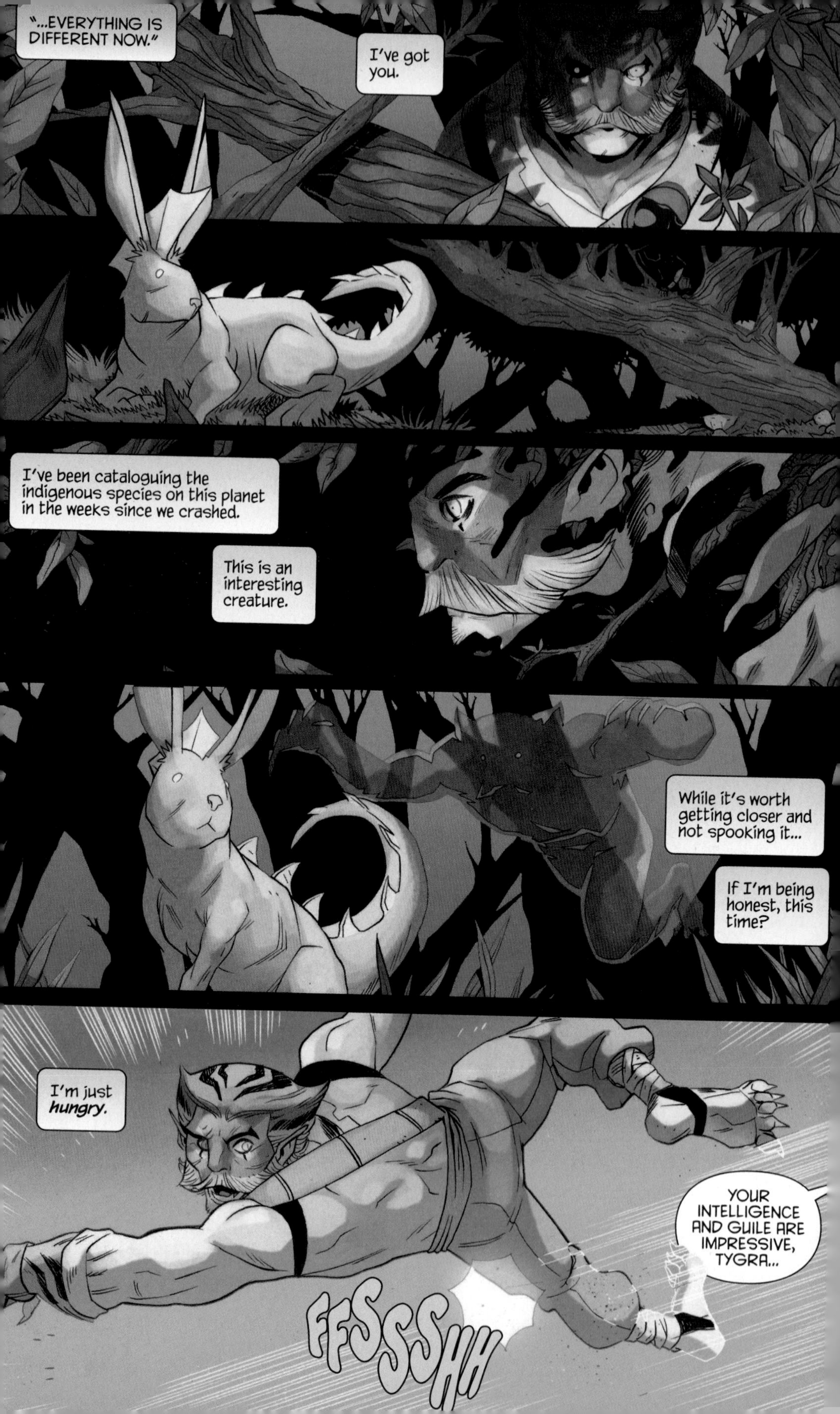
"...EVERYTHING IS DIFFERENT NOW."
I've got you.
I've been cataloguing the indigenous species on this planet in the weeks since we crashed.
This is an interesting creature.
While it's worth getting closer and not spooking it...
If I'm being honest, this time?
I'm just *hungry*.
YOUR INTELLIGENCE AND GUILE ARE IMPRESSIVE, TYGRA...
FFSSSSHH

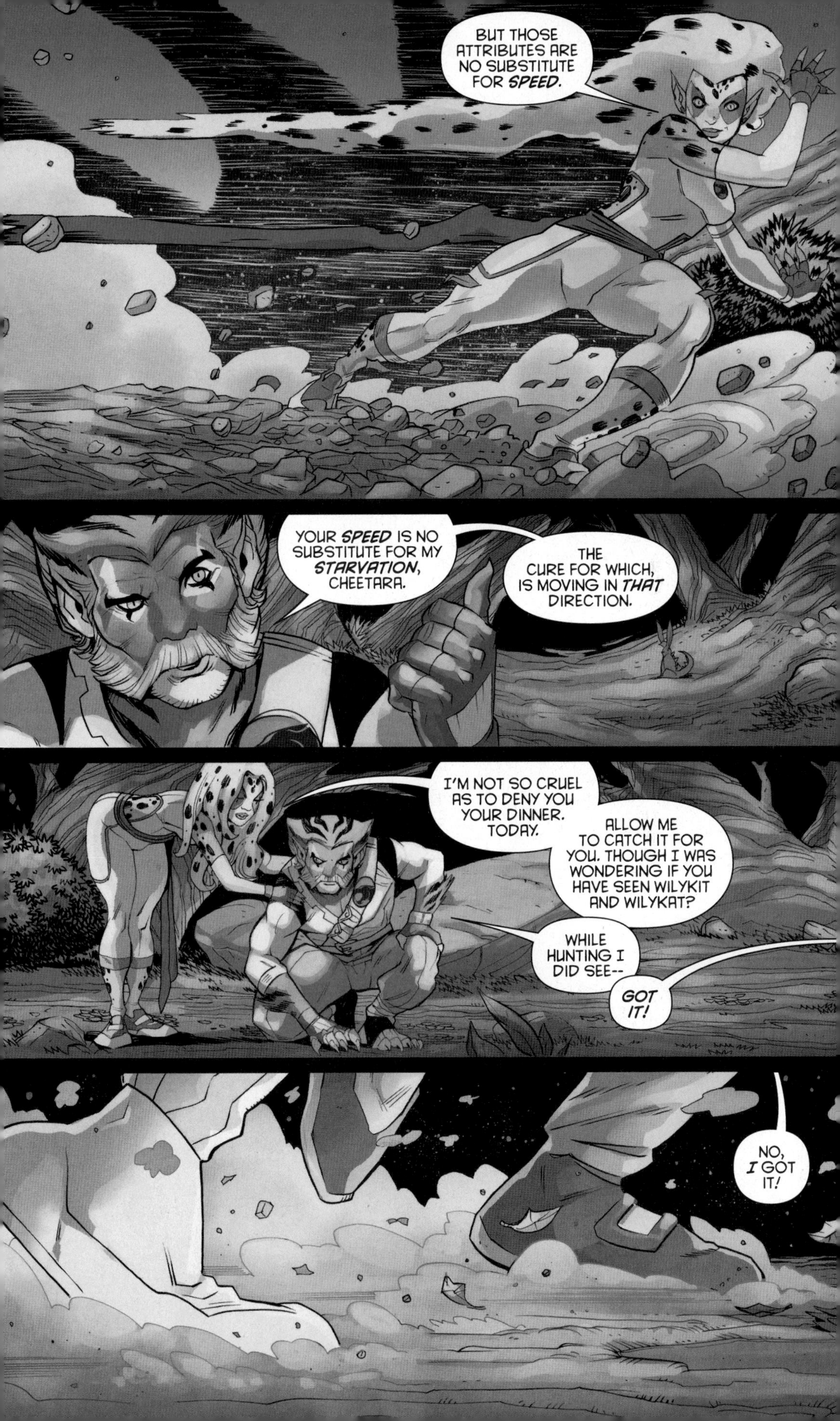
BUT THOSE ATTRIBUTES ARE NO SUBSTITUTE FOR SPEED.
YOUR SPEED IS NO SUBSTITUTE FOR MY STARVATION, CHEETARA.
THE CURE FOR WHICH, IS MOVING IN THAT DIRECTION.
I'M NOT SO CRUEL AS TO DENY YOU YOUR DINNER. TODAY.
ALLOW ME TO CATCH IT FOR YOU. THOUGH I WAS WONDERING IF YOU HAVE SEEN WILYKIT AND WILYKAT?
WHILE HUNTING I DID SEE--
GOT IT!
NO, I GOT IT!

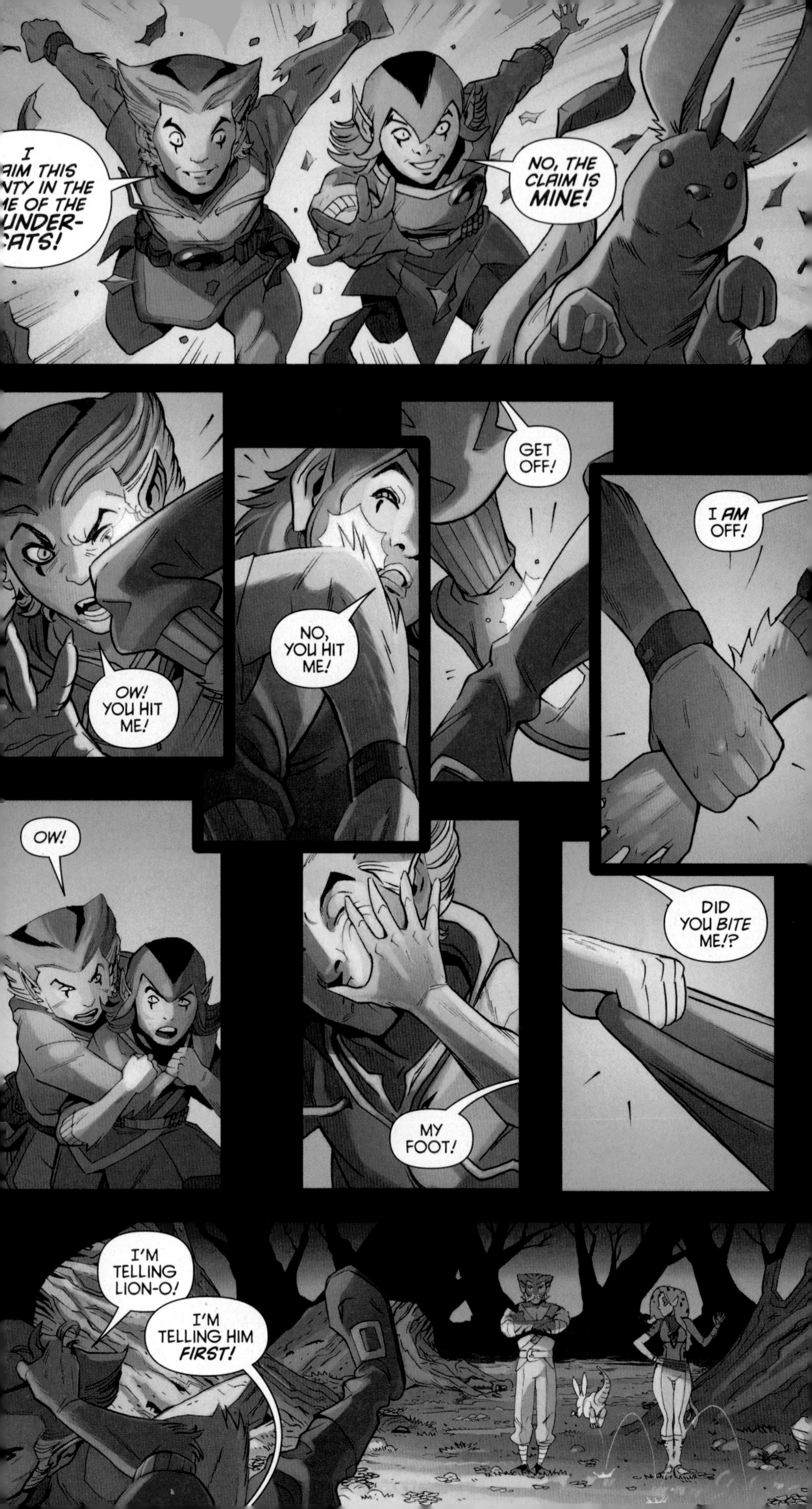
I
AIM THIS
NTY IN THE
ME OF THE
UNDER-
CATS!
NO, THE CLAIM IS MINE!
OW! YOU HIT ME!
NO, YOU HIT ME!
GET OFF!
I AM OFF!
OW!
MY FOOT!
DID YOU BITE ME!?
I'M TELLING LION-O!
I'M TELLING HIM FIRST!

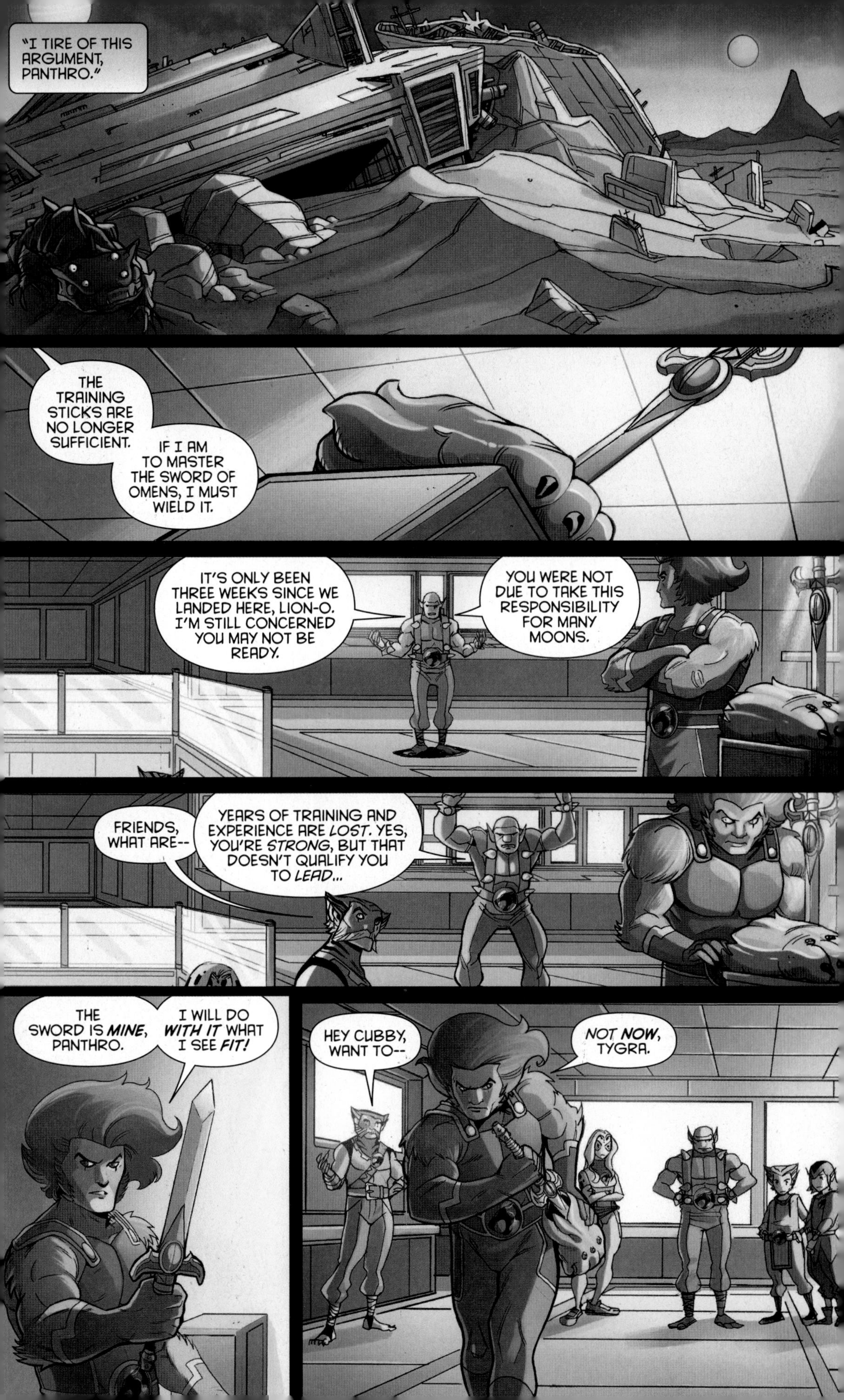
"I TIRE OF THIS ARGUMENT, PANTHRO."
THE TRAINING STICKS ARE NO LONGER SUFFICIENT.
IF I AM TO MASTER THE SWORD OF OMENS, I MUST WIELD IT.
IT'S ONLY BEEN THREE WEEKS SINCE WE LANDED HERE, LION-O. I'M STILL CONCERNED YOU MAY NOT BE READY.
YOU WERE NOT DUE TO TAKE THIS RESPONSIBILITY FOR MANY MOONS.
FRIENDS, WHAT ARE--
YEARS OF TRAINING AND EXPERIENCE ARE *LOST*. YES, YOU'RE *STRONG*, BUT THAT DOESN'T QUALIFY YOU TO *LEAD*...
THE SWORD IS ***MINE***, PANTHRO.
I WILL DO ***WITH IT*** WHAT I SEE ***FIT!***
HEY CUBBY, WANT TO--
*NOT **NOW***, TYGRA.

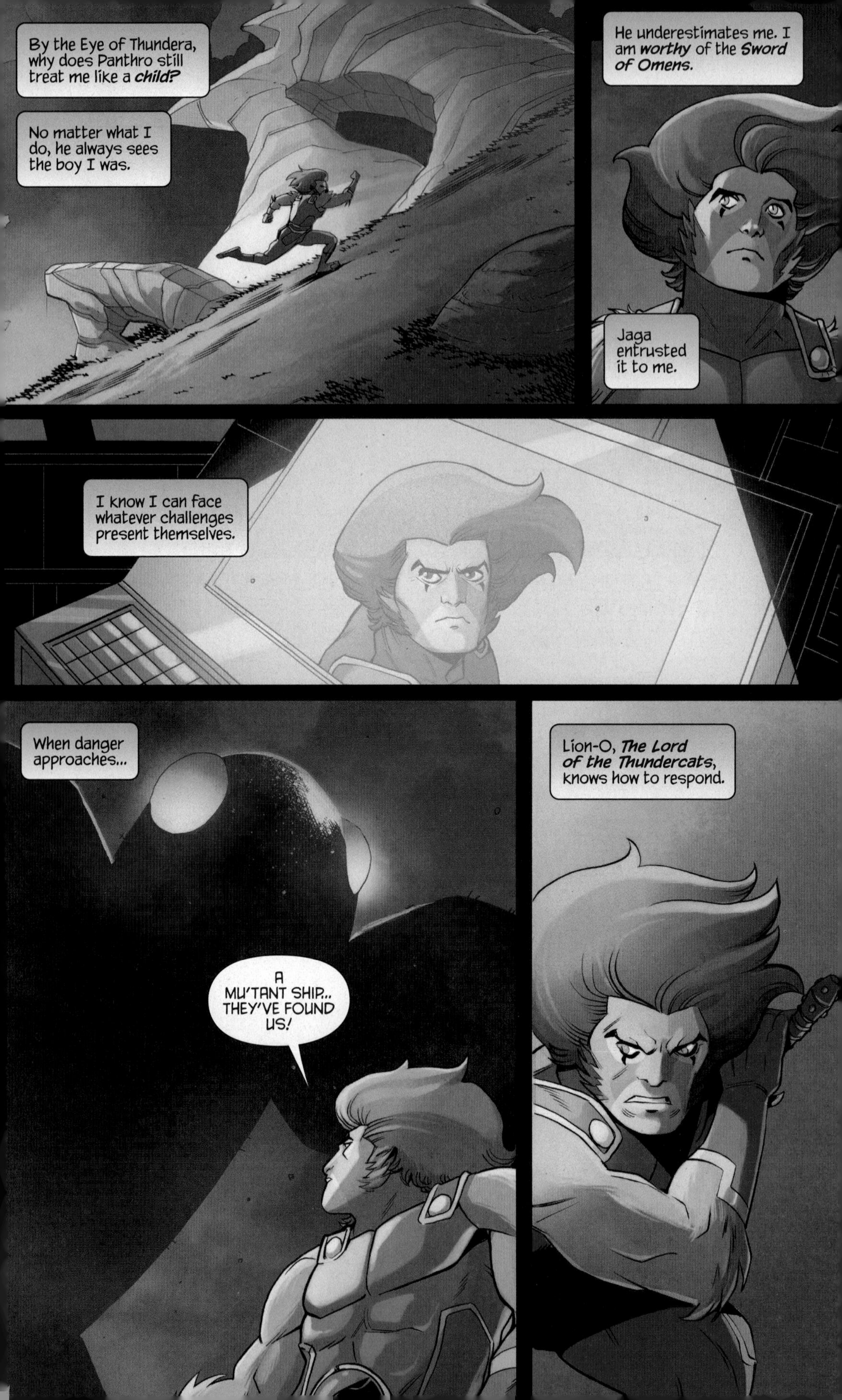
By the Eye of Thundera, why does Panthro still treat me like a *child?*
No matter what I do, he always sees the boy I was.
He underestimates me. I am *worthy* of the *Sword of Omens.*
Jaga entrusted it to me.
I know I can face whatever challenges present themselves.
When danger approaches...
A MU'TANT SHIP.. THEY'VE FOUND US!
Lion-O, *The Lord of the Thundercats,* knows how to respond.

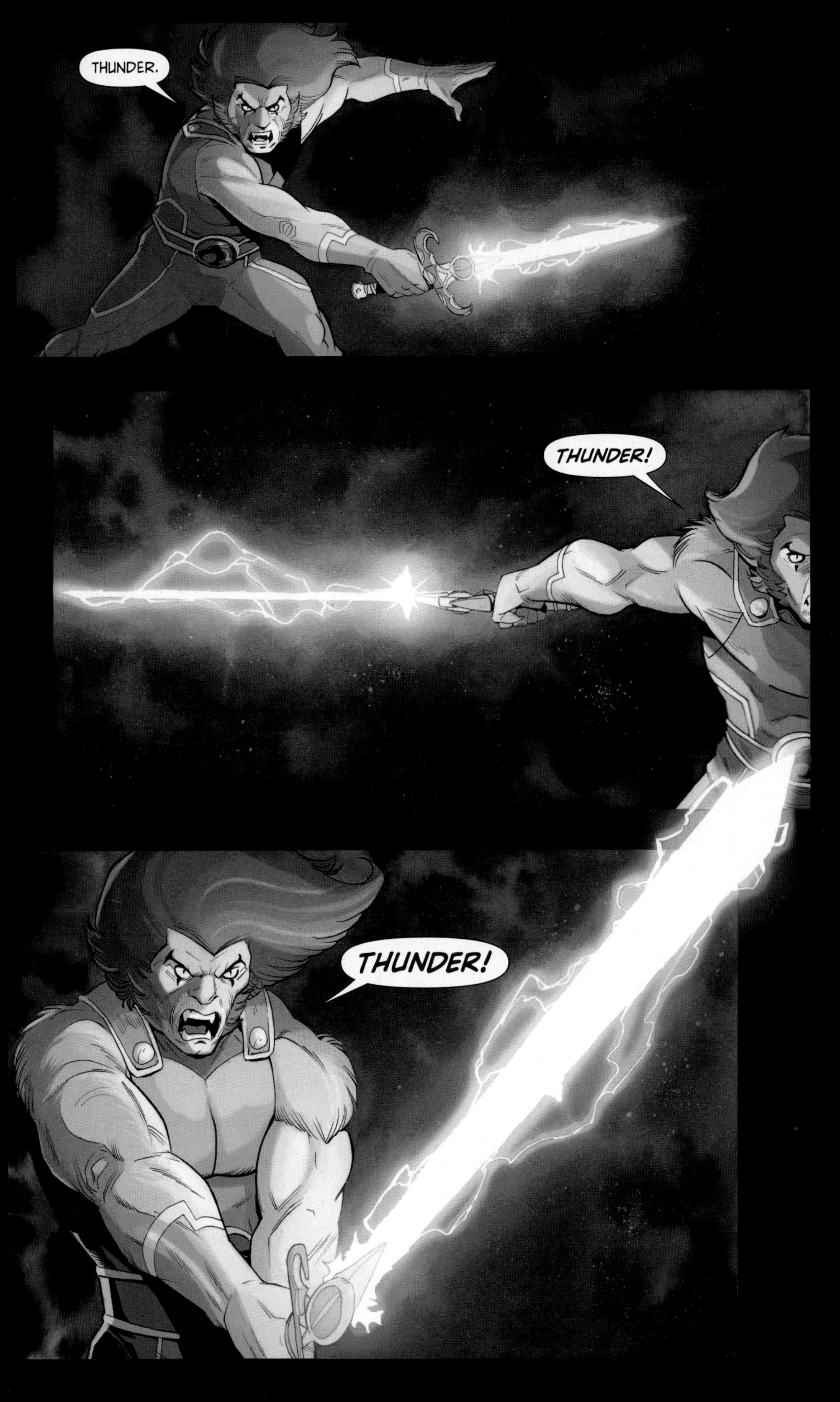
THUNDER.
THUNDER!
THUNDER!

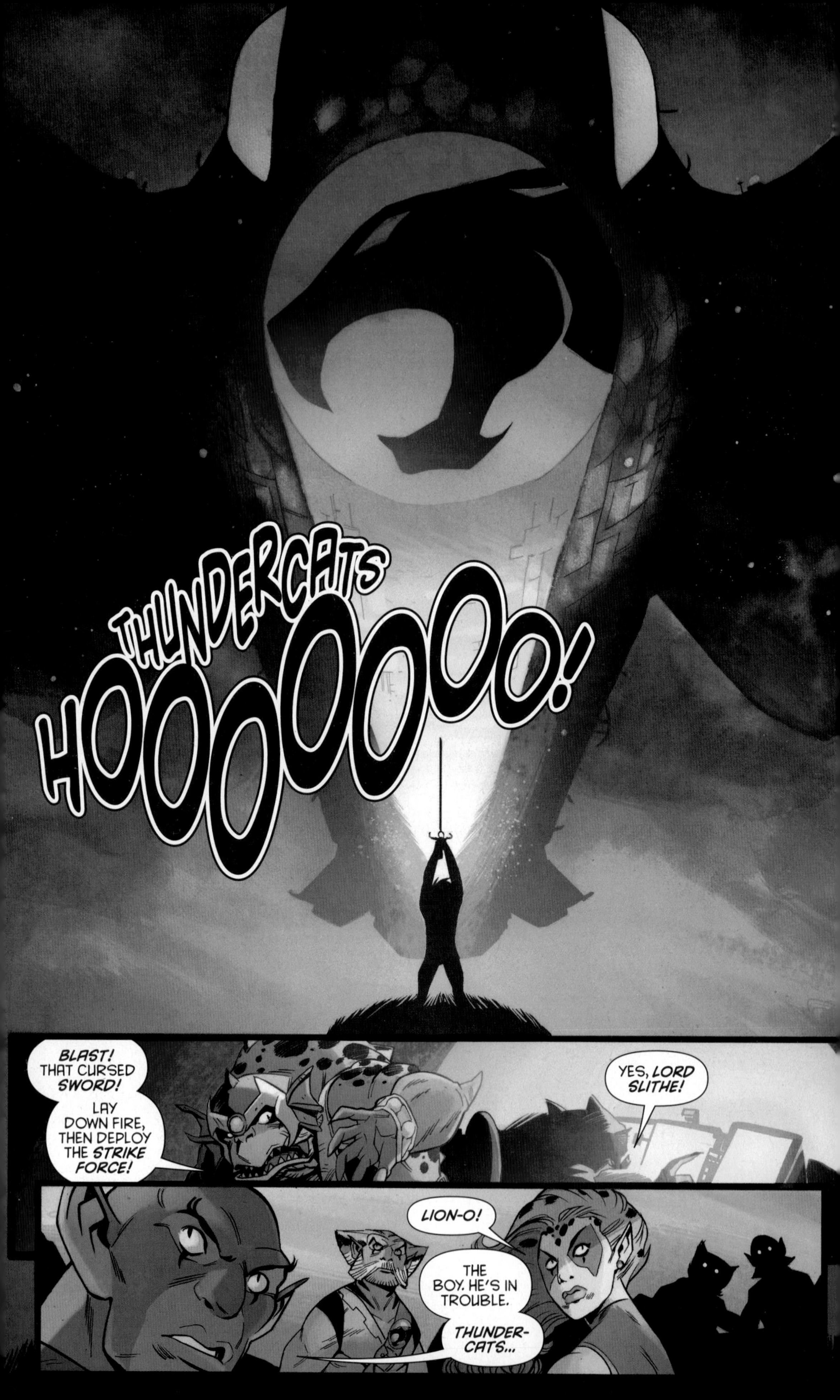
THUNDERCATS HOOOOOOOO!
BLAST! THAT CURSED SWORD!
LAY DOWN FIRE, THEN DEPLOY THE STRIKE FORCE!
YES, LORD SLITHE!
LION-O!
THE BOY. HE'S IN TROUBLE.
THUNDER-CATS...

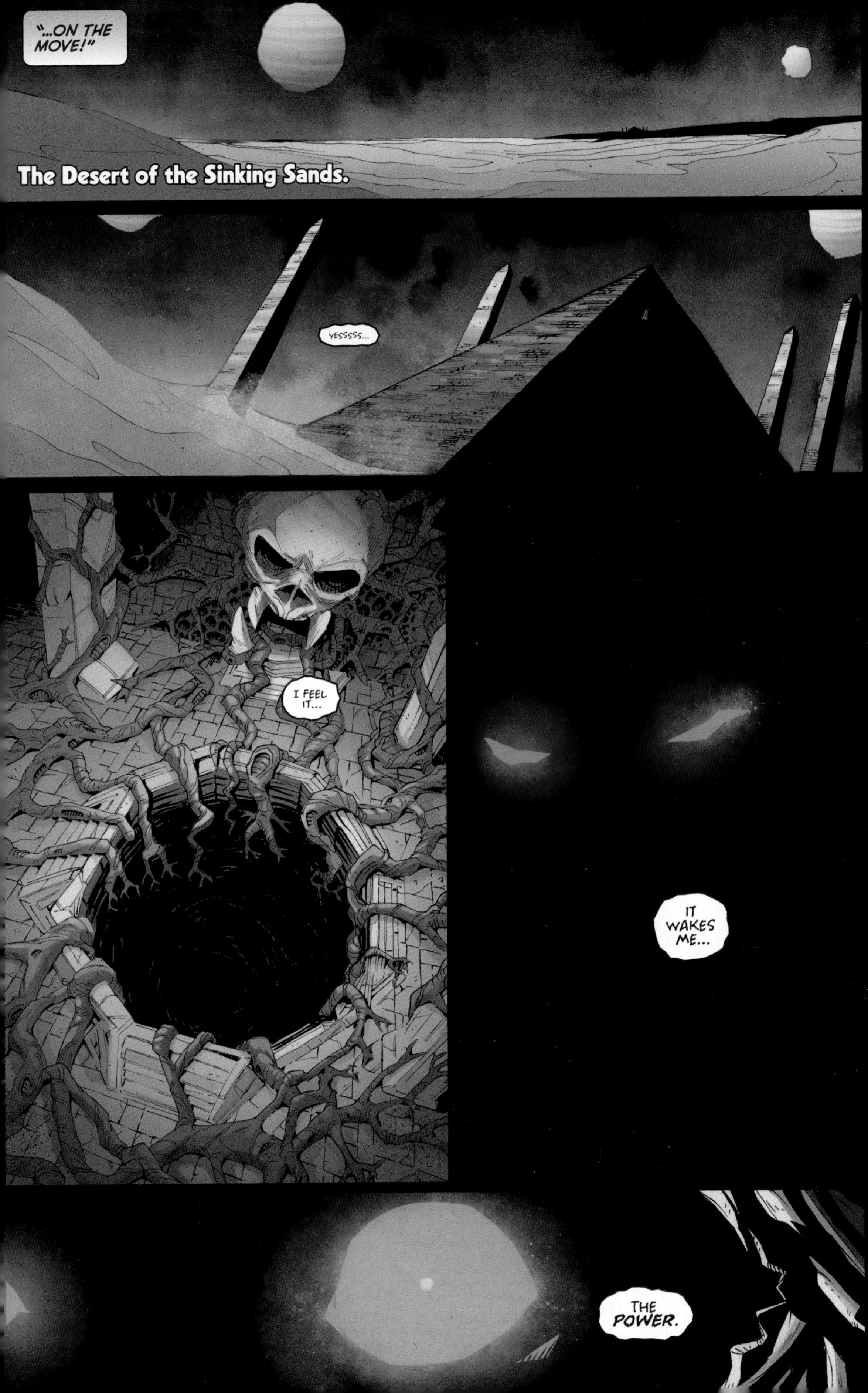
"...ON THE MOVE!"
The Desert of the Sinking Sands.
YESSSSS...
I FEEL IT...
IT WAKES ME...
THE POWER.

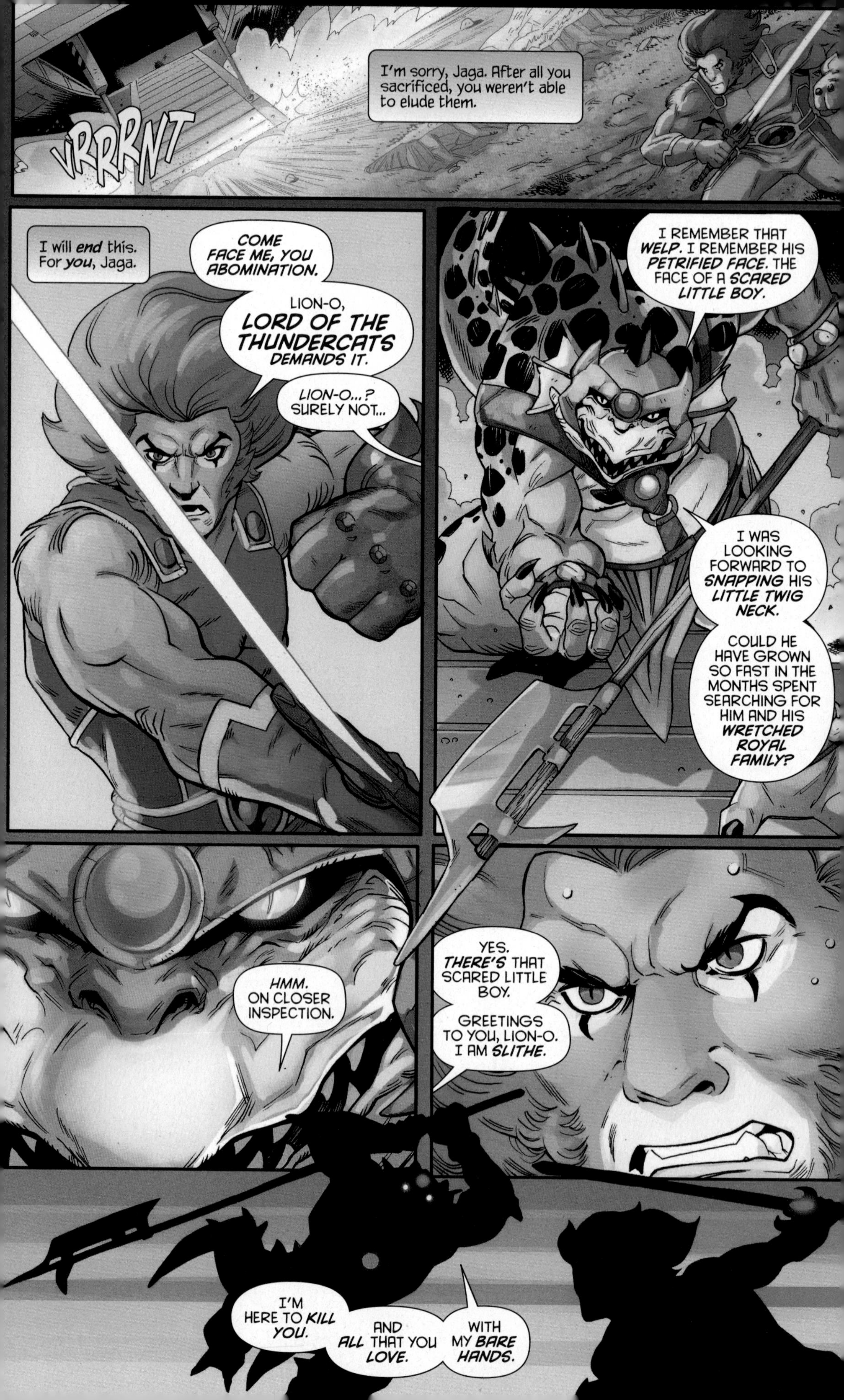

I'm sorry, Jaga. After all you sacrificed, you weren't able to elude them.
VRRRNT
I will end this. For you, Jaga.
COME FACE ME, YOU ABOMINATION.
LION-O, LORD OF THE THUNDERCATS DEMANDS IT.
LION-O...? SURELY NOT...
I REMEMBER THAT WELP. I REMEMBER HIS PETRIFIED FACE. THE FACE OF A SCARED LITTLE BOY.
I WAS LOOKING FORWARD TO SNAPPING HIS LITTLE TWIG NECK.
COULD HE HAVE GROWN SO FAST IN THE MONTHS SPENT SEARCHING FOR HIM AND HIS WRETCHED ROYAL FAMILY?
HMM. ON CLOSER INSPECTION.
YES. THERE'S THAT SCARED LITTLE BOY.
GREETINGS TO YOU, LION-O. I AM SLITHE.
I'M HERE TO KILL YOU.
AND ALL THAT YOU LOVE.
WITH MY BARE HANDS.

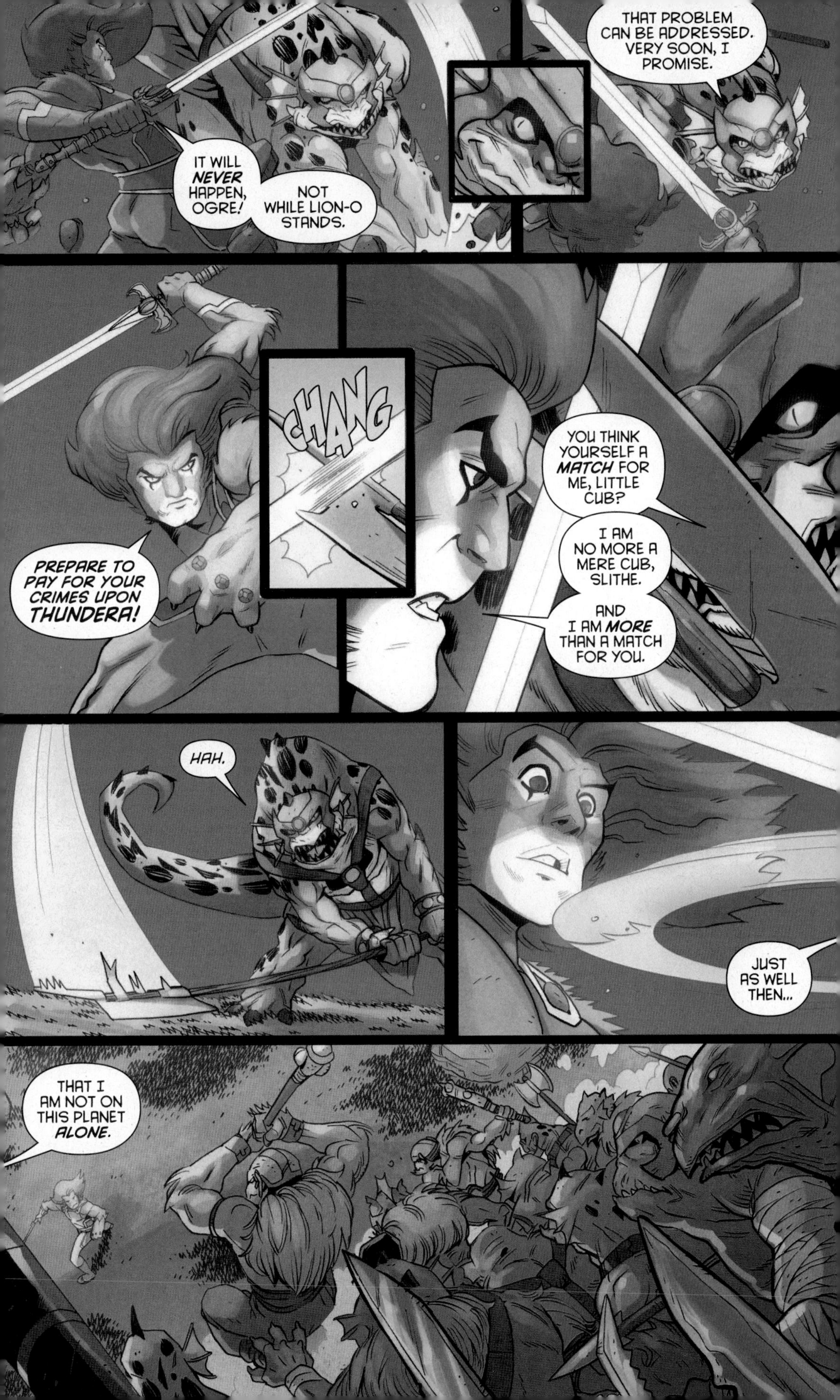
IT WILL NEVER HAPPEN, OGRE!
NOT WHILE LION-O STANDS.
THAT PROBLEM CAN BE ADDRESSED. VERY SOON, I PROMISE.
PREPARE TO PAY FOR YOUR CRIMES UPON THUNDERA!
CHANG
YOU THINK YOURSELF A MATCH FOR ME, LITTLE CUB?
I AM NO MORE A MERE CUB, SLITHE.
AND I AM MORE THAN A MATCH FOR YOU.
HAH.
JUST AS WELL THEN...
THAT I AM NOT ON THIS PLANET ALONE.

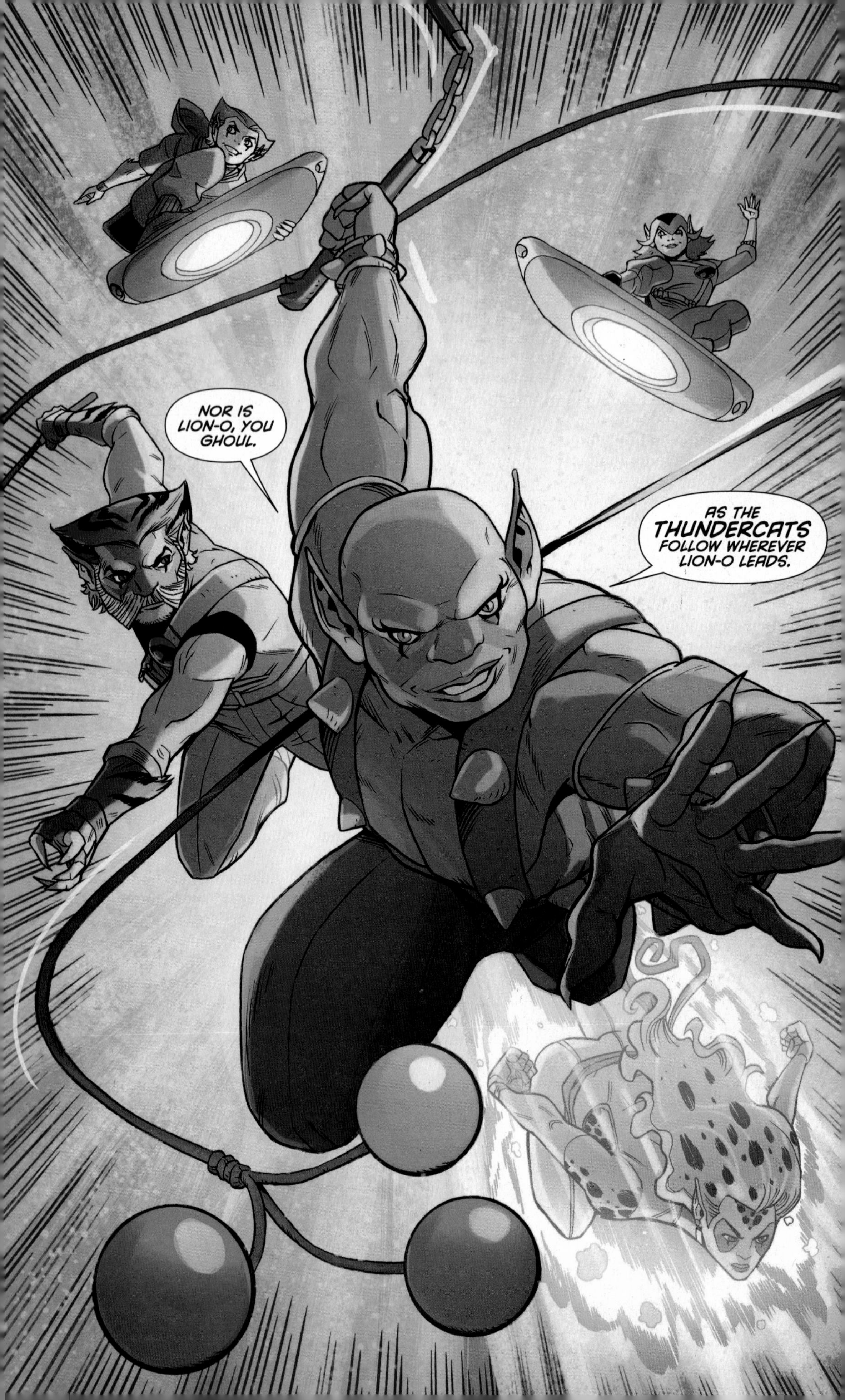
NOR IS LION-O, YOU GHOUL.
AS THE THUNDERCATS FOLLOW WHEREVER LION-O LEADS.

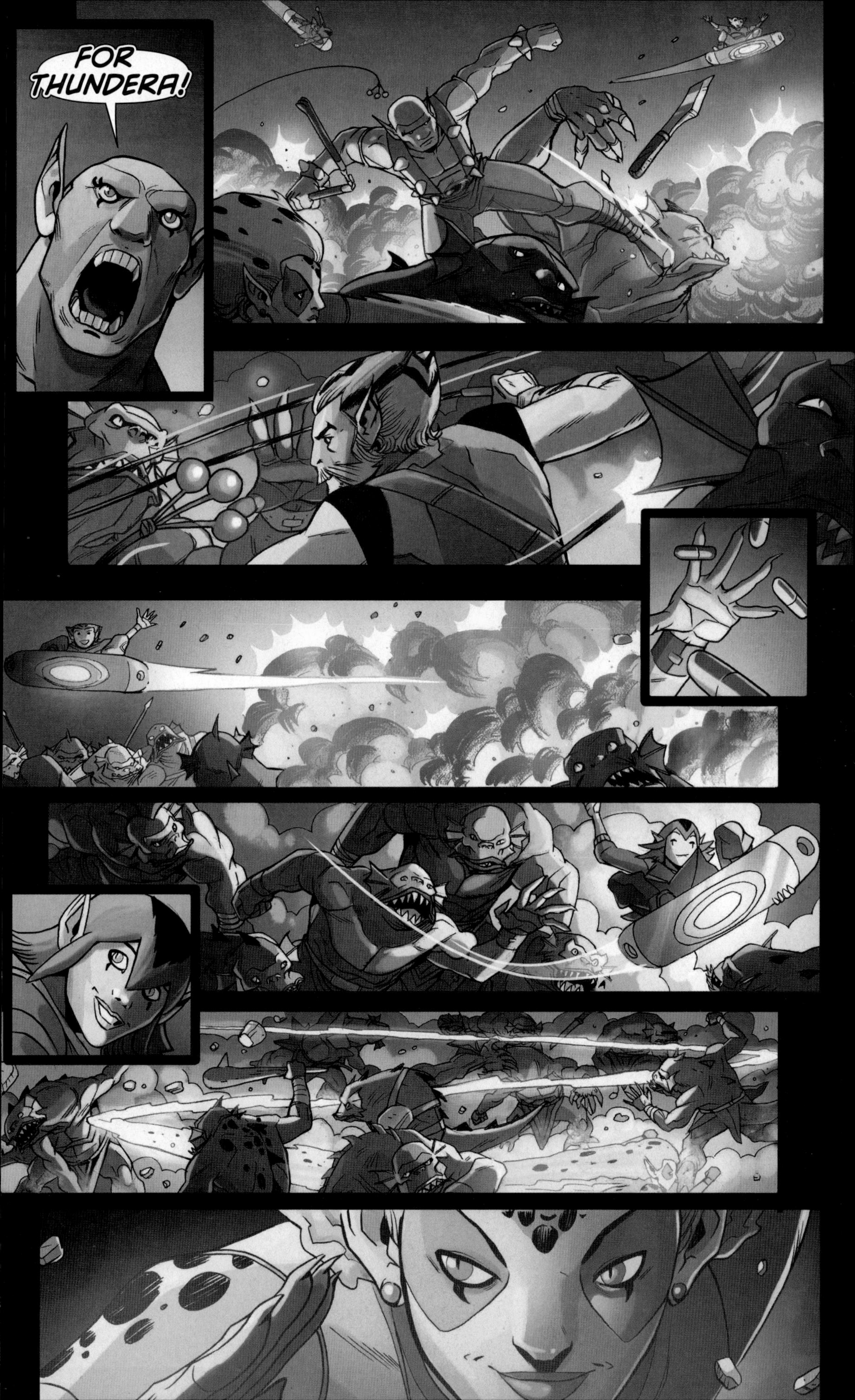
FOR THUNDERA!

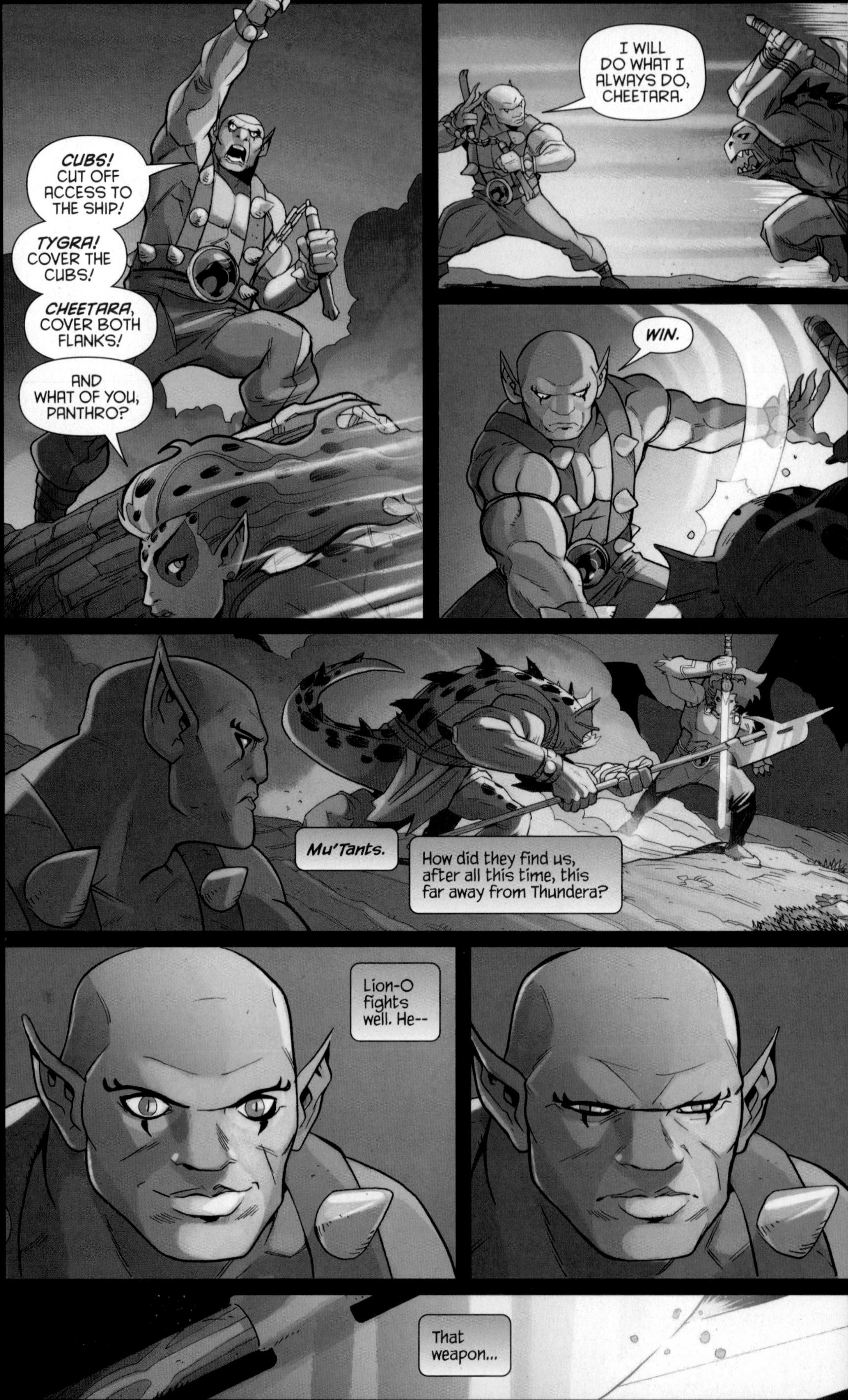
CUBS! CUT OFF ACCESS TO THE SHIP!
TYGRA! COVER THE CUBS!
CHEETARA, COVER BOTH FLANKS!
AND WHAT OF YOU, PANTHRO?
I WILL DO WHAT I ALWAYS DO, CHEETARA.
WIN.
Mu'Tants.
How did they find us, after all this time, this far away from Thundera?
Lion-O fights well. He--
That weapon...

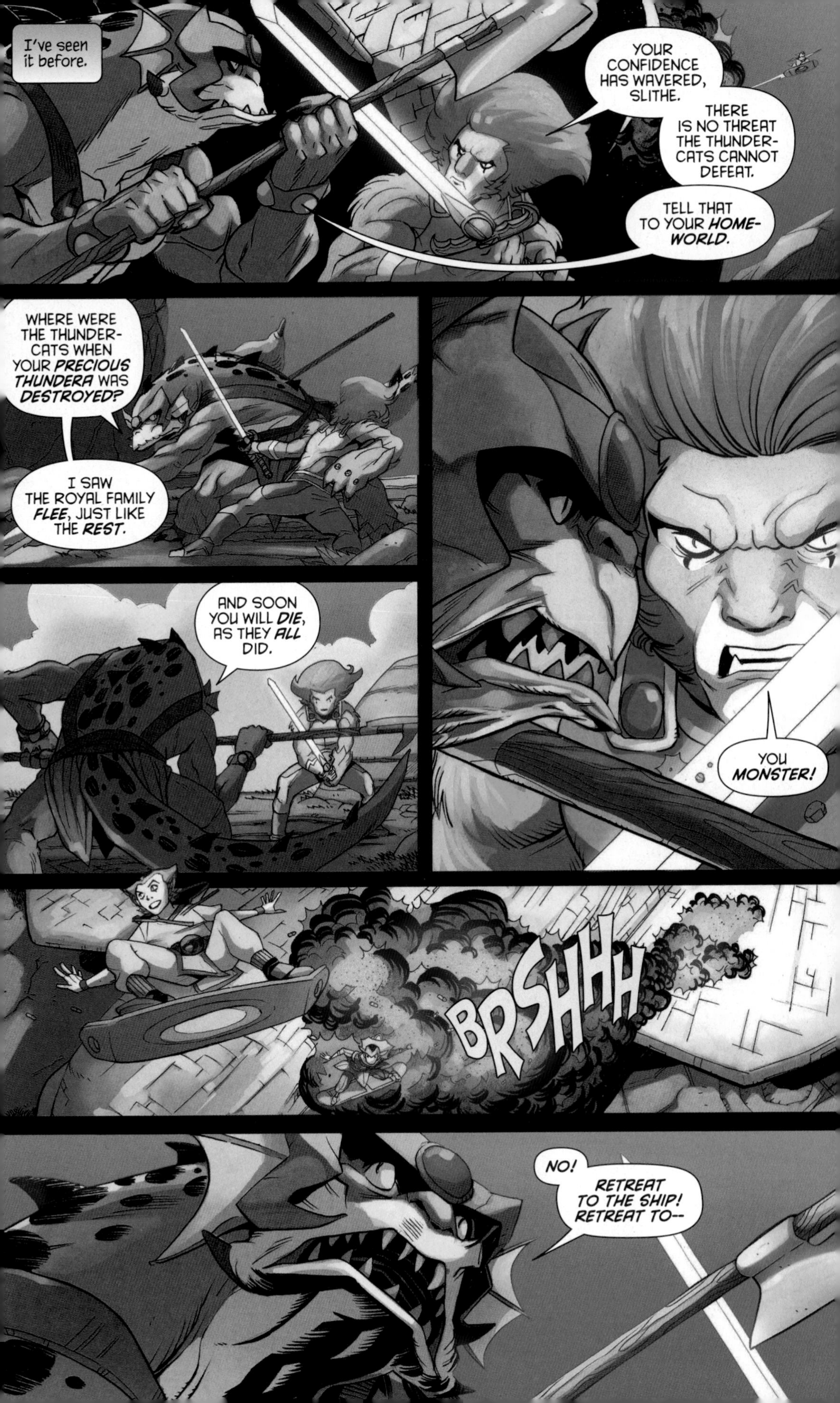
I've seen it before.
YOUR CONFIDENCE HAS WAVERED, SLITHE.
THERE IS NO THREAT THE THUNDER-CATS CANNOT DEFEAT.
TELL THAT TO YOUR HOME-WORLD.
WHERE WERE THE THUNDER-CATS WHEN YOUR PRECIOUS THUNDERA WAS DESTROYED?
I SAW THE ROYAL FAMILY FLEE, JUST LIKE THE REST.
AND SOON YOU WILL DIE, AS THEY ALL DID.
YOU MONSTER!
BRSHHH
NO!
RETREAT TO THE SHIP! RETREAT TO--

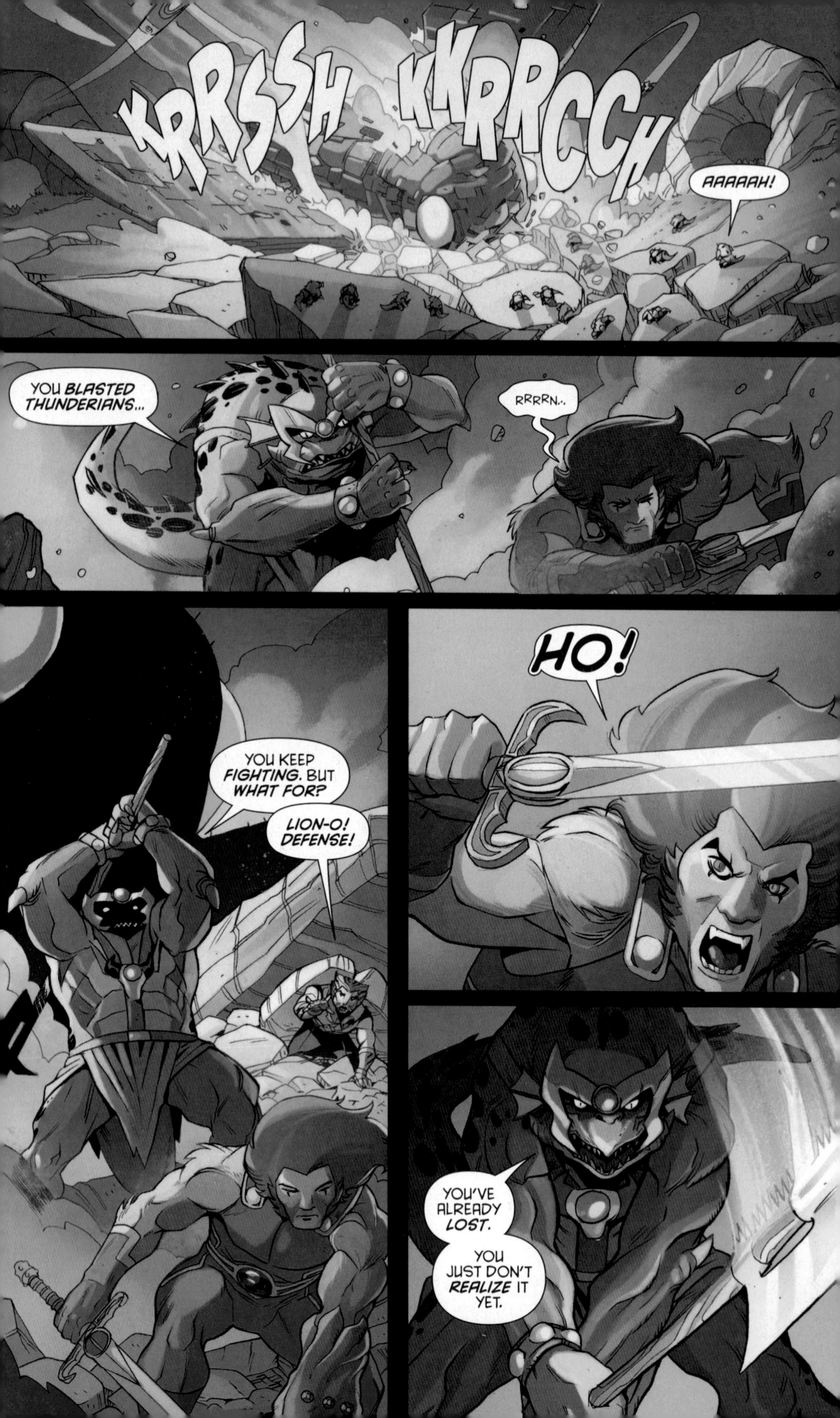
KRRSSH KKRRCCH
AAAAAH!
YOU BLASTED THUNDERIANS...
RRRRN...
YOU KEEP FIGHTING. BUT WHAT FOR?
LION-O! DEFENSE!
HO!
YOU'VE ALREADY LOST.
YOU JUST DON'T REALIZE IT YET.

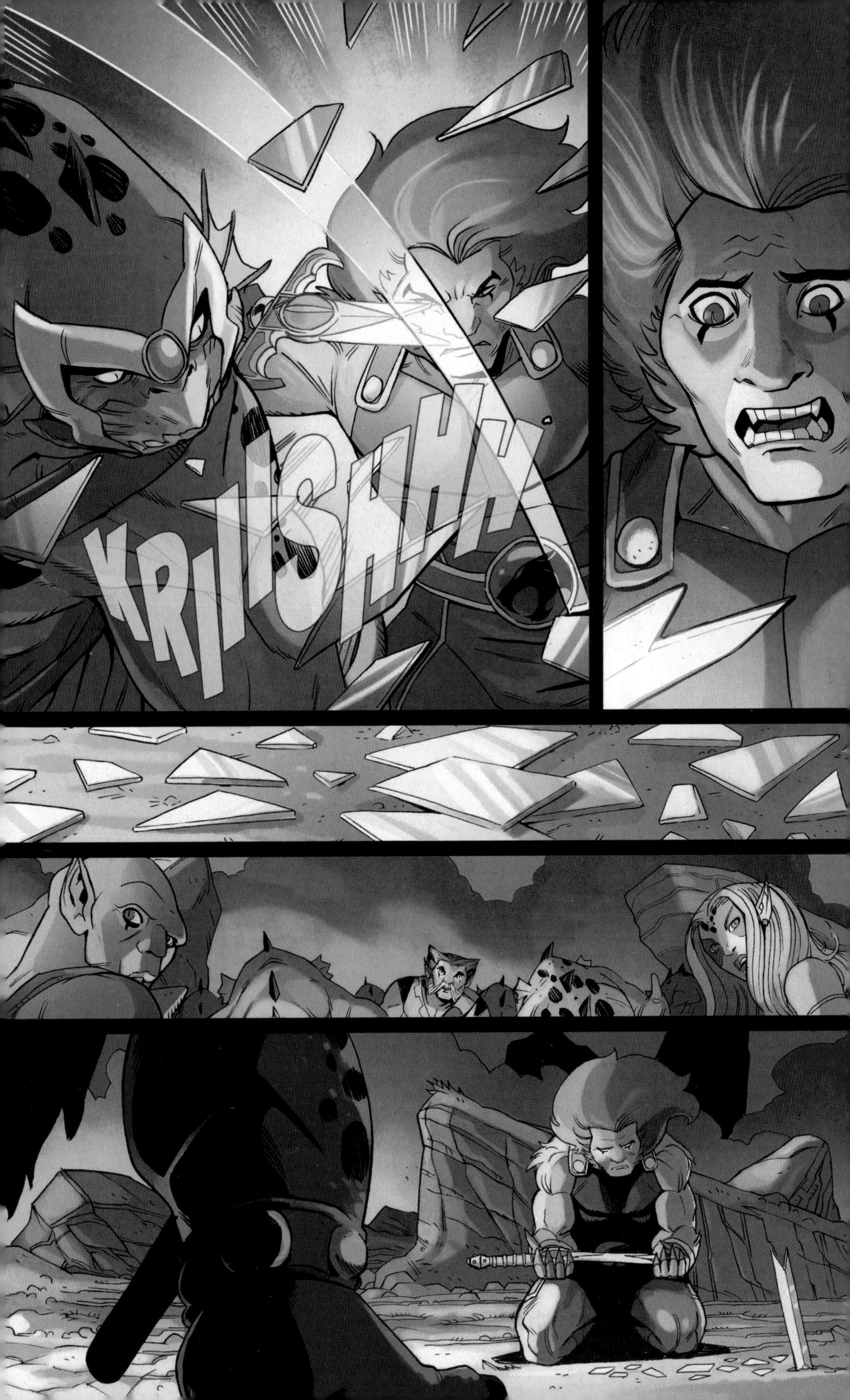
KRIISHHH

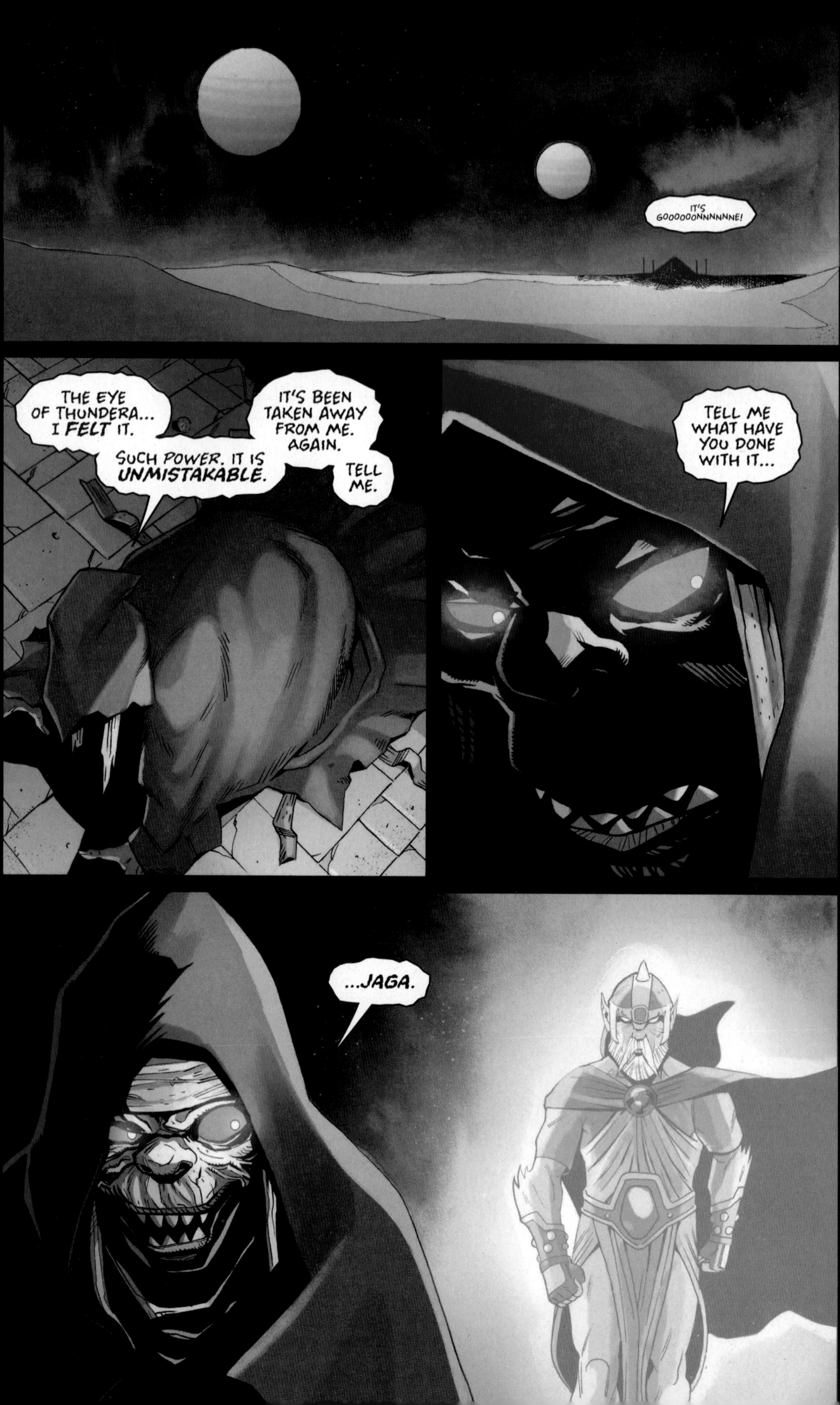
IT'S GOOOOOONNNNNNE!
THE EYE OF THUNDERA... I FELT IT.
SUCH POWER. IT IS UNMISTAKABLE.
IT'S BEEN TAKEN AWAY FROM ME. AGAIN.
TELL ME.
TELL ME WHAT HAVE YOU DONE WITH IT...
...JAGA.

TWO

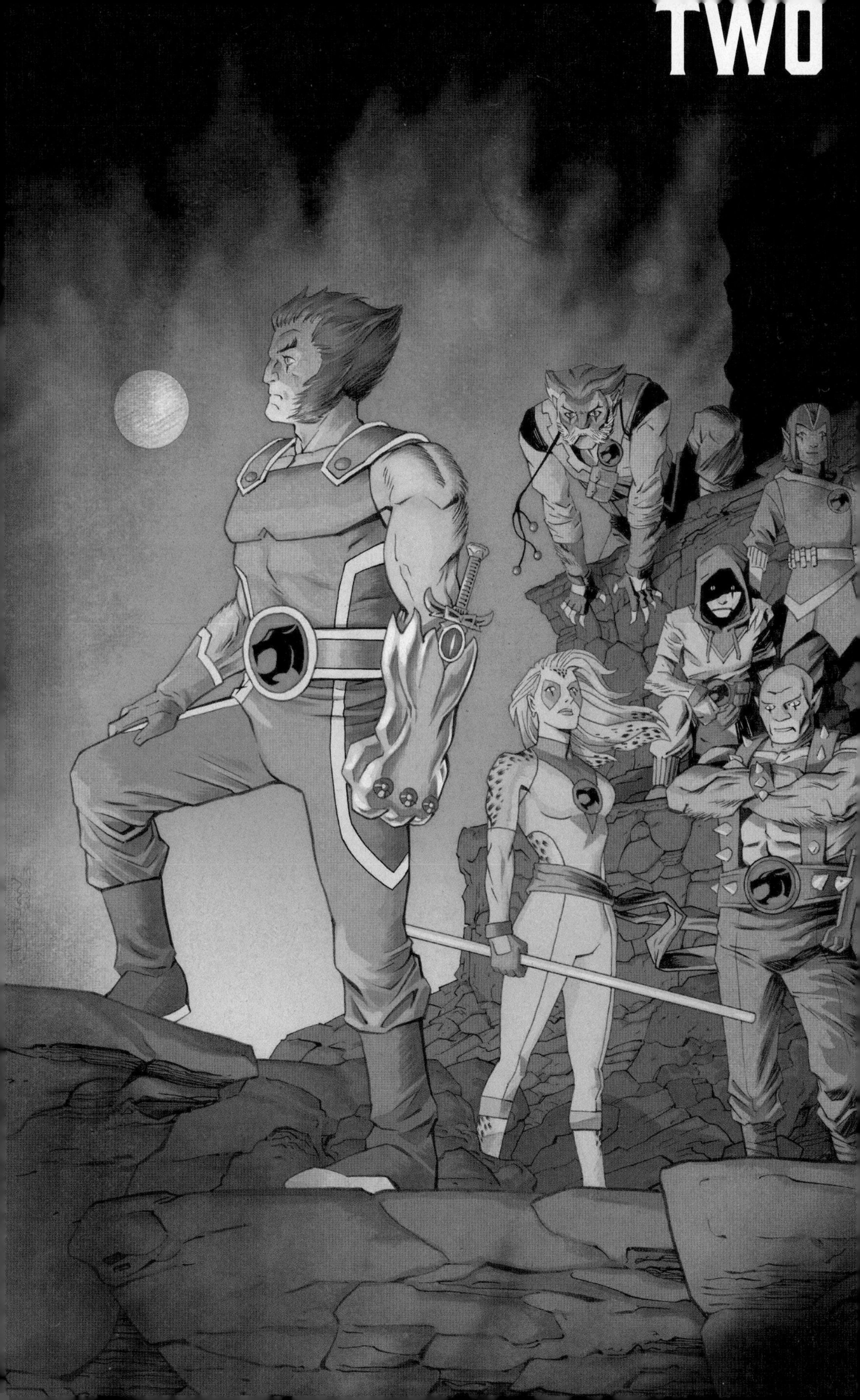

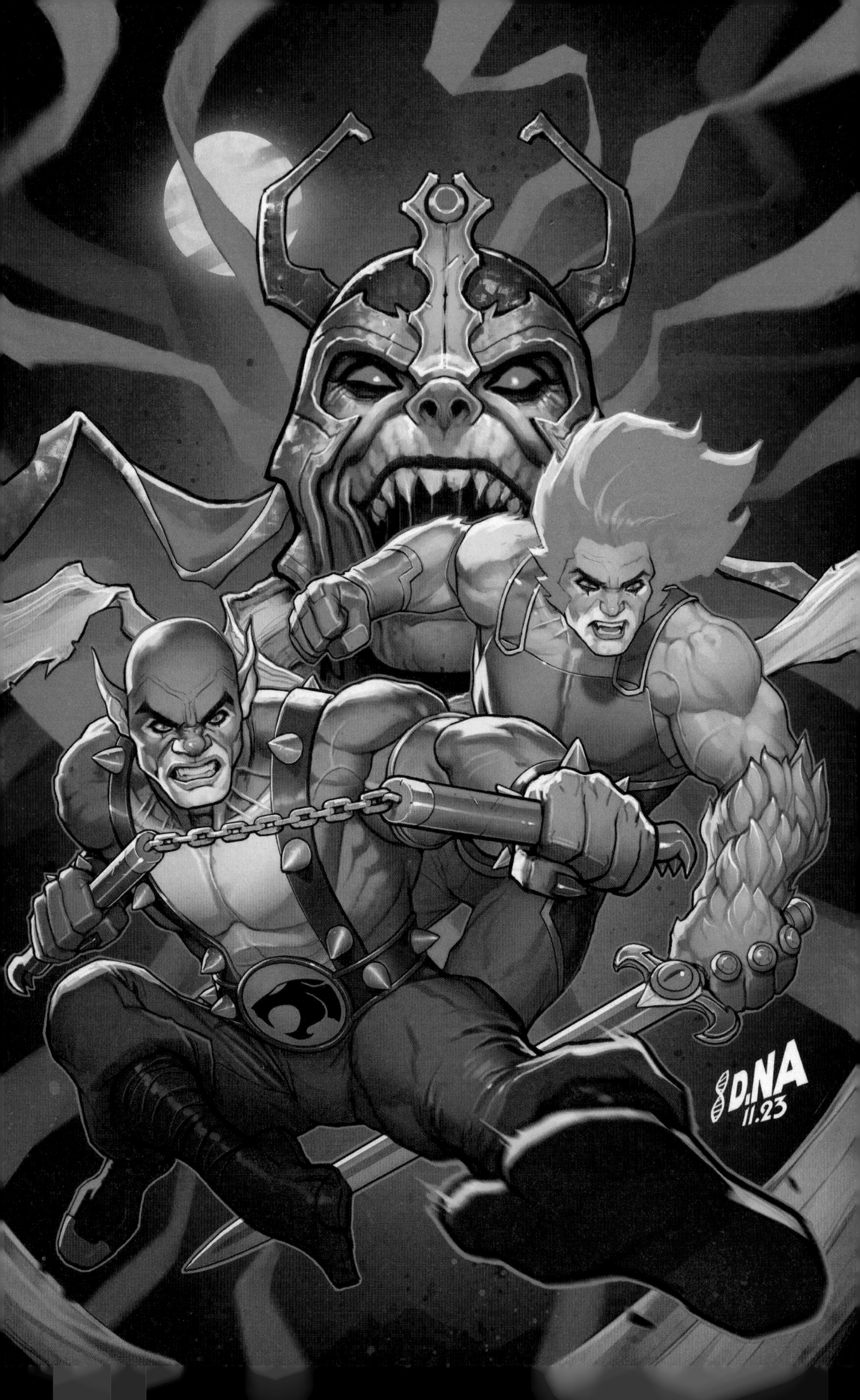
D.NA
11.23

THE GIFT

Shalvey • Moss • Di Francia/Pignedoli • Eckleberry • Cosby

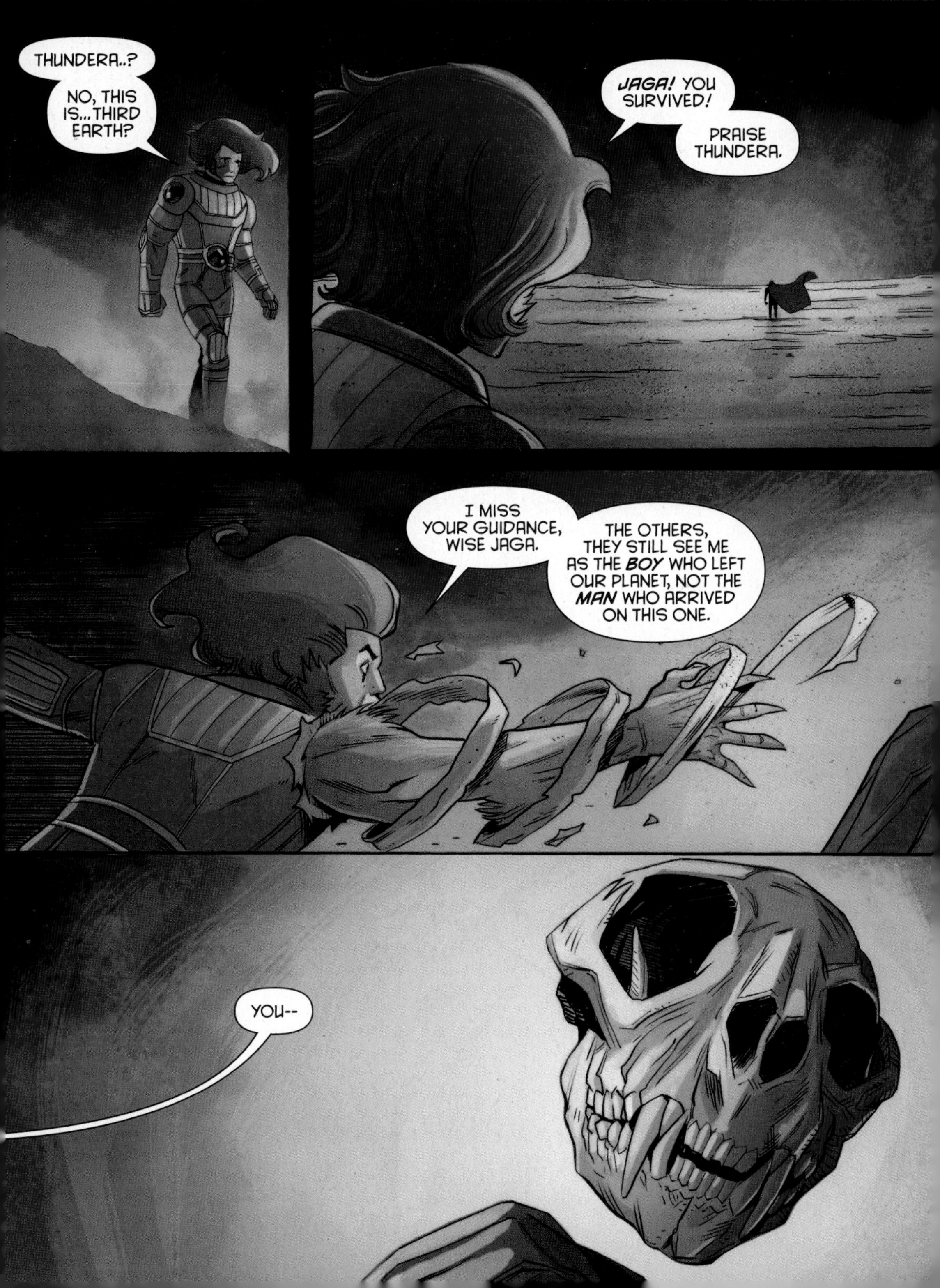
THUNDERA..?
NO, THIS IS...THIRD EARTH?
JAGA! YOU SURVIVED!
PRAISE THUNDERA.
I MISS YOUR GUIDANCE, WISE JAGA.
THE OTHERS, THEY STILL SEE ME AS THE BOY WHO LEFT OUR PLANET, NOT THE MAN WHO ARRIVED ON THIS ONE.
YOU--

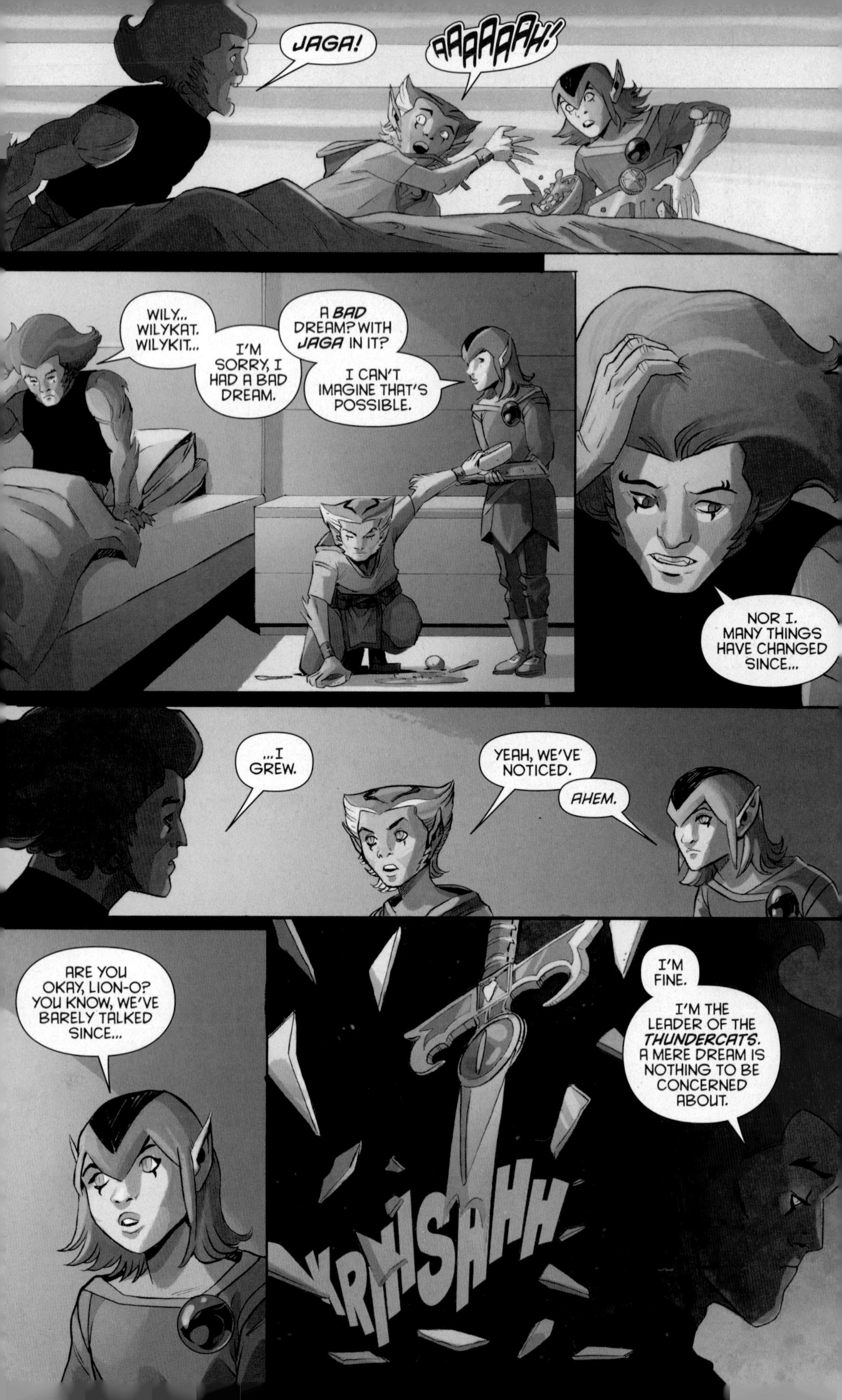
JAGA!
AAAAAAH!
WILY... WILYKAT. WILYKIT...
I'M SORRY, I HAD A BAD DREAM.
A BAD DREAM? WITH JAGA IN IT?
I CAN'T IMAGINE THAT'S POSSIBLE.
NOR I. MANY THINGS HAVE CHANGED SINCE...
...I GREW.
YEAH, WE'VE NOTICED.
AHEM.
ARE YOU OKAY, LION-O? YOU KNOW, WE'VE BARELY TALKED SINCE...
I'M FINE.
I'M THE LEADER OF THE THUNDERCATS. A MERE DREAM IS NOTHING TO BE CONCERNED ABOUT.
KRHHSAHH

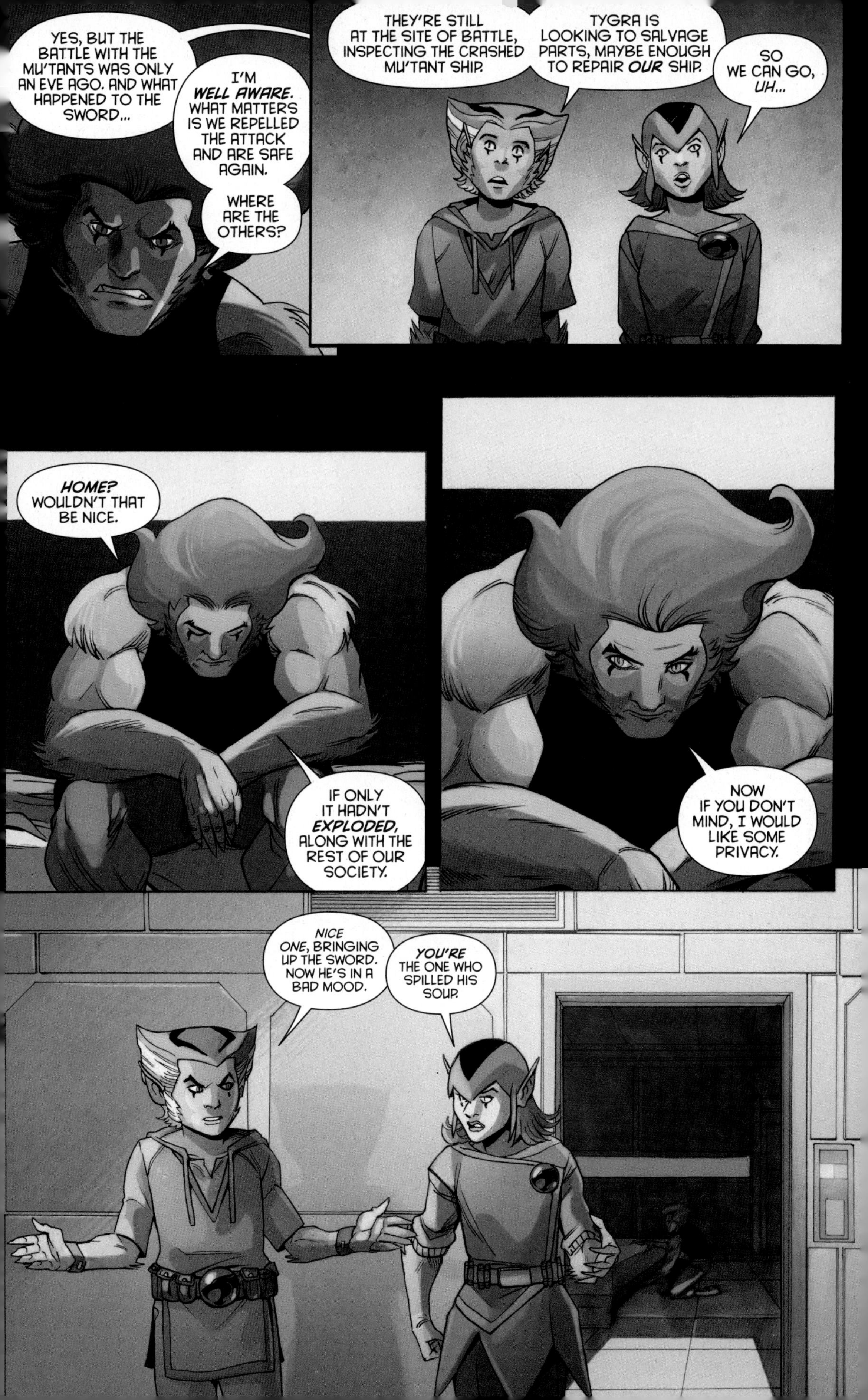
YES, BUT THE BATTLE WITH THE MU'TANTS WAS ONLY AN EVE AGO. AND WHAT HAPPENED TO THE SWORD...
I'M WELL AWARE. WHAT MATTERS IS WE REPELLED THE ATTACK AND ARE SAFE AGAIN.
WHERE ARE THE OTHERS?
THEY'RE STILL AT THE SITE OF BATTLE, INSPECTING THE CRASHED MU'TANT SHIP.
TYGRA IS LOOKING TO SALVAGE PARTS, MAYBE ENOUGH TO REPAIR OUR SHIP.
SO WE CAN GO, UH...
HOME? WOULDN'T THAT BE NICE.
IF ONLY IT HADN'T EXPLODED, ALONG WITH THE REST OF OUR SOCIETY.
NOW IF YOU DON'T MIND, I WOULD LIKE SOME PRIVACY.
NICE ONE, BRINGING UP THE SWORD. NOW HE'S IN A BAD MOOD.
YOU'RE THE ONE WHO SPILLED HIS SOUP.

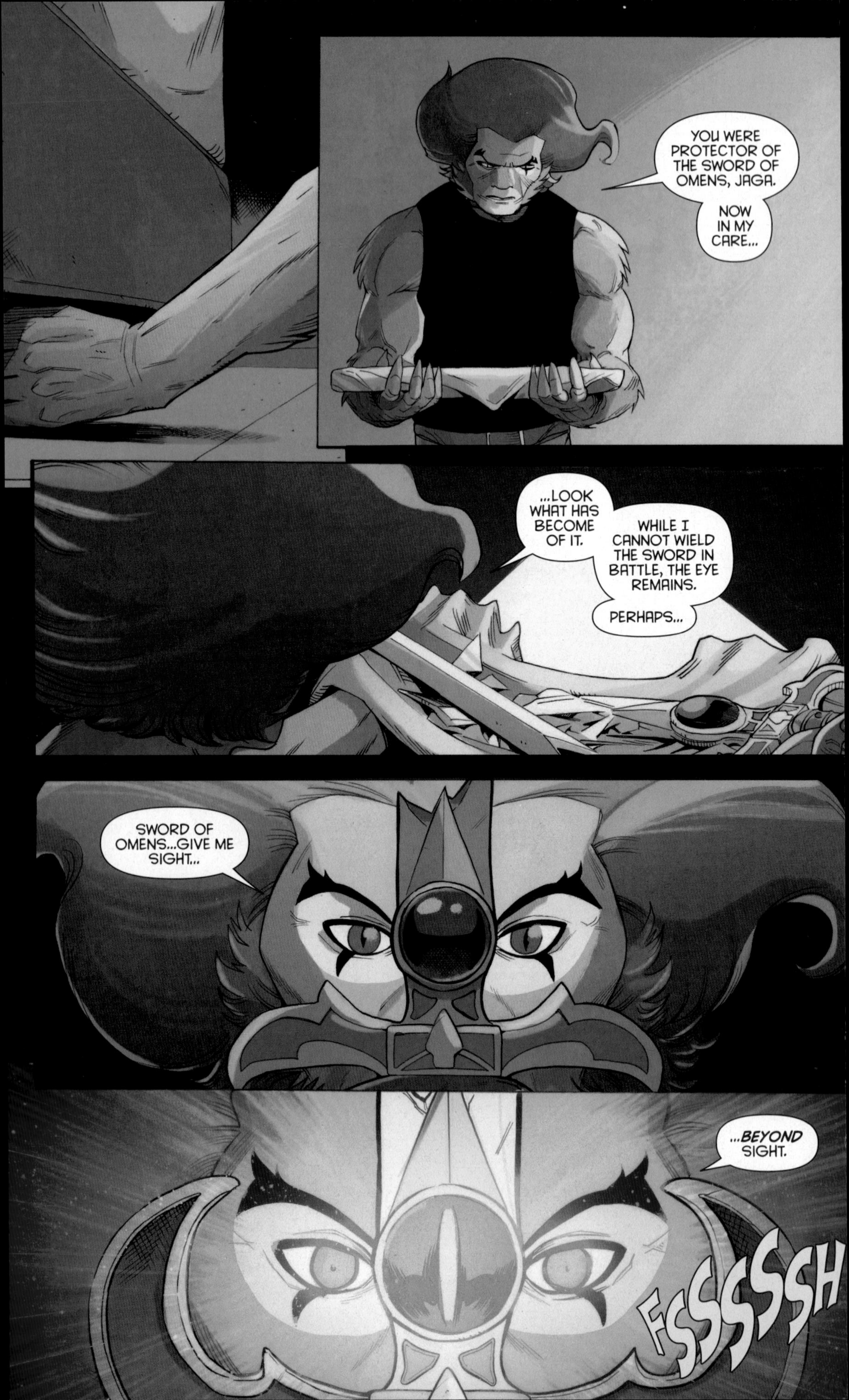
YOU WERE PROTECTOR OF THE SWORD OF OMENS, JAGA.
NOW IN MY CARE...
...LOOK WHAT HAS BECOME OF IT.
WHILE I CANNOT WIELD THE SWORD IN BATTLE, THE EYE REMAINS.
PERHAPS...
SWORD OF OMENS...GIVE ME SIGHT...
...*BEYOND* SIGHT.
FSSSSSH

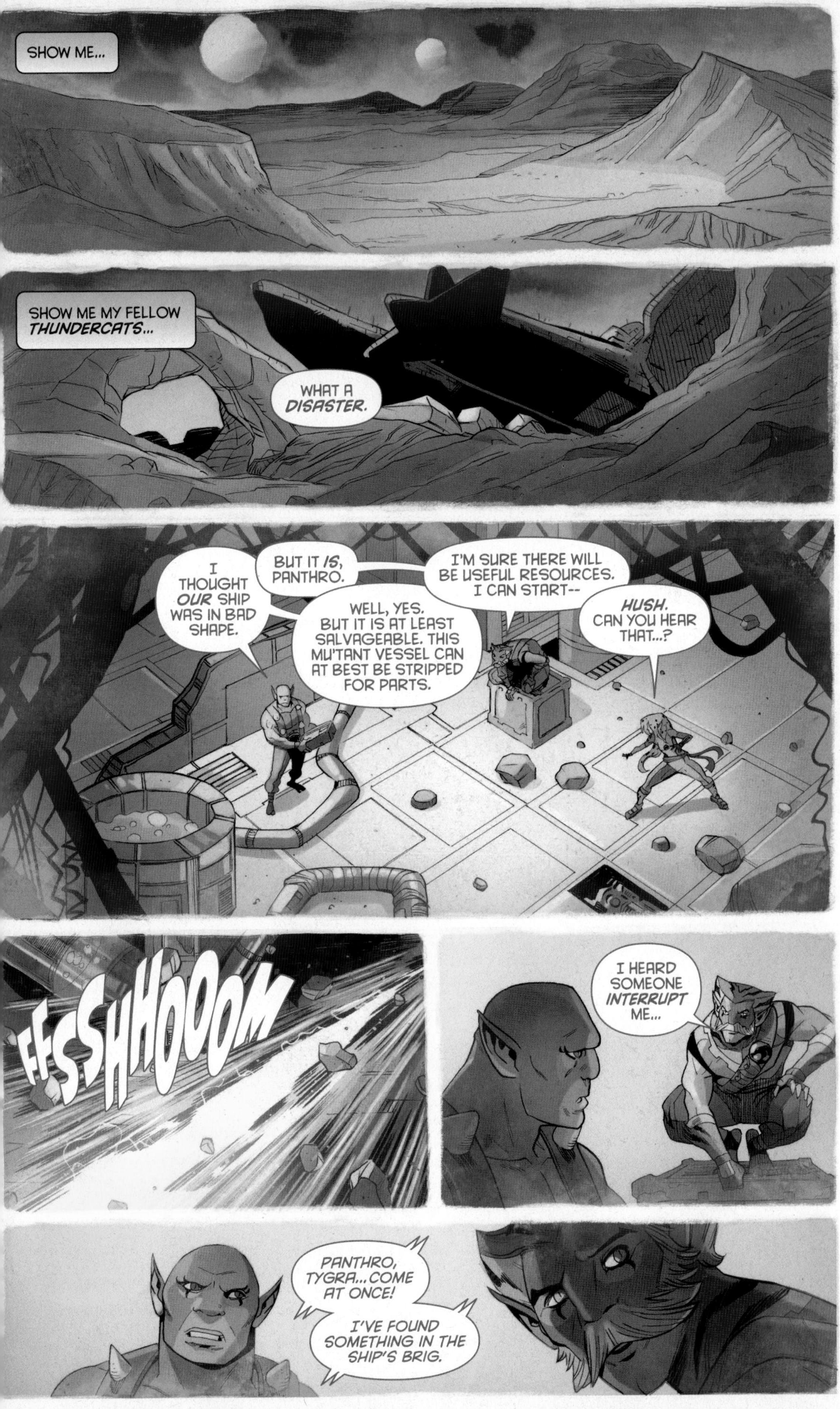
SHOW ME...
SHOW ME MY FELLOW THUNDERCATS...
WHAT A DISASTER.
I THOUGHT OUR SHIP WAS IN BAD SHAPE.
BUT IT IS, PANTHRO.
WELL, YES. BUT IT IS AT LEAST SALVAGEABLE. THIS MU'TANT VESSEL CAN AT BEST BE STRIPPED FOR PARTS.
I'M SURE THERE WILL BE USEFUL RESOURCES. I CAN START--
HUSH. CAN YOU HEAR THAT...?
FFSSHHOOOM
I HEARD SOMEONE INTERRUPT ME...
PANTHRO, TYGRA...COME AT ONCE!
I'VE FOUND SOMETHING IN THE SHIP'S BRIG.

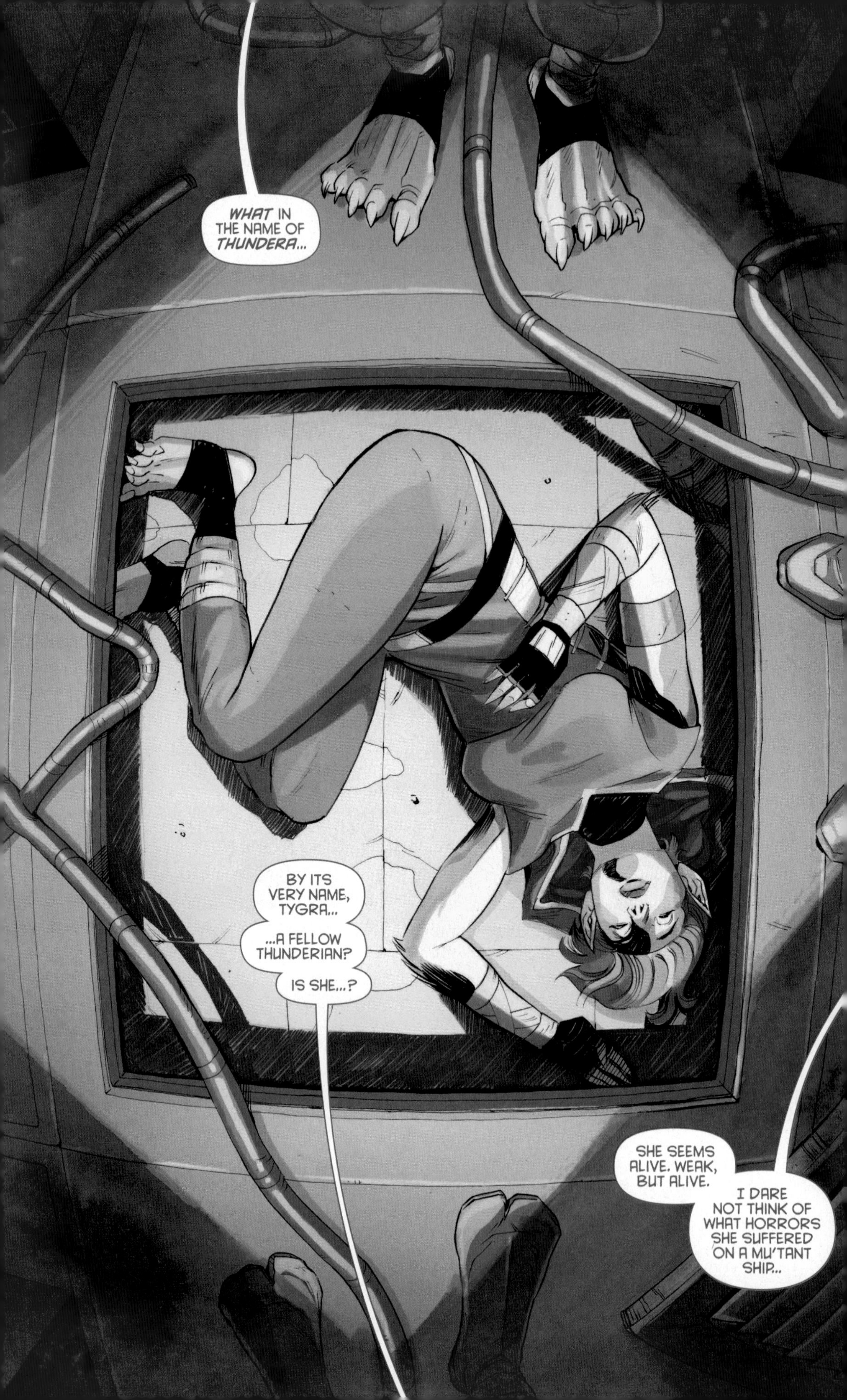
WHAT IN THE NAME OF THUNDERA...
BY ITS VERY NAME, TYGRA...
...A FELLOW THUNDERIAN?
IS SHE...?
SHE SEEMS ALIVE. WEAK, BUT ALIVE.
I DARE NOT THINK OF WHAT HORRORS SHE SUFFERED ON A MU'TANT SHIP...

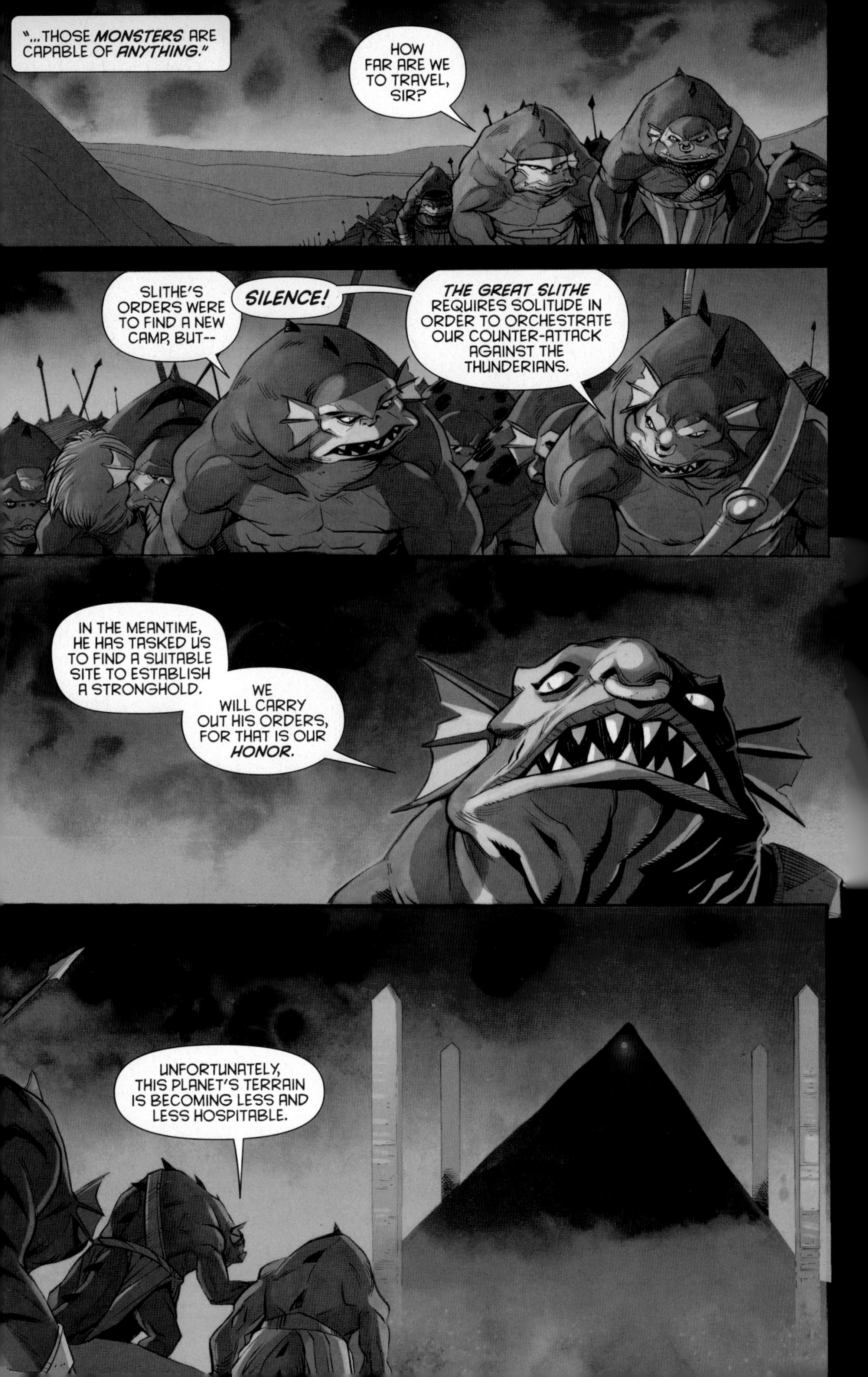
"...THOSE *MONSTERS* ARE CAPABLE OF *ANYTHING*."
HOW FAR ARE WE TO TRAVEL, SIR?
SLITHE'S ORDERS WERE TO FIND A NEW CAMP, BUT--
SILENCE!
THE GREAT SLITHE REQUIRES SOLITUDE IN ORDER TO ORCHESTRATE OUR COUNTER-ATTACK AGAINST THE THUNDERIANS.
IN THE MEANTIME, HE HAS TASKED US TO FIND A SUITABLE SITE TO ESTABLISH A STRONGHOLD.
WE WILL CARRY OUT HIS ORDERS, FOR THAT IS OUR *HONOR*.
UNFORTUNATELY, THIS PLANET'S TERRAIN IS BECOMING LESS AND LESS HOSPITABLE.

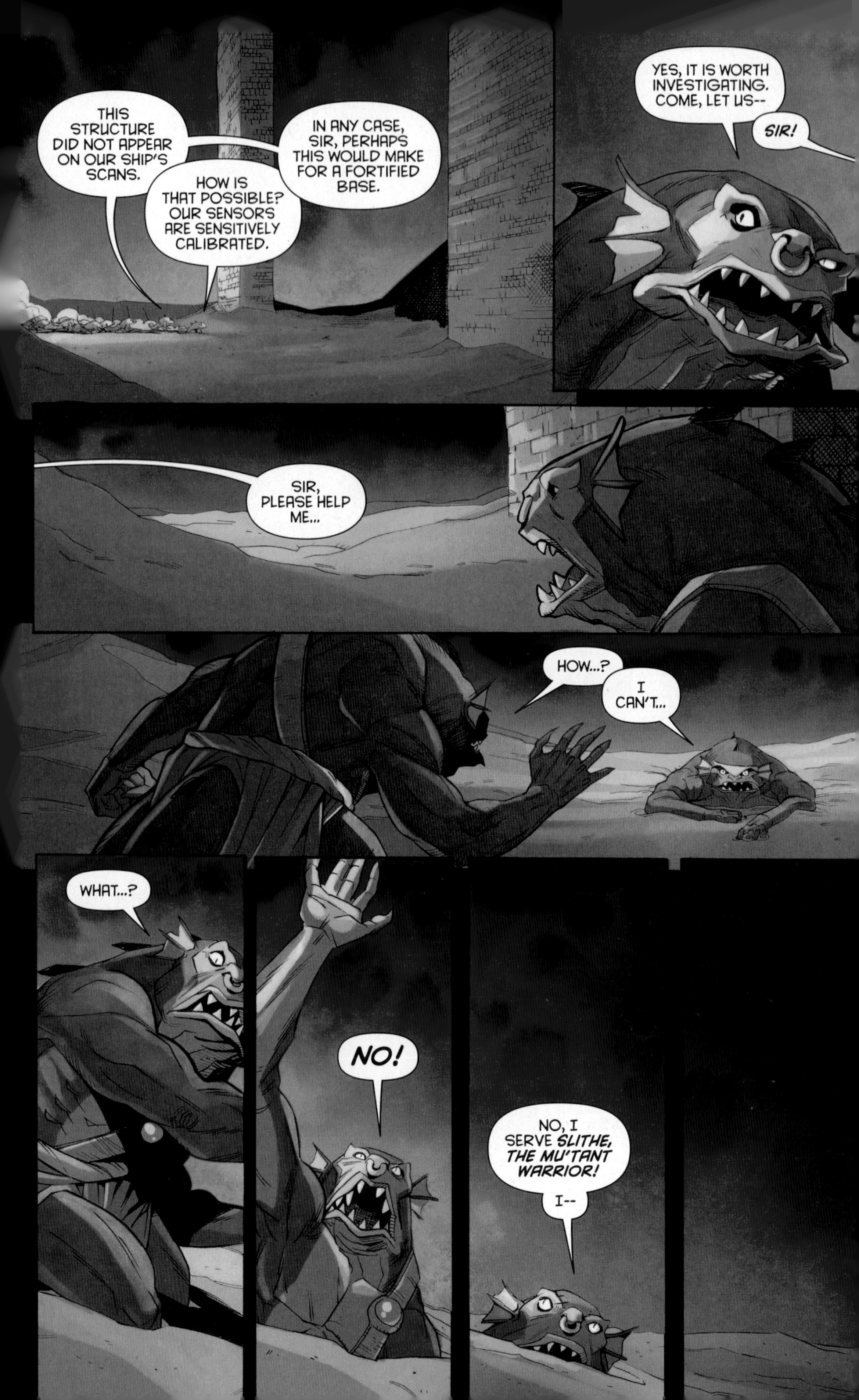
THIS STRUCTURE DID NOT APPEAR ON OUR SHIP'S SCANS.
HOW IS THAT POSSIBLE? OUR SENSORS ARE SENSITIVELY CALIBRATED.
IN ANY CASE, SIR, PERHAPS THIS WOULD MAKE FOR A FORTIFIED BASE.
YES, IT IS WORTH INVESTIGATING. COME, LET US--
SIR!
SIR, PLEASE HELP ME...
HOW...?
I CAN'T...
WHAT...?
NO!
NO, I SERVE SLITHE, THE MU'TANT WARRIOR!
I--

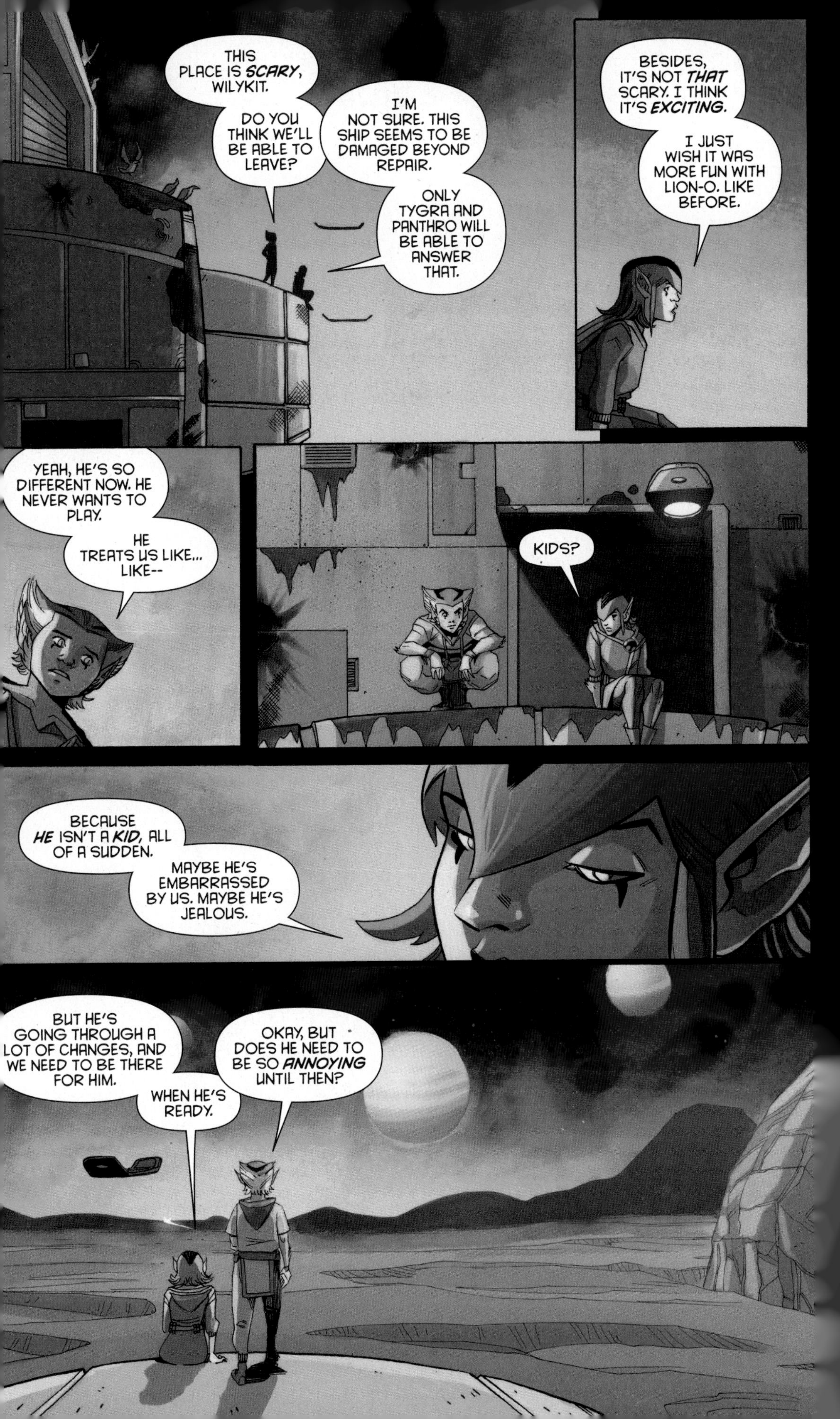
THIS PLACE IS SCARY, WILYKIT.
DO YOU THINK WE'LL BE ABLE TO LEAVE?
I'M NOT SURE. THIS SHIP SEEMS TO BE DAMAGED BEYOND REPAIR.
ONLY TYGRA AND PANTHRO WILL BE ABLE TO ANSWER THAT.
BESIDES, IT'S NOT THAT SCARY. I THINK IT'S EXCITING.
I JUST WISH IT WAS MORE FUN WITH LION-O. LIKE BEFORE.
YEAH, HE'S SO DIFFERENT NOW. HE NEVER WANTS TO PLAY.
HE TREATS US LIKE... LIKE--
KIDS?
BECAUSE HE ISN'T A KID, ALL OF A SUDDEN.
MAYBE HE'S EMBARRASSED BY US. MAYBE HE'S JEALOUS.
BUT HE'S GOING THROUGH A LOT OF CHANGES, AND WE NEED TO BE THERE FOR HIM.
WHEN HE'S READY.
OKAY, BUT DOES HE NEED TO BE SO ANNOYING UNTIL THEN?

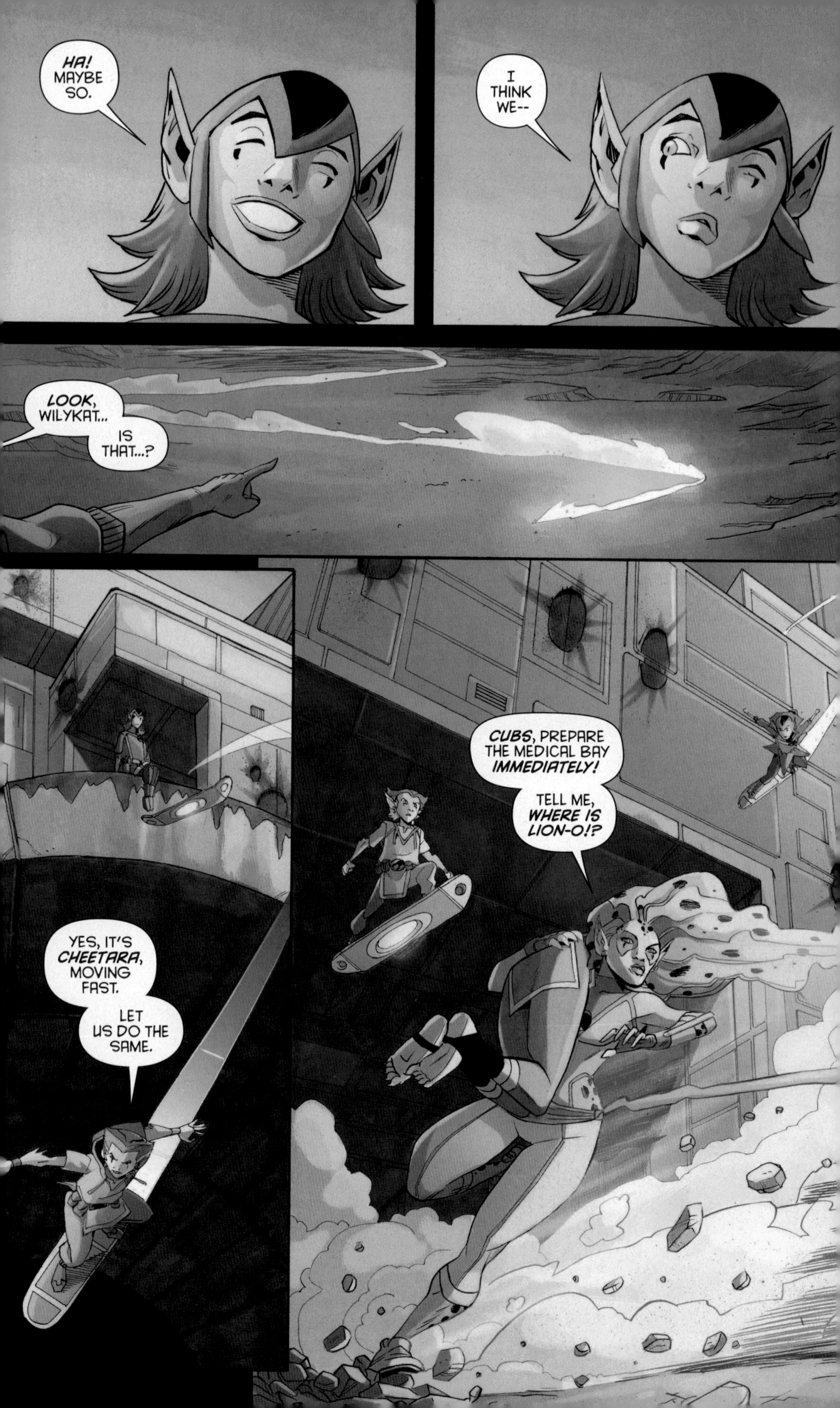
HA! MAYBE SO.
I THINK WE--
LOOK, WILYKAT...
IS THAT...?
YES, IT'S CHEETARA, MOVING FAST.
LET US DO THE SAME.
CUBS, PREPARE THE MEDICAL BAY IMMEDIATELY!
TELL ME, WHERE IS LION-O!?

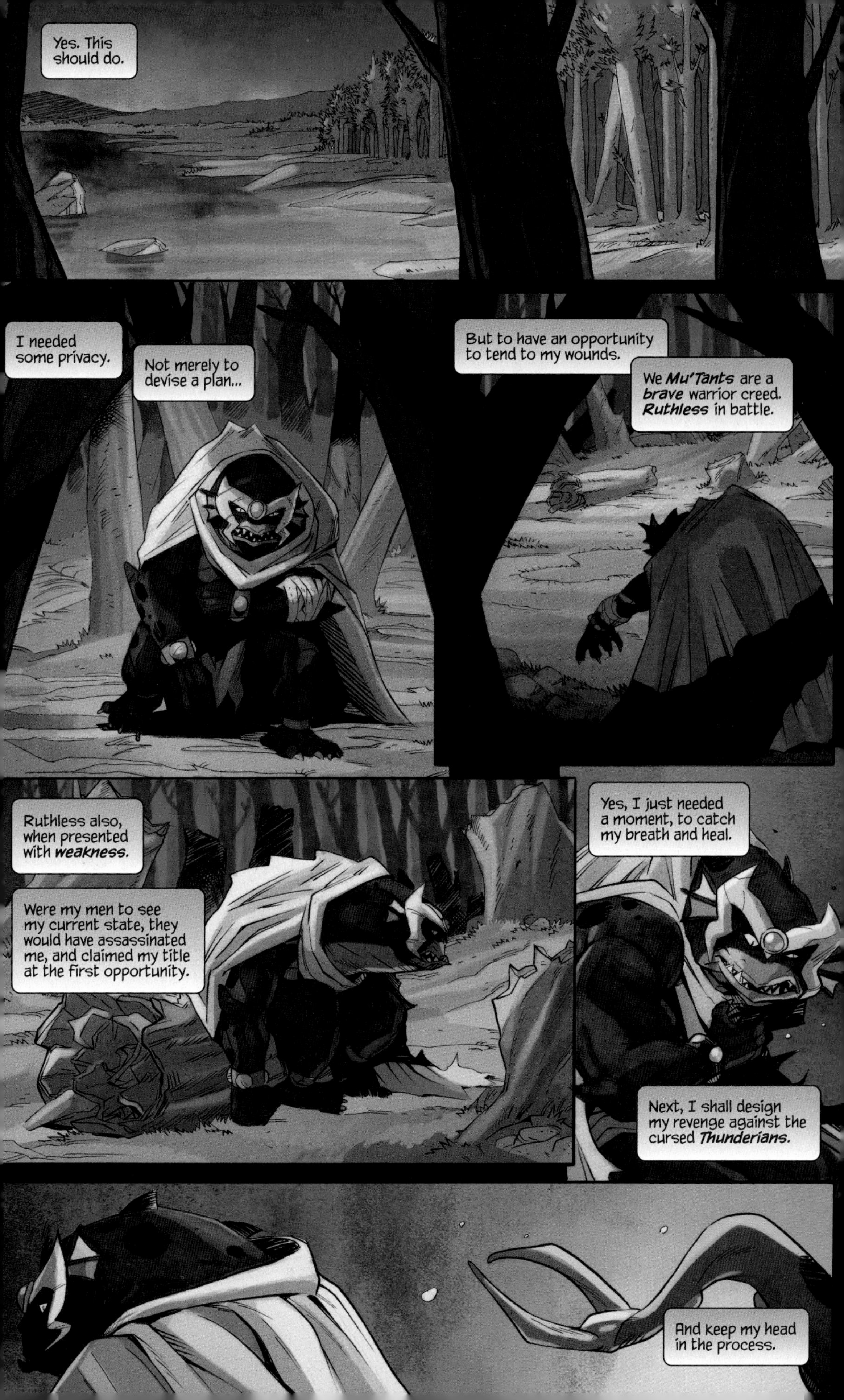
Yes. This should do.
I needed some privacy.
Not merely to devise a plan...
But to have an opportunity to tend to my wounds.
We Mu'Tants are a brave warrior creed. Ruthless in battle.
Ruthless also, when presented with weakness.
Were my men to see my current state, they would have assassinated me, and claimed my title at the first opportunity.
Yes, I just needed a moment, to catch my breath and heal.
Next, I shall design my revenge against the cursed Thunderians.
And keep my head in the process.

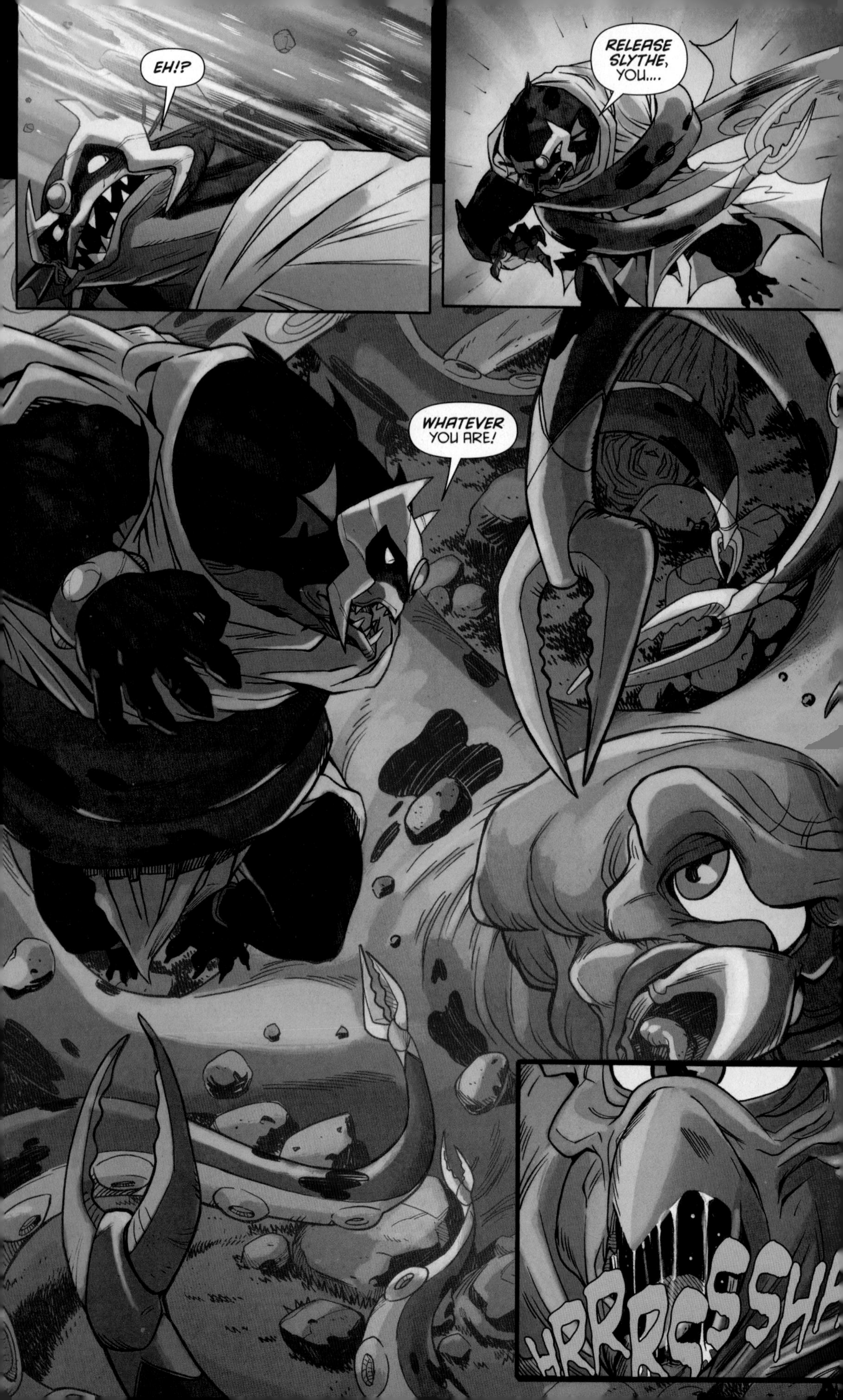
EH!?
RELEASE SLYTHE, YOU....
WHATEVER YOU ARE!
HRRRGSSHA

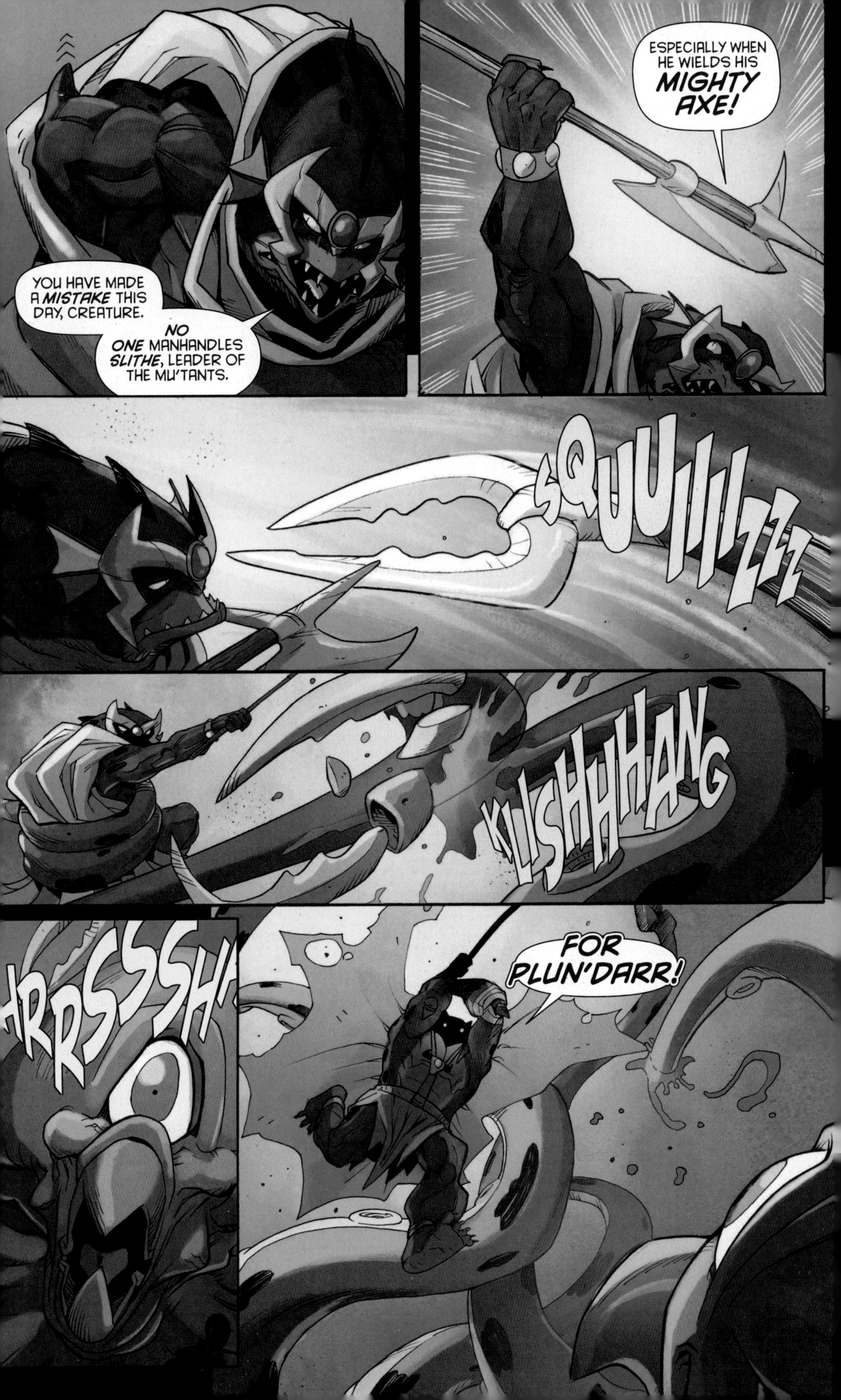
YOU HAVE MADE A *MISTAKE* THIS DAY, CREATURE.
NO ONE MANHANDLES *SLITHE*, LEADER OF THE MU'TANTS.
ESPECIALLY WHEN HE WIELDS HIS *MIGHTY AXE!*
SQUUIIIIZZZ
KLISHHHANG
HRRSSSH
FOR PLUN'DARR!

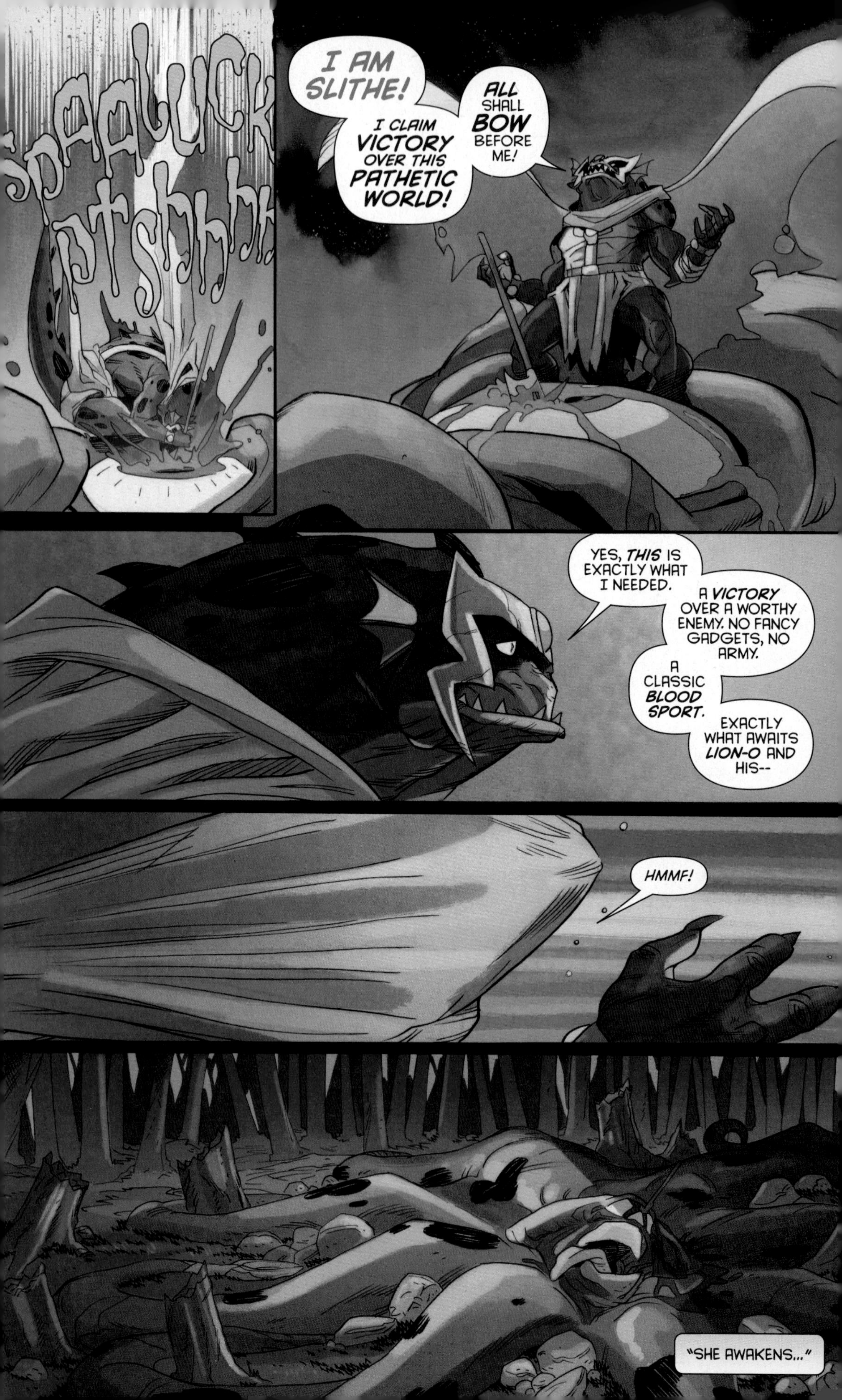
SPAALUCK
PTSHHH!
I AM SLITHE!
I CLAIM VICTORY OVER THIS PATHETIC WORLD!
ALL SHALL BOW BEFORE ME!
YES, THIS IS EXACTLY WHAT I NEEDED.
A VICTORY OVER A WORTHY ENEMY. NO FANCY GADGETS, NO ARMY.
A CLASSIC BLOOD SPORT.
EXACTLY WHAT AWAITS LION-O AND HIS--
HMMF!
"SHE AWAKENS..."

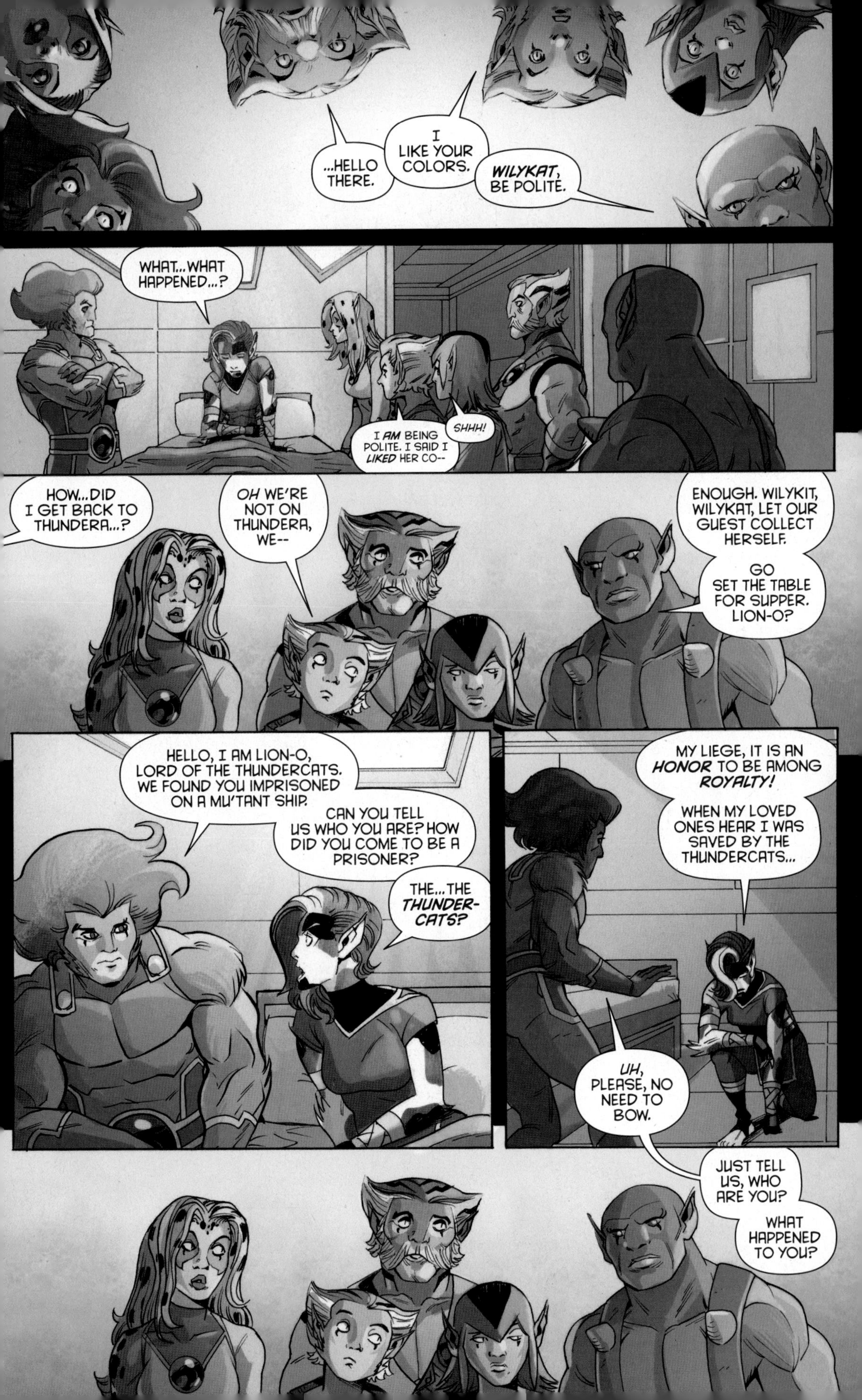
...HELLO THERE.
I LIKE YOUR COLORS.
WILYKAT, BE POLITE.
WHAT...WHAT HAPPENED...?
I AM BEING POLITE. I SAID I LIKED HER CO--
SHHH!
HOW...DID I GET BACK TO THUNDERA...?
OH WE'RE NOT ON THUNDERA, WE--
ENOUGH. WILYKIT, WILYKAT, LET OUR GUEST COLLECT HERSELF.
GO SET THE TABLE FOR SUPPER. LION-O?
HELLO, I AM LION-O, LORD OF THE THUNDERCATS. WE FOUND YOU IMPRISONED ON A MU'TANT SHIP.
CAN YOU TELL US WHO YOU ARE? HOW DID YOU COME TO BE A PRISONER?
THE...THE THUNDER-CATS?
MY LIEGE, IT IS AN HONOR TO BE AMONG ROYALTY!
WHEN MY LOVED ONES HEAR I WAS SAVED BY THE THUNDERCATS...
UH, PLEASE, NO NEED TO BOW.
JUST TELL US, WHO ARE YOU?
WHAT HAPPENED TO YOU?

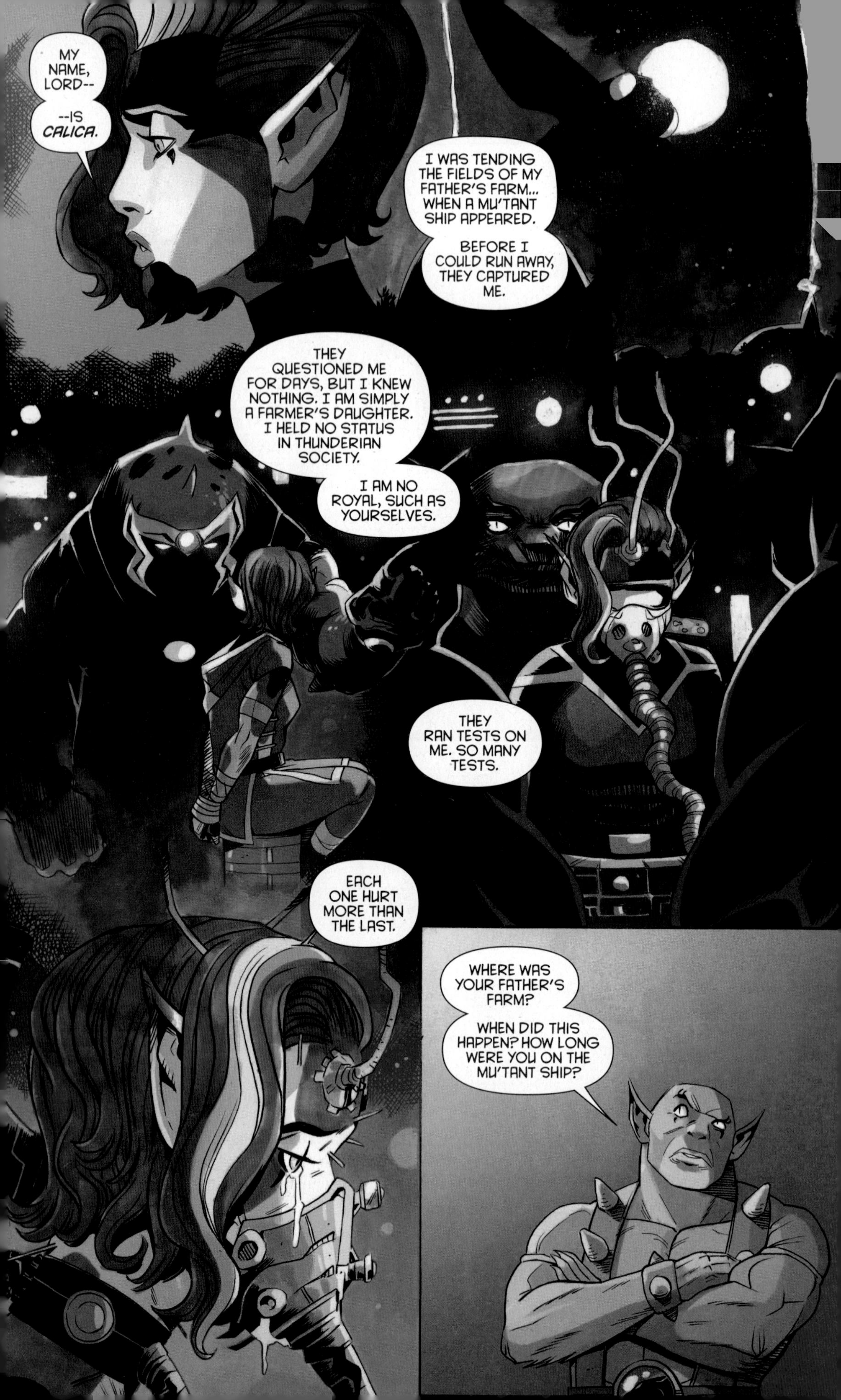

MY NAME, LORD--
--IS *CALICA.*
I WAS TENDING THE FIELDS OF MY FATHER'S FARM... WHEN A MU'TANT SHIP APPEARED.
BEFORE I COULD RUN AWAY, THEY CAPTURED ME.
THEY QUESTIONED ME FOR DAYS, BUT I KNEW NOTHING. I AM SIMPLY A FARMER'S DAUGHTER. I HELD NO STATUS IN THUNDERIAN SOCIETY.
I AM NO ROYAL, SUCH AS YOURSELVES.
THEY RAN TESTS ON ME. SO MANY TESTS.
EACH ONE HURT MORE THAN THE LAST.
WHERE WAS YOUR FATHER'S FARM?
WHEN DID THIS HAPPEN? HOW LONG WERE YOU ON THE MU'TANT SHIP?

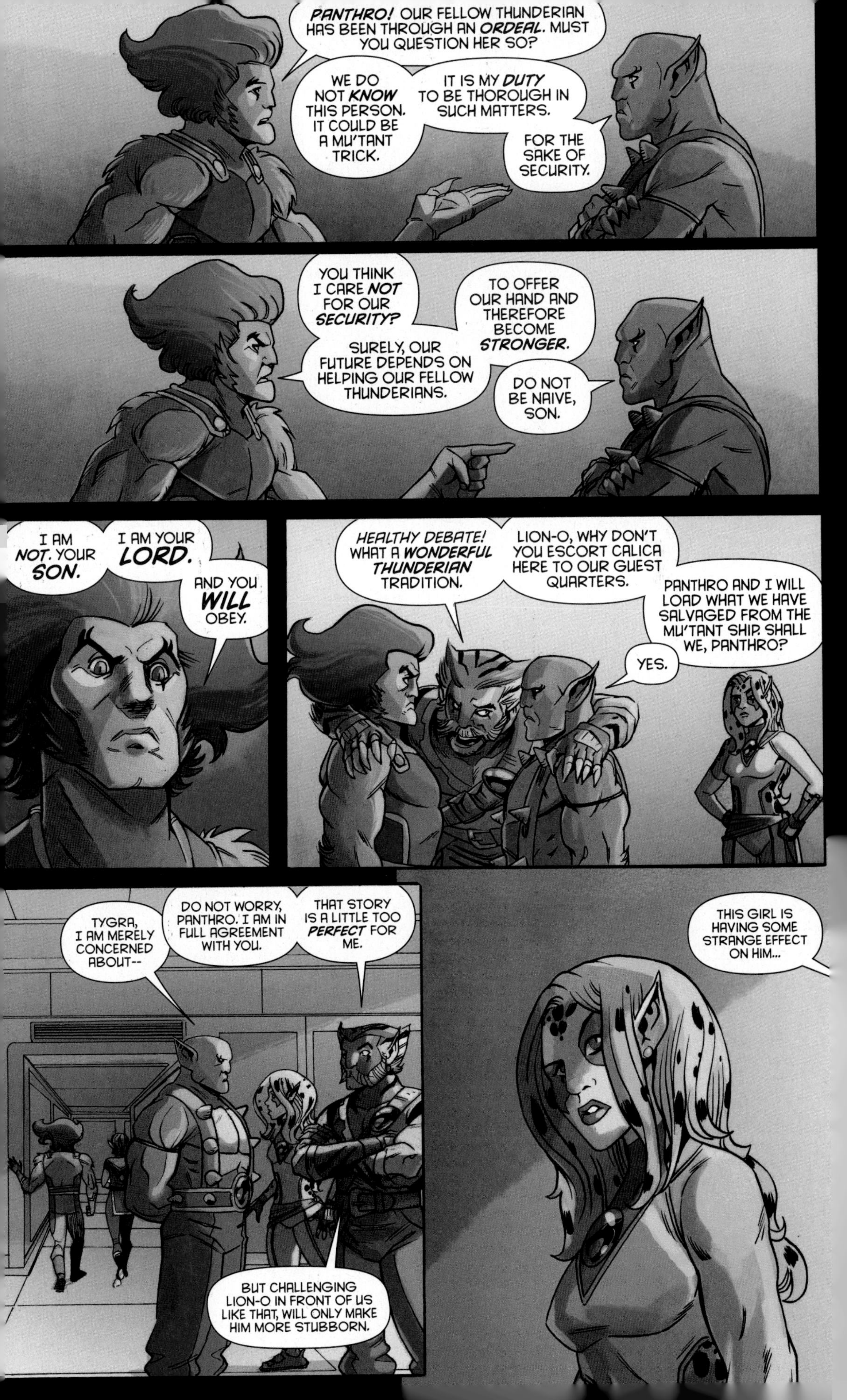
PANTHRO! OUR FELLOW THUNDERIAN HAS BEEN THROUGH AN ORDEAL. MUST YOU QUESTION HER SO?
WE DO NOT KNOW THIS PERSON. IT COULD BE A MU'TANT TRICK.
IT IS MY DUTY TO BE THOROUGH IN SUCH MATTERS.
FOR THE SAKE OF SECURITY.
YOU THINK I CARE NOT FOR OUR SECURITY?
SURELY, OUR FUTURE DEPENDS ON HELPING OUR FELLOW THUNDERIANS.
TO OFFER OUR HAND AND THEREFORE BECOME STRONGER.
DO NOT BE NAIVE, SON.
I AM NOT. YOUR SON.
I AM YOUR LORD.
AND YOU WILL OBEY.
HEALTHY DEBATE! WHAT A WONDERFUL THUNDERIAN TRADITION.
LION-O, WHY DON'T YOU ESCORT CALICA HERE TO OUR GUEST QUARTERS.
PANTHRO AND I WILL LOAD WHAT WE HAVE SALVAGED FROM THE MU'TANT SHIP. SHALL WE, PANTHRO?
YES.
TYGRA, I AM MERELY CONCERNED ABOUT--
DO NOT WORRY, PANTHRO. I AM IN FULL AGREEMENT WITH YOU.
THAT STORY IS A LITTLE TOO PERFECT FOR ME.
BUT CHALLENGING LION-O IN FRONT OF US LIKE THAT, WILL ONLY MAKE HIM MORE STUBBORN.
THIS GIRL IS HAVING SOME STRANGE EFFECT ON HIM...

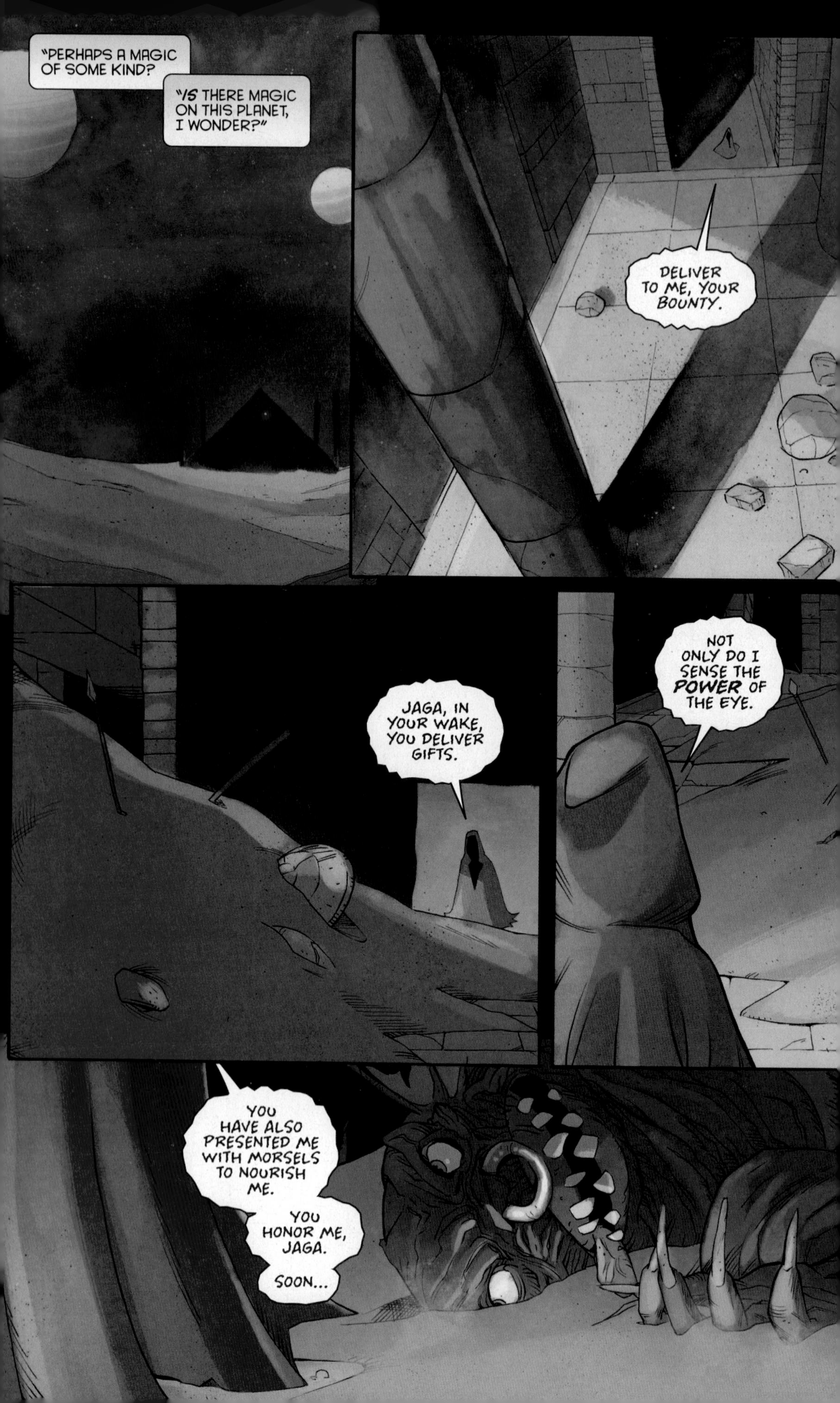
"PERHAPS A MAGIC OF SOME KIND?
"IS THERE MAGIC ON THIS PLANET, I WONDER?"
DELIVER TO ME, YOUR BOUNTY.
JAGA, IN YOUR WAKE, YOU DELIVER GIFTS.
NOT ONLY DO I SENSE THE POWER OF THE EYE.
YOU HAVE ALSO PRESENTED ME WITH MORSELS TO NOURISH ME.
YOU HONOR ME, JAGA.
SOON...

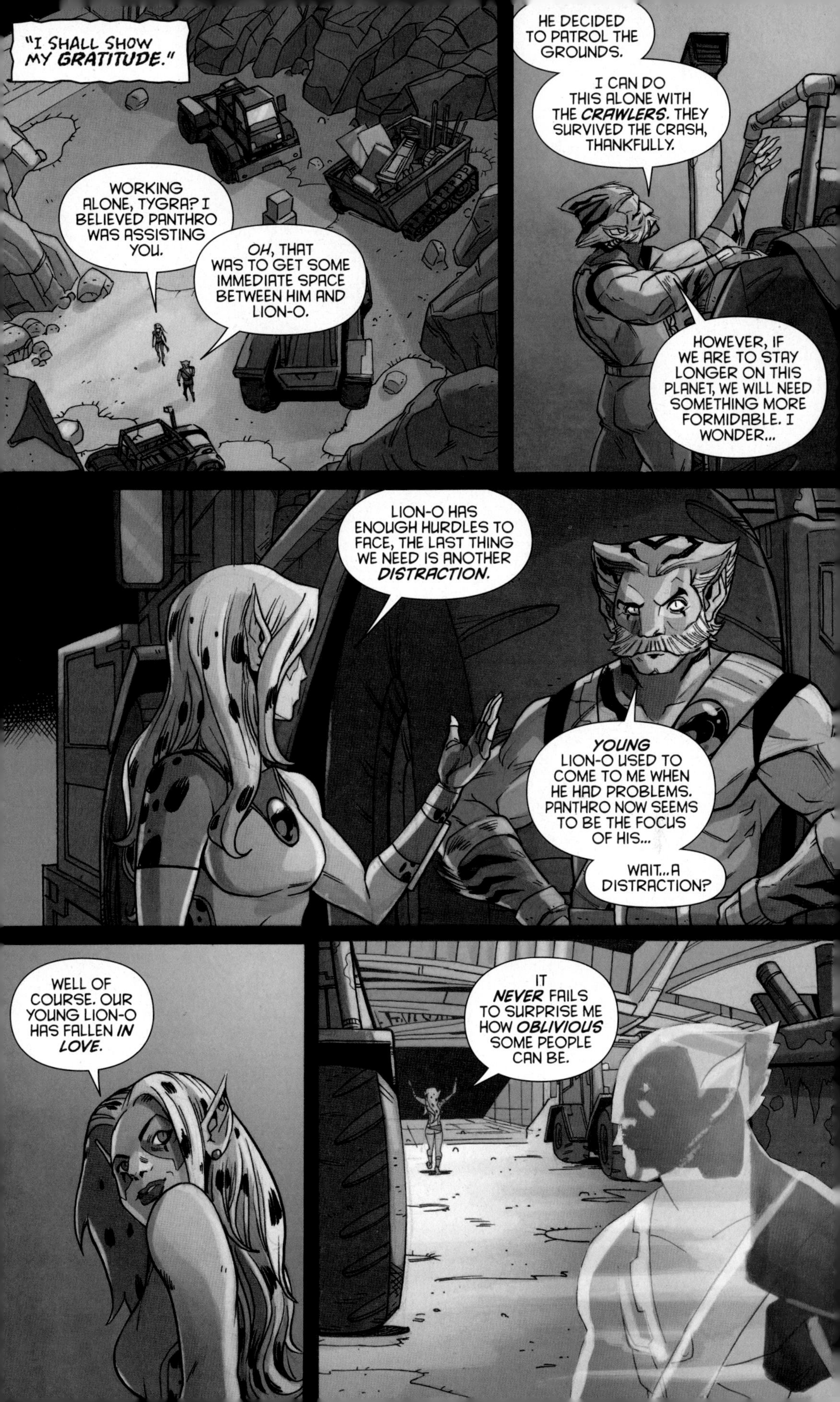
"I SHALL SHOW MY GRATITUDE."
WORKING ALONE, TYGRA? I BELIEVED PANTHRO WAS ASSISTING YOU.
OH, THAT WAS TO GET SOME IMMEDIATE SPACE BETWEEN HIM AND LION-O.
HE DECIDED TO PATROL THE GROUNDS.
I CAN DO THIS ALONE WITH THE CRAWLERS. THEY SURVIVED THE CRASH, THANKFULLY.
HOWEVER, IF WE ARE TO STAY LONGER ON THIS PLANET, WE WILL NEED SOMETHING MORE FORMIDABLE. I WONDER...
LION-O HAS ENOUGH HURDLES TO FACE, THE LAST THING WE NEED IS ANOTHER DISTRACTION.
YOUNG LION-O USED TO COME TO ME WHEN HE HAD PROBLEMS. PANTHRO NOW SEEMS TO BE THE FOCUS OF HIS...
WAIT...A DISTRACTION?
WELL OF COURSE. OUR YOUNG LION-O HAS FALLEN IN LOVE.
IT NEVER FAILS TO SURPRISE ME HOW OBLIVIOUS SOME PEOPLE CAN BE.

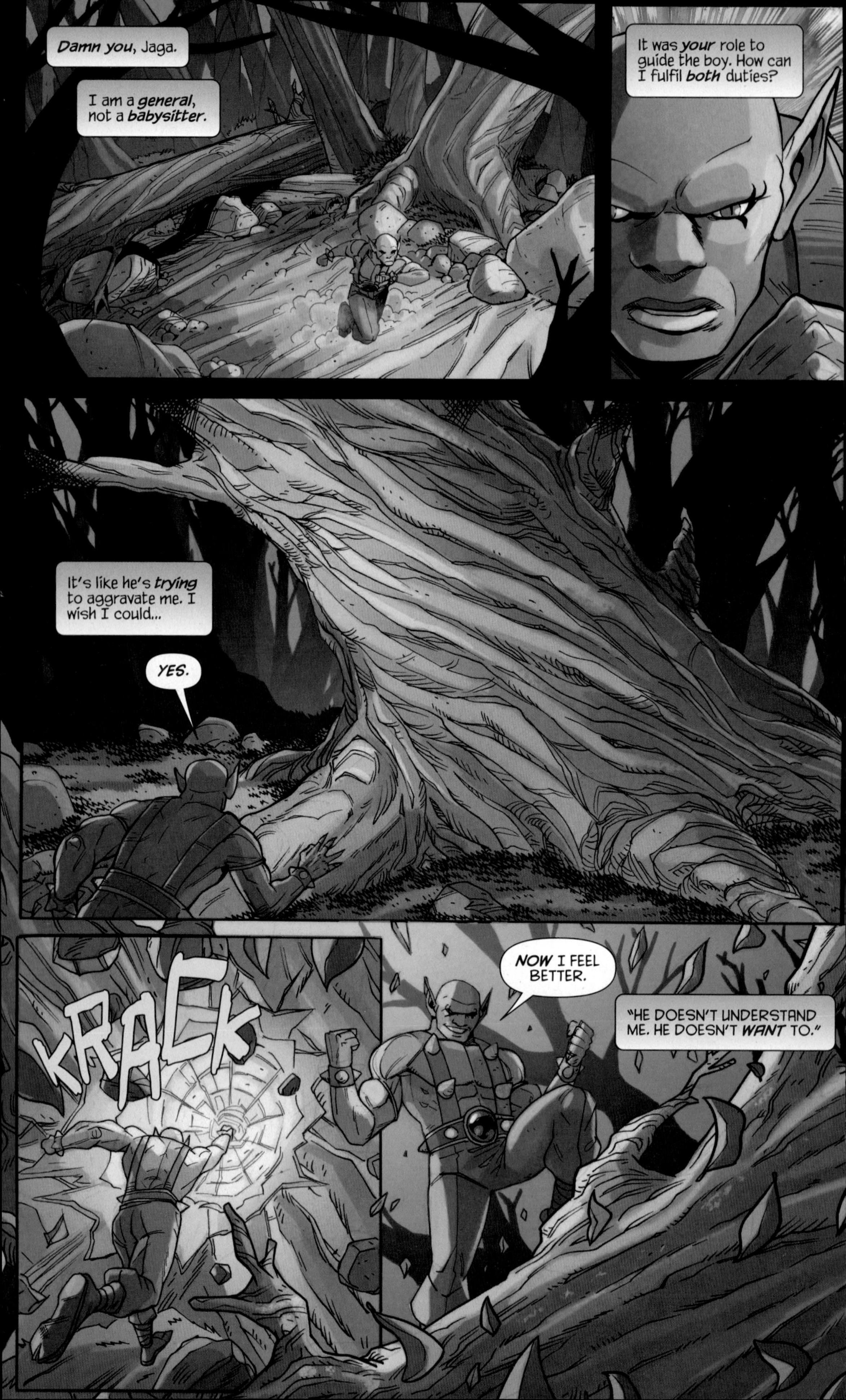
Damn you, Jaga.
I am a general, not a babysitter.
It was your role to guide the boy. How can I fulfil both duties?
It's like he's trying to aggravate me. I wish I could...
YES.
KRACK
NOW I FEEL BETTER.
"HE DOESN'T UNDERSTAND ME. HE DOESN'T WANT TO."

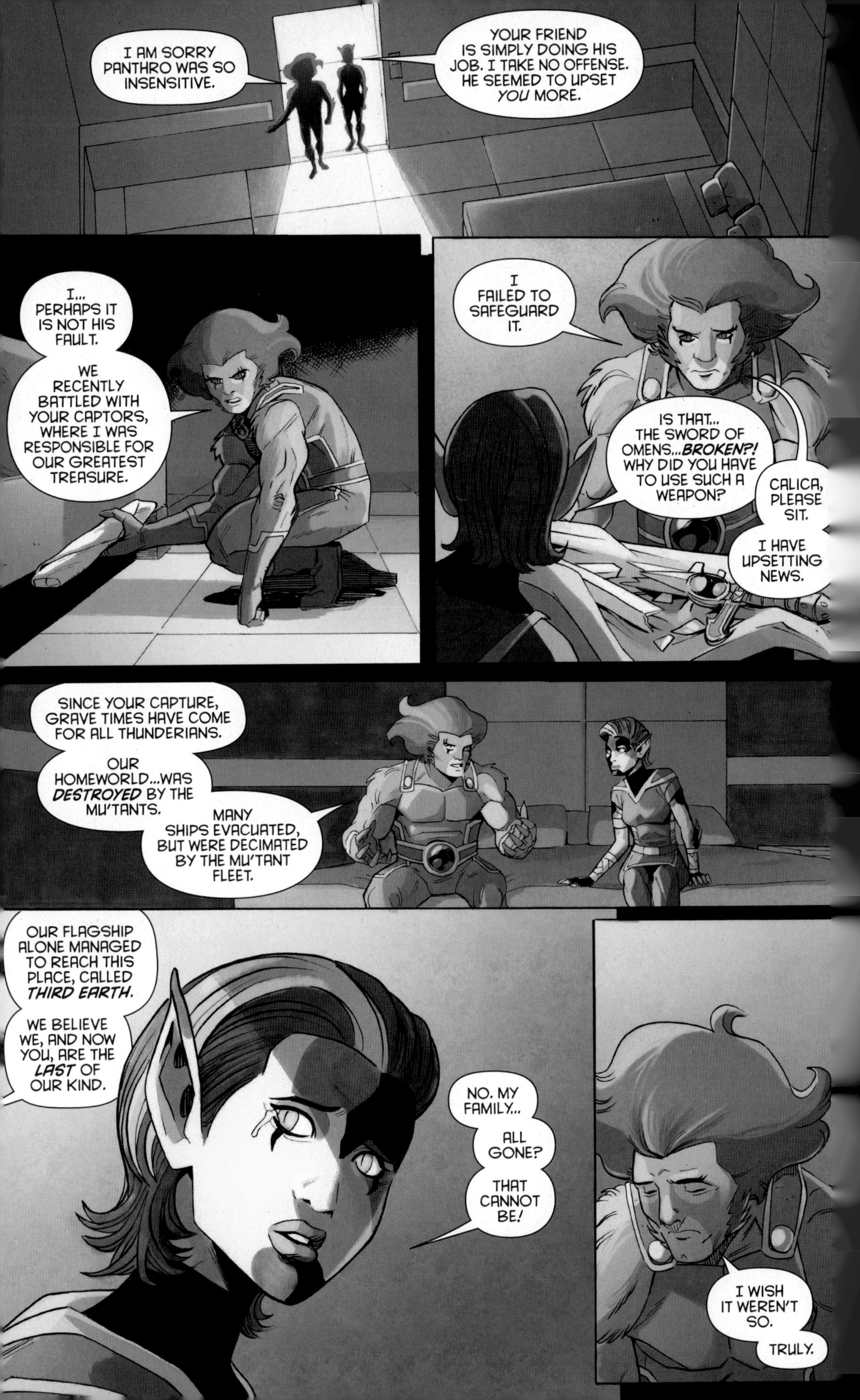
I AM SORRY PANTHRO WAS SO INSENSITIVE.
YOUR FRIEND IS SIMPLY DOING HIS JOB. I TAKE NO OFFENSE. HE SEEMED TO UPSET *YOU* MORE.
I... PERHAPS IT IS NOT HIS FAULT.
WE RECENTLY BATTLED WITH YOUR CAPTORS, WHERE I WAS RESPONSIBLE FOR OUR GREATEST TREASURE.
I FAILED TO SAFEGUARD IT.
IS THAT... THE SWORD OF OMENS...***BROKEN?!*** WHY DID YOU HAVE TO USE SUCH A WEAPON?
CALICA, PLEASE SIT.
I HAVE UPSETTING NEWS.
SINCE YOUR CAPTURE, GRAVE TIMES HAVE COME FOR ALL THUNDERIANS.
OUR HOMEWORLD...WAS ***DESTROYED*** BY THE MU'TANTS.
MANY SHIPS EVACUATED, BUT WERE DECIMATED BY THE MU'TANT FLEET.
OUR FLAGSHIP ALONE MANAGED TO REACH THIS PLACE, CALLED ***THIRD EARTH***.
WE BELIEVE WE, AND NOW YOU, ARE THE ***LAST*** OF OUR KIND.
NO. MY FAMILY...
ALL GONE?
THAT CANNOT BE!
I WISH IT WEREN'T SO.
TRULY.

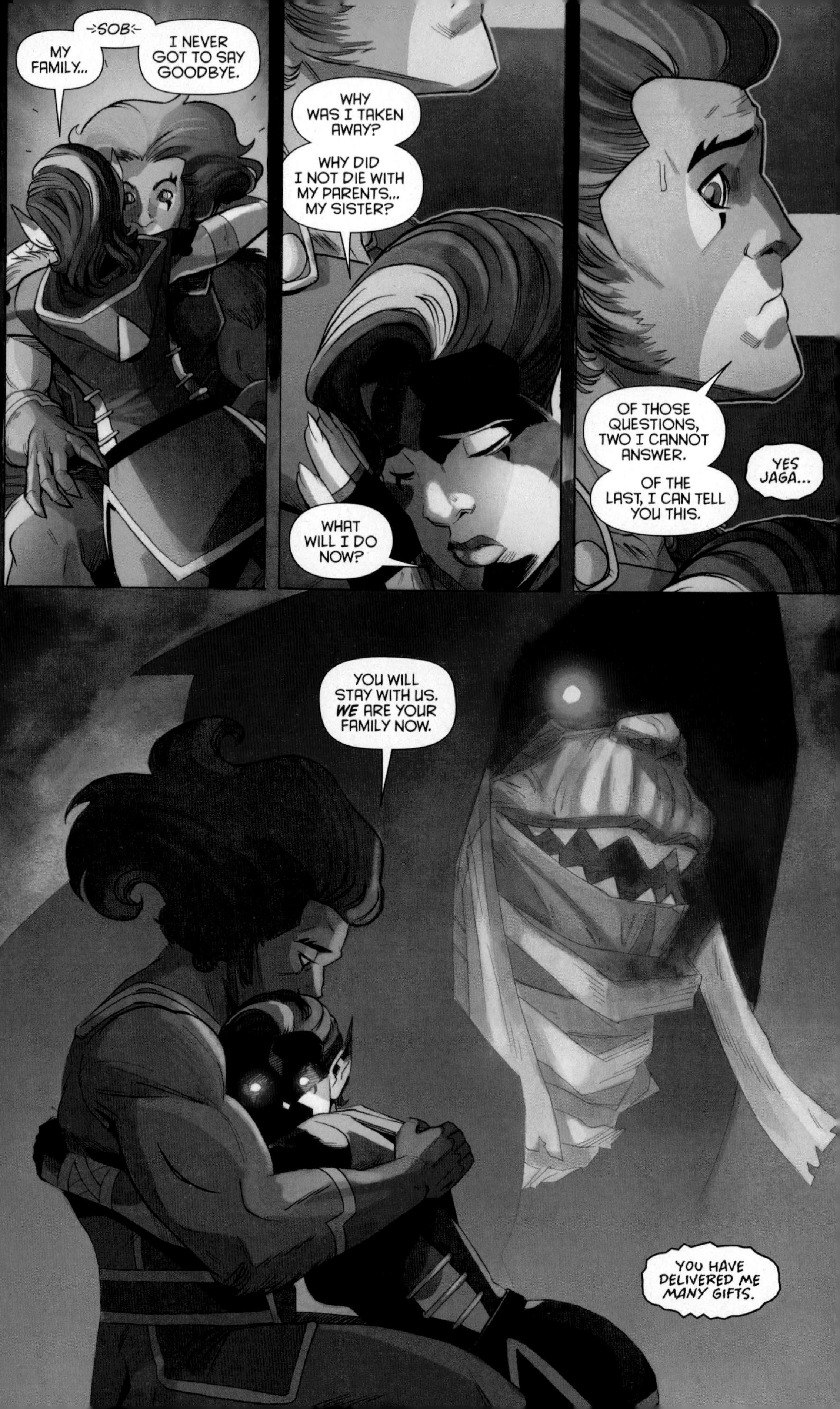
MY FAMILY...
SOB
I NEVER GOT TO SAY GOODBYE.
WHY WAS I TAKEN AWAY?
WHY DID I NOT DIE WITH MY PARENTS... MY SISTER?
WHAT WILL I DO NOW?
OF THOSE QUESTIONS, TWO I CANNOT ANSWER.
OF THE LAST, I CAN TELL YOU THIS.
YES JAGA...
YOU WILL STAY WITH US. WE ARE YOUR FAMILY NOW.
YOU HAVE DELIVERED ME MANY GIFTS.

THREE

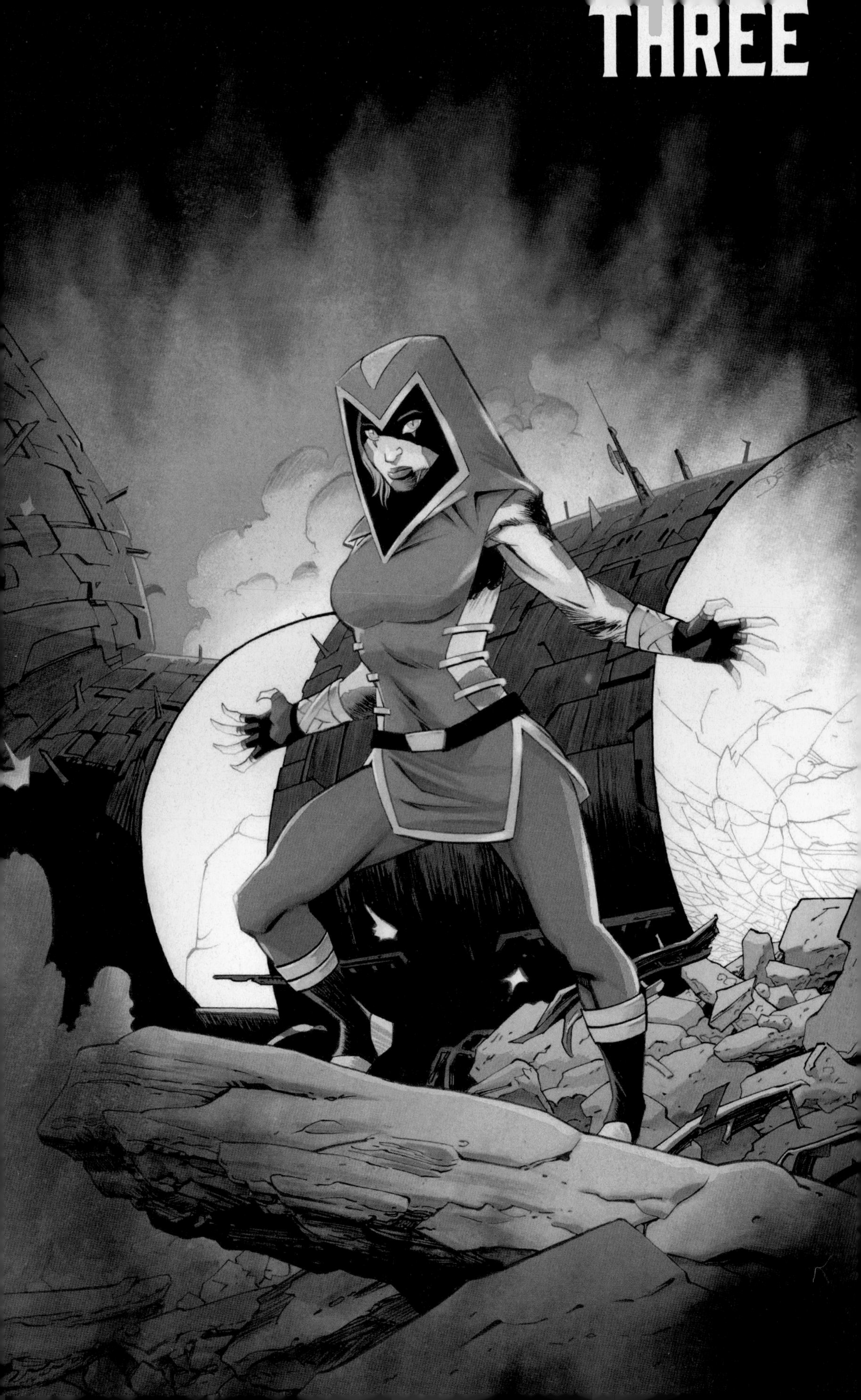

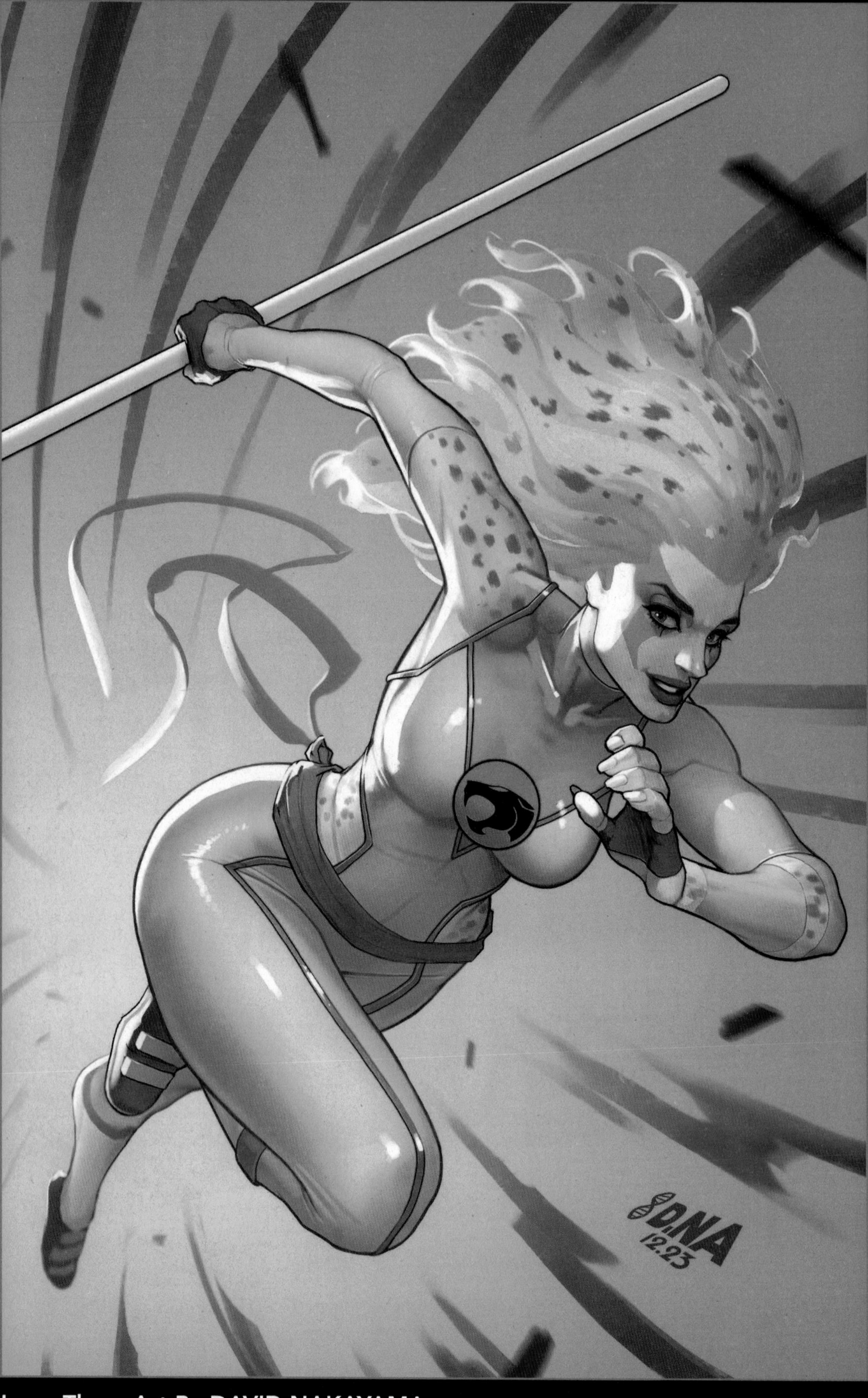
D.NA
12.23

Issue Three Art By DAVID NAKAYAMA

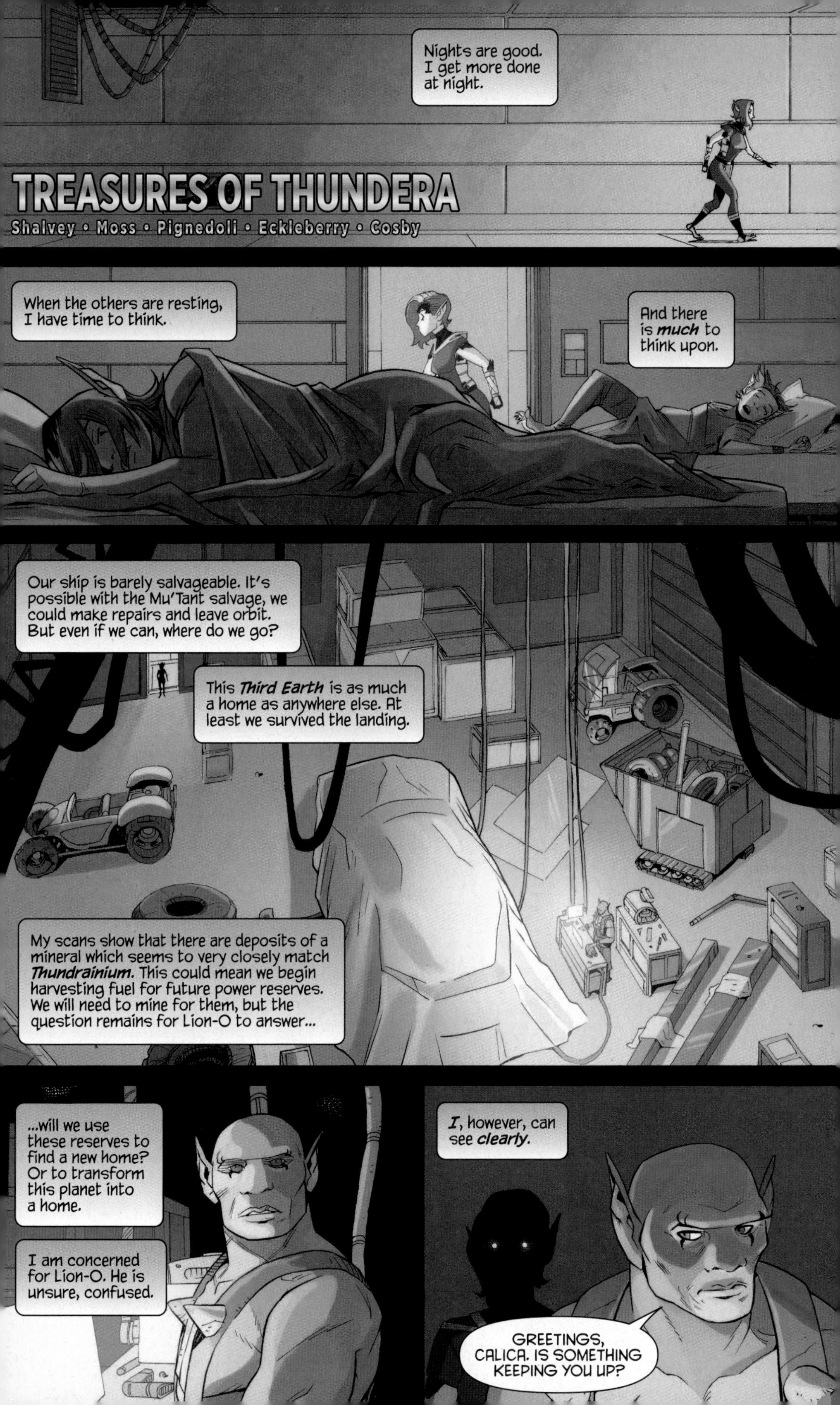
Nights are good. I get more done at night.
TREASURES OF THUNDERA
Shalvey • Moss • Pignedoli • Eckleberry • Cosby
When the others are resting, I have time to think.
And there is *much* to think upon.
Our ship is barely salvageable. It's possible with the Mu'Tant salvage, we could make repairs and leave orbit. But even if we can, where do we go?
This *Third Earth* is as much a home as anywhere else. At least we survived the landing.
My scans show that there are deposits of a mineral which seems to very closely match *Thundrainium*. This could mean we begin harvesting fuel for future power reserves. We will need to mine for them, but the question remains for Lion-O to answer...
...will we use these reserves to find a new home? Or to transform this planet into a home.
I am concerned for Lion-O. He is unsure, confused.
I, however, can see *clearly*.
GREETINGS, CALICA. IS SOMETHING KEEPING YOU UP?

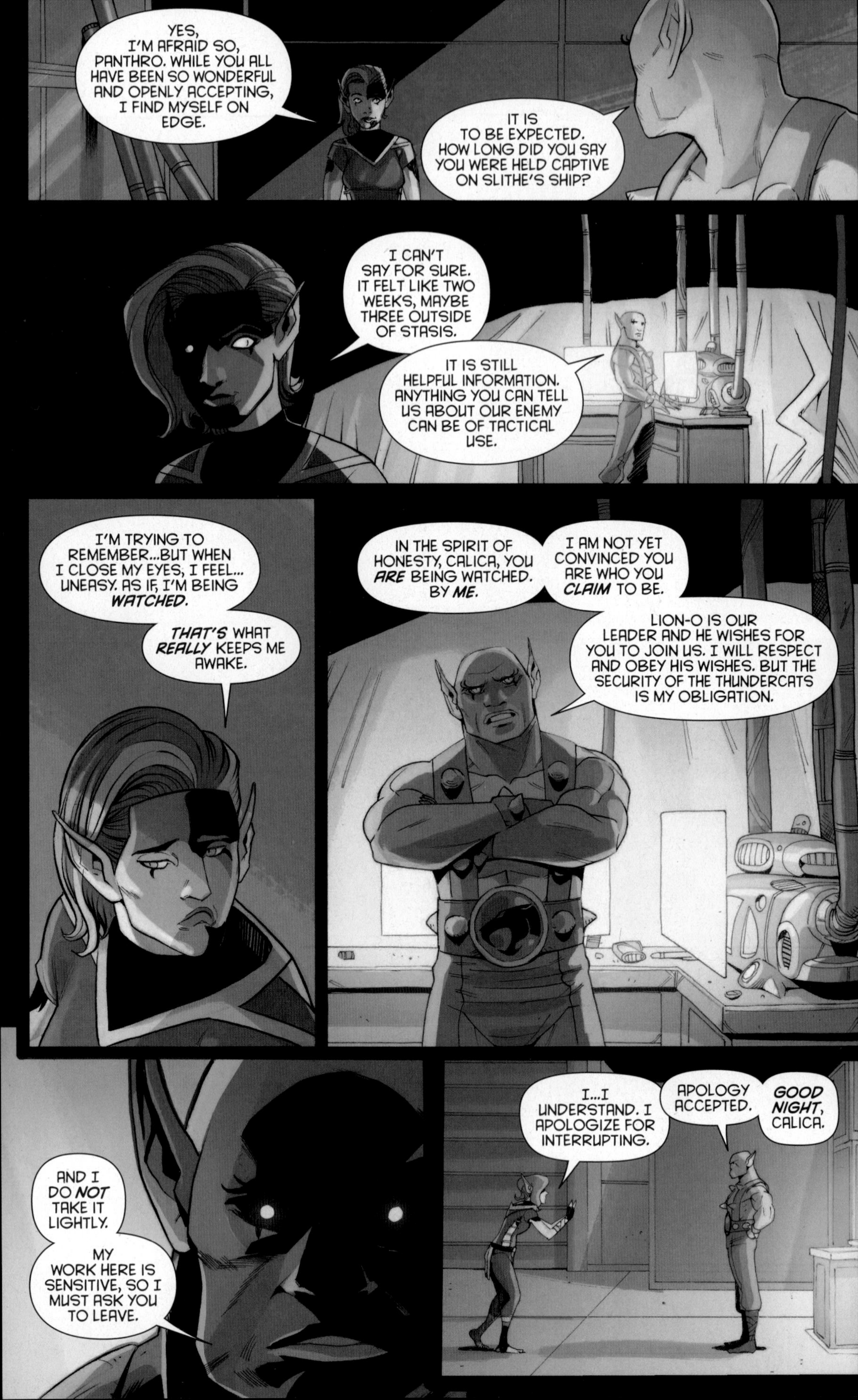
YES, I'M AFRAID SO, PANTHRO. WHILE YOU ALL HAVE BEEN SO WONDERFUL AND OPENLY ACCEPTING, I FIND MYSELF ON EDGE.
IT IS TO BE EXPECTED. HOW LONG DID YOU SAY YOU WERE HELD CAPTIVE ON SLITHE'S SHIP?
I CAN'T SAY FOR SURE. IT FELT LIKE TWO WEEKS, MAYBE THREE OUTSIDE OF STASIS.
IT IS STILL HELPFUL INFORMATION. ANYTHING YOU CAN TELL US ABOUT OUR ENEMY CAN BE OF TACTICAL USE.
I'M TRYING TO REMEMBER...BUT WHEN I CLOSE MY EYES, I FEEL... UNEASY. AS IF, I'M BEING WATCHED.
THAT'S WHAT REALLY KEEPS ME AWAKE.
IN THE SPIRIT OF HONESTY, CALICA, YOU ARE BEING WATCHED. BY ME.
I AM NOT YET CONVINCED YOU ARE WHO YOU CLAIM TO BE.
LION-O IS OUR LEADER AND HE WISHES FOR YOU TO JOIN US. I WILL RESPECT AND OBEY HIS WISHES. BUT THE SECURITY OF THE THUNDERCATS IS MY OBLIGATION.
AND I DO NOT TAKE IT LIGHTLY.
MY WORK HERE IS SENSITIVE, SO I MUST ASK YOU TO LEAVE.
I...I UNDERSTAND. I APOLOGIZE FOR INTERRUPTING.
APOLOGY ACCEPTED.
GOOD NIGHT, CALICA.

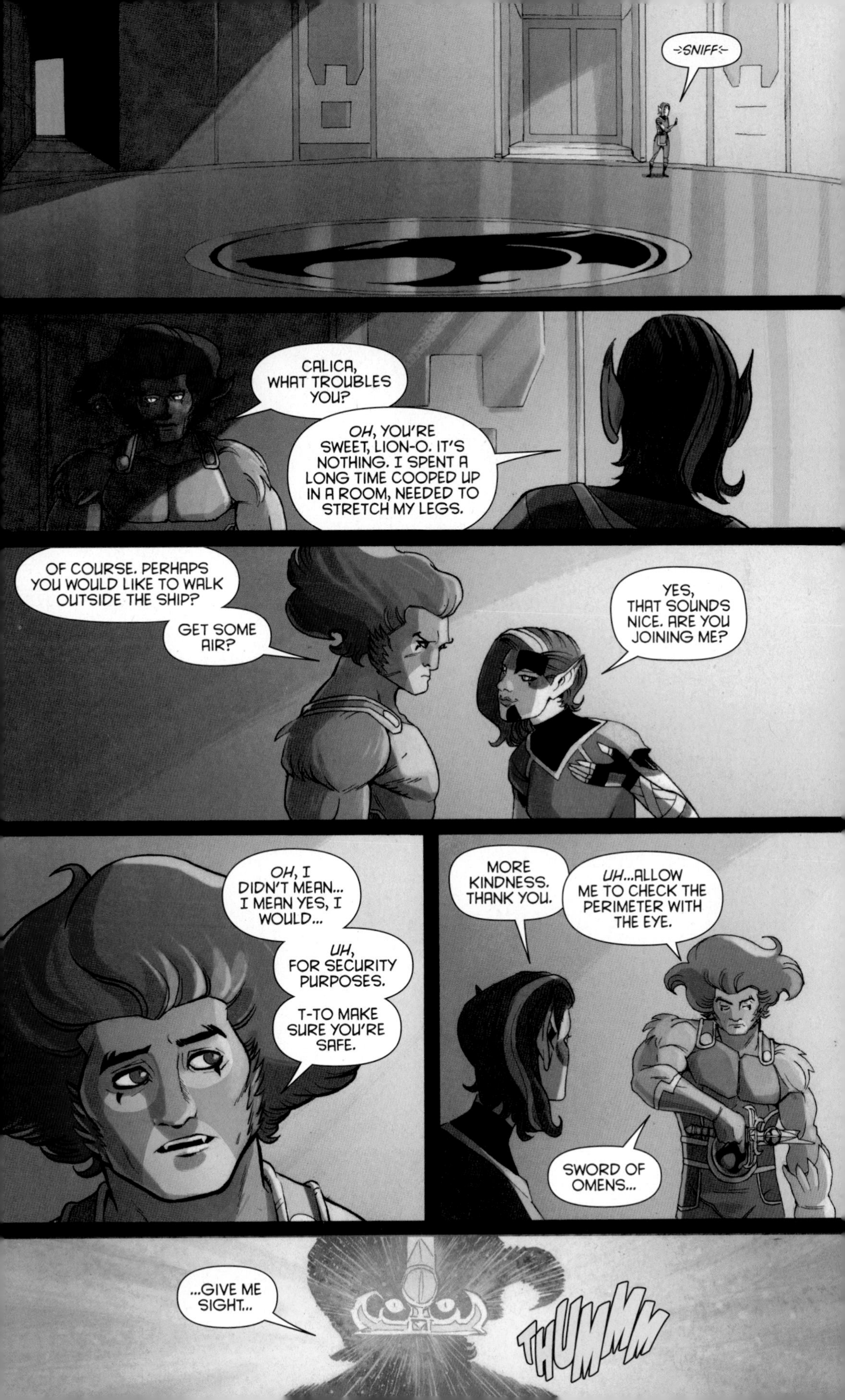
SNIFF
CALICA, WHAT TROUBLES YOU?
OH, YOU'RE SWEET, LION-O. IT'S NOTHING. I SPENT A LONG TIME COOPED UP IN A ROOM, NEEDED TO STRETCH MY LEGS.
OF COURSE. PERHAPS YOU WOULD LIKE TO WALK OUTSIDE THE SHIP?
GET SOME AIR?
YES, THAT SOUNDS NICE. ARE YOU JOINING ME?
OH, I DIDN'T MEAN... I MEAN YES, I WOULD...
UH, FOR SECURITY PURPOSES.
T-TO MAKE SURE YOU'RE SAFE.
MORE KINDNESS. THANK YOU.
UH...ALLOW ME TO CHECK THE PERIMETER WITH THE EYE.
SWORD OF OMENS...
...GIVE ME SIGHT...
THUMMMM

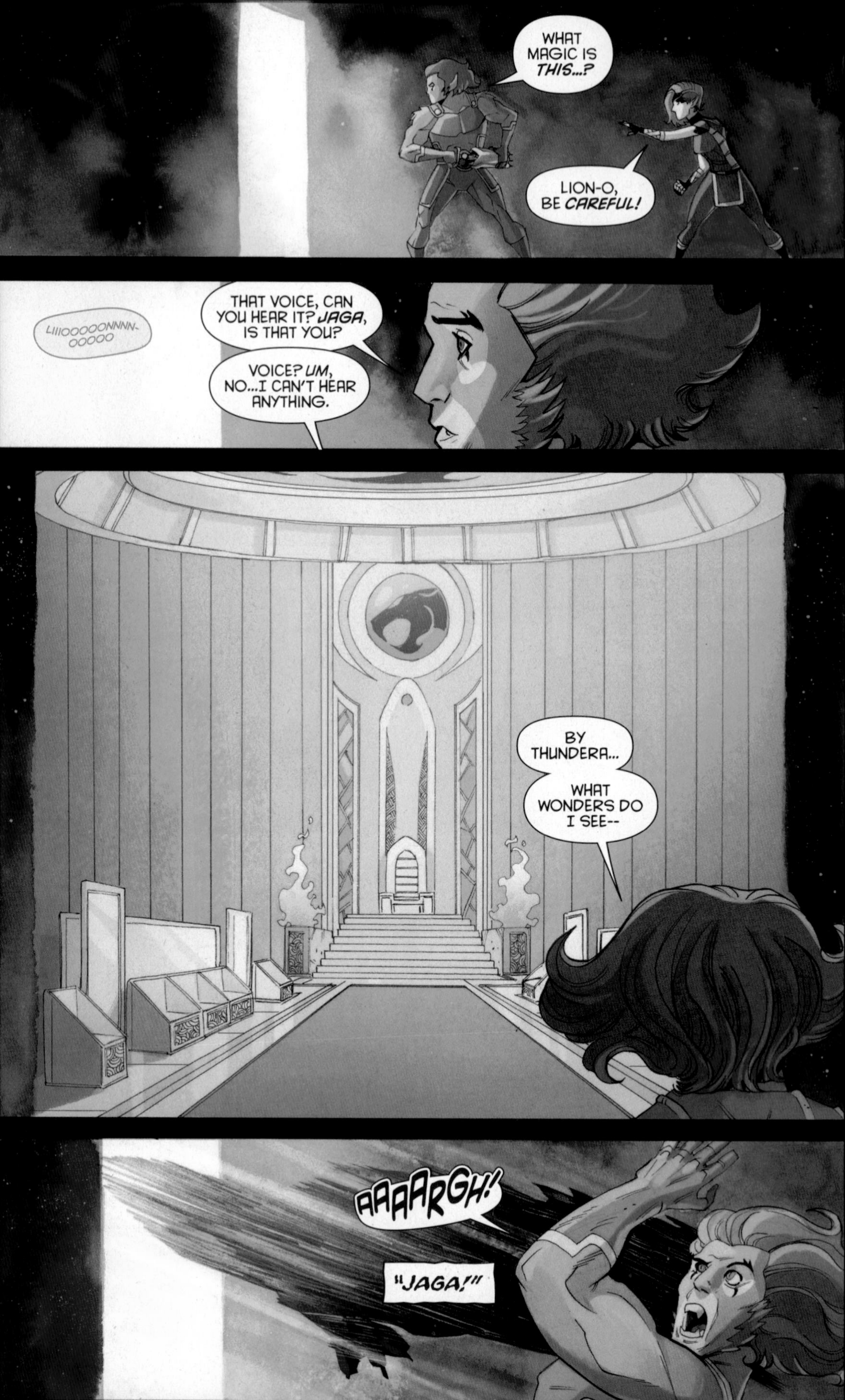
WHAT MAGIC IS THIS...?
LION-O, BE CAREFUL!
LIIIOOOOONNNN-OOOOO
THAT VOICE, CAN YOU HEAR IT? JAGA, IS THAT YOU?
VOICE? UM, NO...I CAN'T HEAR ANYTHING.
BY THUNDERA...
WHAT WONDERS DO I SEE--
AAAARGH!
"JAGA!"

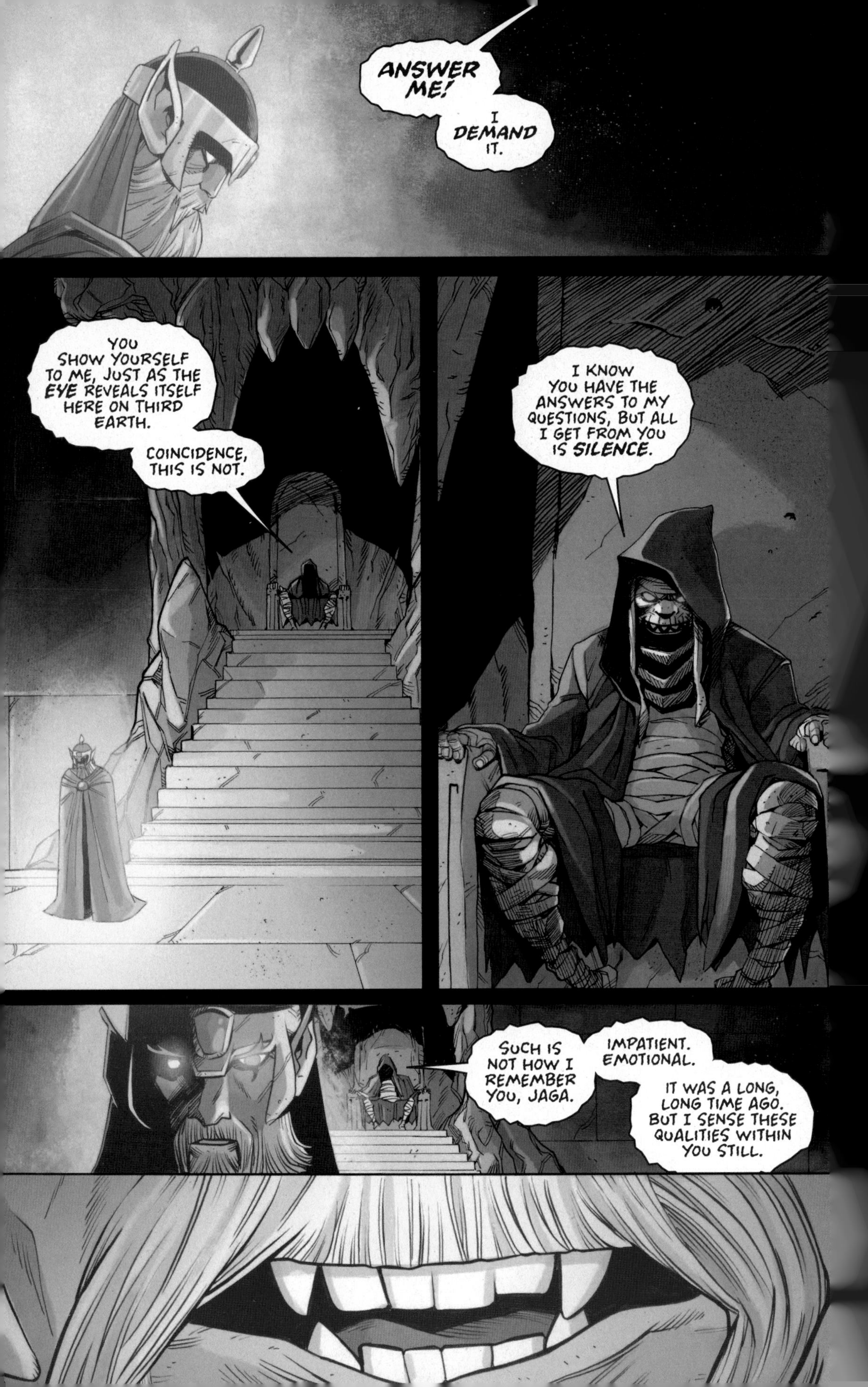

ANSWER ME!
I DEMAND IT.
YOU SHOW YOURSELF TO ME, JUST AS THE EYE REVEALS ITSELF HERE ON THIRD EARTH.
COINCIDENCE, THIS IS NOT.
I KNOW YOU HAVE THE ANSWERS TO MY QUESTIONS, BUT ALL I GET FROM YOU IS SILENCE.
SUCH IS NOT HOW I REMEMBER YOU, JAGA.
IMPATIENT. EMOTIONAL.
IT WAS A LONG, LONG TIME AGO. BUT I SENSE THESE QUALITIES WITHIN YOU STILL.

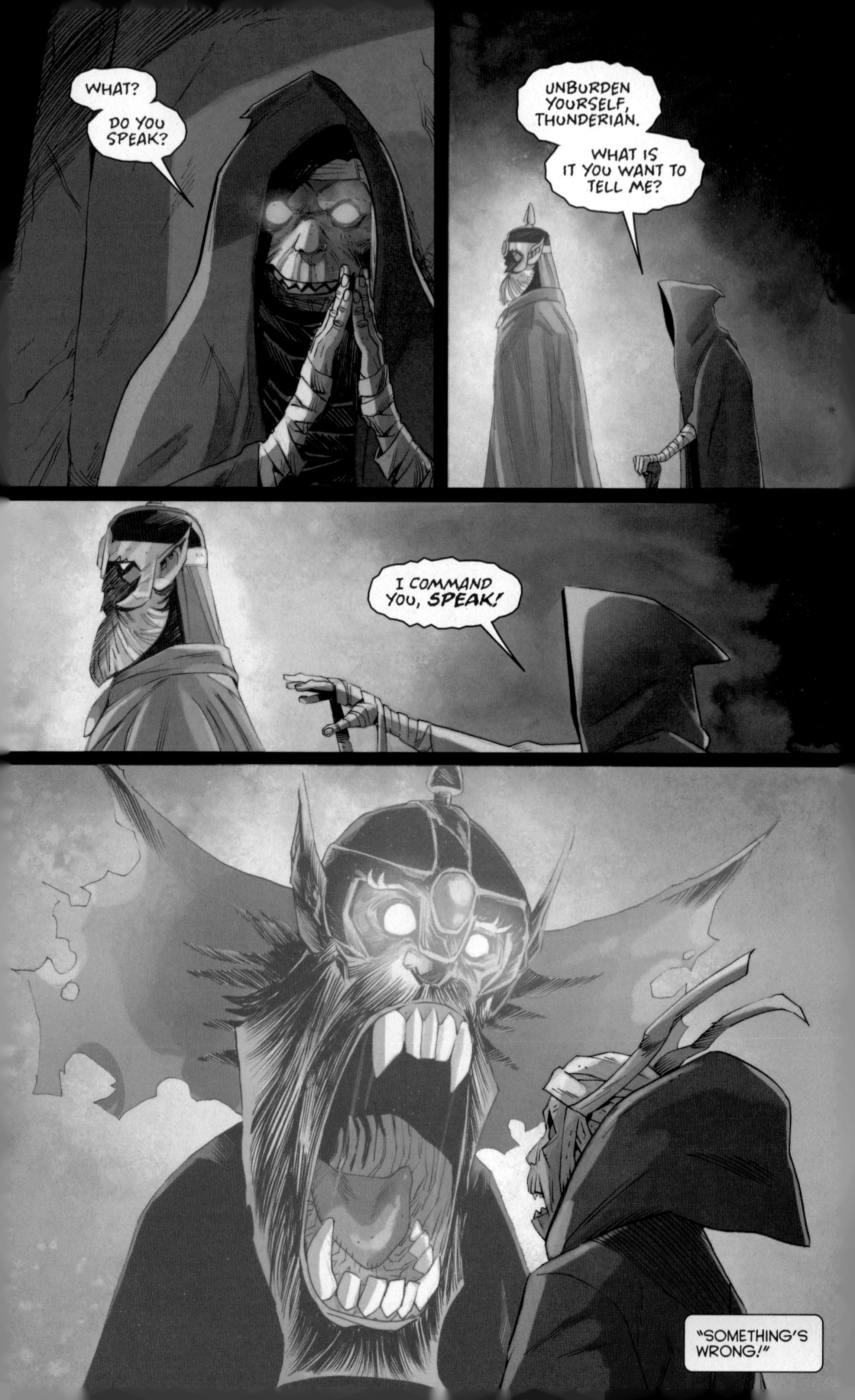

WHAT?
DO YOU SPEAK?
UNBURDEN YOURSELF, THUNDERIAN.
WHAT IS IT YOU WANT TO TELL ME?
I COMMAND YOU, **SPEAK!**
"SOMETHING'S WRONG!"

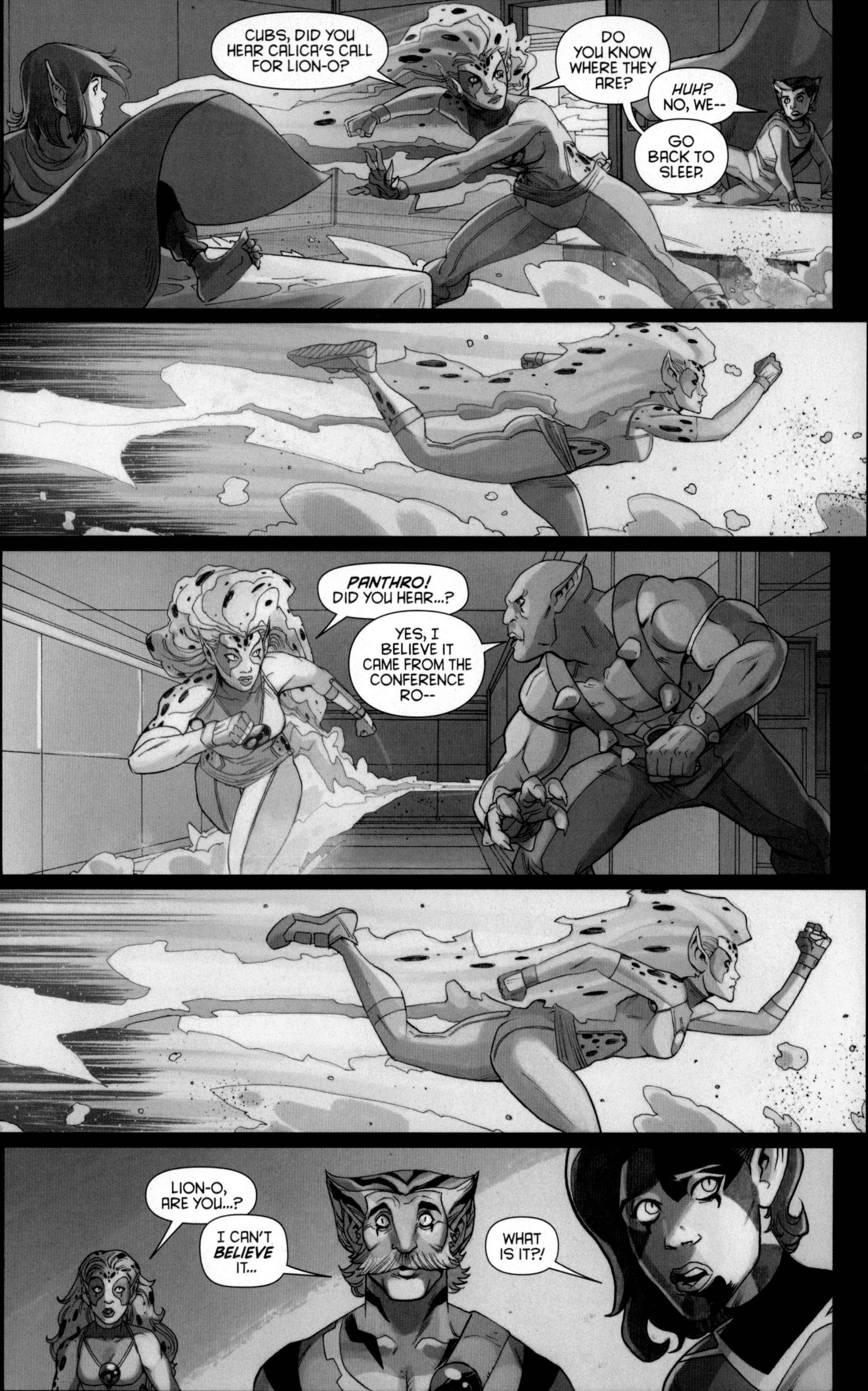
CUBS, DID YOU HEAR CALICA'S CALL FOR LION-O?
DO YOU KNOW WHERE THEY ARE?
HUH? NO, WE--
GO BACK TO SLEEP.
PANTHRO! DID YOU HEAR...?
YES, I BELIEVE IT CAME FROM THE CONFERENCE RO--
LION-O, ARE YOU...?
I CAN'T ***BELIEVE*** IT...
WHAT IS IT?!

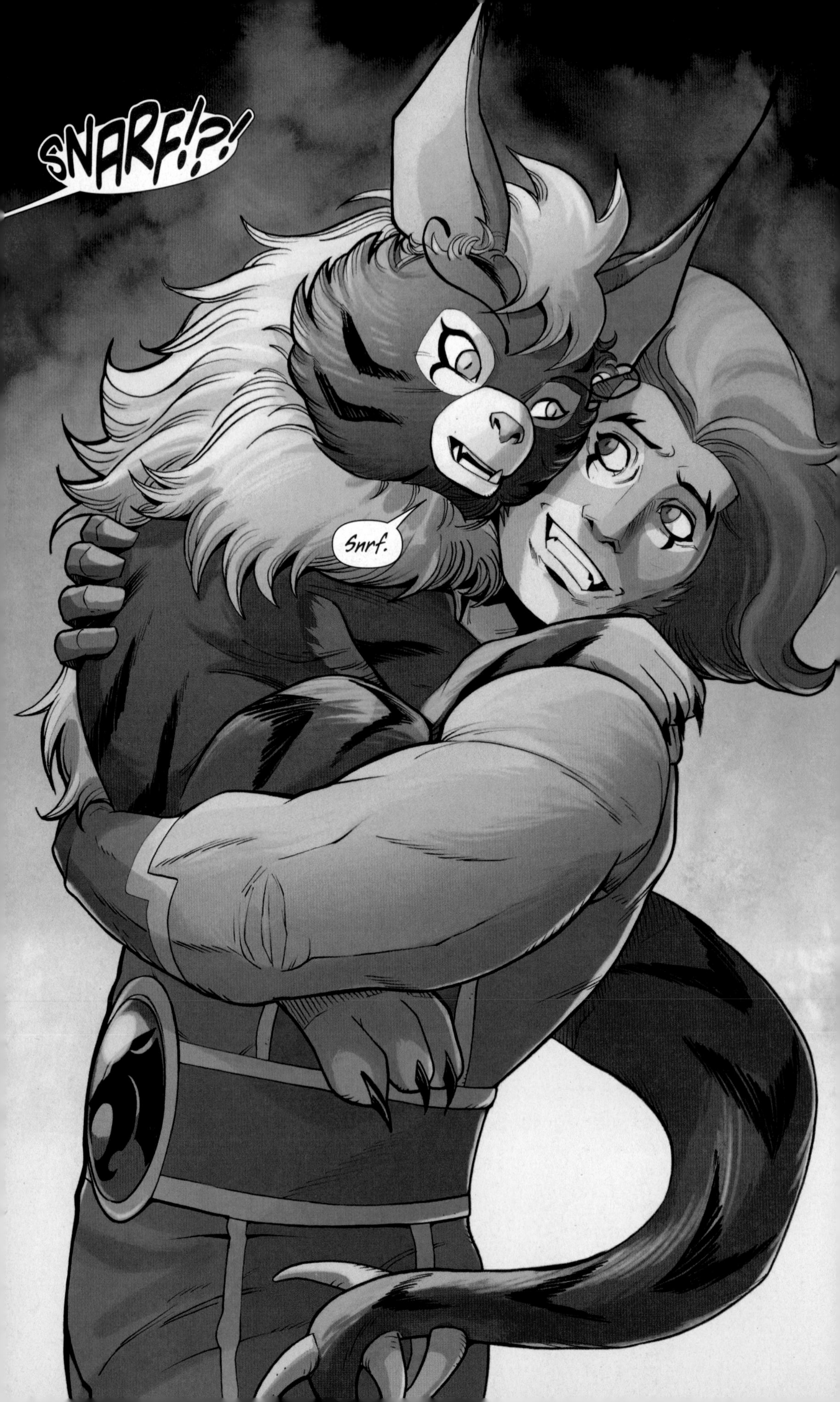
SNARF!?!
Snrf.

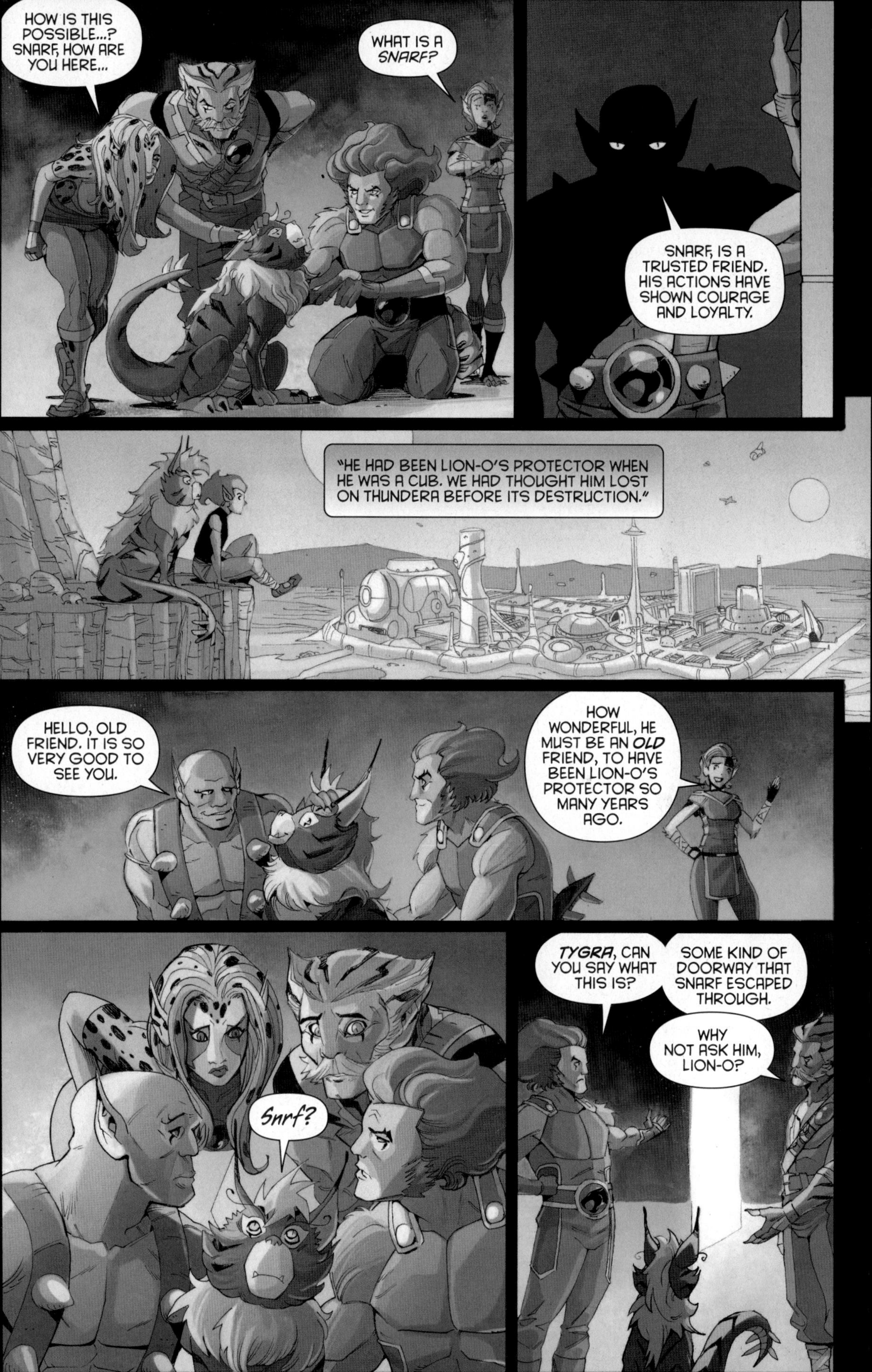
HOW IS THIS POSSIBLE...? SNARF, HOW ARE YOU HERE...
WHAT IS A SNARF?
SNARF, IS A TRUSTED FRIEND. HIS ACTIONS HAVE SHOWN COURAGE AND LOYALTY.
"HE HAD BEEN LION-O'S PROTECTOR WHEN HE WAS A CUB. WE HAD THOUGHT HIM LOST ON THUNDERA BEFORE ITS DESTRUCTION."
HELLO, OLD FRIEND. IT IS SO VERY GOOD TO SEE YOU.
HOW WONDERFUL, HE MUST BE AN OLD FRIEND, TO HAVE BEEN LION-O'S PROTECTOR SO MANY YEARS AGO.
Snrf?
TYGRA, CAN YOU SAY WHAT THIS IS?
SOME KIND OF DOORWAY THAT SNARF ESCAPED THROUGH.
WHY NOT ASK HIM, LION-O?

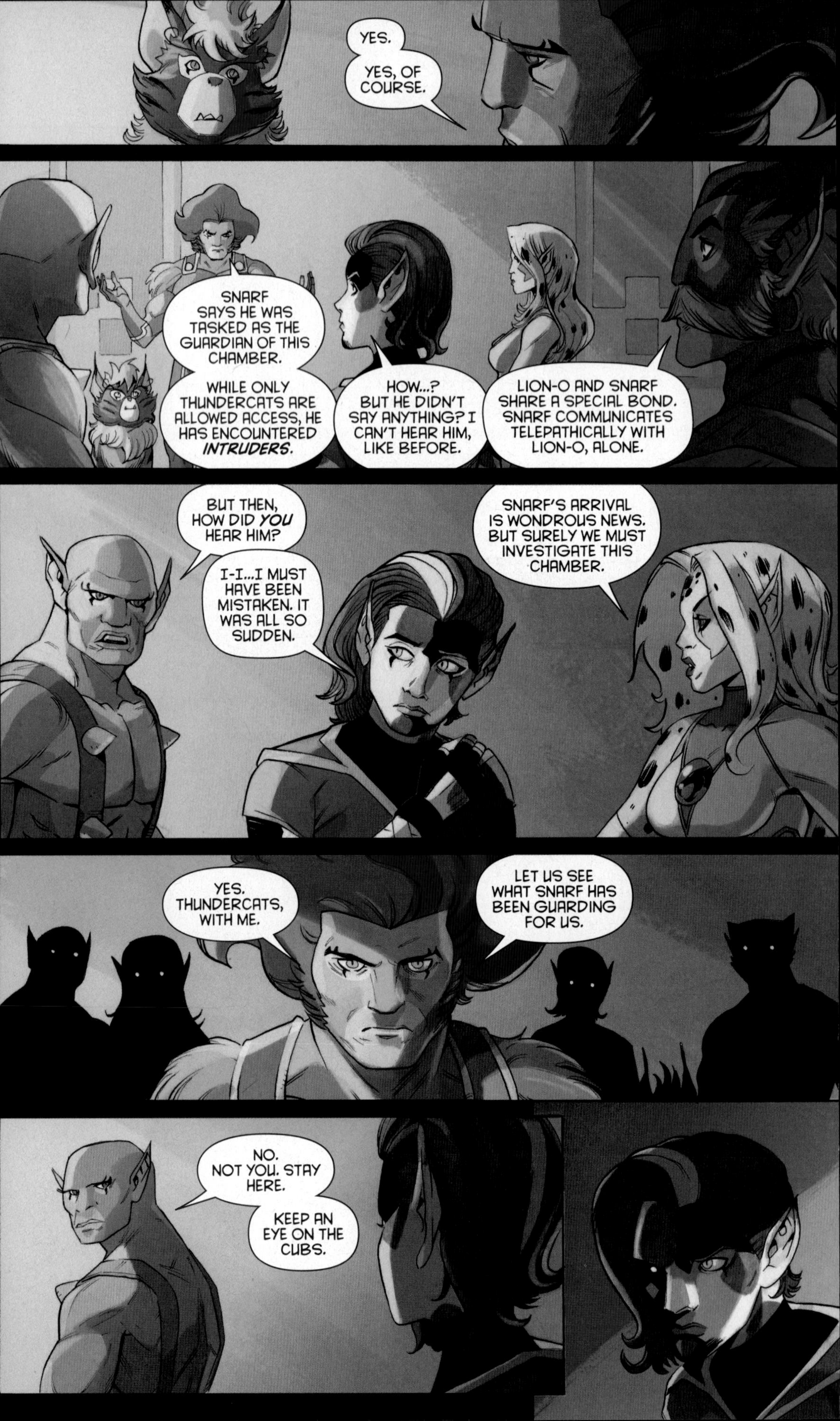
YES.
YES, OF COURSE.
SNARF SAYS HE WAS TASKED AS THE GUARDIAN OF THIS CHAMBER.
WHILE ONLY THUNDERCATS ARE ALLOWED ACCESS, HE HAS ENCOUNTERED *INTRUDERS*.
HOW...? BUT HE DIDN'T SAY ANYTHING? I CAN'T HEAR HIM, LIKE BEFORE.
LION-O AND SNARF SHARE A SPECIAL BOND. SNARF COMMUNICATES TELEPATHICALLY WITH LION-O, ALONE.
BUT THEN, HOW DID *YOU* HEAR HIM?
I-I...I MUST HAVE BEEN MISTAKEN. IT WAS ALL SO SUDDEN.
SNARF'S ARRIVAL IS WONDROUS NEWS. BUT SURELY WE MUST INVESTIGATE THIS CHAMBER.
YES. THUNDERCATS, WITH ME.
LET US SEE WHAT SNARF HAS BEEN GUARDING FOR US.
NO. NOT YOU. STAY HERE.
KEEP AN EYE ON THE CUBS.

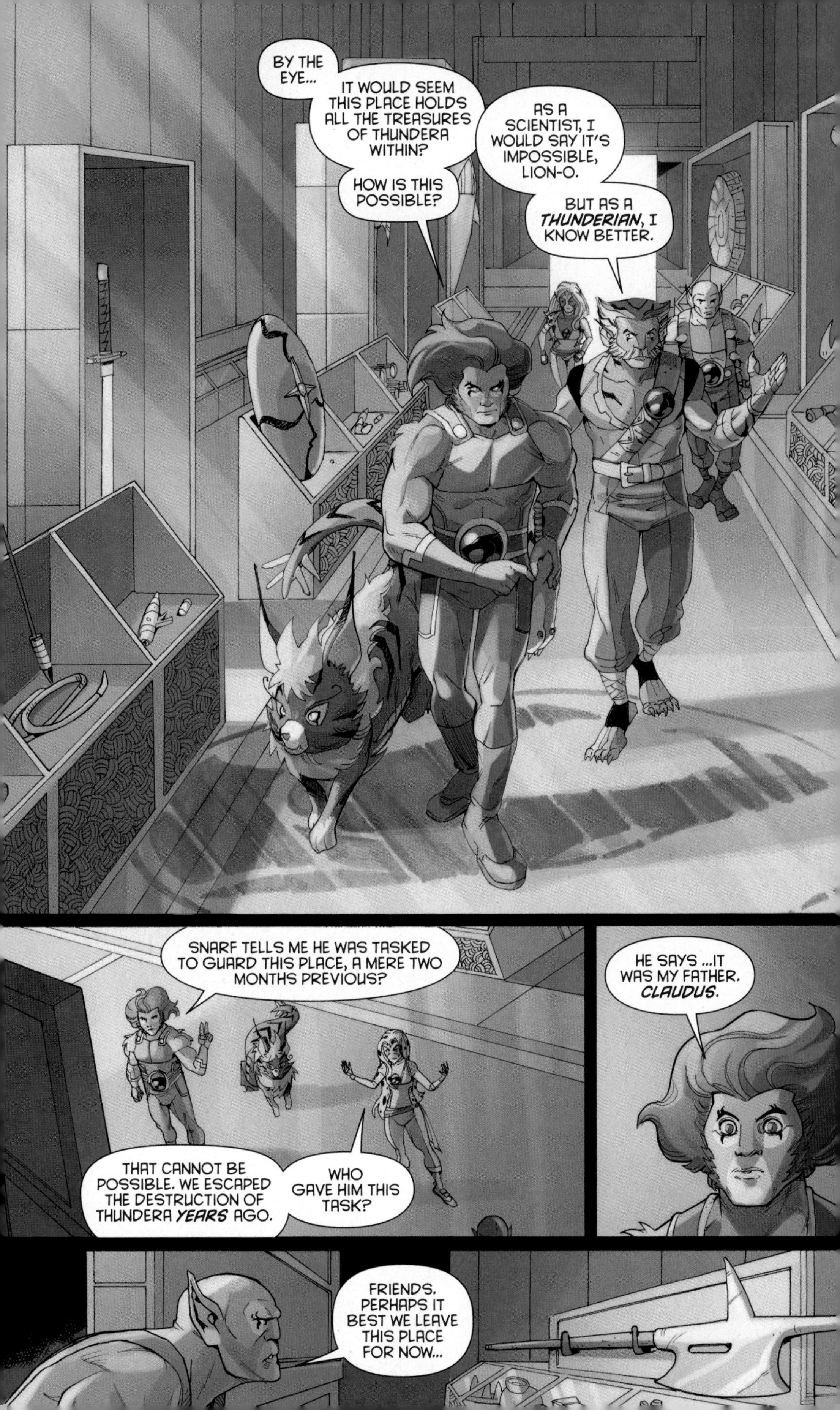
BY THE EYE...
IT WOULD SEEM THIS PLACE HOLDS ALL THE TREASURES OF THUNDERA WITHIN?
HOW IS THIS POSSIBLE?
AS A SCIENTIST, I WOULD SAY IT'S IMPOSSIBLE, LION-O.
BUT AS A *THUNDERIAN*, I KNOW BETTER.
SNARF TELLS ME HE WAS TASKED TO GUARD THIS PLACE, A MERE TWO MONTHS PREVIOUS?
THAT CANNOT BE POSSIBLE. WE ESCAPED THE DESTRUCTION OF THUNDERA *YEARS* AGO.
WHO GAVE HIM THIS TASK?
HE SAYS ...IT WAS MY FATHER. *CLAUDUS*.
FRIENDS. PERHAPS IT BEST WE LEAVE THIS PLACE FOR NOW...

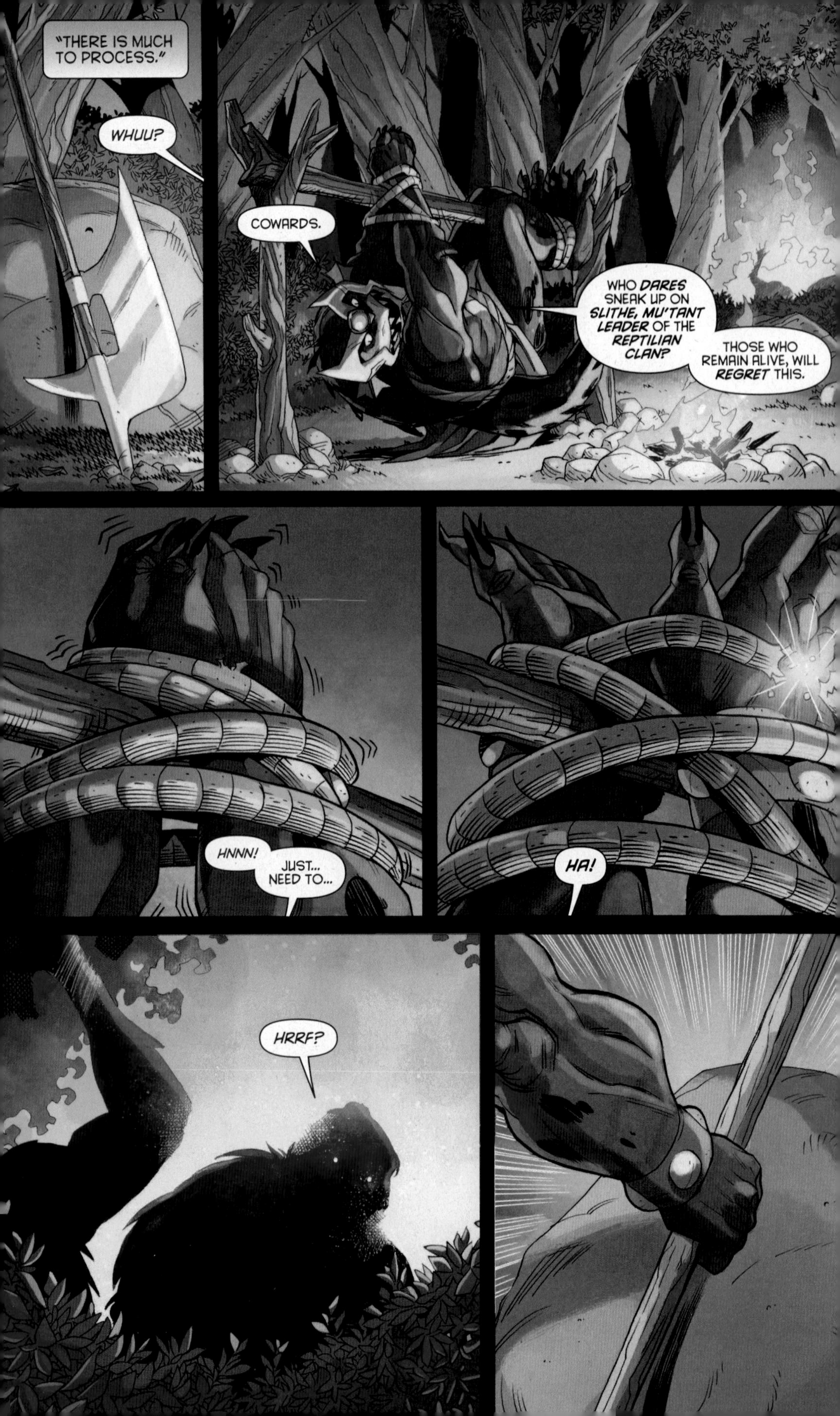
"THERE IS MUCH TO PROCESS."
WHUU?
COWARDS.
WHO DARES SNEAK UP ON SLITHE, MU'TANT LEADER OF THE REPTILIAN CLAN?
THOSE WHO REMAIN ALIVE, WILL REGRET THIS.
HNNN!
JUST... NEED TO...
HA!
HRRF?

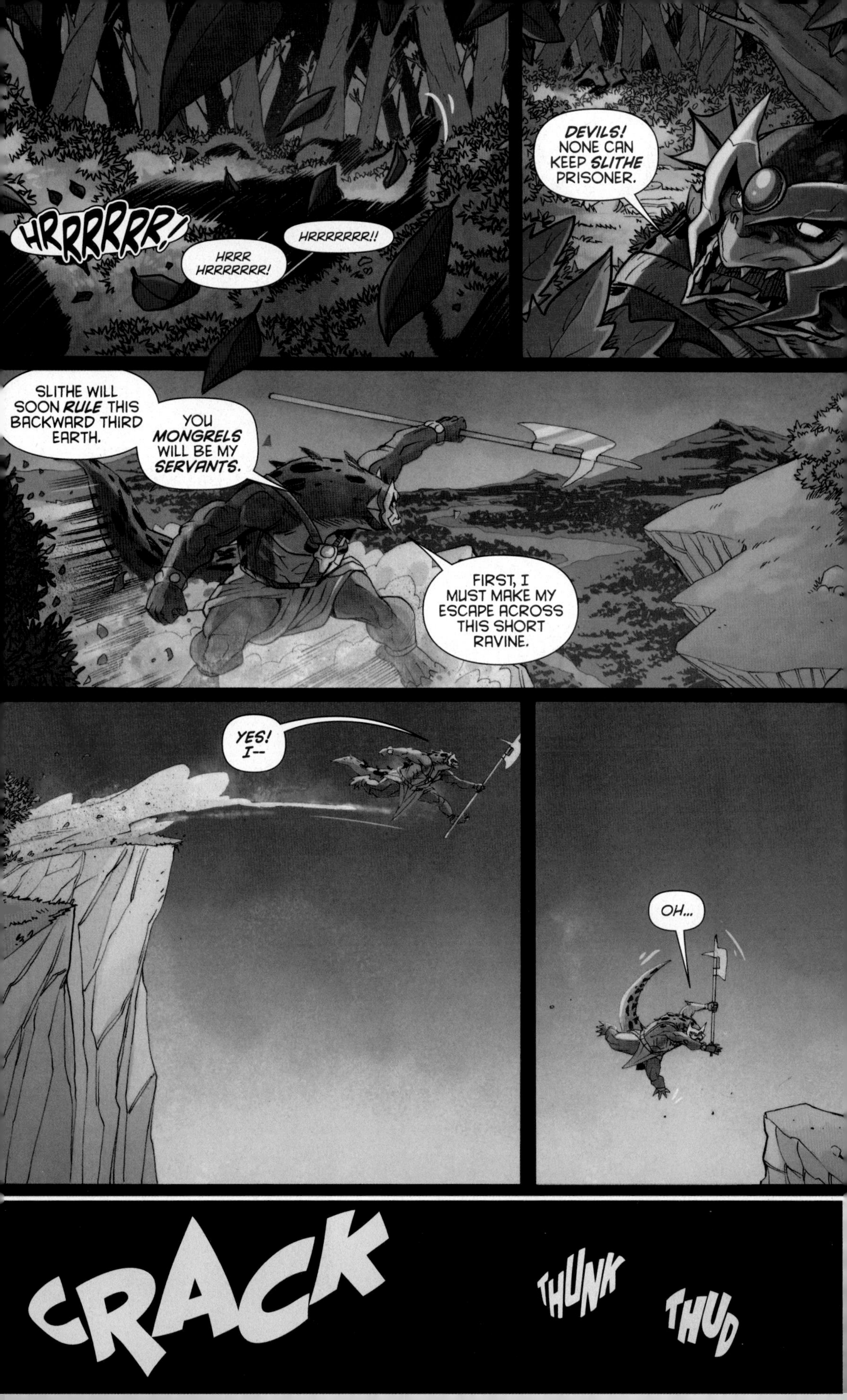
HRRRRRR!
HRRR HRRRRRRR!
HRRRRRRR!!
DEVILS! NONE CAN KEEP SLITHE PRISONER.
SLITHE WILL SOON RULE THIS BACKWARD THIRD EARTH.
YOU MONGRELS WILL BE MY SERVANTS.
FIRST, I MUST MAKE MY ESCAPE ACROSS THIS SHORT RAVINE.
YES! I--
OH...
CRACK
THUNK
THUD

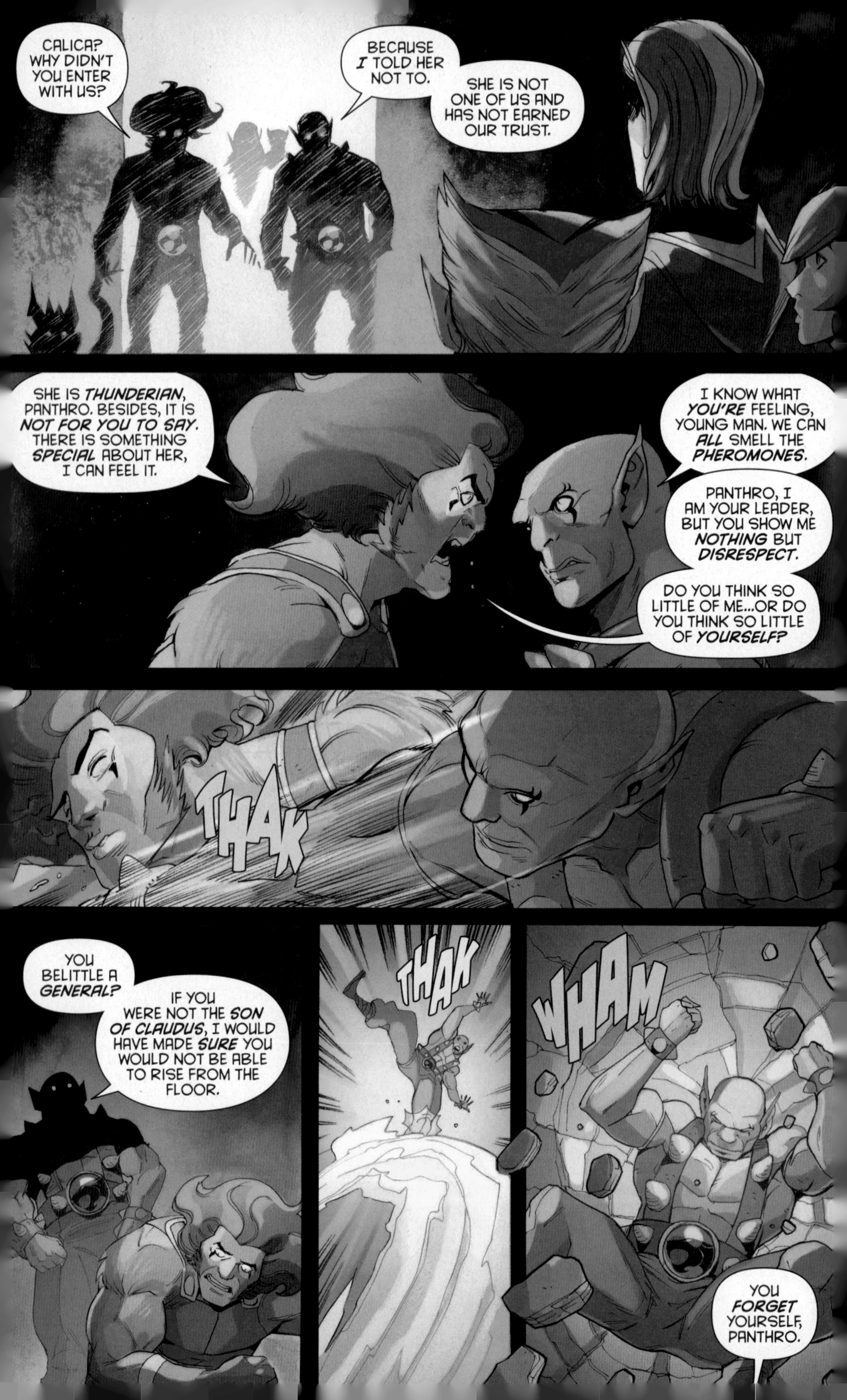
CALICA? WHY DIDN'T YOU ENTER WITH US?
BECAUSE I TOLD HER NOT TO.
SHE IS NOT ONE OF US AND HAS NOT EARNED OUR TRUST.
SHE IS THUNDERIAN, PANTHRO. BESIDES, IT IS NOT FOR YOU TO SAY. THERE IS SOMETHING SPECIAL ABOUT HER, I CAN FEEL IT.
I KNOW WHAT YOU'RE FEELING, YOUNG MAN. WE CAN ALL SMELL THE PHEROMONES.
PANTHRO, I AM YOUR LEADER, BUT YOU SHOW ME NOTHING BUT DISRESPECT.
DO YOU THINK SO LITTLE OF ME...OR DO YOU THINK SO LITTLE OF YOURSELF?
THAK
YOU BELITTLE A GENERAL?
IF YOU WERE NOT THE SON OF CLAUDUS, I WOULD HAVE MADE SURE YOU WOULD NOT BE ABLE TO RISE FROM THE FLOOR.
THAK
WHAM
YOU FORGET YOURSELF, PANTHRO.

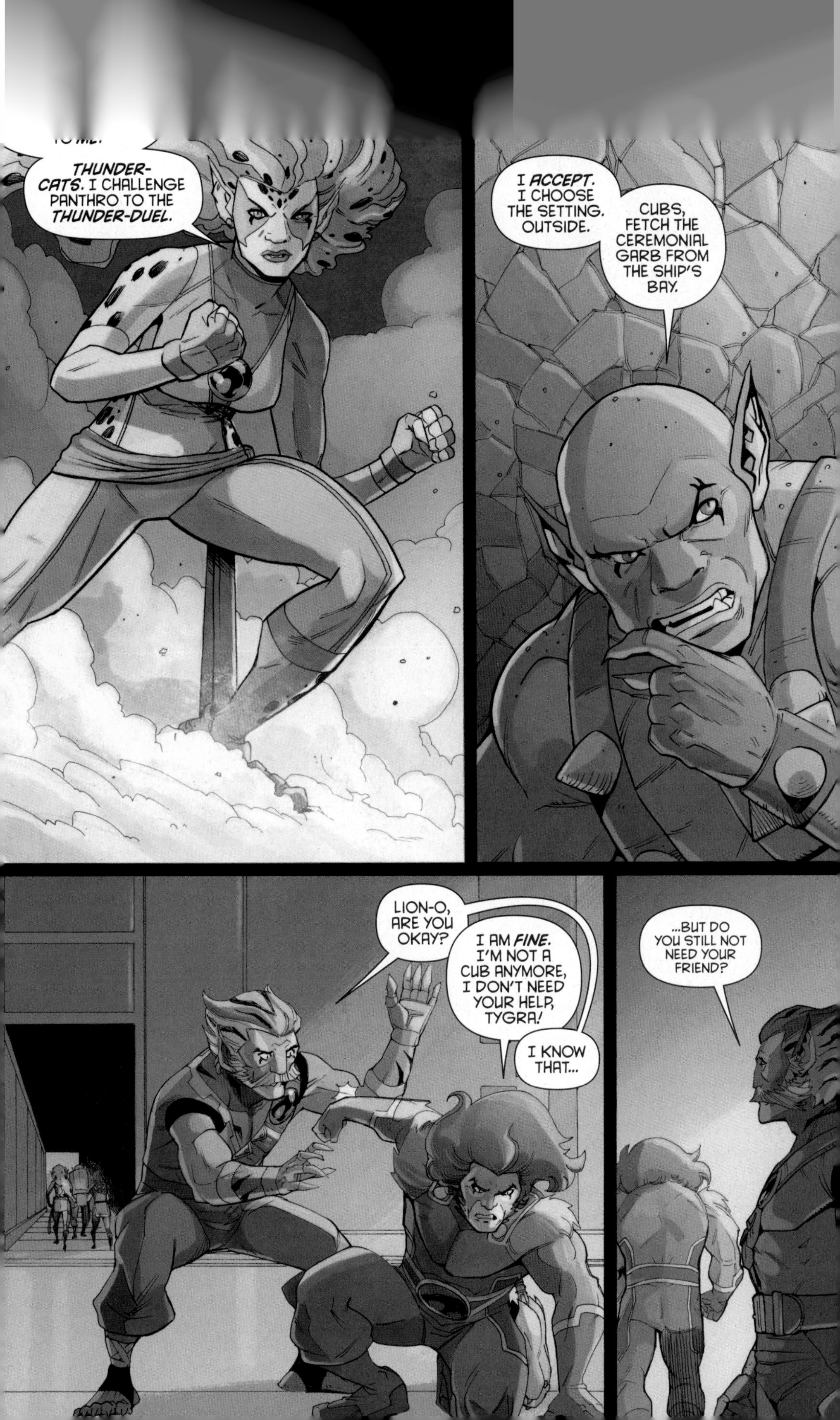
THUNDER-CATS. I CHALLENGE PANTHRO TO THE THUNDER-DUEL.
I ACCEPT. I CHOOSE THE SETTING. OUTSIDE.
CUBS, FETCH THE CEREMONIAL GARB FROM THE SHIP'S BAY.
LION-O, ARE YOU OKAY?
I AM FINE. I'M NOT A CUB ANYMORE, I DON'T NEED YOUR HELP, TYGRA!
I KNOW THAT...
...BUT DO YOU STILL NOT NEED YOUR FRIEND?

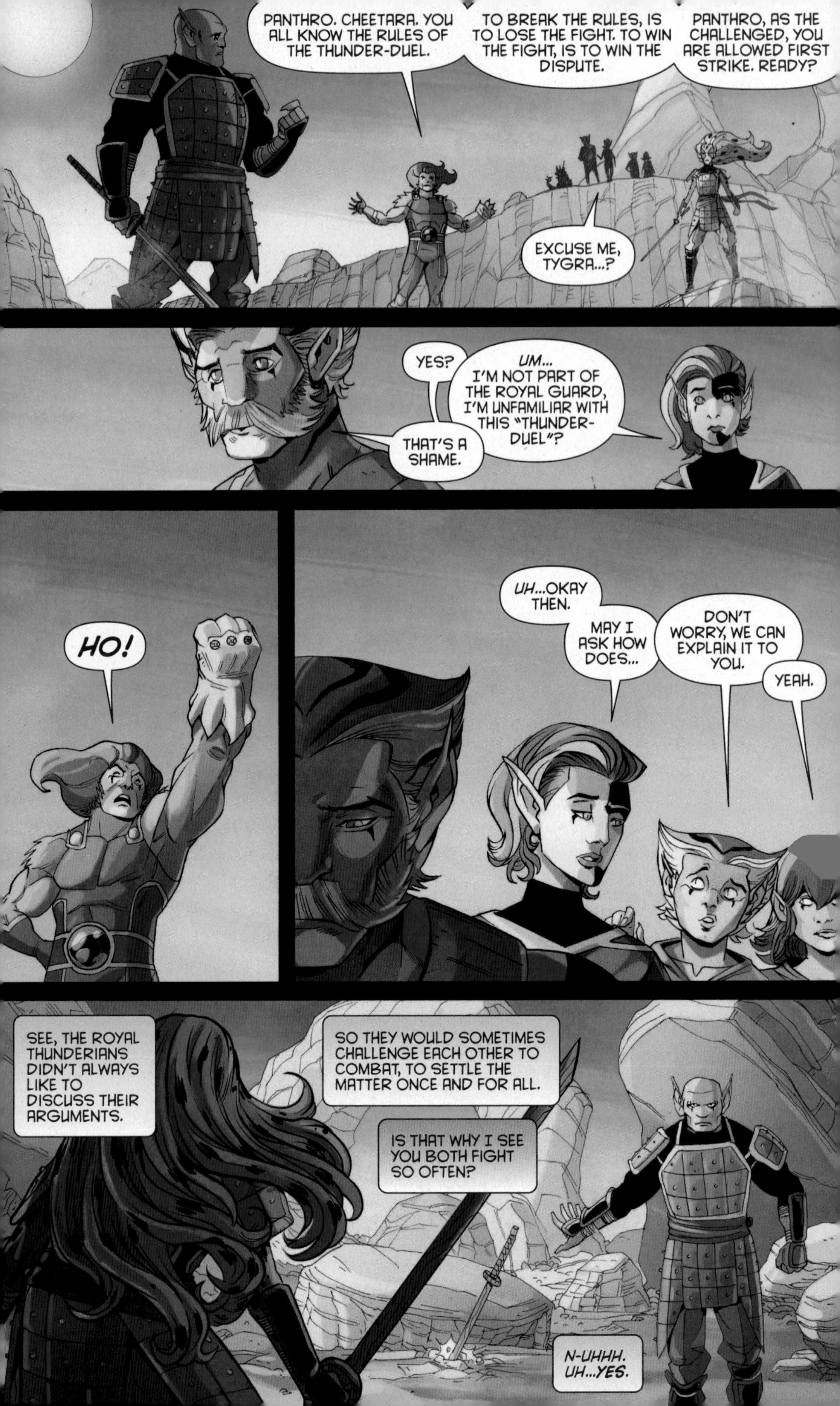
PANTHRO. CHEETARA. YOU ALL KNOW THE RULES OF THE THUNDER-DUEL.
TO BREAK THE RULES, IS TO LOSE THE FIGHT. TO WIN THE FIGHT, IS TO WIN THE DISPUTE.
PANTHRO, AS THE CHALLENGED, YOU ARE ALLOWED FIRST STRIKE. READY?
EXCUSE ME, TYGRA...?
YES?
UM... I'M NOT PART OF THE ROYAL GUARD, I'M UNFAMILIAR WITH THIS "THUNDER-DUEL"?
THAT'S A SHAME.
HO!
UH...OKAY THEN.
MAY I ASK HOW DOES...
DON'T WORRY, WE CAN EXPLAIN IT TO YOU.
YEAH.
SEE, THE ROYAL THUNDERIANS DIDN'T ALWAYS LIKE TO DISCUSS THEIR ARGUMENTS.
SO THEY WOULD SOMETIMES CHALLENGE EACH OTHER TO COMBAT, TO SETTLE THE MATTER ONCE AND FOR ALL.
IS THAT WHY I SEE YOU BOTH FIGHT SO OFTEN?
N-UHHH. UH...YES.

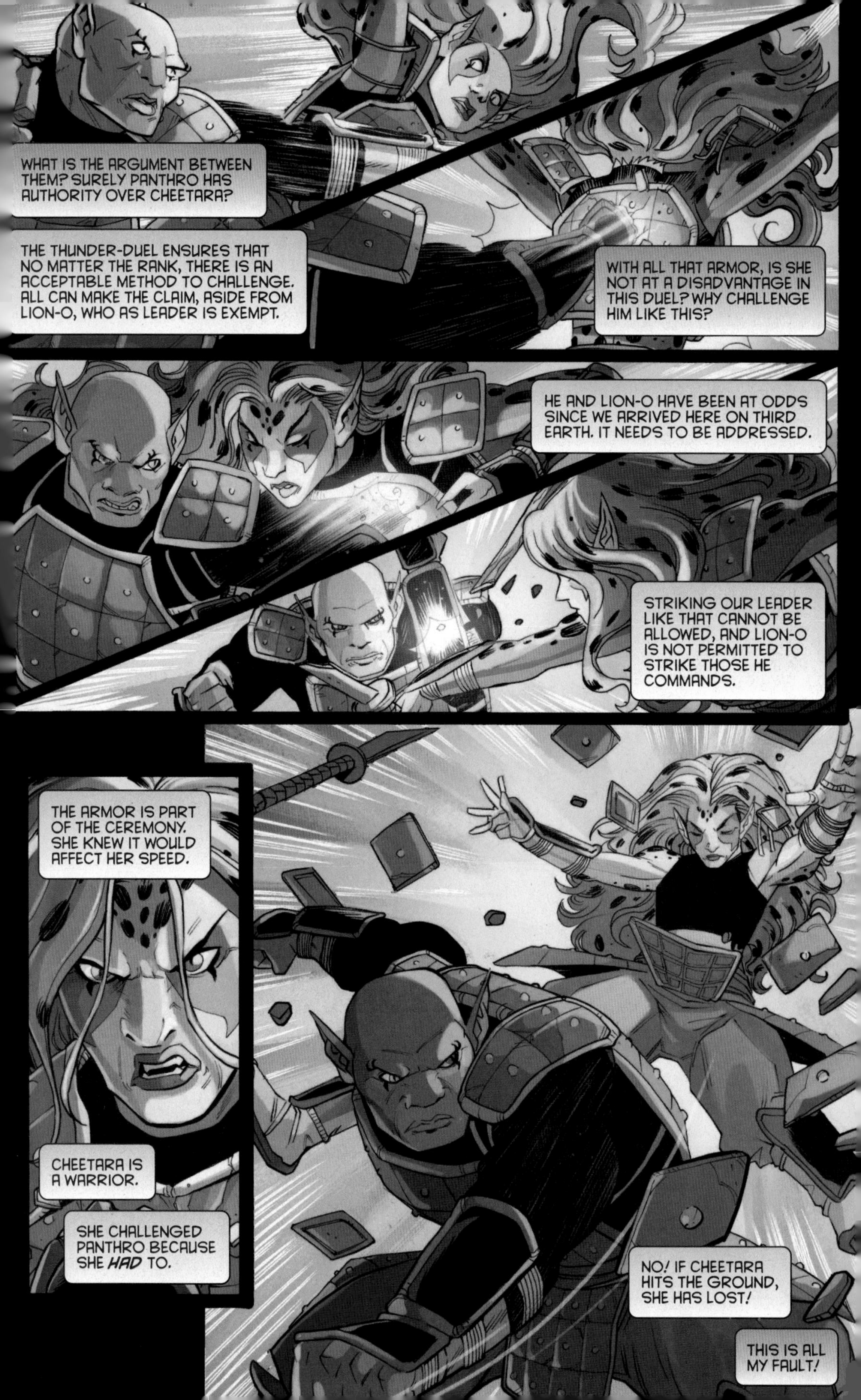
WHAT IS THE ARGUMENT BETWEEN THEM? SURELY PANTHRO HAS AUTHORITY OVER CHEETARA?
THE THUNDER-DUEL ENSURES THAT NO MATTER THE RANK, THERE IS AN ACCEPTABLE METHOD TO CHALLENGE. ALL CAN MAKE THE CLAIM, ASIDE FROM LION-O, WHO AS LEADER IS EXEMPT.
WITH ALL THAT ARMOR, IS SHE NOT AT A DISADVANTAGE IN THIS DUEL? WHY CHALLENGE HIM LIKE THIS?
HE AND LION-O HAVE BEEN AT ODDS SINCE WE ARRIVED HERE ON THIRD EARTH. IT NEEDS TO BE ADDRESSED.
STRIKING OUR LEADER LIKE THAT CANNOT BE ALLOWED, AND LION-O IS NOT PERMITTED TO STRIKE THOSE HE COMMANDS.
THE ARMOR IS PART OF THE CEREMONY. SHE KNEW IT WOULD AFFECT HER SPEED.
CHEETARA IS A WARRIOR.
SHE CHALLENGED PANTHRO BECAUSE SHE *HAD* TO.
NO! IF CHEETARA HITS THE GROUND, SHE HAS LOST!
THIS IS ALL MY FAULT!

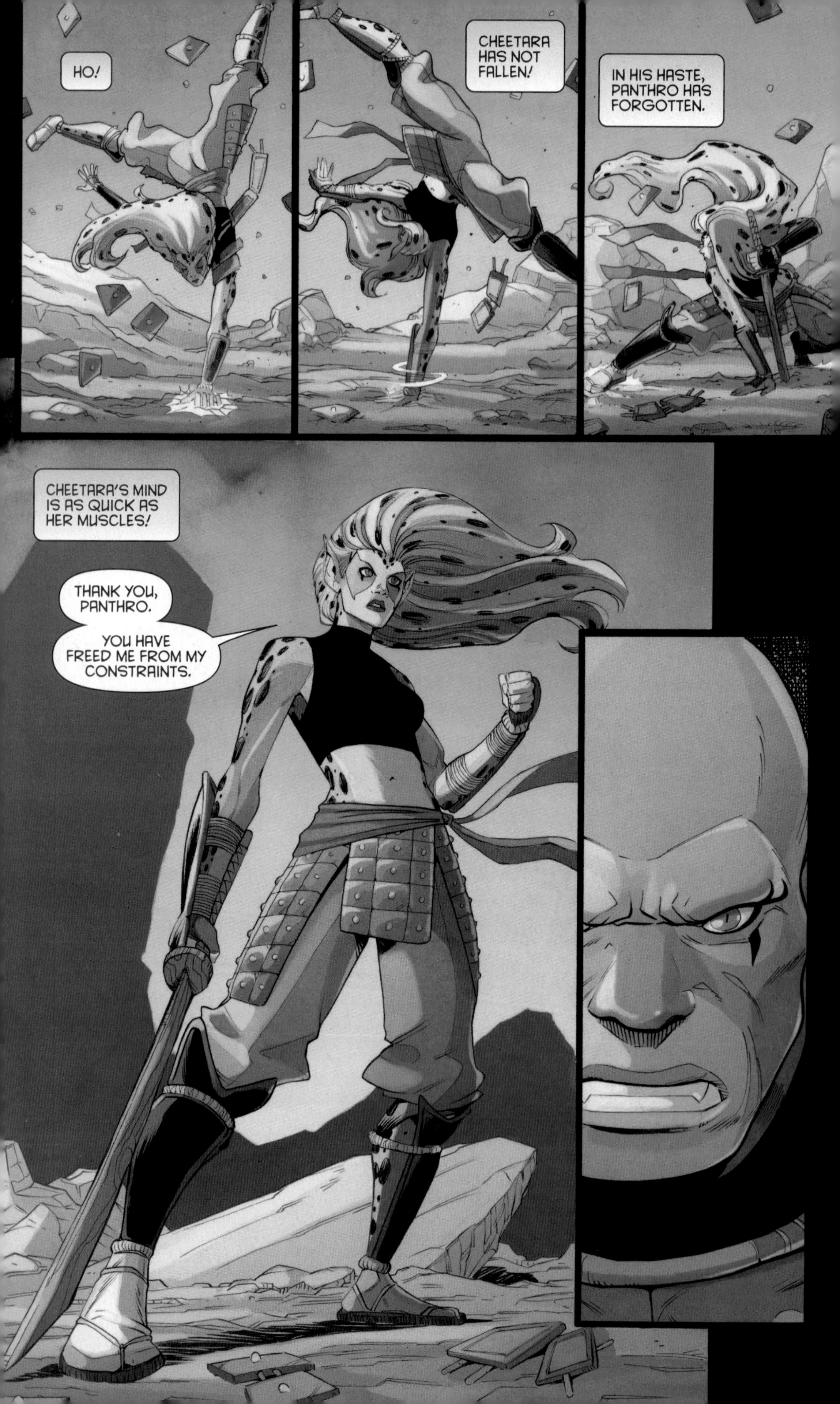
HO!
CHEETARA HAS NOT FALLEN!
IN HIS HASTE, PANTHRO HAS FORGOTTEN.
CHEETARA'S MIND IS AS QUICK AS HER MUSCLES!
THANK YOU, PANTHRO.
YOU HAVE FREED ME FROM MY CONSTRAINTS.

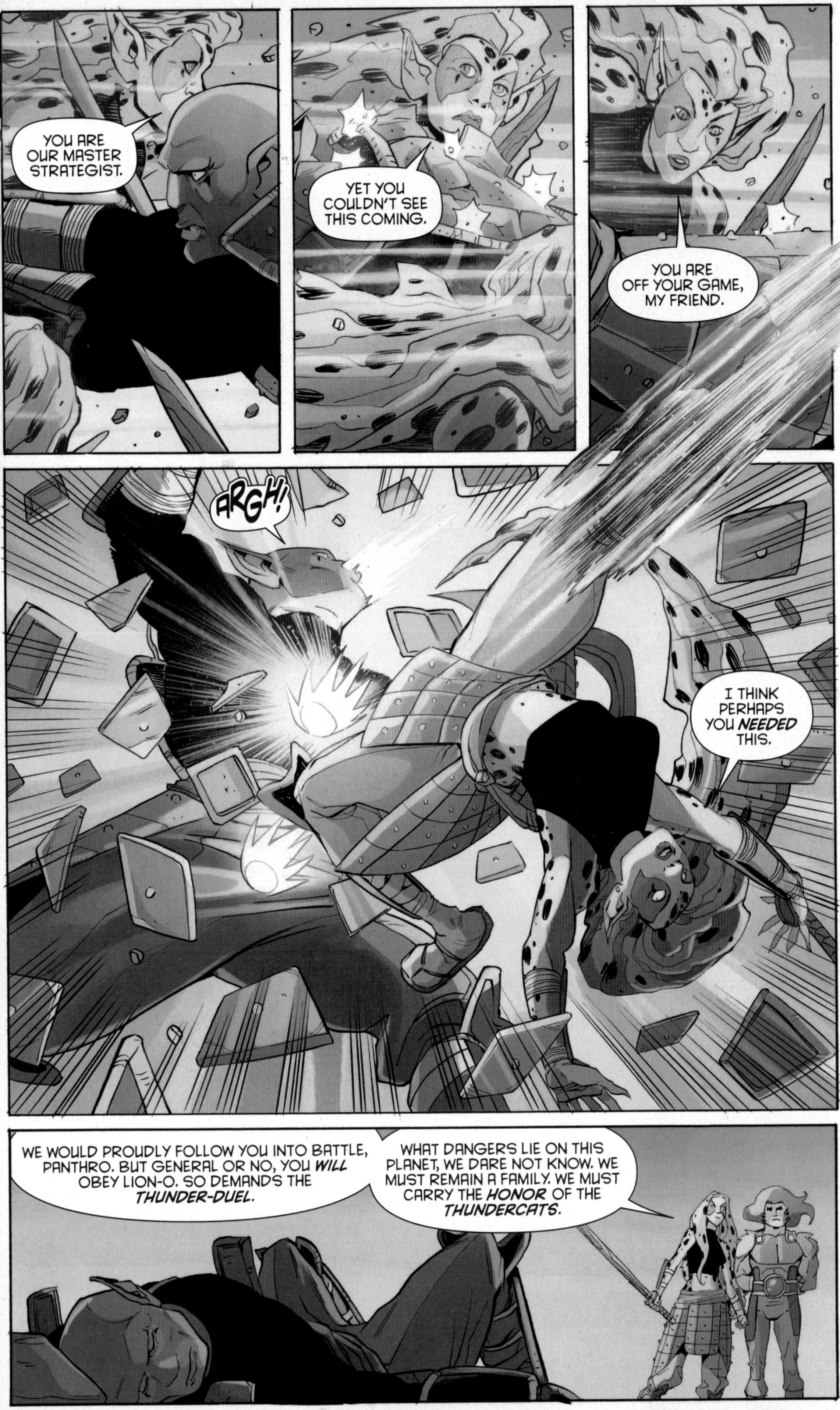
YOU ARE OUR MASTER STRATEGIST.
YET YOU COULDN'T SEE THIS COMING.
YOU ARE OFF YOUR GAME, MY FRIEND.
ARGH!
I THINK PERHAPS YOU *NEEDED* THIS.
WE WOULD PROUDLY FOLLOW YOU INTO BATTLE, PANTHRO. BUT GENERAL OR NO, YOU *WILL* OBEY LION-O. SO DEMANDS THE *THUNDER-DUEL*.
WHAT DANGERS LIE ON THIS PLANET, WE DARE NOT KNOW. WE MUST REMAIN A FAMILY. WE MUST CARRY THE *HONOR* OF THE *THUNDERCATS*.

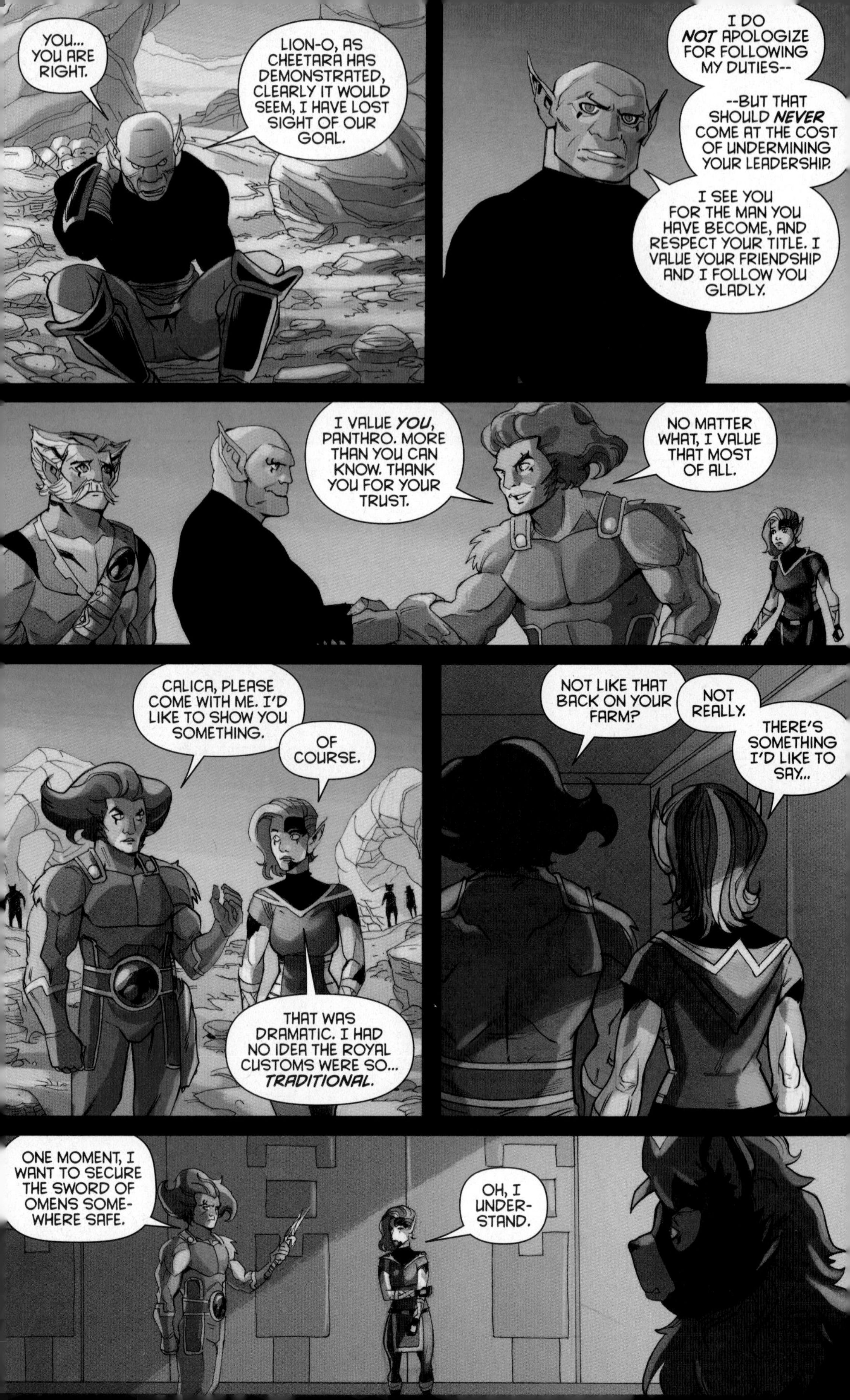
YOU... YOU ARE RIGHT.
LION-O, AS CHEETARA HAS DEMONSTRATED, CLEARLY IT WOULD SEEM, I HAVE LOST SIGHT OF OUR GOAL.
I DO *NOT* APOLOGIZE FOR FOLLOWING MY DUTIES--
--BUT THAT SHOULD *NEVER* COME AT THE COST OF UNDERMINING YOUR LEADERSHIP.
I SEE YOU FOR THE MAN YOU HAVE BECOME, AND RESPECT YOUR TITLE. I VALUE YOUR FRIENDSHIP AND I FOLLOW YOU GLADLY.
I VALUE *YOU*, PANTHRO. MORE THAN YOU CAN KNOW. THANK YOU FOR YOUR TRUST.
NO MATTER WHAT, I VALUE THAT MOST OF ALL.
CALICA, PLEASE COME WITH ME. I'D LIKE TO SHOW YOU SOMETHING.
OF COURSE.
THAT WAS DRAMATIC. I HAD NO IDEA THE ROYAL CUSTOMS WERE SO... *TRADITIONAL*.
NOT LIKE THAT BACK ON YOUR FARM?
NOT REALLY.
THERE'S SOMETHING I'D LIKE TO SAY...
ONE MOMENT, I WANT TO SECURE THE SWORD OF OMENS SOME-WHERE SAFE.
OH, I UNDER-STAND.

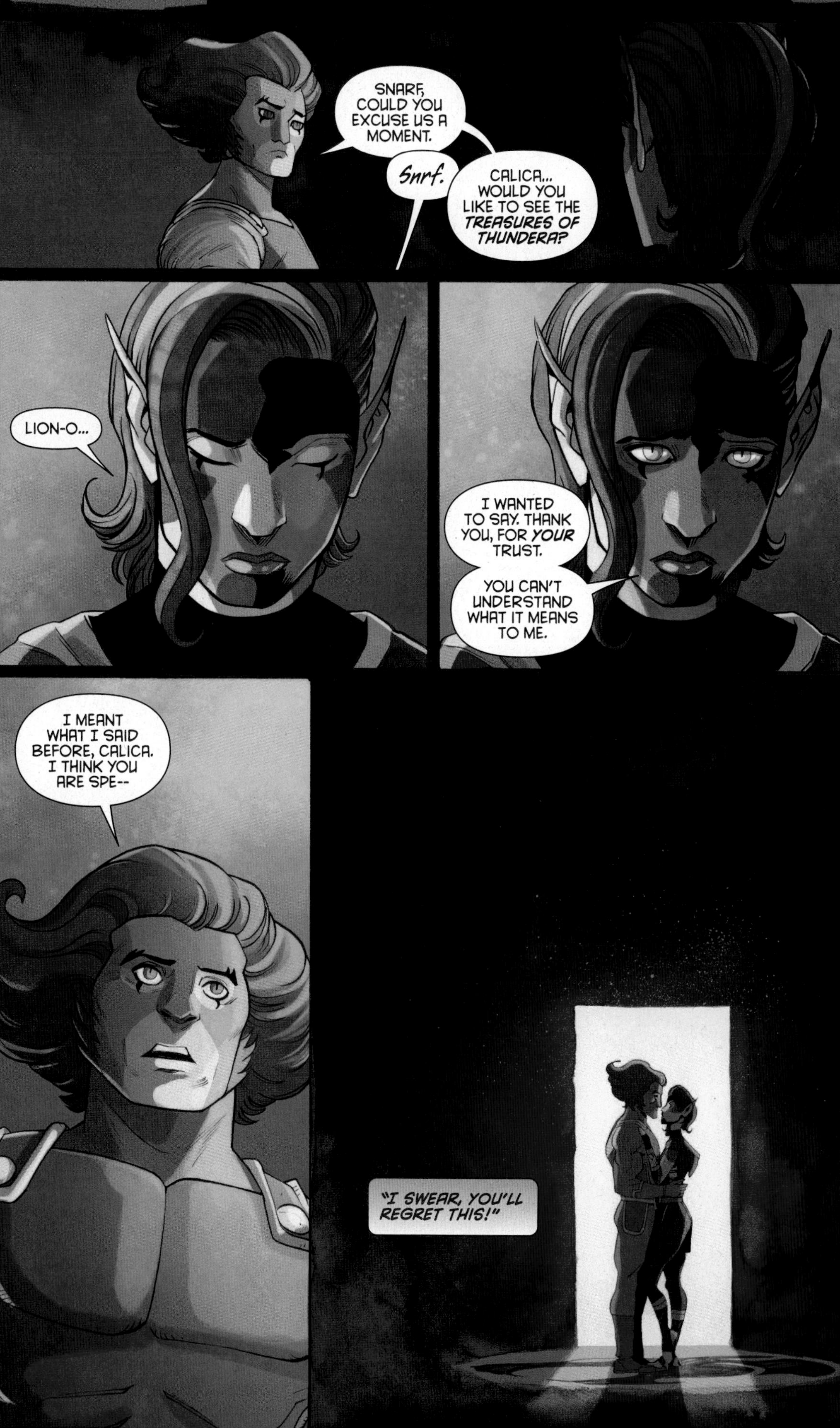

SNARF, COULD YOU EXCUSE US A MOMENT.
Snrf.
CALICA... WOULD YOU LIKE TO SEE THE *TREASURES OF THUNDERA?*
LION-O...
I WANTED TO SAY. THANK YOU, FOR *YOUR* TRUST.
YOU CAN'T UNDERSTAND WHAT IT MEANS TO ME.
I MEANT WHAT I SAID BEFORE, CALICA. I THINK YOU ARE SPE--
"I SWEAR, YOU'LL REGRET THIS!"

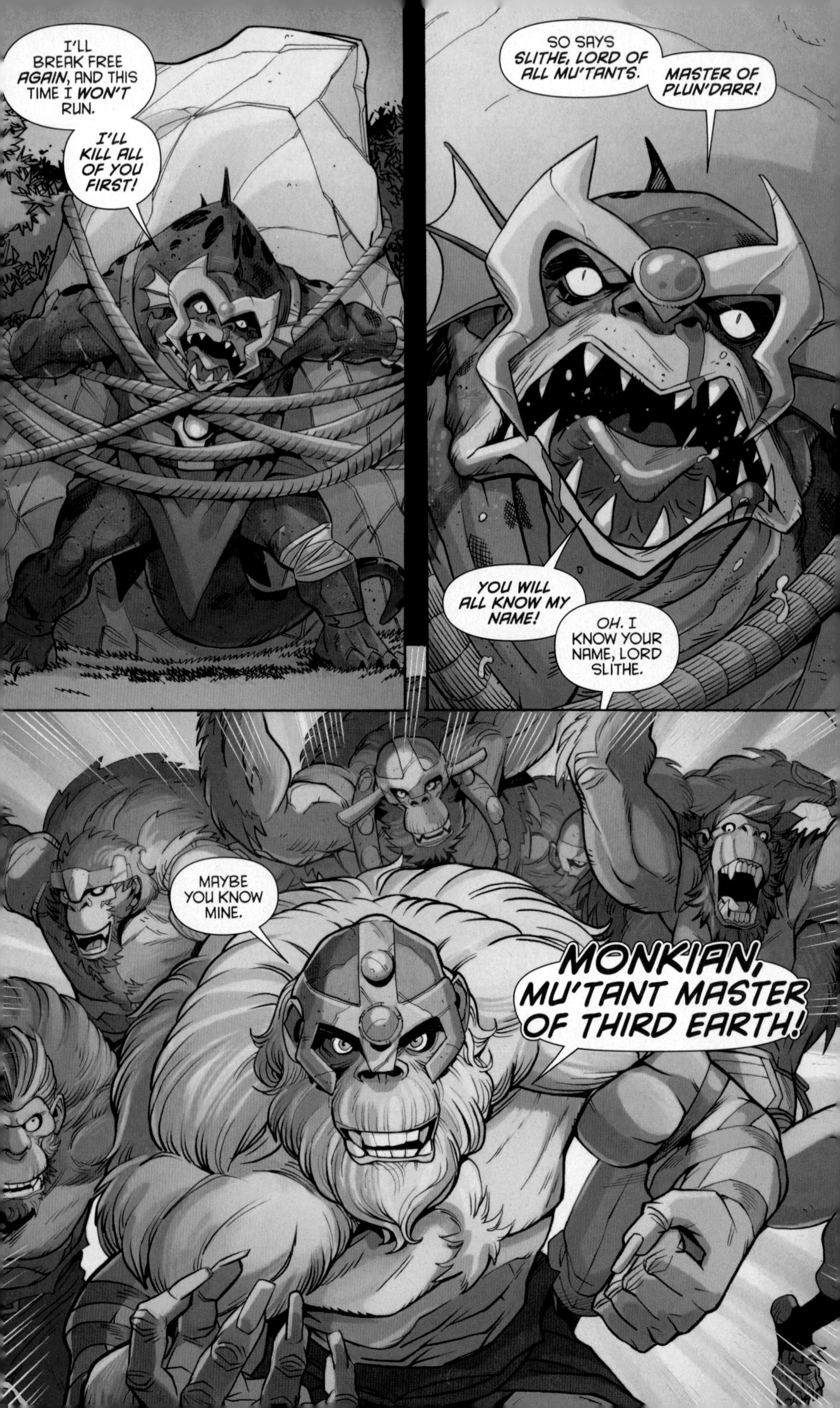
I'LL BREAK FREE AGAIN, AND THIS TIME I WON'T RUN.
I'LL KILL ALL OF YOU FIRST!
SO SAYS SLITHE, LORD OF ALL MU'TANTS.
MASTER OF PLUN'DARR!
YOU WILL ALL KNOW MY NAME!
OH. I KNOW YOUR NAME, LORD SLITHE.
MAYBE YOU KNOW MINE.
MONKIAN, MU'TANT MASTER OF THIRD EARTH!

FOUR

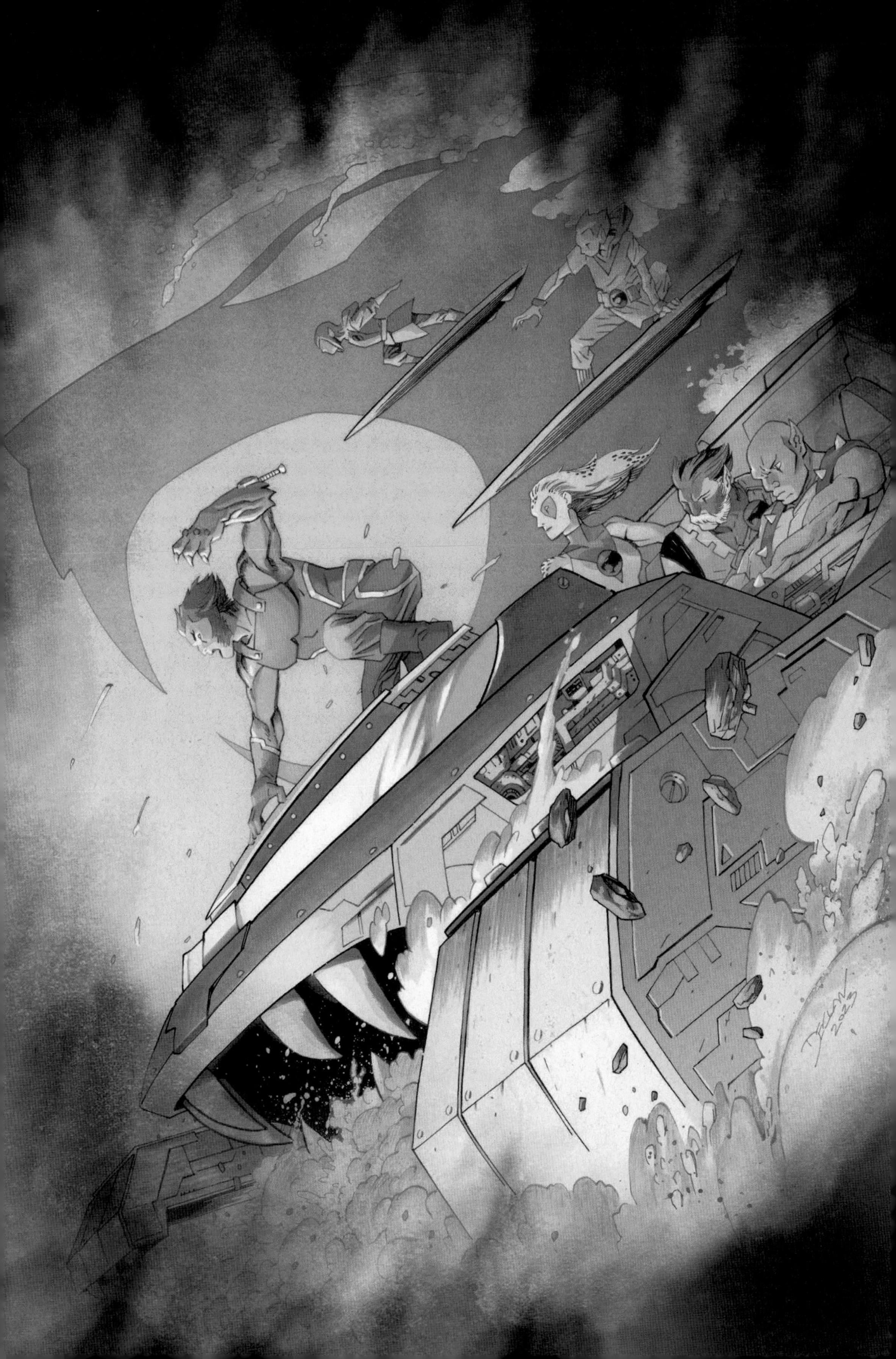

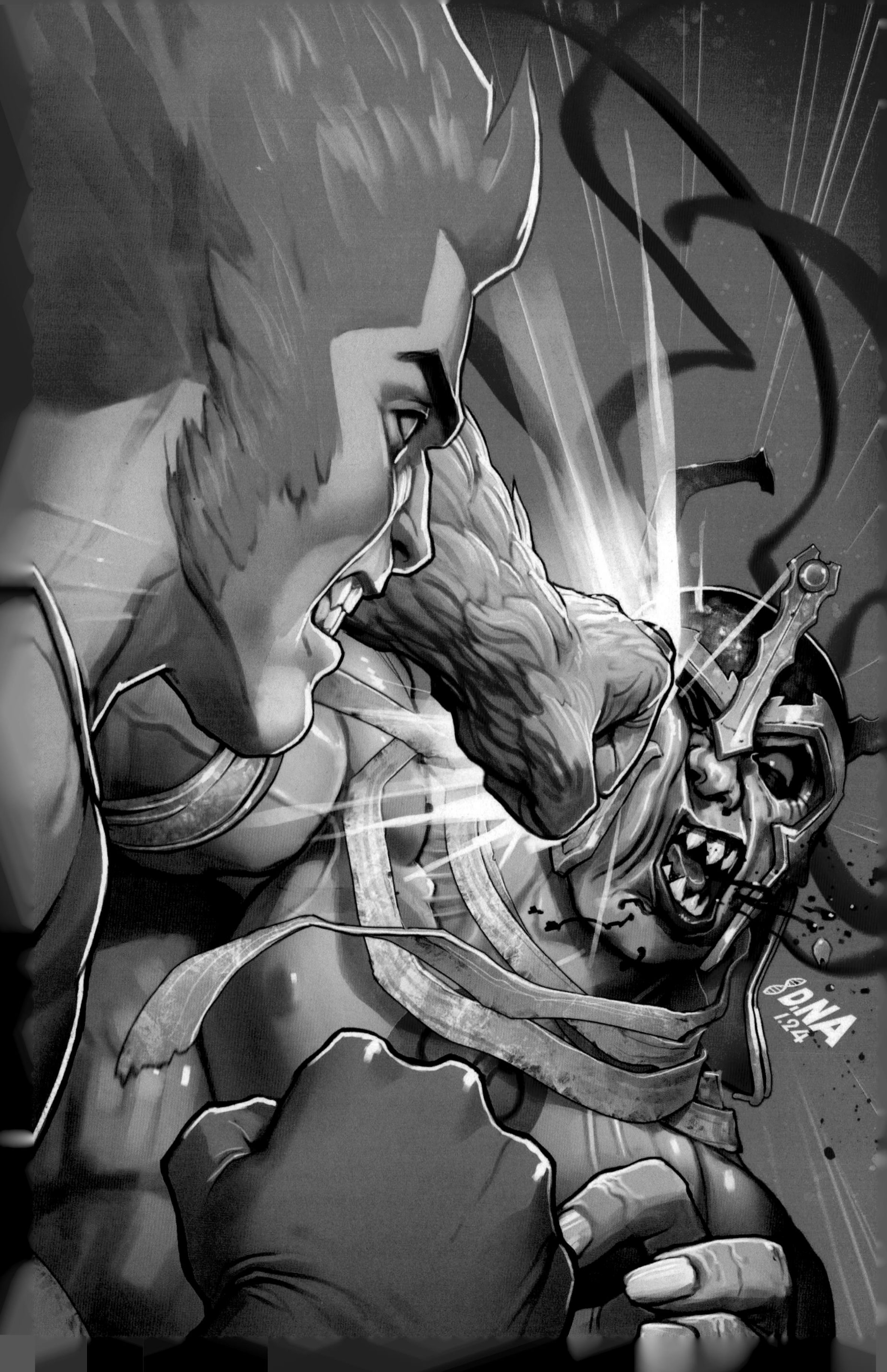
D.NA
1:24

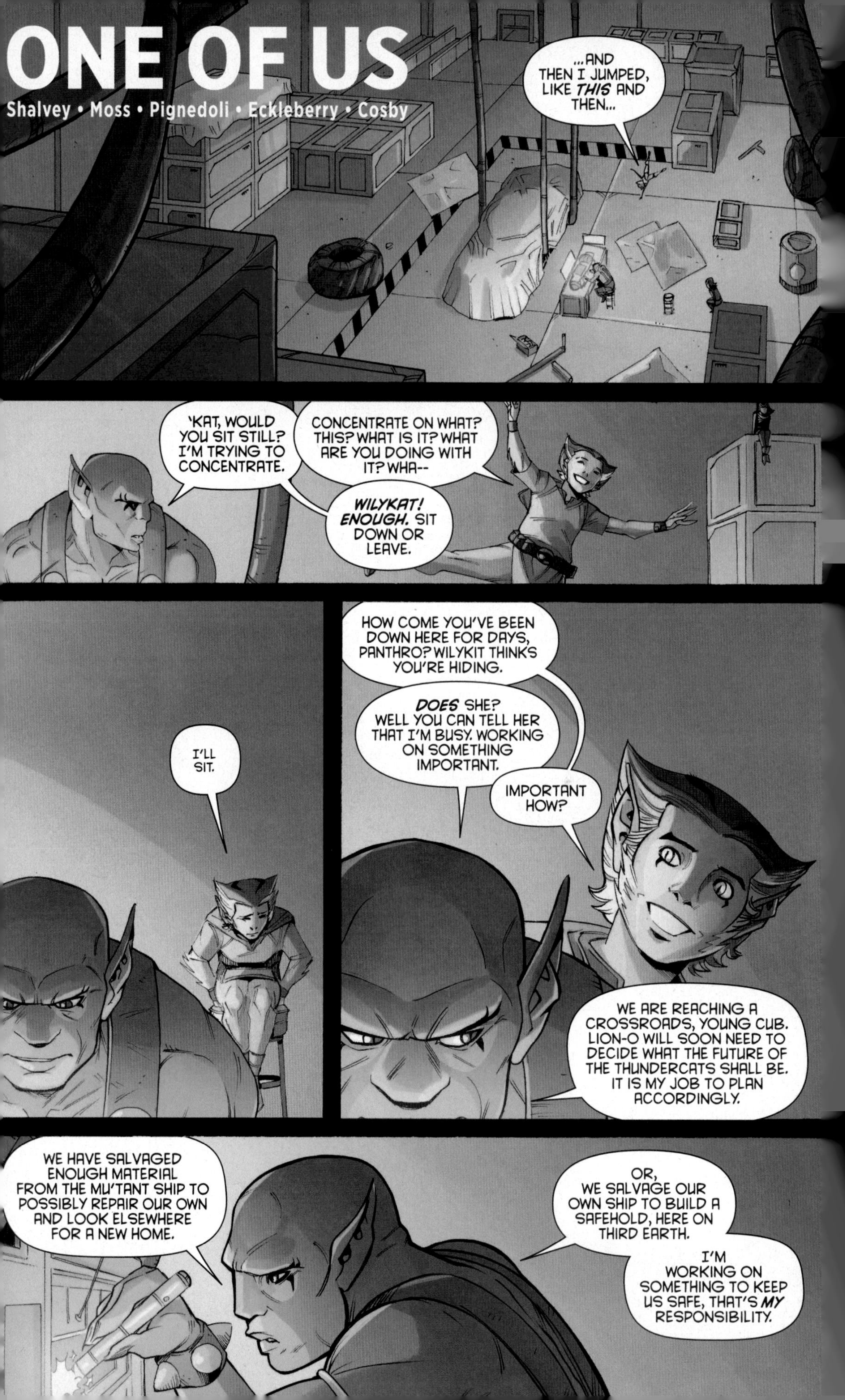
ONE OF US
Shalvey • Moss • Pignedoli • Eckleberry • Cosby
...AND THEN I JUMPED, LIKE *THIS* AND THEN...
'KAT, WOULD YOU SIT STILL? I'M TRYING TO CONCENTRATE.
CONCENTRATE ON WHAT? THIS? WHAT IS IT? WHAT ARE YOU DOING WITH IT? WHA--
WILYKAT! ENOUGH. SIT DOWN OR LEAVE.
I'LL SIT.
HOW COME YOU'VE BEEN DOWN HERE FOR DAYS, PANTHRO? WILYKIT THINKS YOU'RE HIDING.
DOES SHE? WELL YOU CAN TELL HER THAT I'M BUSY. WORKING ON SOMETHING IMPORTANT.
IMPORTANT HOW?
WE ARE REACHING A CROSSROADS, YOUNG CUB. LION-O WILL SOON NEED TO DECIDE WHAT THE FUTURE OF THE THUNDERCATS SHALL BE. IT IS MY JOB TO PLAN ACCORDINGLY.
WE HAVE SALVAGED ENOUGH MATERIAL FROM THE MU'TANT SHIP TO POSSIBLY REPAIR OUR OWN AND LOOK ELSEWHERE FOR A NEW HOME.
OR, WE SALVAGE OUR OWN SHIP TO BUILD A SAFEHOLD, HERE ON THIRD EARTH.
I'M WORKING ON SOMETHING TO KEEP US SAFE, THAT'S *MY* RESPONSIBILITY.

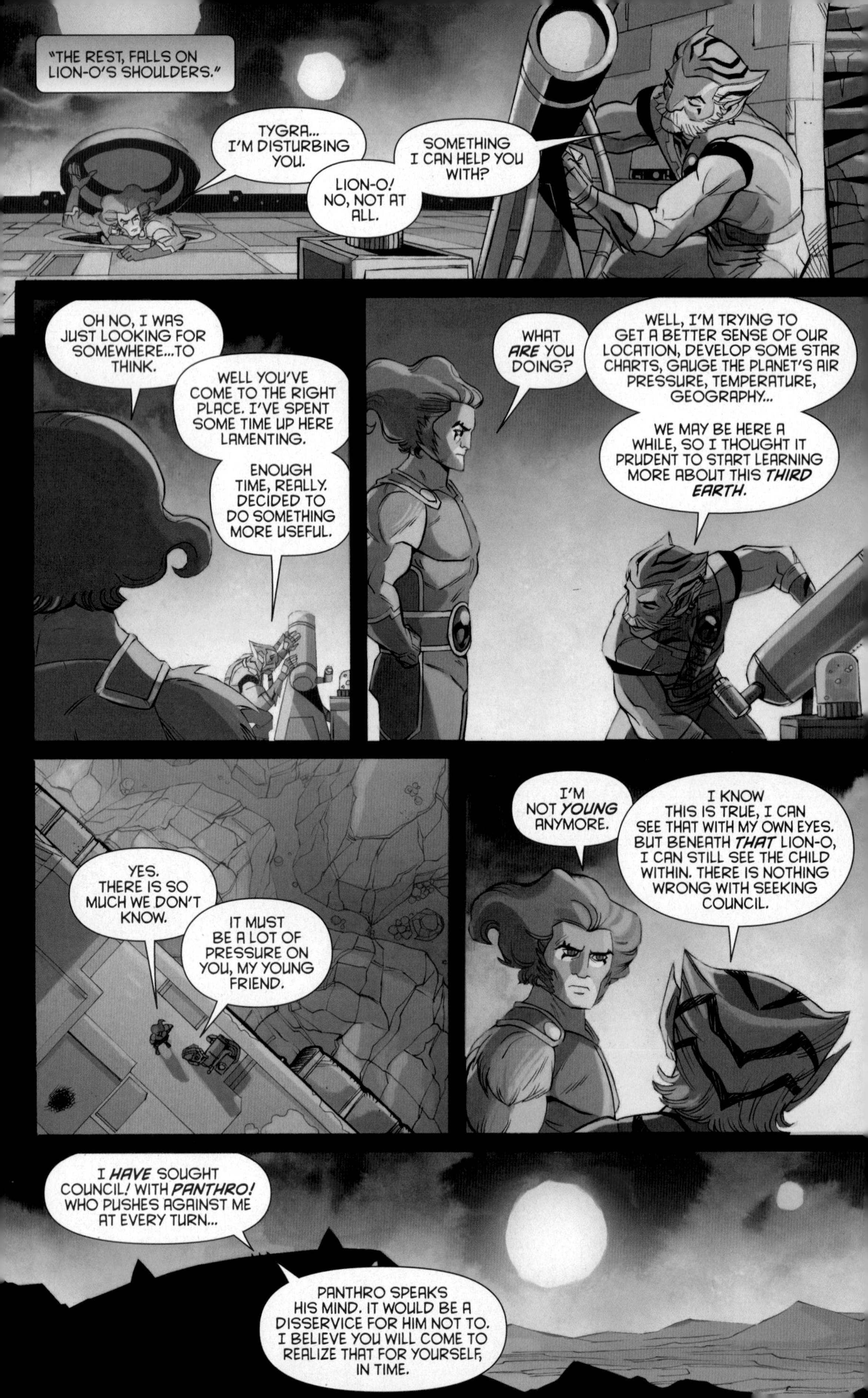
"THE REST, FALLS ON LION-O'S SHOULDERS."
TYGRA... I'M DISTURBING YOU.
LION-O! NO, NOT AT ALL.
SOMETHING I CAN HELP YOU WITH?
OH NO, I WAS JUST LOOKING FOR SOMEWHERE...TO THINK.
WELL YOU'VE COME TO THE RIGHT PLACE. I'VE SPENT SOME TIME UP HERE LAMENTING.
ENOUGH TIME, REALLY. DECIDED TO DO SOMETHING MORE USEFUL.
WHAT *ARE* YOU DOING?
WELL, I'M TRYING TO GET A BETTER SENSE OF OUR LOCATION, DEVELOP SOME STAR CHARTS, GAUGE THE PLANET'S AIR PRESSURE, TEMPERATURE, GEOGRAPHY...
WE MAY BE HERE A WHILE, SO I THOUGHT IT PRUDENT TO START LEARNING MORE ABOUT THIS *THIRD EARTH*.
YES. THERE IS SO MUCH WE DON'T KNOW.
IT MUST BE A LOT OF PRESSURE ON YOU, MY YOUNG FRIEND.
I'M NOT *YOUNG* ANYMORE.
I KNOW THIS IS TRUE, I CAN SEE THAT WITH MY OWN EYES. BUT BENEATH *THAT* LION-O, I CAN STILL SEE THE CHILD WITHIN. THERE IS NOTHING WRONG WITH SEEKING COUNCIL.
I *HAVE* SOUGHT COUNCIL! WITH *PANTHRO!* WHO PUSHES AGAINST ME AT EVERY TURN...
PANTHRO SPEAKS HIS MIND. IT WOULD BE A DISSERVICE FOR HIM NOT TO. I BELIEVE YOU WILL COME TO REALIZE THAT FOR YOURSELF, IN TIME.

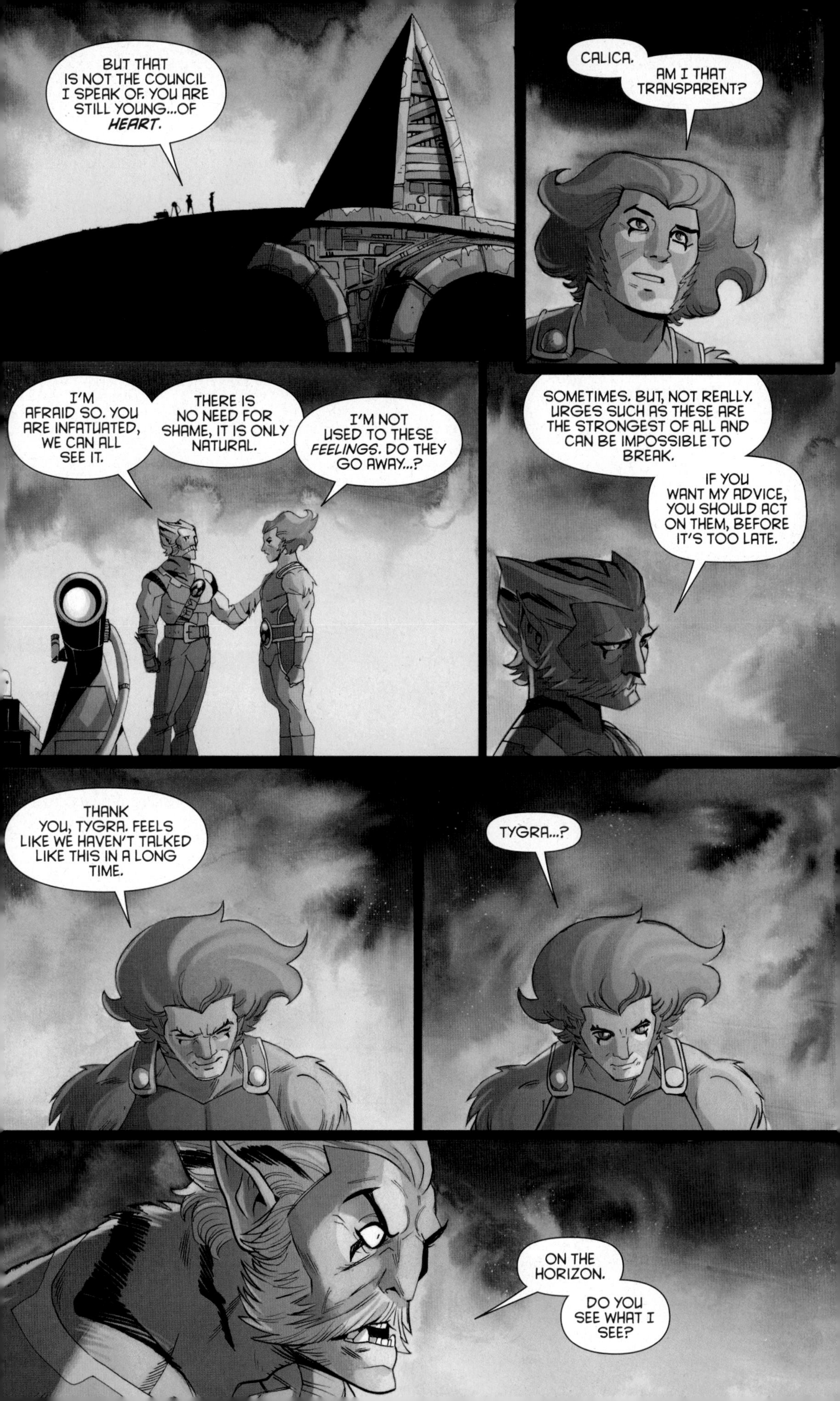

BUT THAT IS NOT THE COUNCIL I SPEAK OF. YOU ARE STILL YOUNG...OF *HEART*.
CALICA.
AM I THAT TRANSPARENT?
I'M AFRAID SO. YOU ARE INFATUATED, WE CAN ALL SEE IT.
THERE IS NO NEED FOR SHAME, IT IS ONLY NATURAL.
I'M NOT USED TO THESE *FEELINGS*. DO THEY GO AWAY...?
SOMETIMES. BUT, NOT REALLY. URGES SUCH AS THESE ARE THE STRONGEST OF ALL AND CAN BE IMPOSSIBLE TO BREAK.
IF YOU WANT MY ADVICE, YOU SHOULD ACT ON THEM, BEFORE IT'S TOO LATE.
THANK YOU, TYGRA. FEELS LIKE WE HAVEN'T TALKED LIKE THIS IN A LONG TIME.
TYGRA...?
ON THE HORIZON.
DO YOU SEE WHAT I SEE?

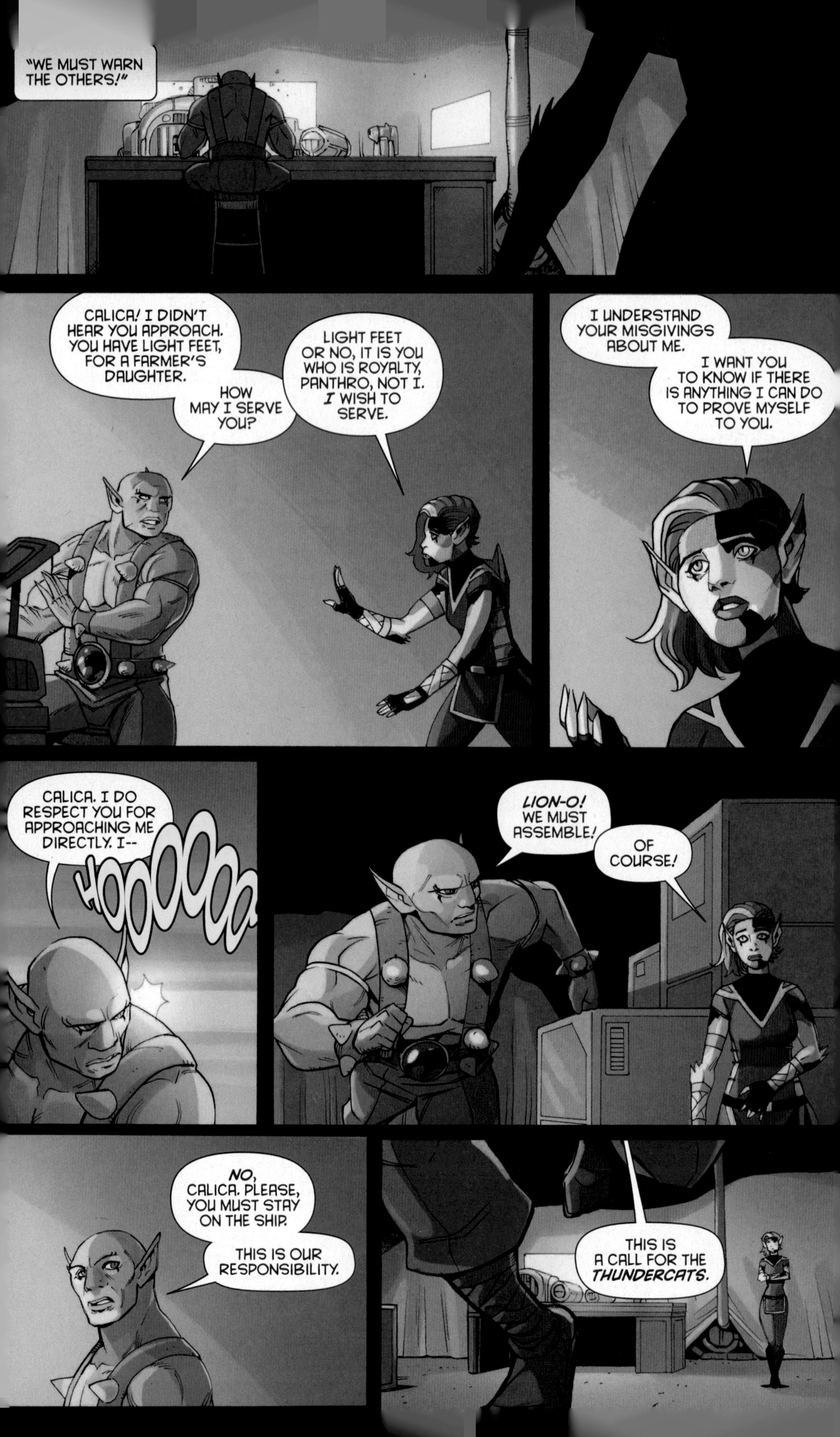
"WE MUST WARN THE OTHERS!"
CALICA! I DIDN'T HEAR YOU APPROACH. YOU HAVE LIGHT FEET, FOR A FARMER'S DAUGHTER.
HOW MAY I SERVE YOU?
LIGHT FEET OR NO, IT IS YOU WHO IS ROYALTY, PANTHRO, NOT I. *I* WISH TO SERVE.
I UNDERSTAND YOUR MISGIVINGS ABOUT ME.
I WANT YOU TO KNOW IF THERE IS ANYTHING I CAN DO TO PROVE MYSELF TO YOU.
CALICA. I DO RESPECT YOU FOR APPROACHING ME DIRECTLY. I--
HOOOOOO
LION-O! WE MUST ASSEMBLE!
OF COURSE!
NO, CALICA. PLEASE, YOU MUST STAY ON THE SHIP.
THIS IS OUR RESPONSIBILITY.
THIS IS A CALL FOR THE *THUNDERCATS.*

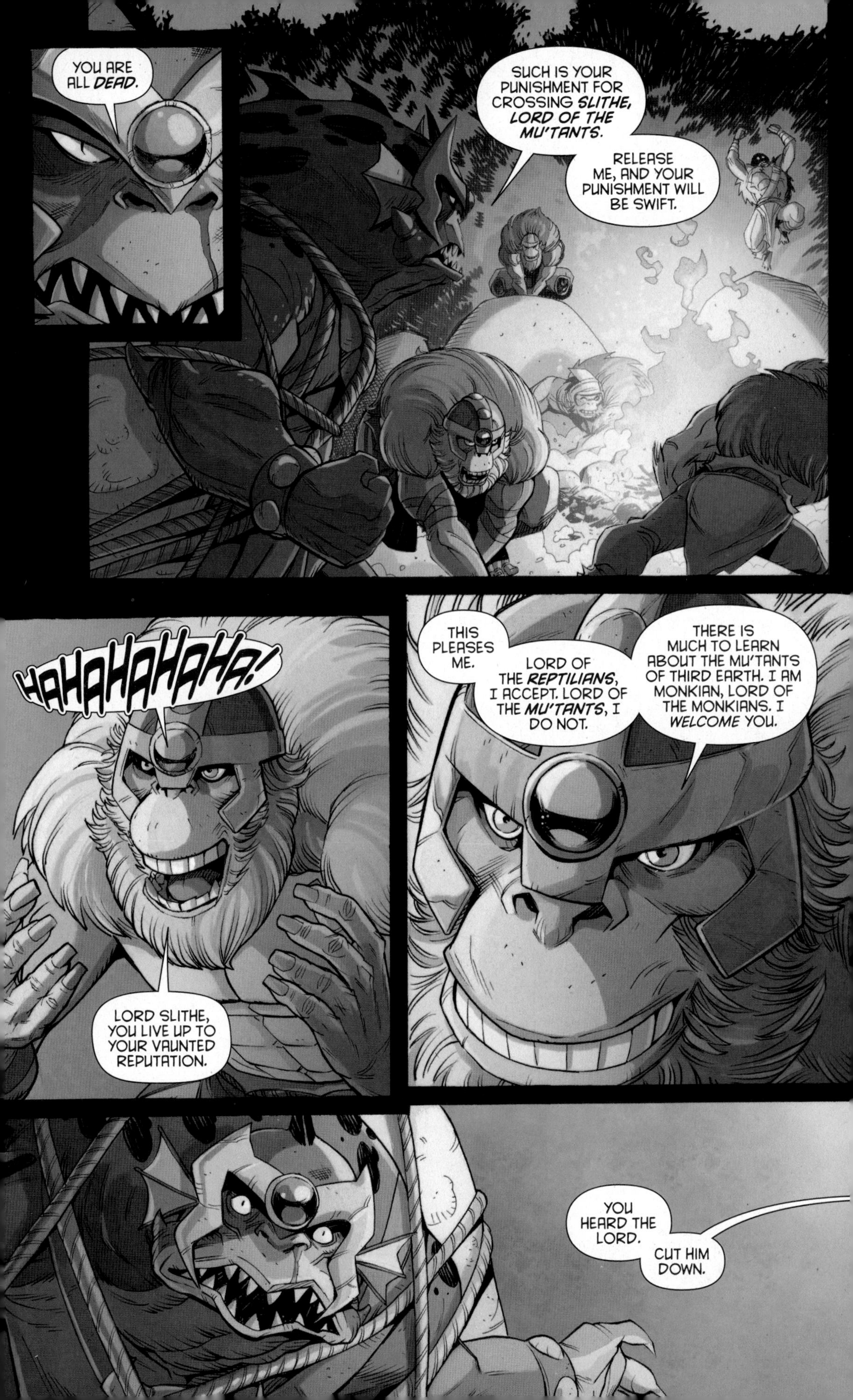
YOU ARE ALL DEAD.
SUCH IS YOUR PUNISHMENT FOR CROSSING SLITHE, LORD OF THE MU'TANTS.
RELEASE ME, AND YOUR PUNISHMENT WILL BE SWIFT.
HAHAHAHAHAHA!
LORD SLITHE, YOU LIVE UP TO YOUR VAUNTED REPUTATION.
THIS PLEASES ME.
LORD OF THE REPTILIANS, I ACCEPT. LORD OF THE MU'TANTS, I DO NOT.
THERE IS MUCH TO LEARN ABOUT THE MU'TANTS OF THIRD EARTH. I AM MONKIAN, LORD OF THE MONKIANS. I WELCOME YOU.
YOU HEARD THE LORD.
CUT HIM DOWN.

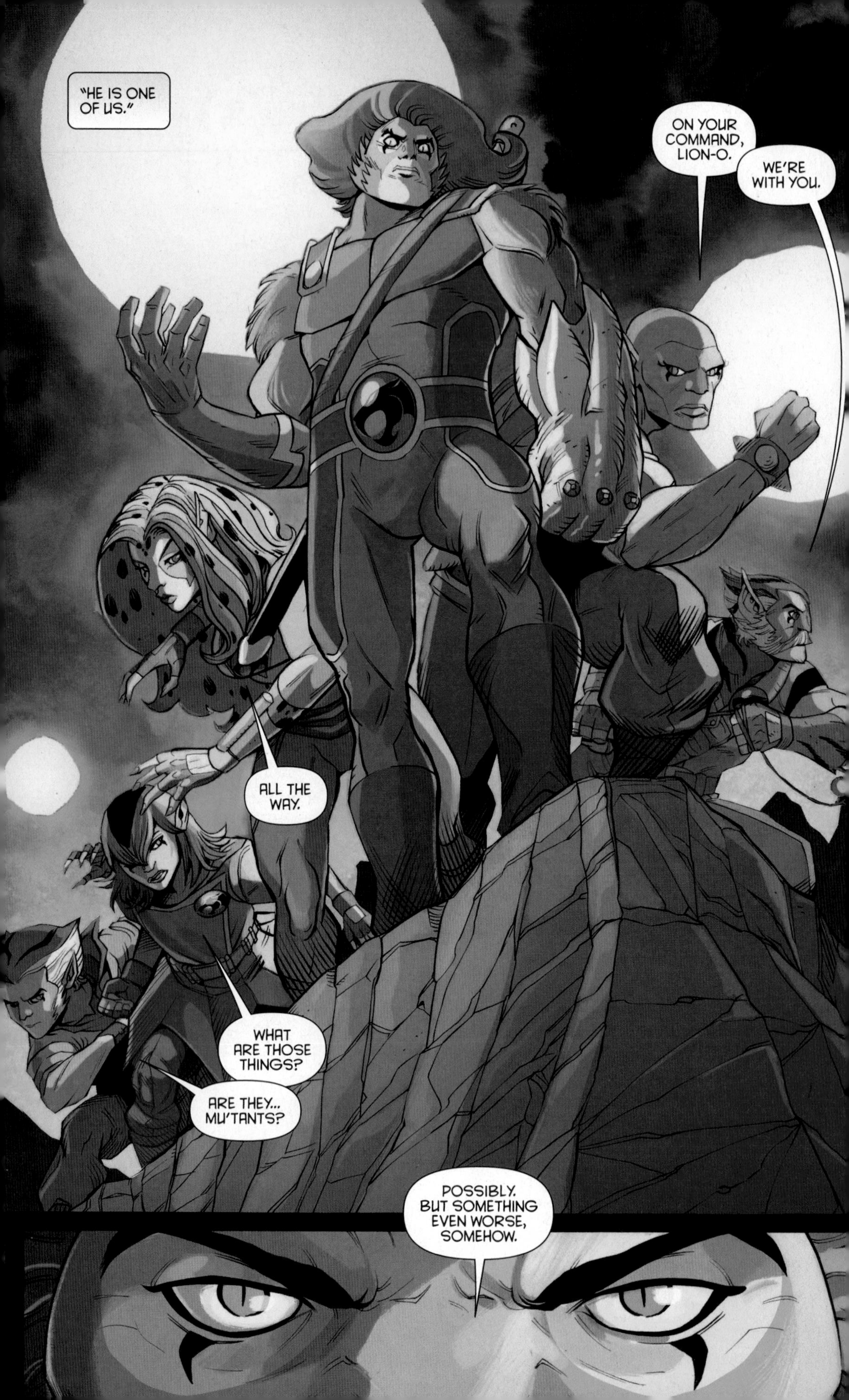
"HE IS ONE OF US."
ON YOUR COMMAND, LION-O.
WE'RE WITH YOU.
ALL THE WAY.
WHAT ARE THOSE THINGS?
ARE THEY... MU'TANTS?
POSSIBLY. BUT SOMETHING EVEN WORSE, SOMEHOW.

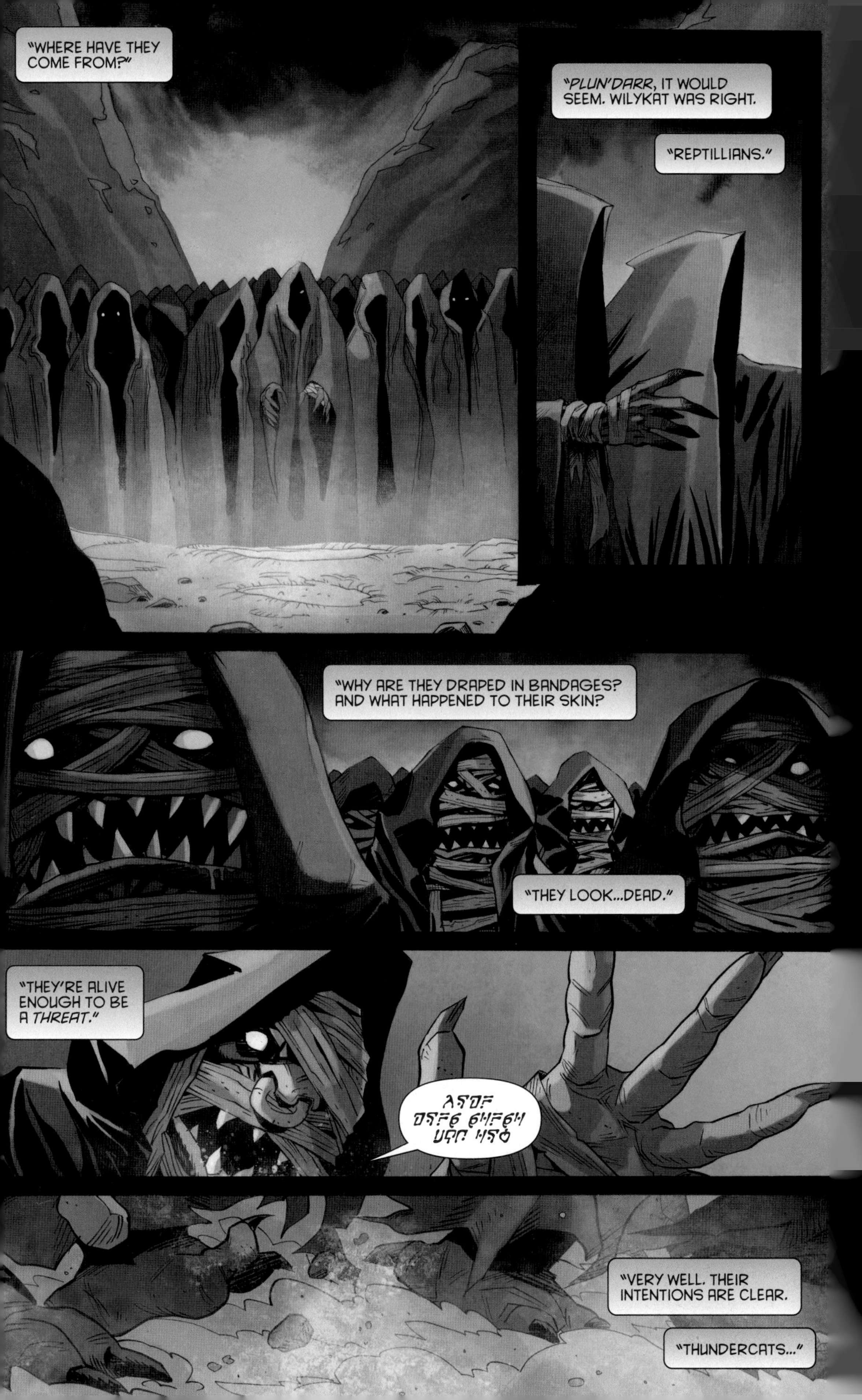
"WHERE HAVE THEY COME FROM?"
"PLUN'DARR, IT WOULD SEEM. WILYKAT WAS RIGHT.
"REPTILLIANS."
"WHY ARE THEY DRAPED IN BANDAGES? AND WHAT HAPPENED TO THEIR SKIN?
"THEY LOOK...DEAD."
"THEY'RE ALIVE ENOUGH TO BE A THREAT."
"VERY WELL. THEIR INTENTIONS ARE CLEAR.
"THUNDERCATS..."

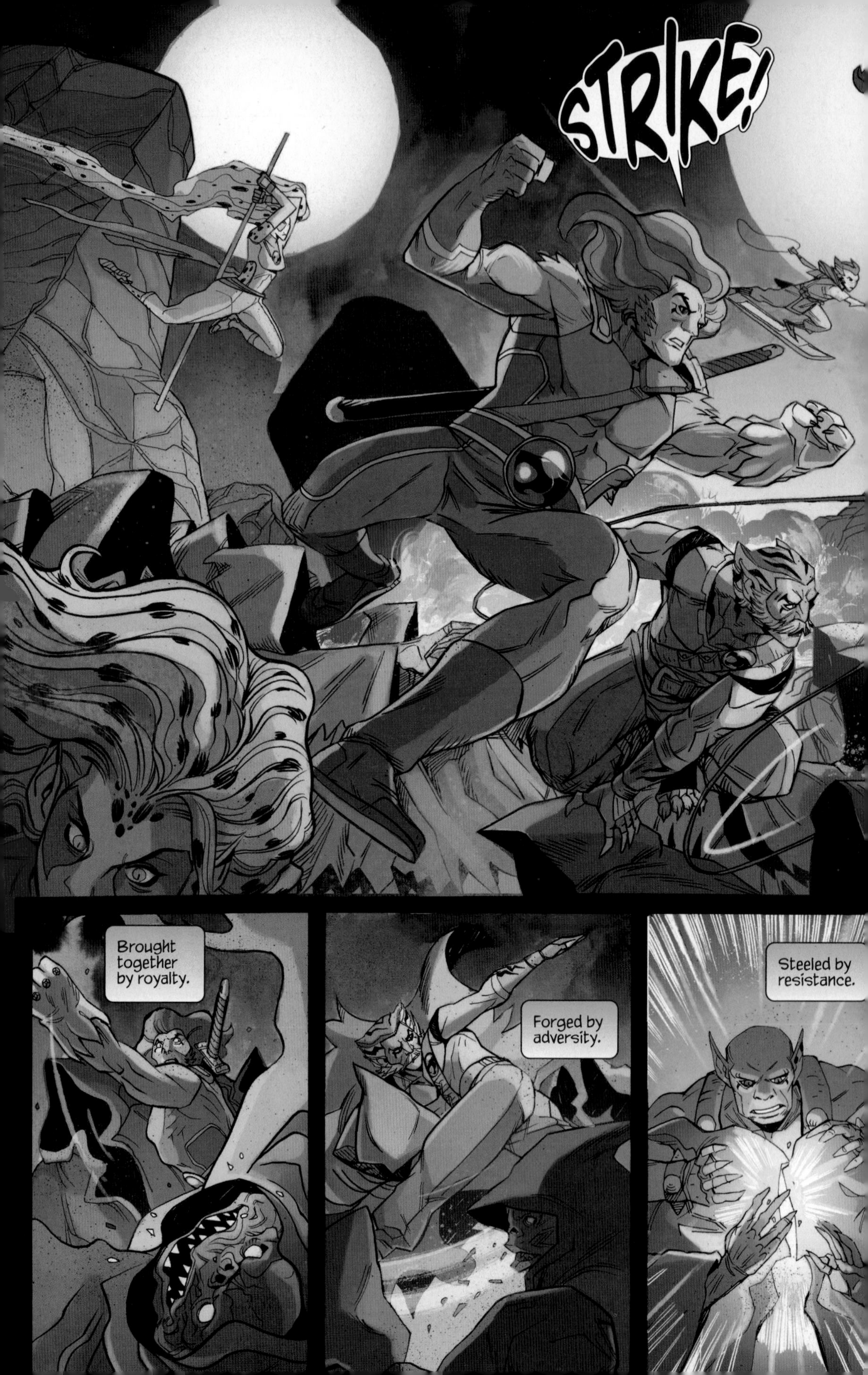
STRIKE!
Brought together by royalty.
Forged by adversity.
Steeled by resistance.

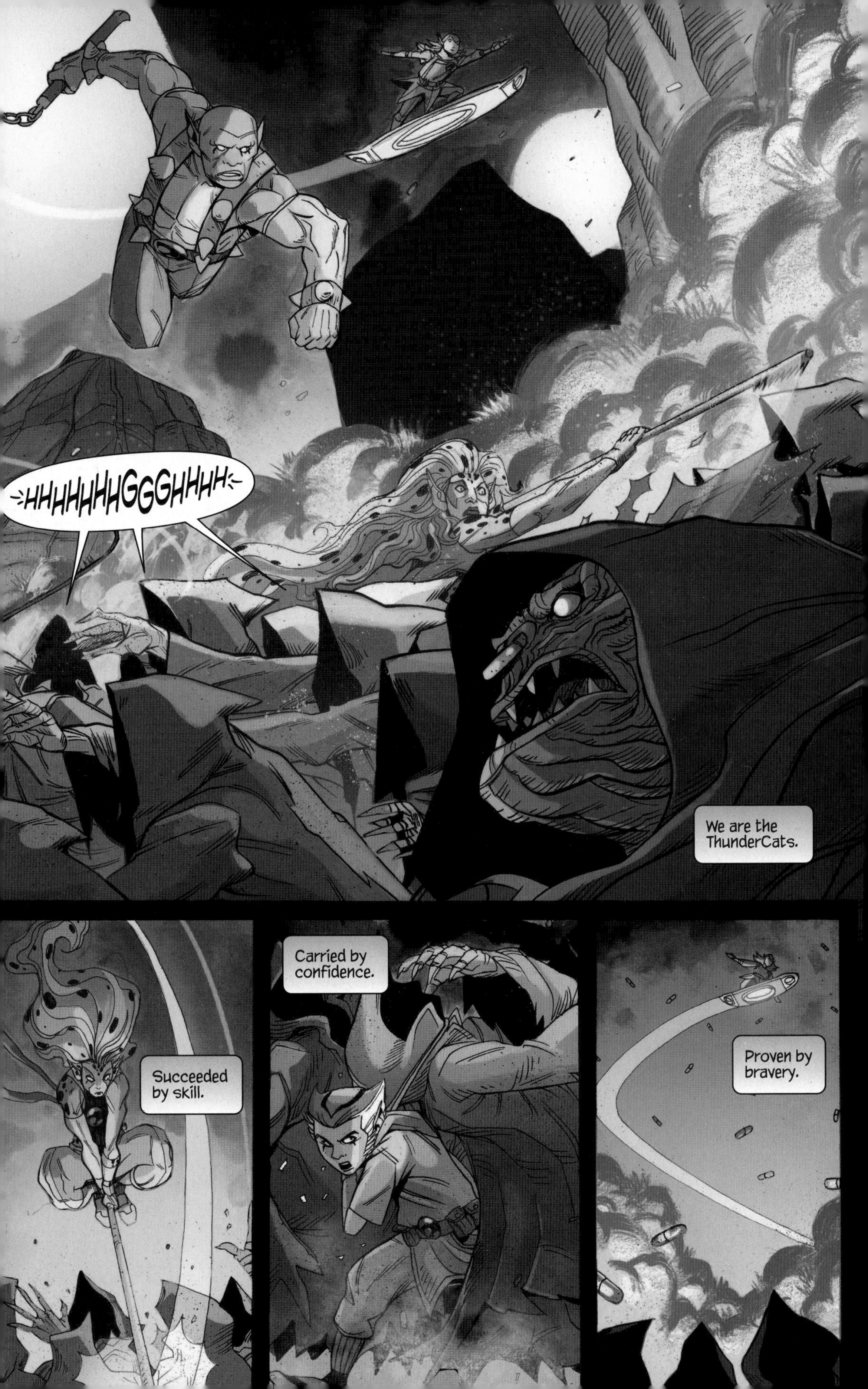
HHHHHHHGGGHHHH
We are the ThunderCats.
Succeeded by skill.
Carried by confidence.
Proven by bravery.

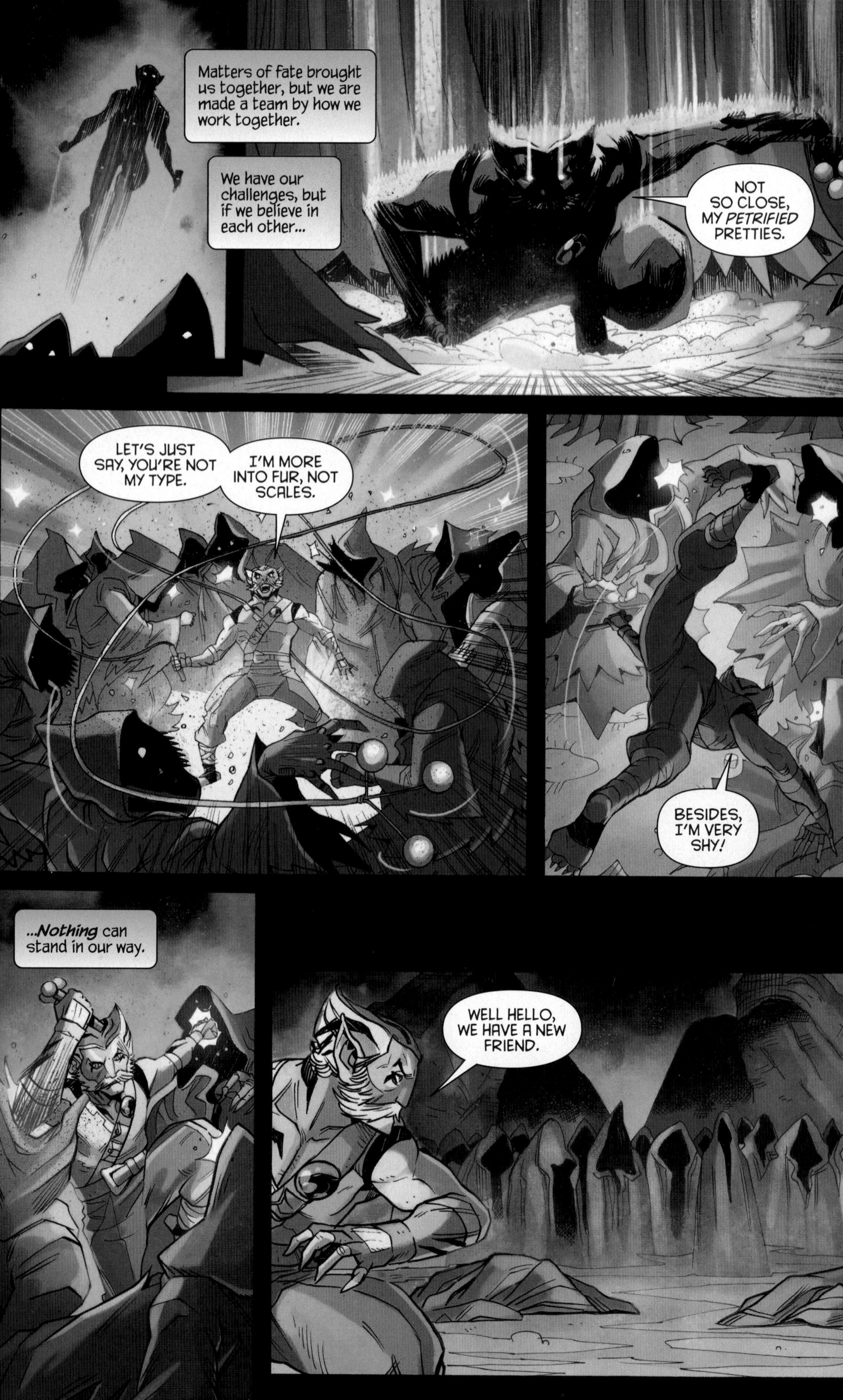
Matters of fate brought us together, but we are made a team by how we work together.
We have our challenges, but if we believe in each other...
NOT SO CLOSE, MY *PETRIFIED* PRETTIES.
LET'S JUST SAY, YOU'RE NOT MY TYPE.
I'M MORE INTO FUR, NOT SCALES.
BESIDES, I'M VERY SHY!
...*Nothing* can stand in our way.
WELL HELLO, WE HAVE A NEW FRIEND.

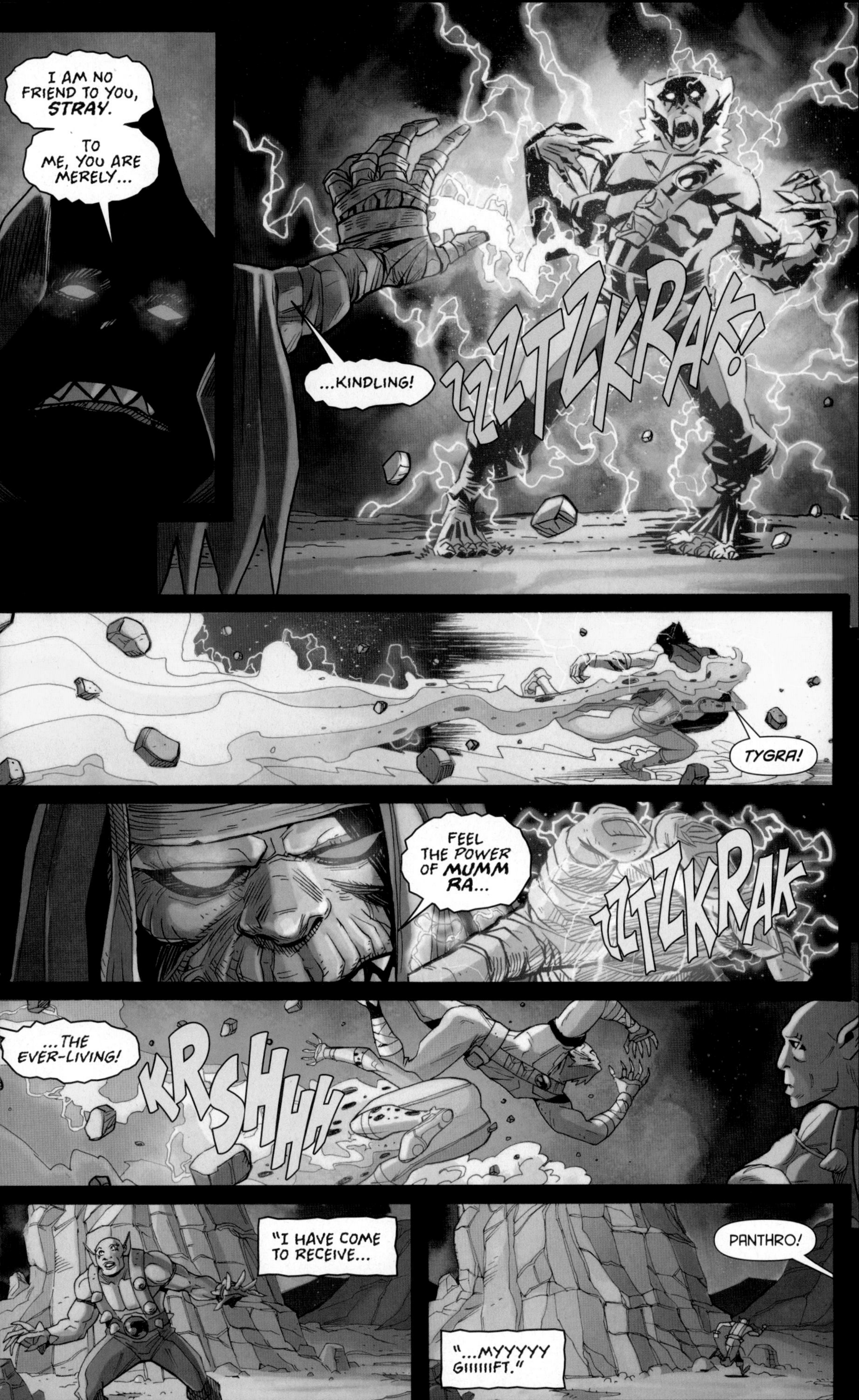
I AM NO FRIEND TO YOU, STRAY.
TO ME, YOU ARE MERELY...
...KINDLING!
ZZZZTZKRAK!
TYGRA!
FEEL THE POWER OF MUMM RA...
ZZZTZKRAK
...THE EVER-LIVING!
KRSHHH
"I HAVE COME TO RECEIVE...
PANTHRO!
"...MYYYYY GIIIIIFT."

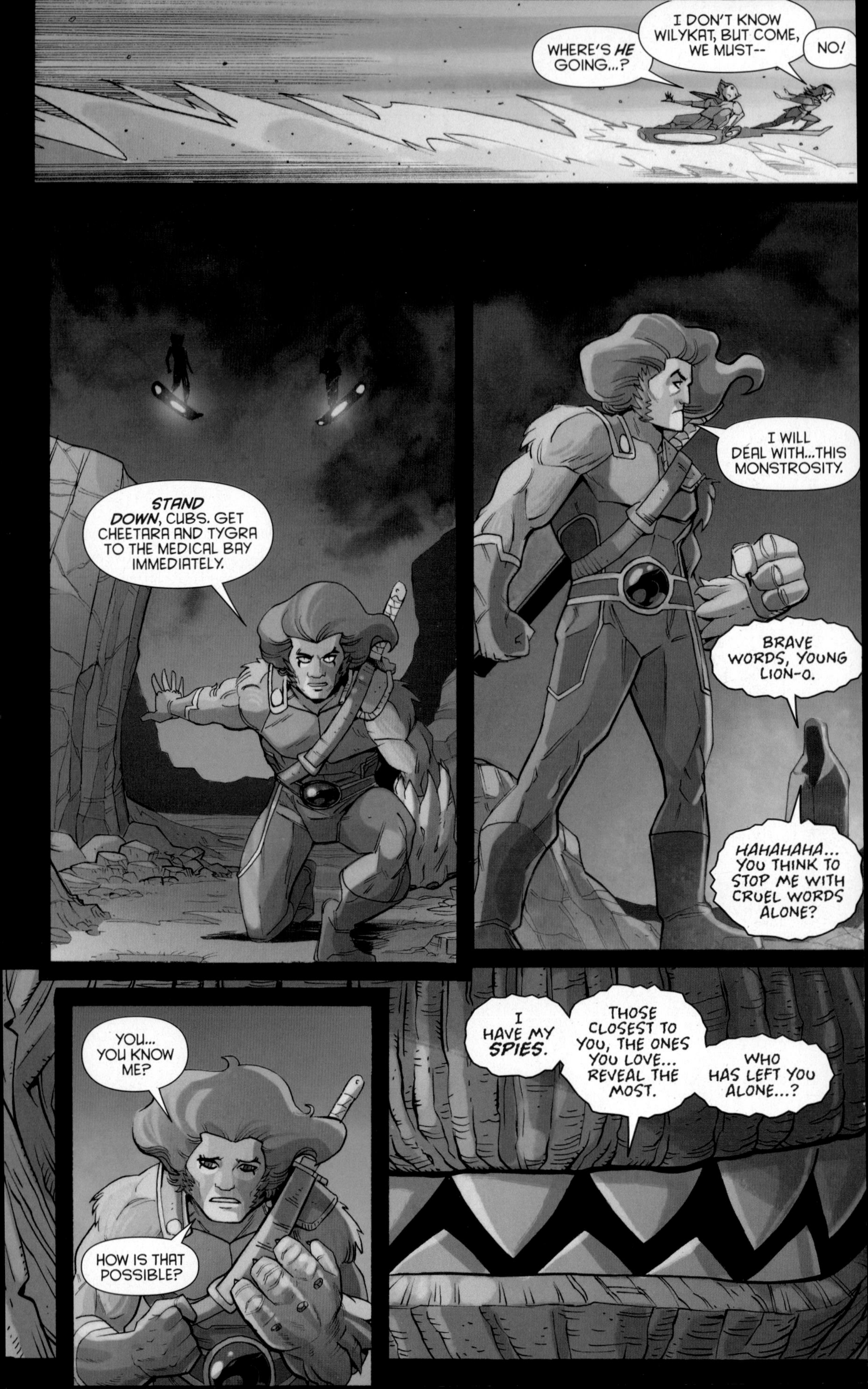
WHERE'S HE GOING...?
I DON'T KNOW WILYKAT, BUT COME, WE MUST--
NO!
STAND DOWN, CUBS. GET CHEETARA AND TYGRA TO THE MEDICAL BAY IMMEDIATELY.
I WILL DEAL WITH...THIS MONSTROSITY.
BRAVE WORDS, YOUNG LION-O.
HAHAHAHA... YOU THINK TO STOP ME WITH CRUEL WORDS ALONE?
YOU... YOU KNOW ME?
HOW IS THAT POSSIBLE?
I HAVE MY SPIES.
THOSE CLOSEST TO YOU, THE ONES YOU LOVE... REVEAL THE MOST.
WHO HAS LEFT YOU ALONE...?

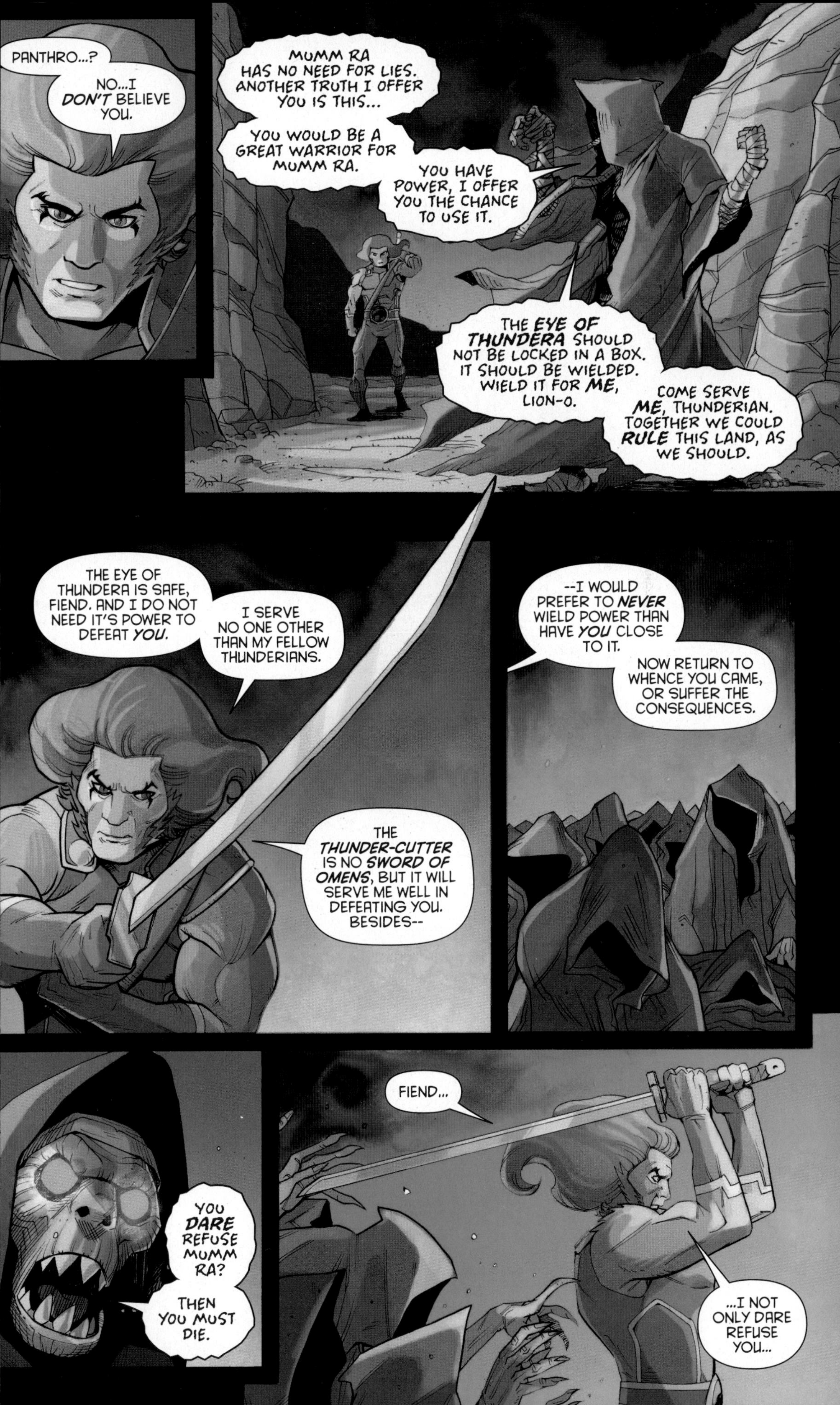
PANTHRO...?
NO...I DON'T BELIEVE YOU.
MUMM RA HAS NO NEED FOR LIES. ANOTHER TRUTH I OFFER YOU IS THIS...
YOU WOULD BE A GREAT WARRIOR FOR MUMM RA.
YOU HAVE POWER, I OFFER YOU THE CHANCE TO USE IT.
THE EYE OF THUNDERA SHOULD NOT BE LOCKED IN A BOX. IT SHOULD BE WIELDED. WIELD IT FOR ME, LION-O.
COME SERVE ME, THUNDERIAN. TOGETHER WE COULD RULE THIS LAND, AS WE SHOULD.
THE EYE OF THUNDERA IS SAFE, FIEND. AND I DO NOT NEED IT'S POWER TO DEFEAT YOU.
I SERVE NO ONE OTHER THAN MY FELLOW THUNDERIANS.
THE THUNDER-CUTTER IS NO SWORD OF OMENS, BUT IT WILL SERVE ME WELL IN DEFEATING YOU. BESIDES--
--I WOULD PREFER TO NEVER WIELD POWER THAN HAVE YOU CLOSE TO IT.
NOW RETURN TO WHENCE YOU CAME, OR SUFFER THE CONSEQUENCES.
YOU DARE REFUSE MUMM RA?
THEN YOU MUST DIE.
FIEND...
...I NOT ONLY DARE REFUSE YOU...

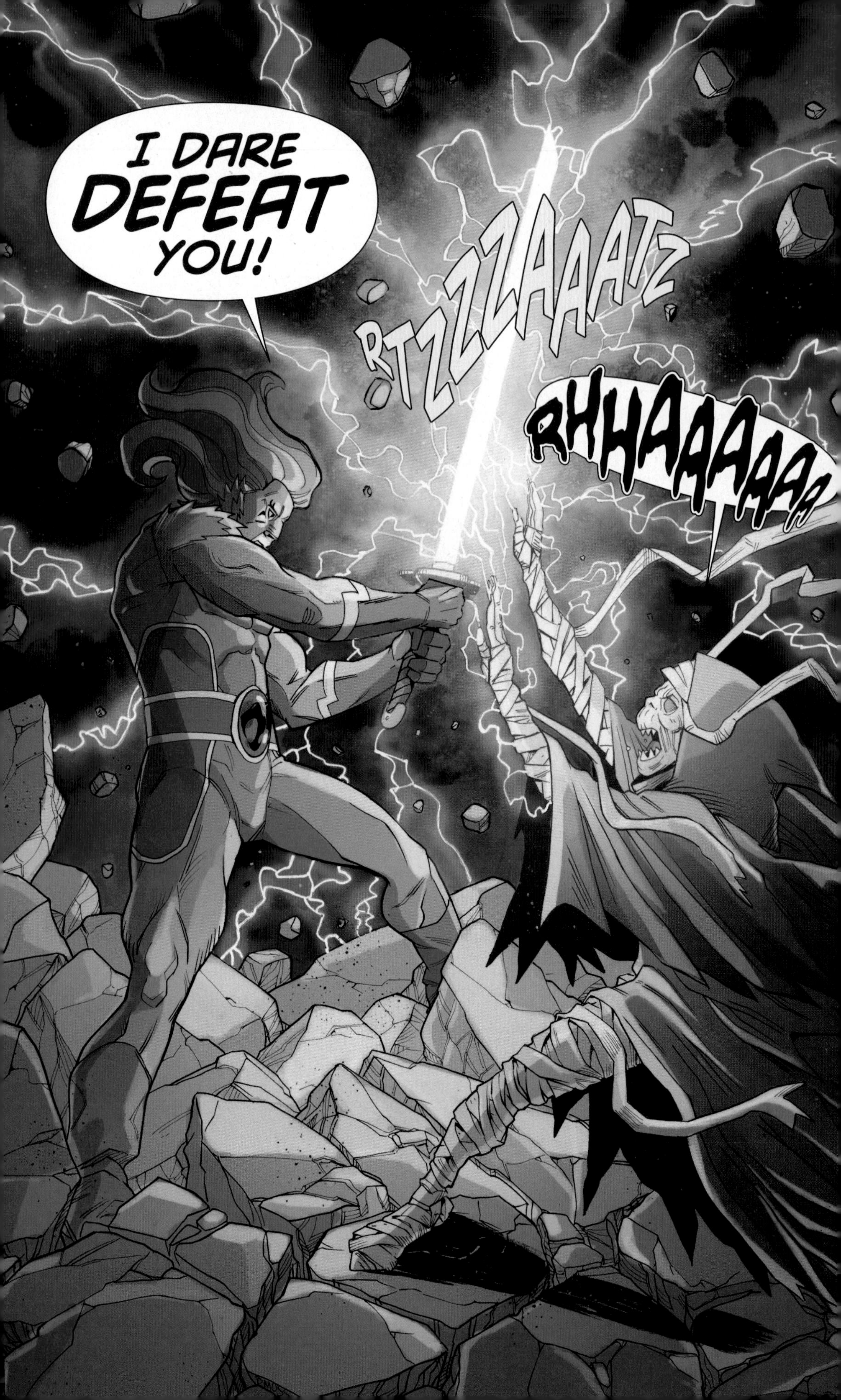
I DARE DEFEAT YOU!
RTZZZAAATZ
RHHAAAAAAA

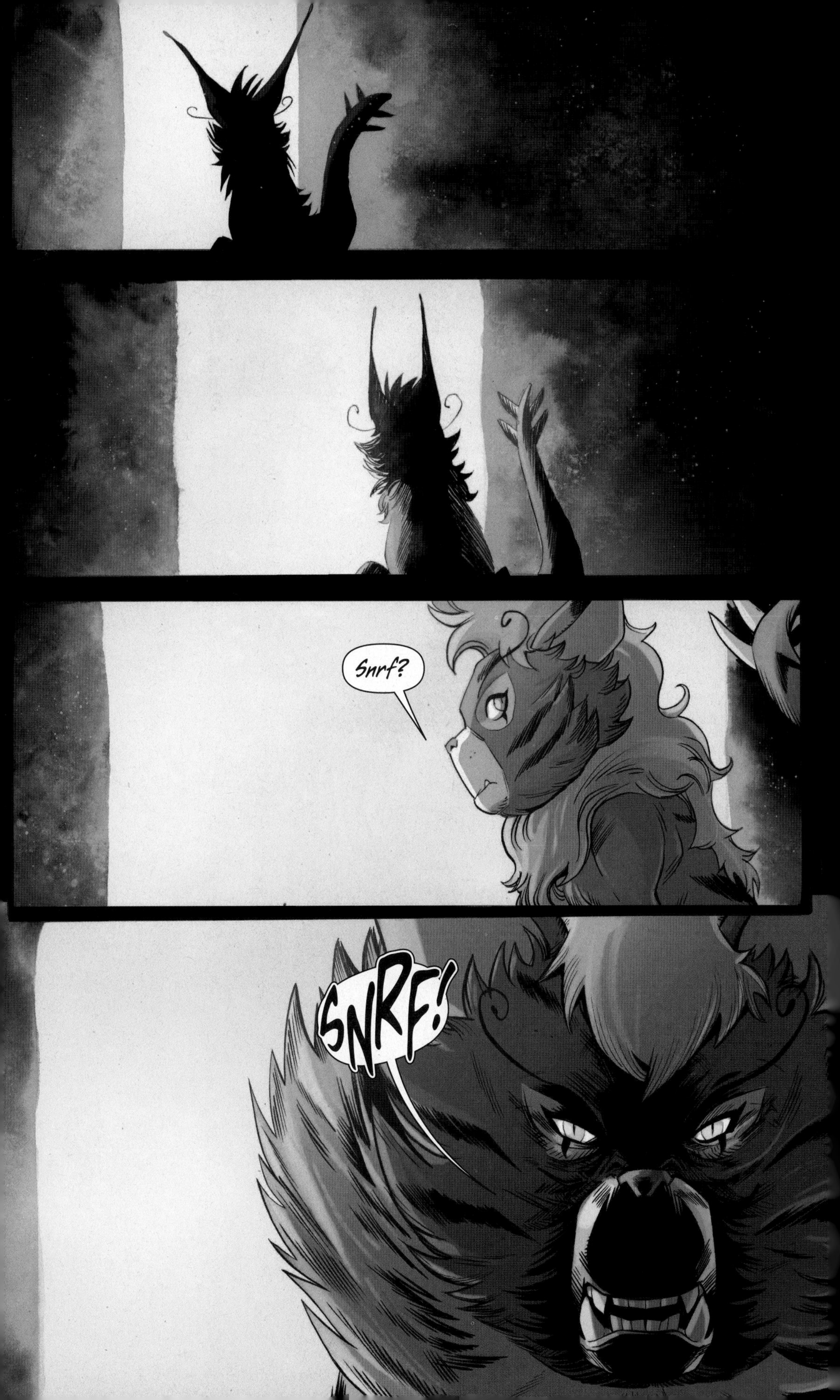
Snrf?
SNRF!

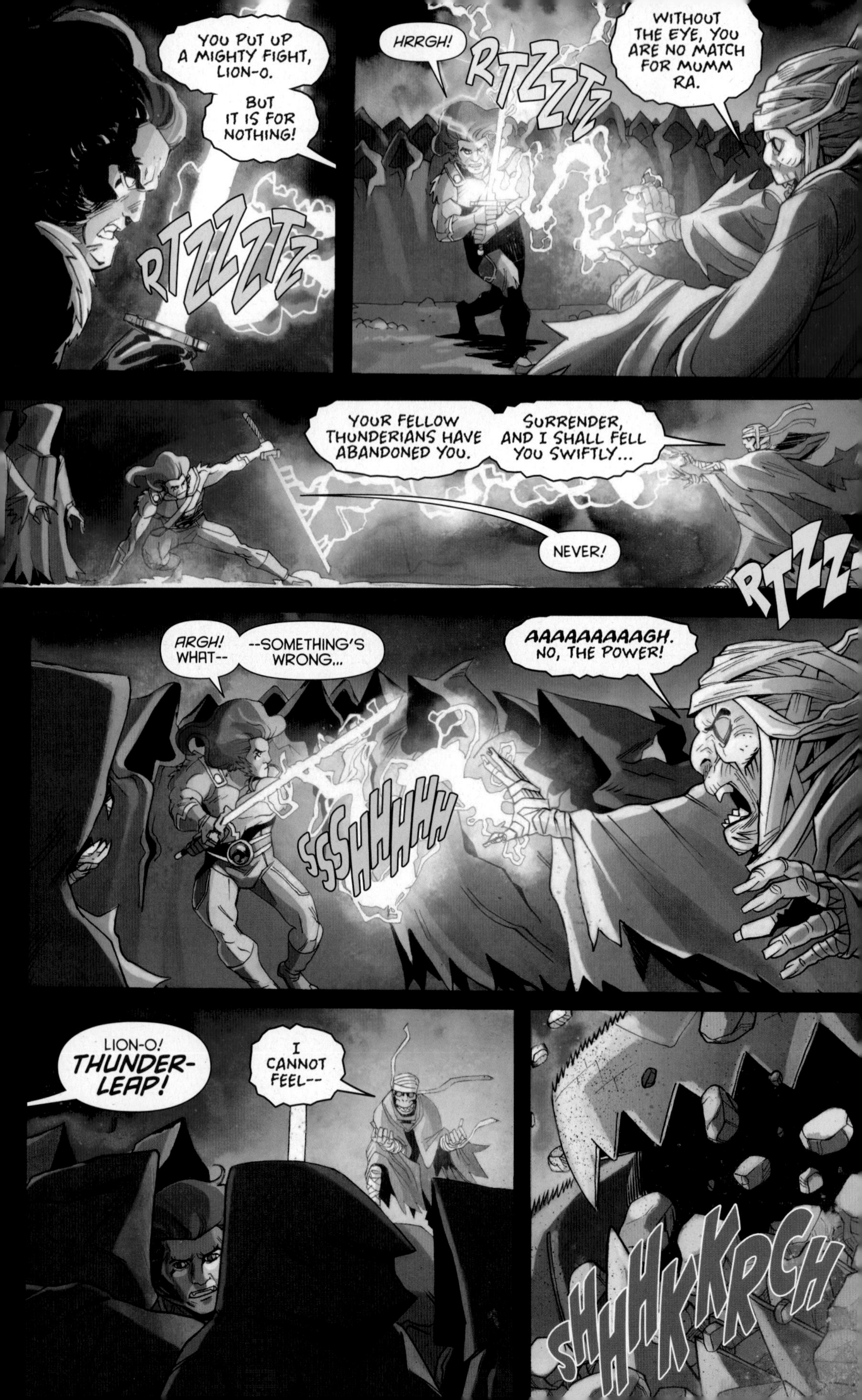
YOU PUT UP A MIGHTY FIGHT, LION-O.
BUT IT IS FOR NOTHING!
RTZZZTZ
HRRGH!
RTZZZTZ
WITHOUT THE EYE, YOU ARE NO MATCH FOR MUMM RA.
YOUR FELLOW THUNDERIANS HAVE ABANDONED YOU.
SURRENDER, AND I SHALL FELL YOU SWIFTLY...
NEVER!
RTZZ
ARGH! WHAT--
--SOMETHING'S WRONG...
AAAAAAAAAGH. NO, THE POWER!
SSSHHHHH
LION-O! THUNDER-LEAP!
I CANNOT FEEL--
SHHHKRCH

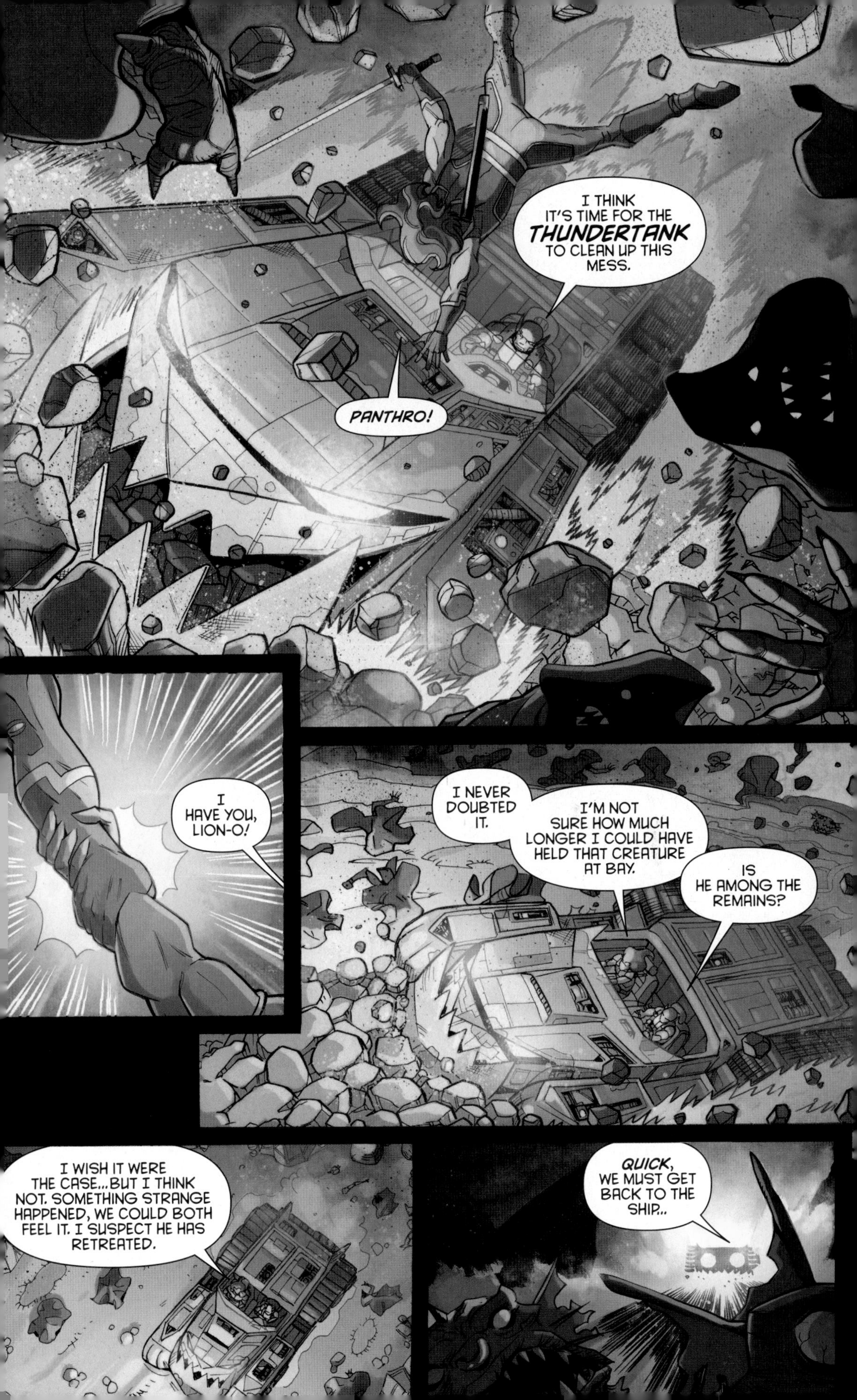

I THINK IT'S TIME FOR THE THUNDERTANK TO CLEAN UP THIS MESS.
PANTHRO!
I HAVE YOU, LION-O!
I NEVER DOUBTED IT.
I'M NOT SURE HOW MUCH LONGER I COULD HAVE HELD THAT CREATURE AT BAY.
IS HE AMONG THE REMAINS?
I WISH IT WERE THE CASE...BUT I THINK NOT. SOMETHING STRANGE HAPPENED, WE COULD BOTH FEEL IT. I SUSPECT HE HAS RETREATED.
QUICK, WE MUST GET BACK TO THE SHIP...

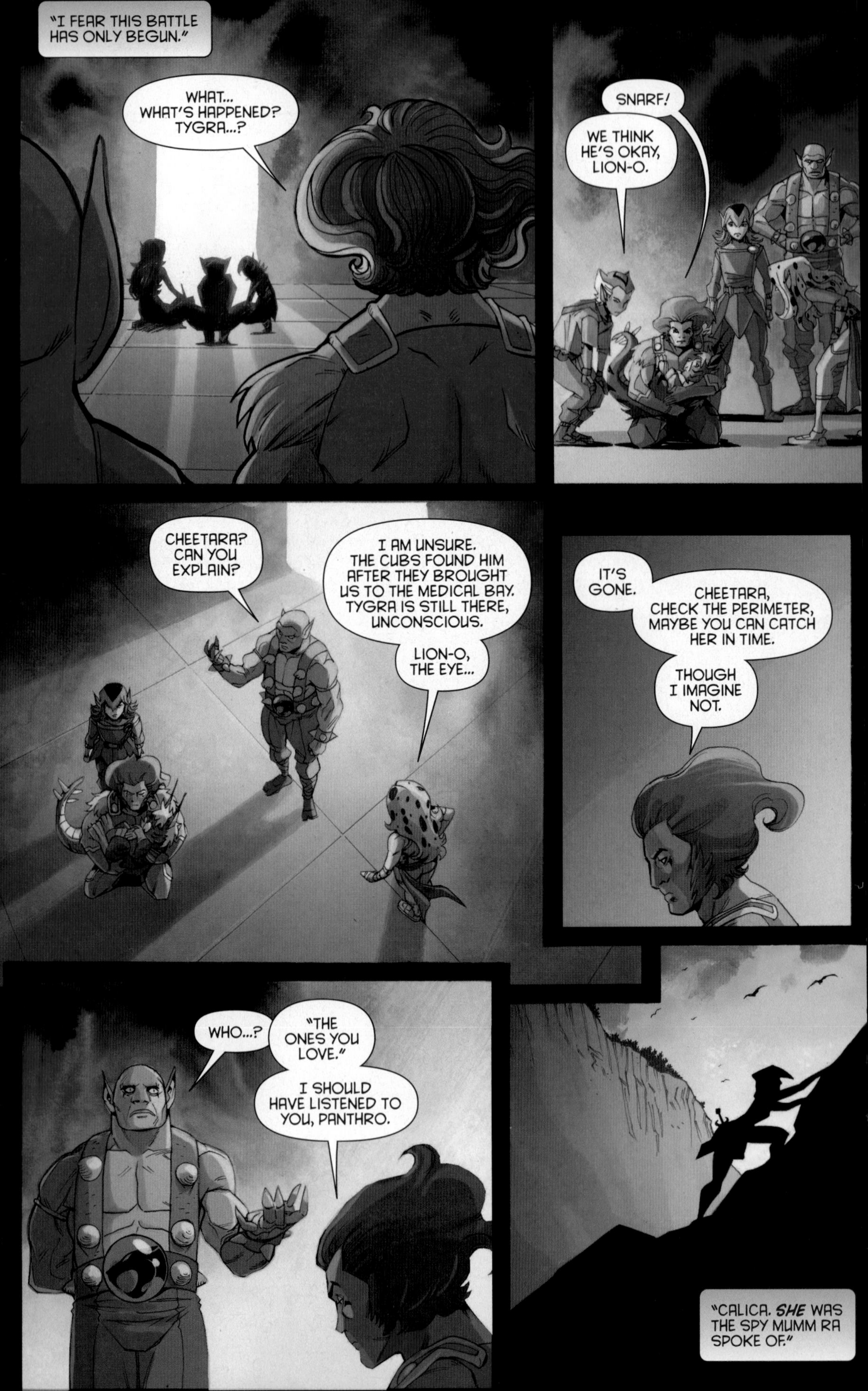
"I FEAR THIS BATTLE HAS ONLY BEGUN."
WHAT... WHAT'S HAPPENED? TYGRA...?
SNARF!
WE THINK HE'S OKAY, LION-O.
CHEETARA? CAN YOU EXPLAIN?
I AM UNSURE. THE CUBS FOUND HIM AFTER THEY BROUGHT US TO THE MEDICAL BAY. TYGRA IS STILL THERE, UNCONSCIOUS.
LION-O, THE EYE...
IT'S GONE.
CHEETARA, CHECK THE PERIMETER, MAYBE YOU CAN CATCH HER IN TIME.
THOUGH I IMAGINE NOT.
WHO...?
"THE ONES YOU LOVE."
I SHOULD HAVE LISTENED TO YOU, PANTHRO.
"CALICA. *SHE* WAS THE SPY MUMM RA SPOKE OF."

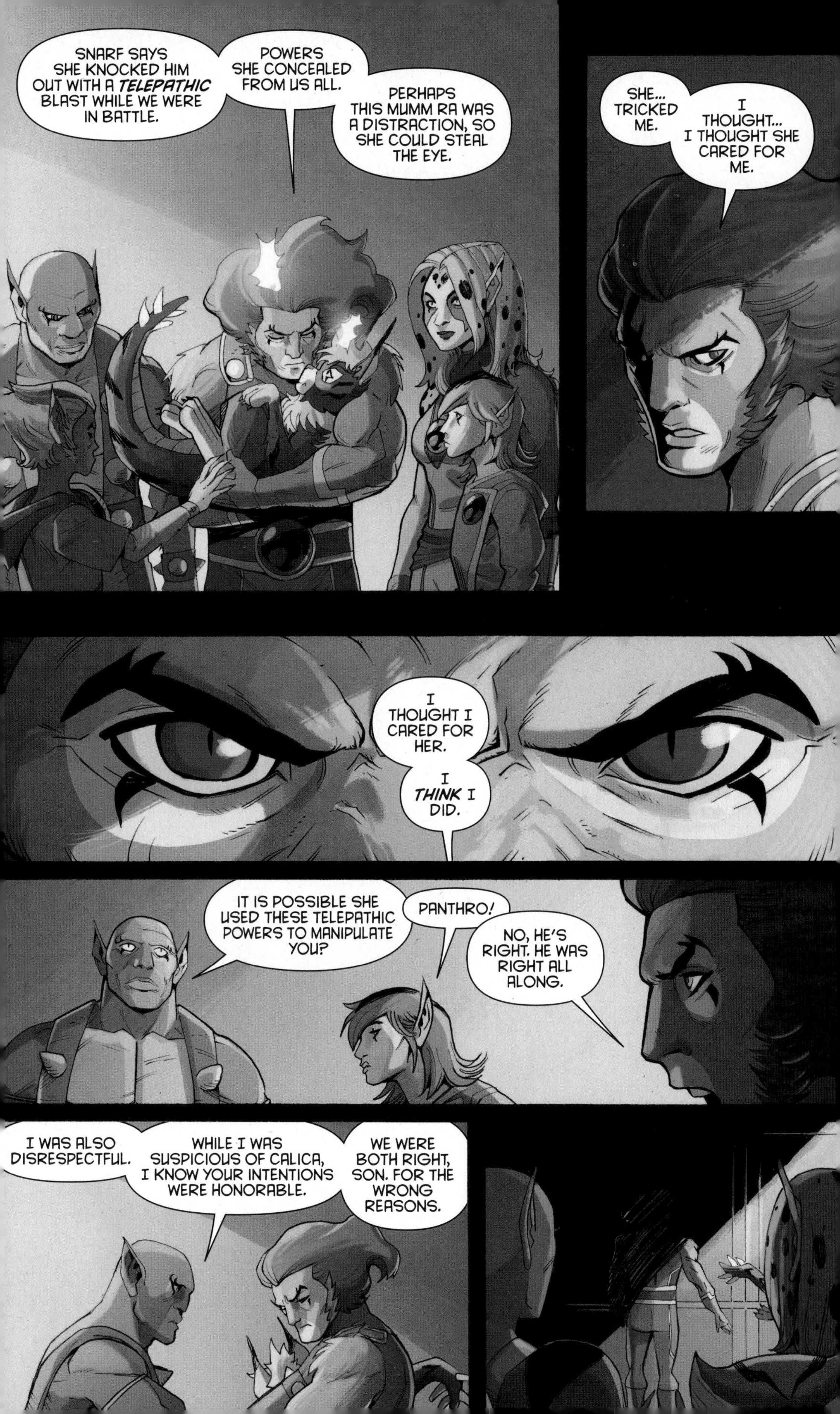
SNARF SAYS SHE KNOCKED HIM OUT WITH A *TELEPATHIC* BLAST WHILE WE WERE IN BATTLE.
POWERS SHE CONCEALED FROM US ALL.
PERHAPS THIS MUMM RA WAS A DISTRACTION, SO SHE COULD STEAL THE EYE.
SHE... TRICKED ME.
I THOUGHT... I THOUGHT SHE CARED FOR ME.
I THOUGHT I CARED FOR HER.
I *THINK* I DID.
IT IS POSSIBLE SHE USED THESE TELEPATHIC POWERS TO MANIPULATE YOU?
PANTHRO!
NO, HE'S RIGHT. HE WAS RIGHT ALL ALONG.
I WAS ALSO DISRESPECTFUL.
WHILE I WAS SUSPICIOUS OF CALICA, I KNOW YOUR INTENTIONS WERE HONORABLE.
WE WERE BOTH RIGHT, SON. FOR THE WRONG REASONS.

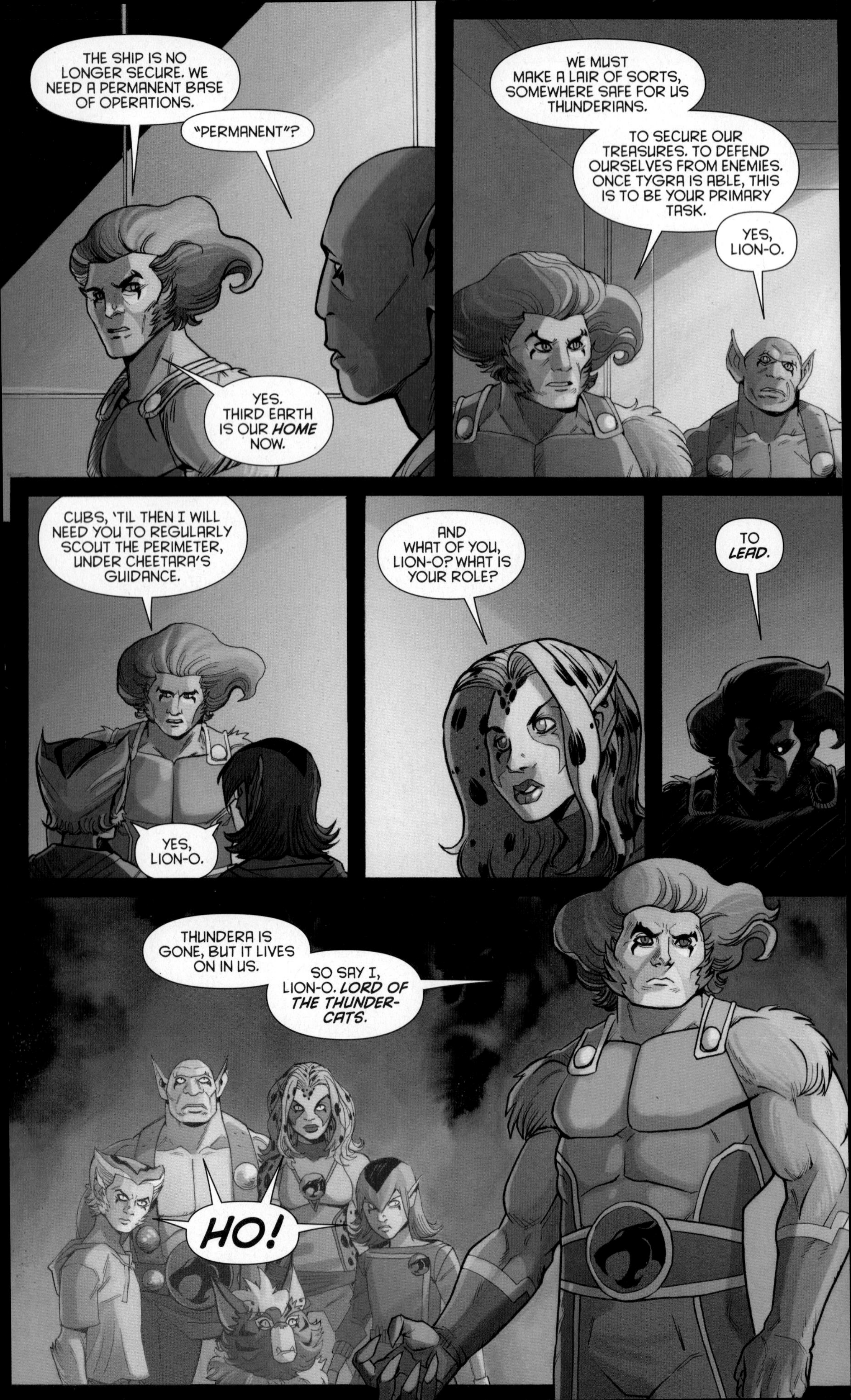
THE SHIP IS NO LONGER SECURE. WE NEED A PERMANENT BASE OF OPERATIONS.
"PERMANENT"?
YES. THIRD EARTH IS OUR *HOME* NOW.
WE MUST MAKE A LAIR OF SORTS, SOMEWHERE SAFE FOR US THUNDERIANS.
TO SECURE OUR TREASURES. TO DEFEND OURSELVES FROM ENEMIES. ONCE TYGRA IS ABLE, THIS IS TO BE YOUR PRIMARY TASK.
YES, LION-O.
CUBS, 'TIL THEN I WILL NEED YOU TO REGULARLY SCOUT THE PERIMETER, UNDER CHEETARA'S GUIDANCE.
YES, LION-O.
AND WHAT OF YOU, LION-O? WHAT IS YOUR ROLE?
TO *LEAD*.
THUNDERA IS GONE, BUT IT LIVES ON IN US.
SO SAY I, LION-O. *LORD OF THE THUNDER-CATS.*
HO!

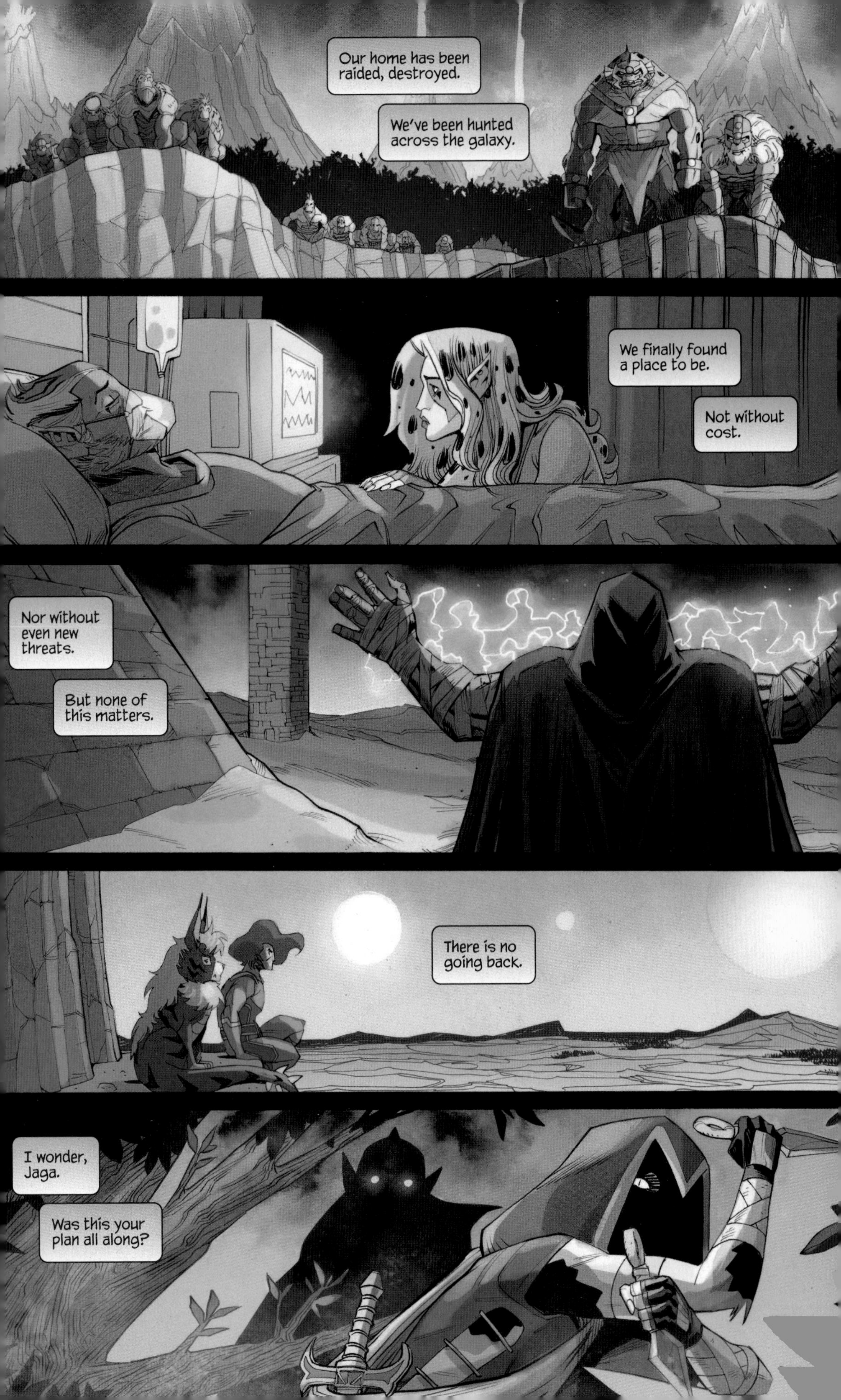
Our home has been raided, destroyed.
We've been hunted across the galaxy.
We finally found a place to be.
Not without cost.
Nor without even new threats.
But none of this matters.
There is no going back.
I wonder, Jaga.
Was this your plan all along?

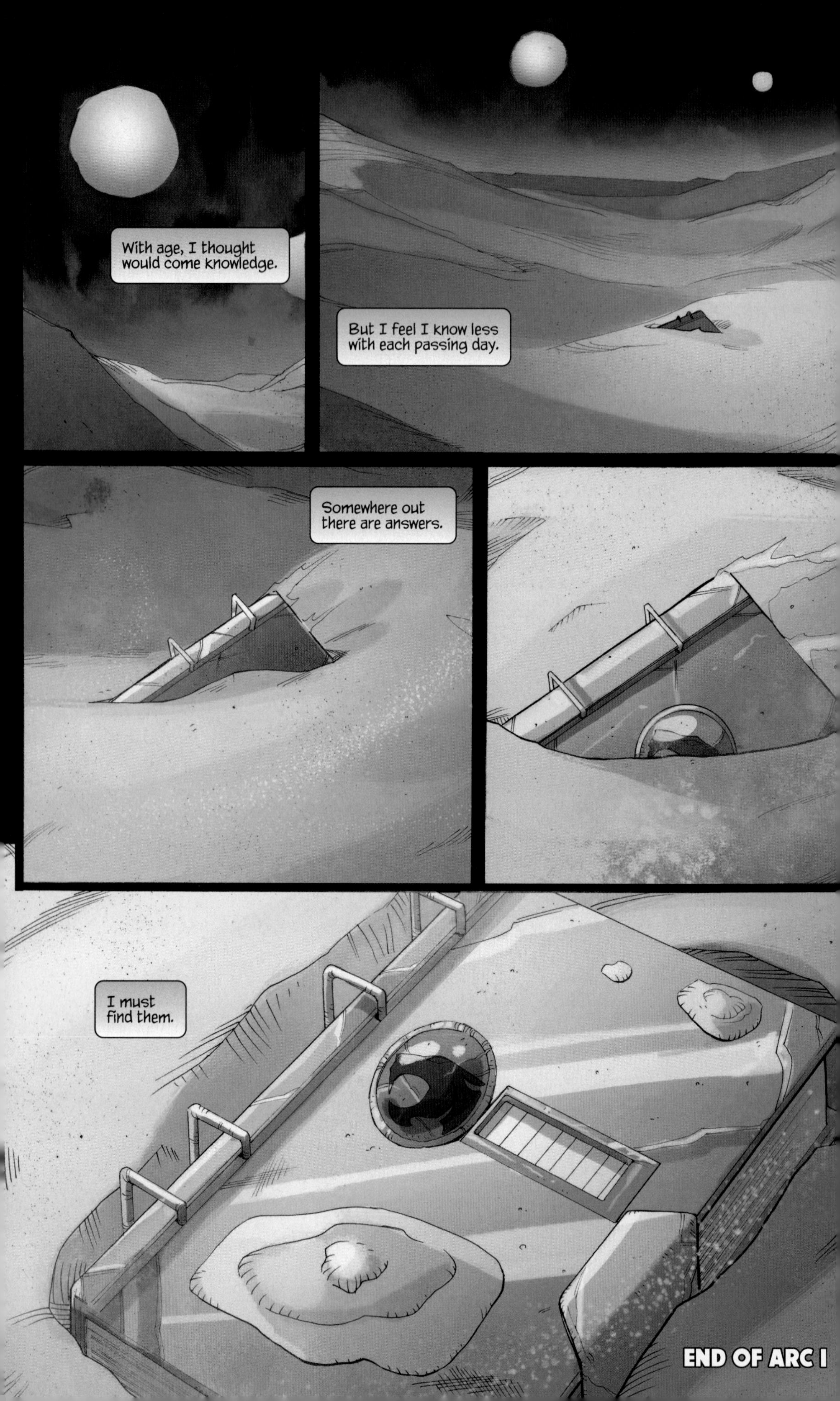
With age, I thought would come knowledge.
But I feel I know less with each passing day.
Somewhere out there are answers.
I must find them.
END OF ARC I

FIVE

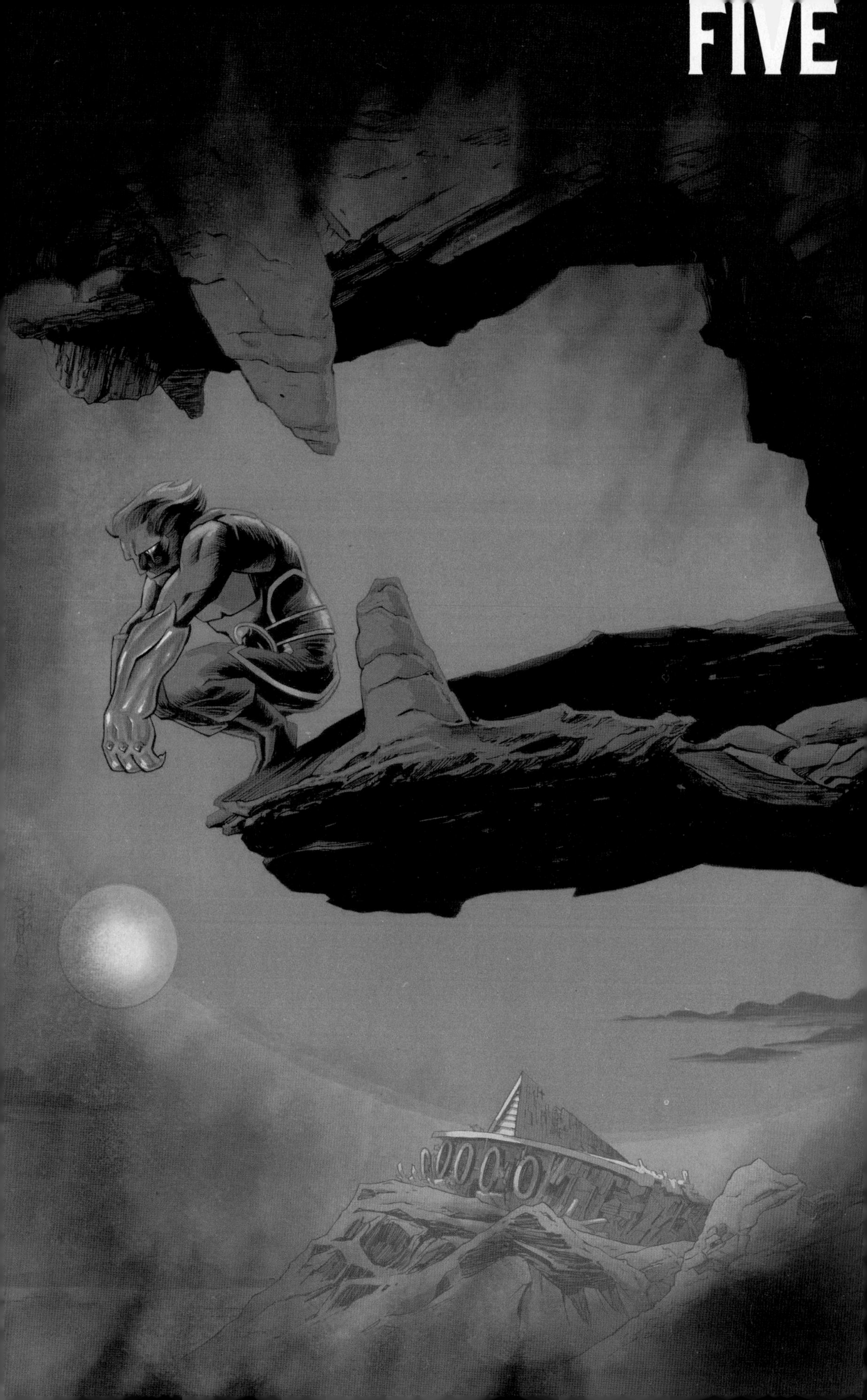

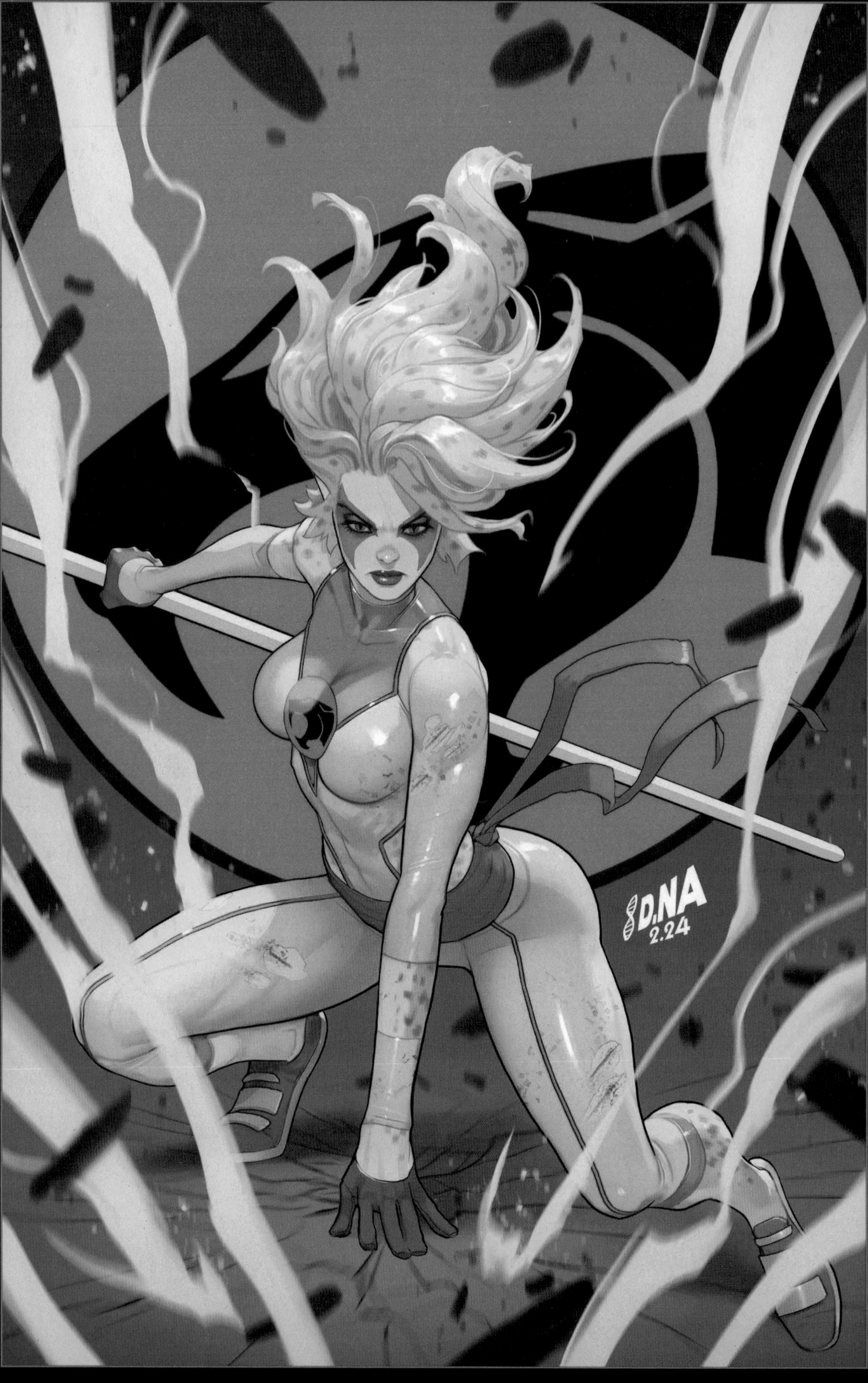
D.NA
2.24
Issue Five Art By DAVID NAKAYAMA

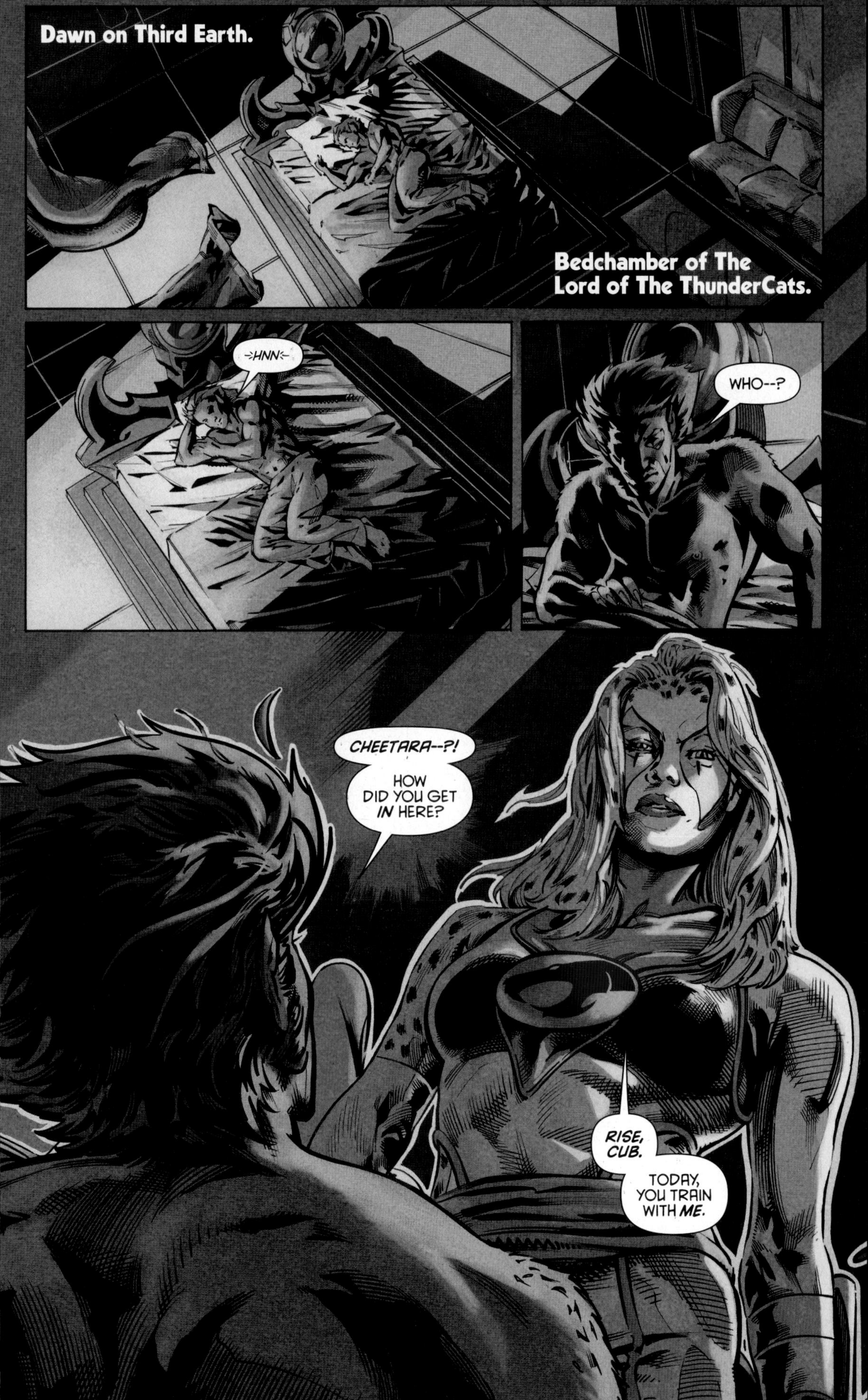
Dawn on Third Earth.
Bedchamber of The Lord of The ThunderCats.
HNN
WHO--?
CHEETARA--?!
HOW DID YOU GET *IN* HERE?
RISE, CUB.
TODAY, YOU TRAIN WITH *ME*.

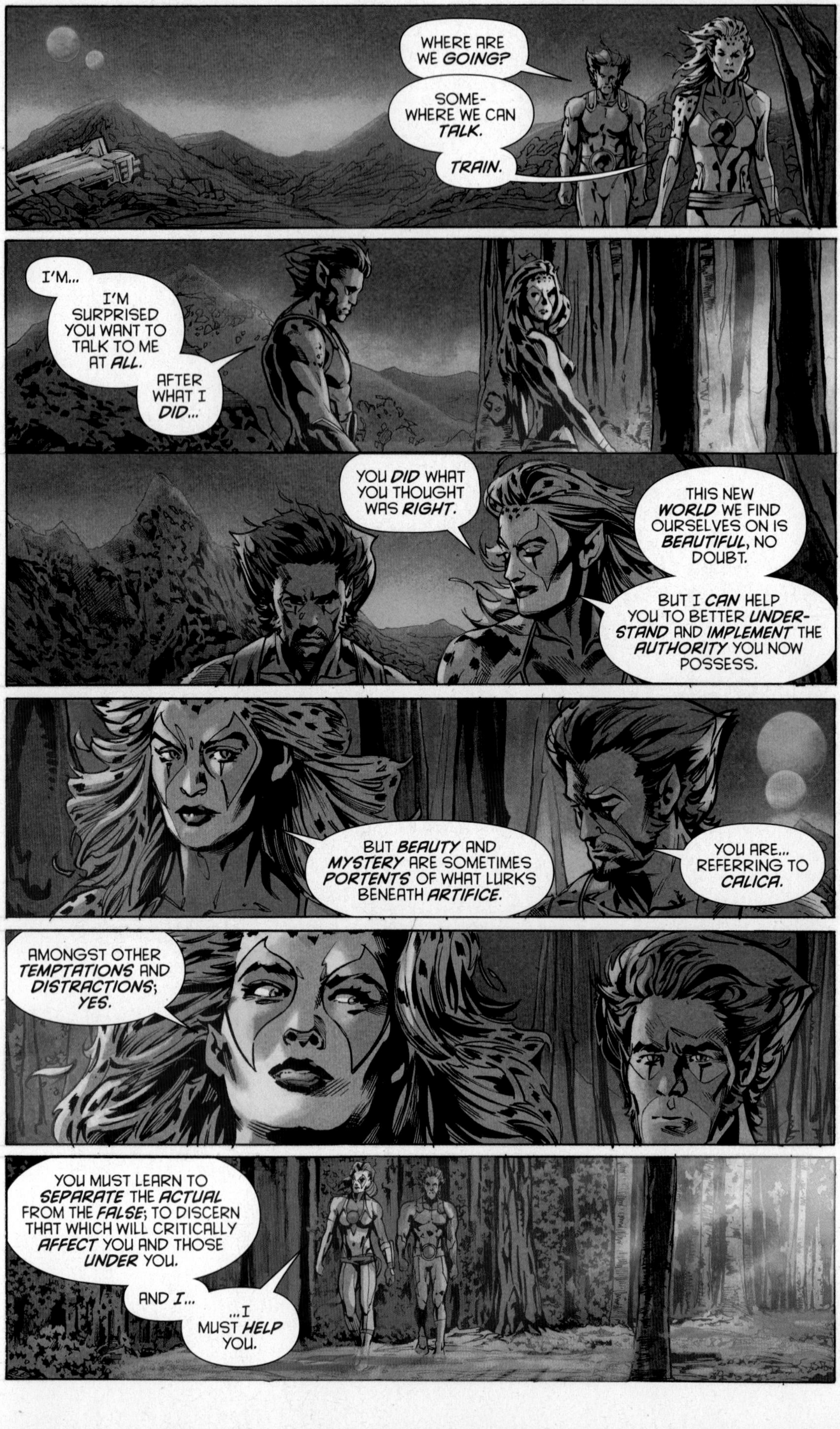
WHERE ARE WE GOING?
SOME-WHERE WE CAN TALK.
TRAIN.
I'M...
I'M SURPRISED YOU WANT TO TALK TO ME AT ALL.
AFTER WHAT I DID...
YOU DID WHAT YOU THOUGHT WAS RIGHT.
THIS NEW WORLD WE FIND OURSELVES ON IS BEAUTIFUL, NO DOUBT.
BUT I CAN HELP YOU TO BETTER UNDER-STAND AND IMPLEMENT THE AUTHORITY YOU NOW POSSESS.
BUT BEAUTY AND MYSTERY ARE SOMETIMES PORTENTS OF WHAT LURKS BENEATH ARTIFICE.
YOU ARE... REFERRING TO CALICA.
AMONGST OTHER TEMPTATIONS AND DISTRACTIONS; YES.
YOU MUST LEARN TO SEPARATE THE ACTUAL FROM THE FALSE; TO DISCERN THAT WHICH WILL CRITICALLY AFFECT YOU AND THOSE UNDER YOU.
AND I...
...I MUST HELP YOU.

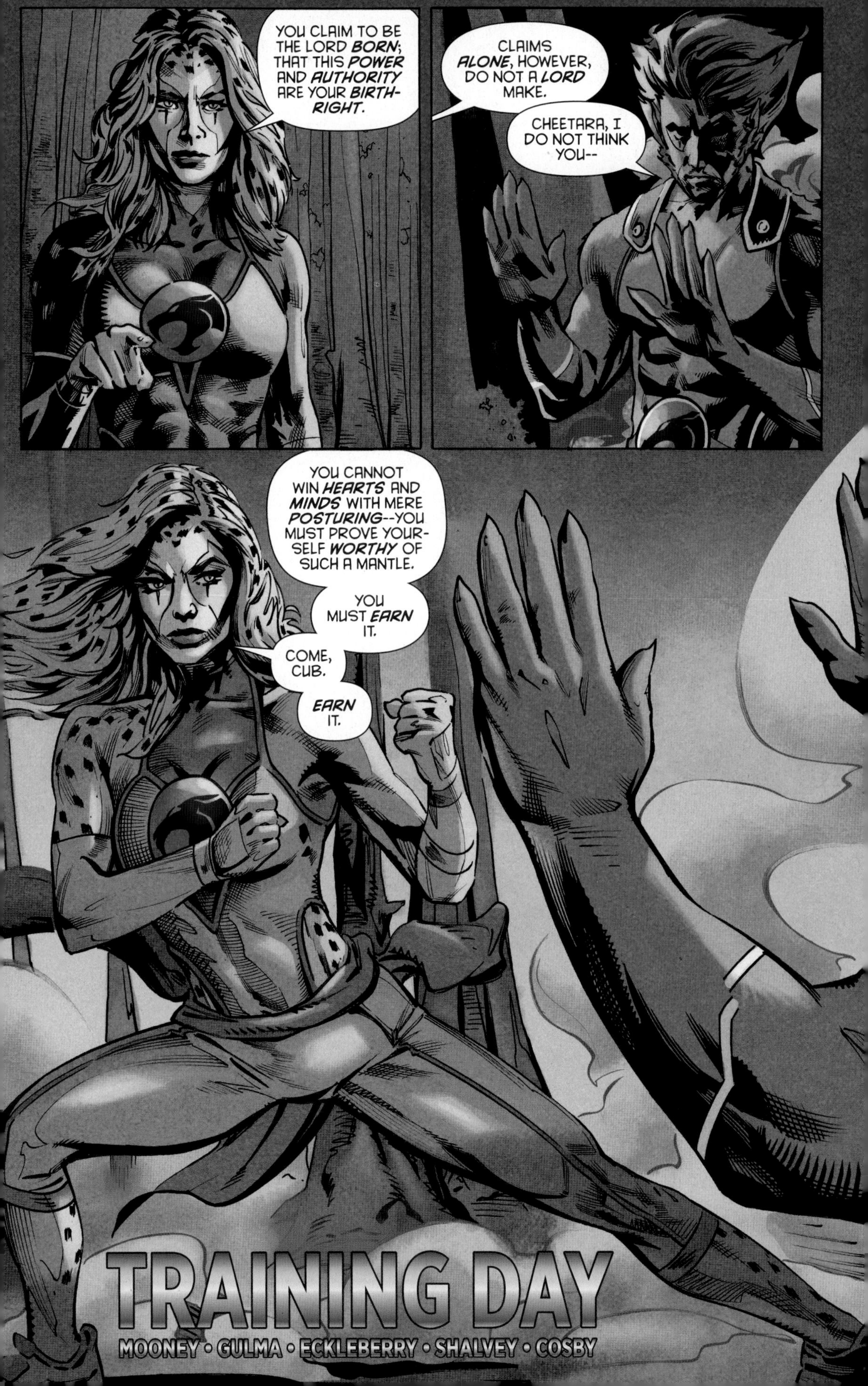

YOU CLAIM TO BE THE LORD BORN; THAT THIS POWER AND AUTHORITY ARE YOUR BIRTH-RIGHT.
CLAIMS ALONE, HOWEVER, DO NOT A LORD MAKE.
CHEETARA, I DO NOT THINK YOU--
YOU CANNOT WIN HEARTS AND MINDS WITH MERE POSTURING--YOU MUST PROVE YOUR-SELF WORTHY OF SUCH A MANTLE.
YOU MUST EARN IT.
COME, CUB.
EARN IT.
TRAINING DAY
MOONEY • GULMA • ECKLEBERRY • SHALVEY • COSBY

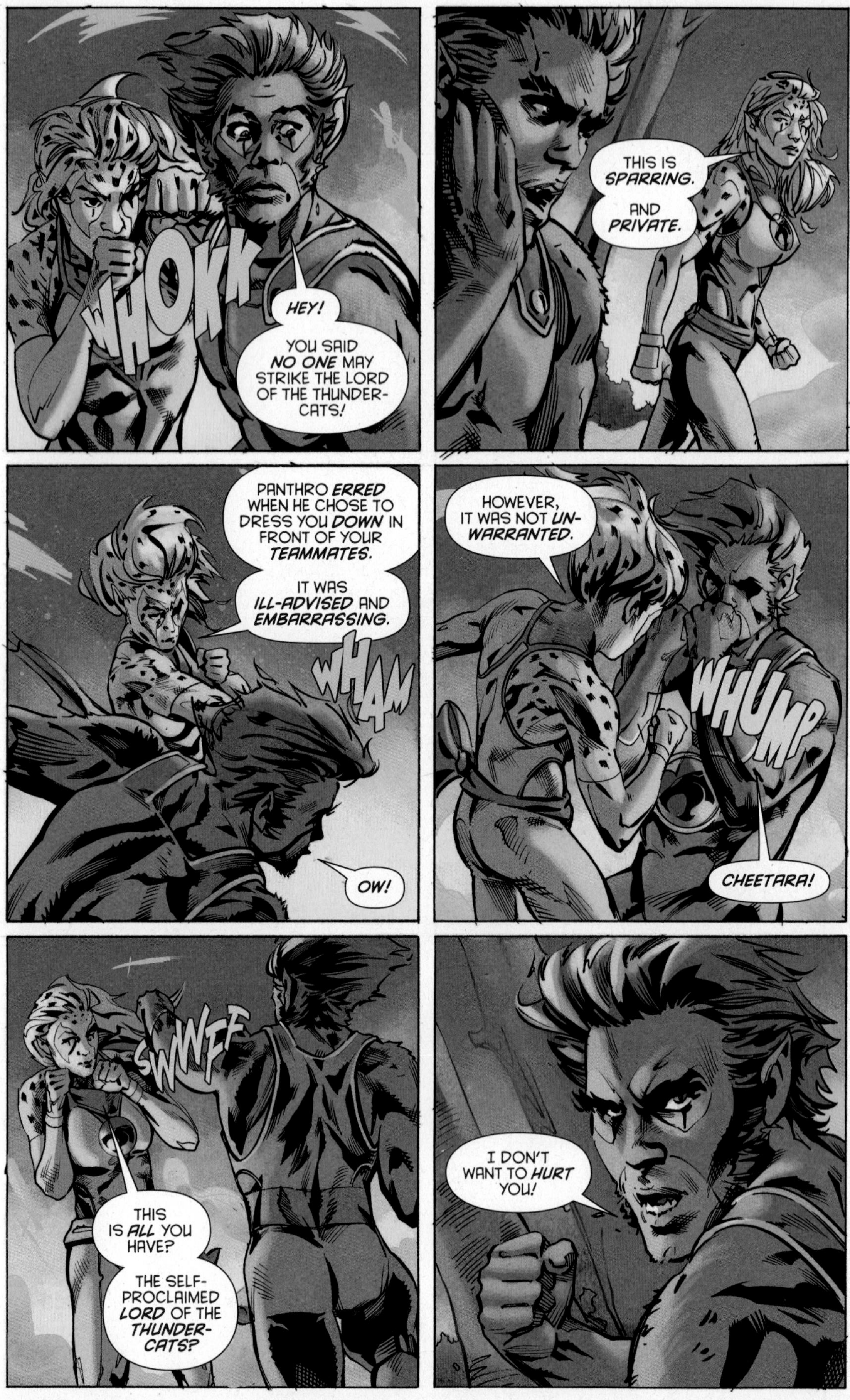
WHOKK
HEY!
YOU SAID NO ONE MAY STRIKE THE LORD OF THE THUNDER-CATS!
THIS IS SPARRING.
AND PRIVATE.
PANTHRO ERRED WHEN HE CHOSE TO DRESS YOU DOWN IN FRONT OF YOUR TEAMMATES.
IT WAS ILL-ADVISED AND EMBARRASSING.
WHAM
OW!
HOWEVER, IT WAS NOT UN-WARRANTED.
WHUMP
CHEETARA!
SWWFF
THIS IS ALL YOU HAVE?
THE SELF-PROCLAIMED LORD OF THE THUNDER-CATS?
I DON'T WANT TO HURT YOU!

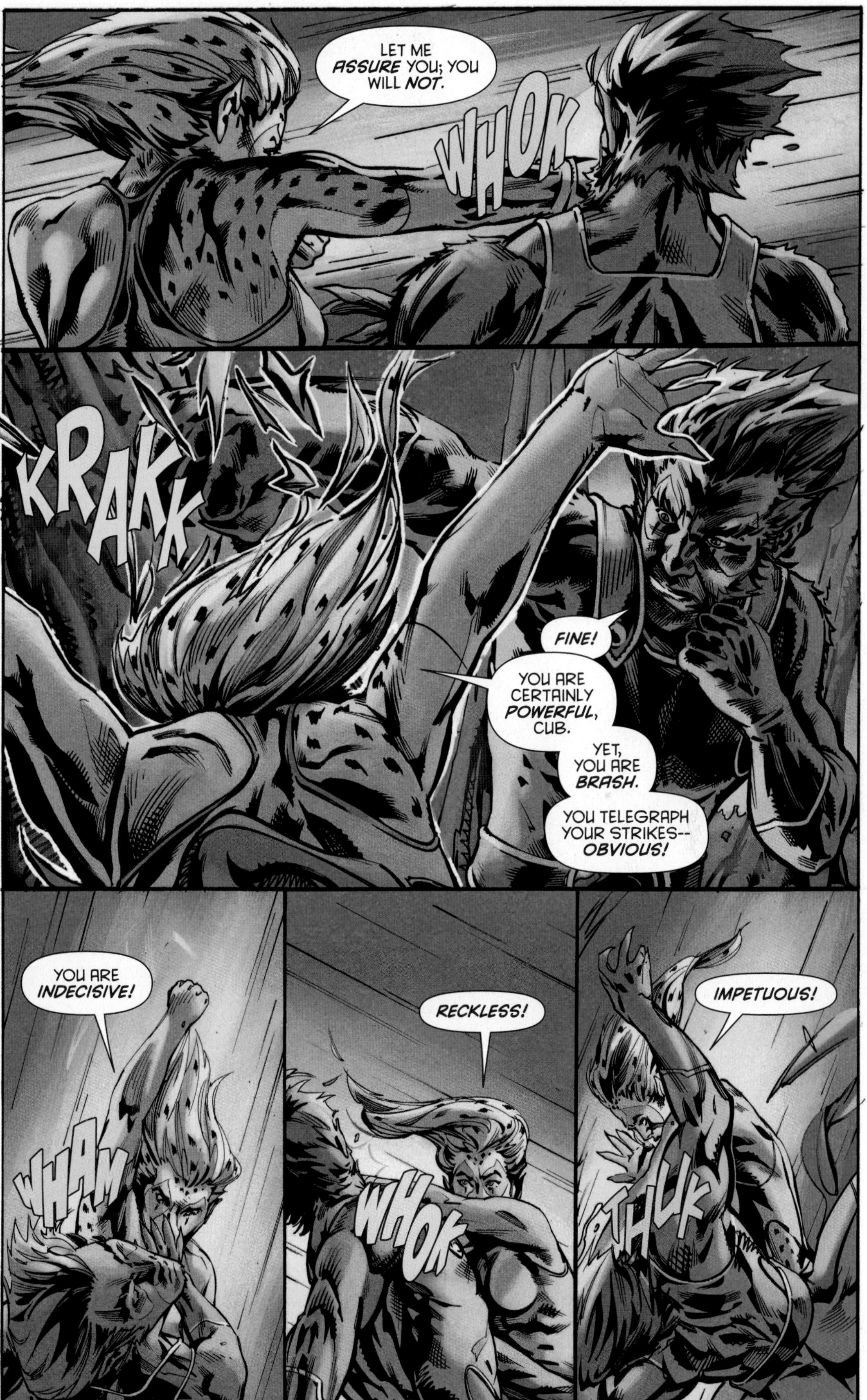
LET ME *ASSURE* YOU; YOU WILL *NOT*.
WHOK
KRAKK
FINE!
YOU ARE CERTAINLY *POWERFUL*, CUB.
YET, YOU ARE *BRASH*.
YOU TELEGRAPH YOUR STRIKES-- *OBVIOUS!*
YOU ARE *INDECISIVE!*
WHAM
RECKLESS!
WHOK
IMPETUOUS!
THUK

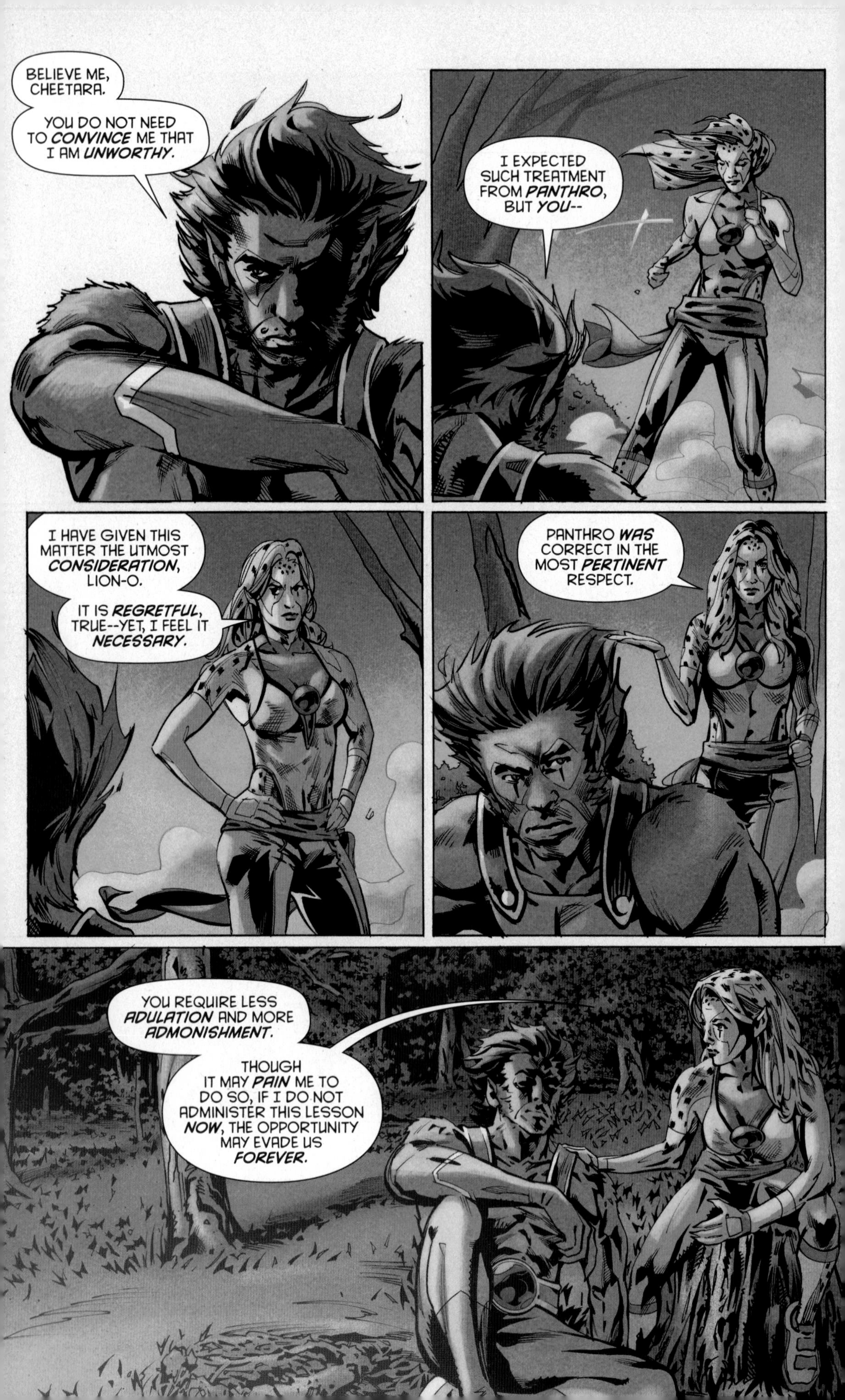
BELIEVE ME, CHEETARA.
YOU DO NOT NEED TO *CONVINCE* ME THAT I AM *UNWORTHY*.
I EXPECTED SUCH TREATMENT FROM *PANTHRO*, BUT *YOU*--
I HAVE GIVEN THIS MATTER THE UTMOST *CONSIDERATION*, LION-O.
IT IS *REGRETFUL*, TRUE--YET, I FEEL IT *NECESSARY*.
PANTHRO *WAS* CORRECT IN THE MOST *PERTINENT* RESPECT.
YOU REQUIRE LESS *ADULATION* AND MORE *ADMONISHMENT*.
THOUGH IT MAY *PAIN* ME TO DO SO, IF I DO NOT ADMINISTER THIS LESSON *NOW*, THE OPPORTUNITY MAY EVADE US *FOREVER*.

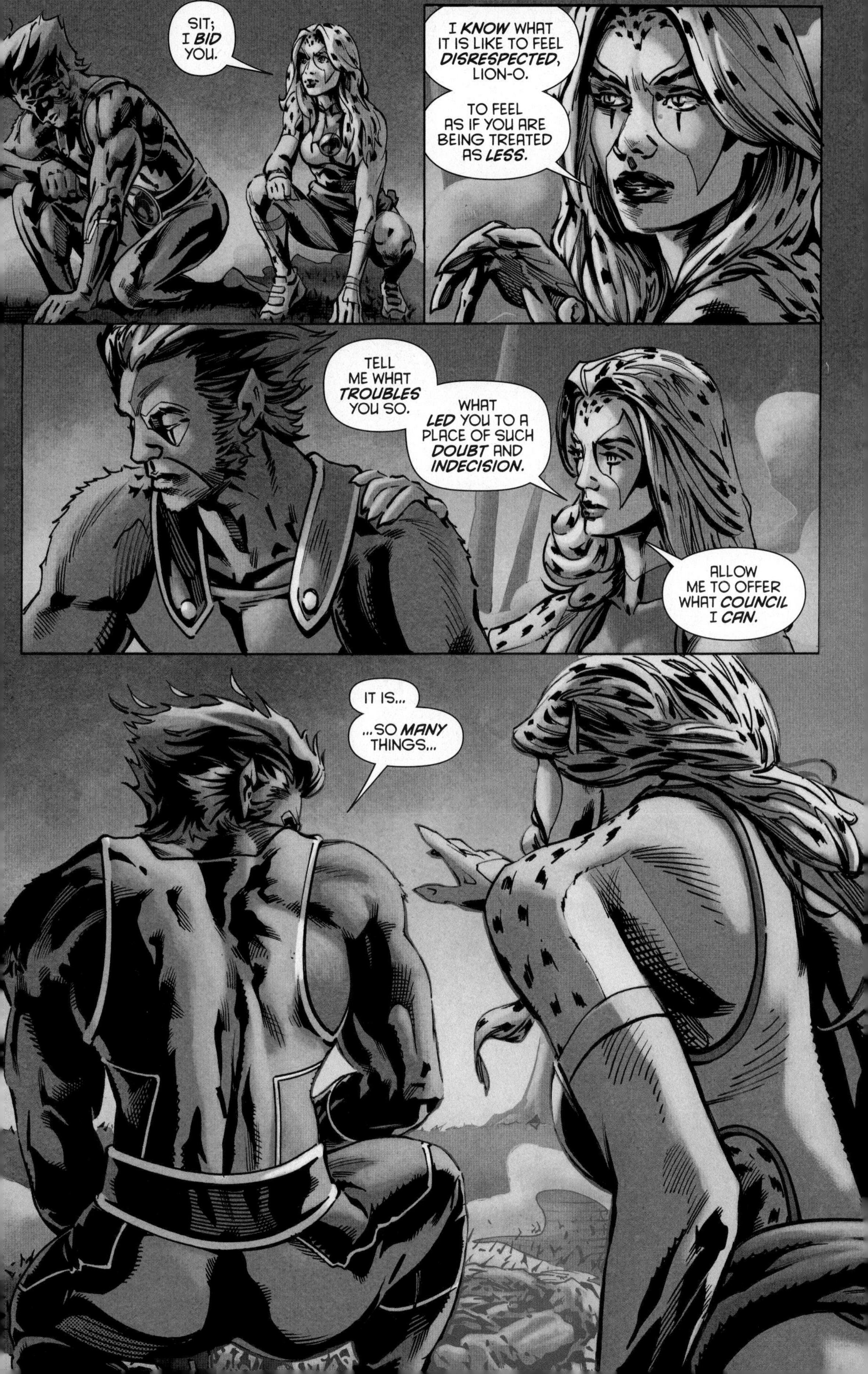
SIT; I BID YOU.
I KNOW WHAT IT IS LIKE TO FEEL DISRESPECTED, LION-O.
TO FEEL AS IF YOU ARE BEING TREATED AS LESS.
TELL ME WHAT TROUBLES YOU SO.
WHAT LED YOU TO A PLACE OF SUCH DOUBT AND INDECISION.
ALLOW ME TO OFFER WHAT COUNCIL I CAN.
IT IS...
...SO MANY THINGS...

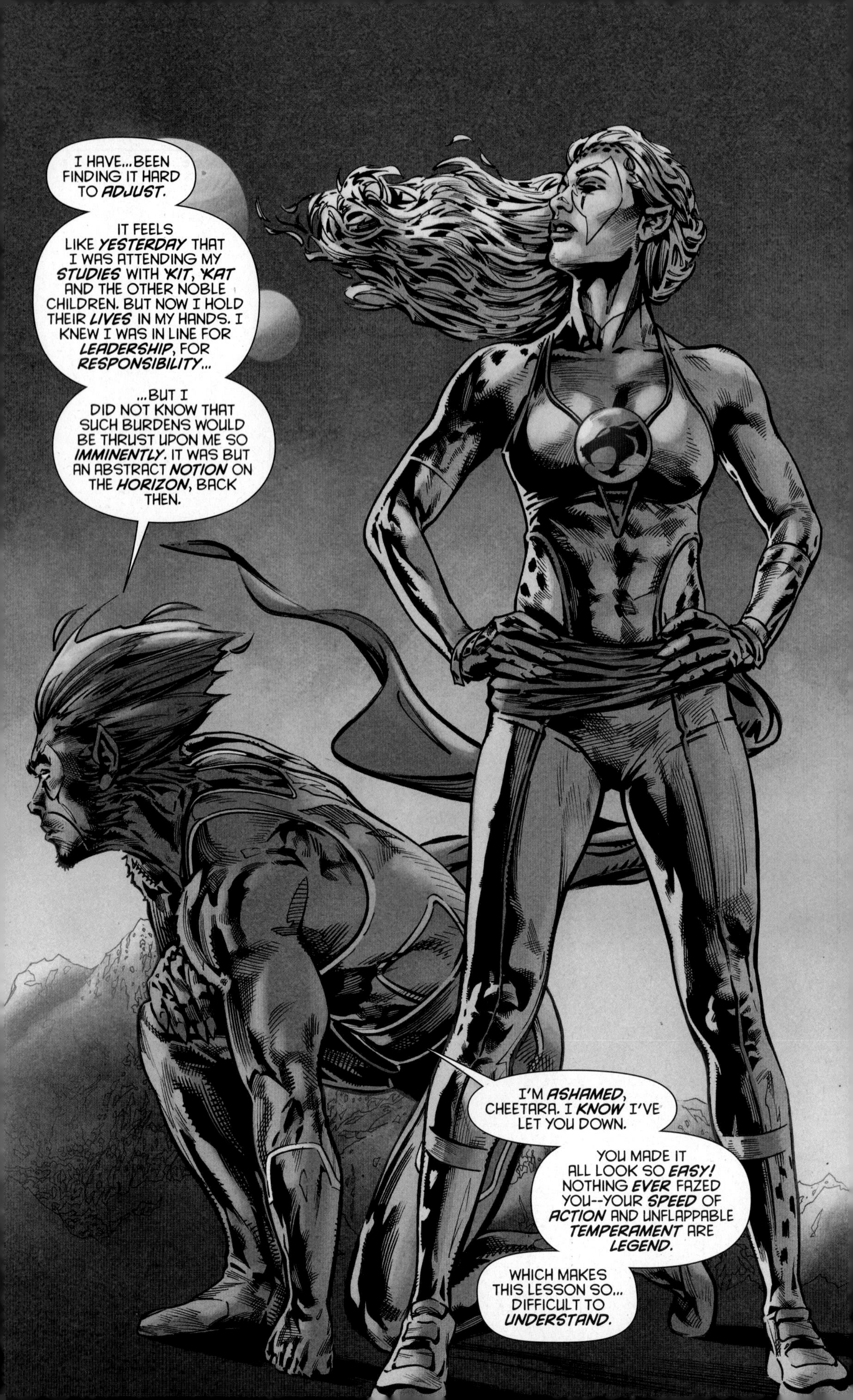
I HAVE...BEEN FINDING IT HARD TO ADJUST.
IT FEELS LIKE YESTERDAY THAT I WAS ATTENDING MY STUDIES WITH 'KIT, 'KAT AND THE OTHER NOBLE CHILDREN. BUT NOW I HOLD THEIR LIVES IN MY HANDS. I KNEW I WAS IN LINE FOR LEADERSHIP, FOR RESPONSIBILITY...
...BUT I DID NOT KNOW THAT SUCH BURDENS WOULD BE THRUST UPON ME SO IMMINENTLY. IT WAS BUT AN ABSTRACT NOTION ON THE HORIZON, BACK THEN.
I'M ASHAMED, CHEETARA. I KNOW I'VE LET YOU DOWN.
YOU MADE IT ALL LOOK SO EASY! NOTHING EVER FAZED YOU--YOUR SPEED OF ACTION AND UNFLAPPABLE TEMPERAMENT ARE LEGEND.
WHICH MAKES THIS LESSON SO... DIFFICULT TO UNDERSTAND.

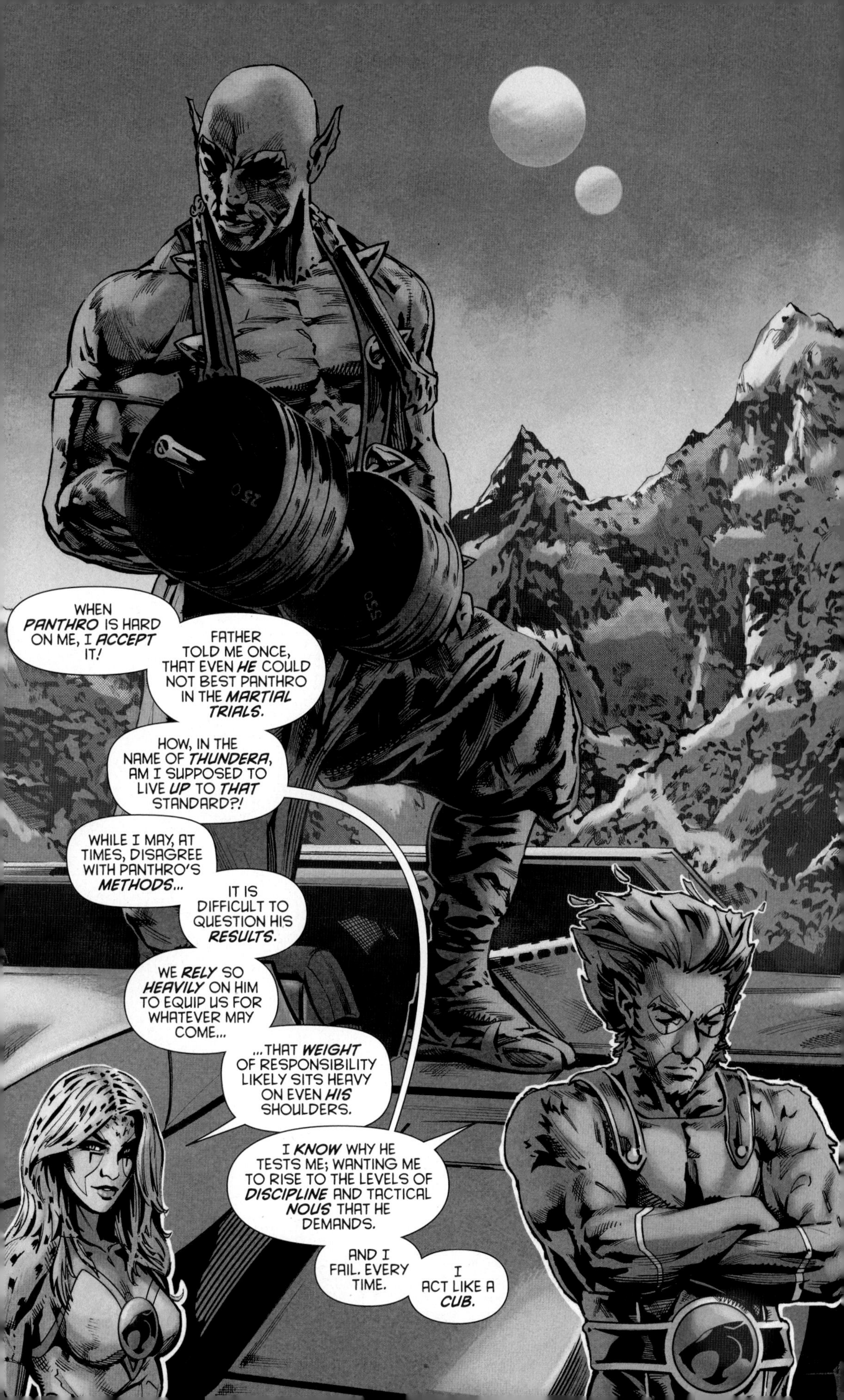
WHEN PANTHRO IS HARD ON ME, I ACCEPT IT!
FATHER TOLD ME ONCE, THAT EVEN HE COULD NOT BEST PANTHRO IN THE MARTIAL TRIALS.
HOW, IN THE NAME OF THUNDERA, AM I SUPPOSED TO LIVE UP TO THAT STANDARD?!
WHILE I MAY, AT TIMES, DISAGREE WITH PANTHRO'S METHODS...
IT IS DIFFICULT TO QUESTION HIS RESULTS.
WE RELY SO HEAVILY ON HIM TO EQUIP US FOR WHATEVER MAY COME...
...THAT WEIGHT OF RESPONSIBILITY LIKELY SITS HEAVY ON EVEN HIS SHOULDERS.
I KNOW WHY HE TESTS ME; WANTING ME TO RISE TO THE LEVELS OF DISCIPLINE AND TACTICAL NOUS THAT HE DEMANDS.
AND I FAIL. EVERY TIME.
I ACT LIKE A CUB.

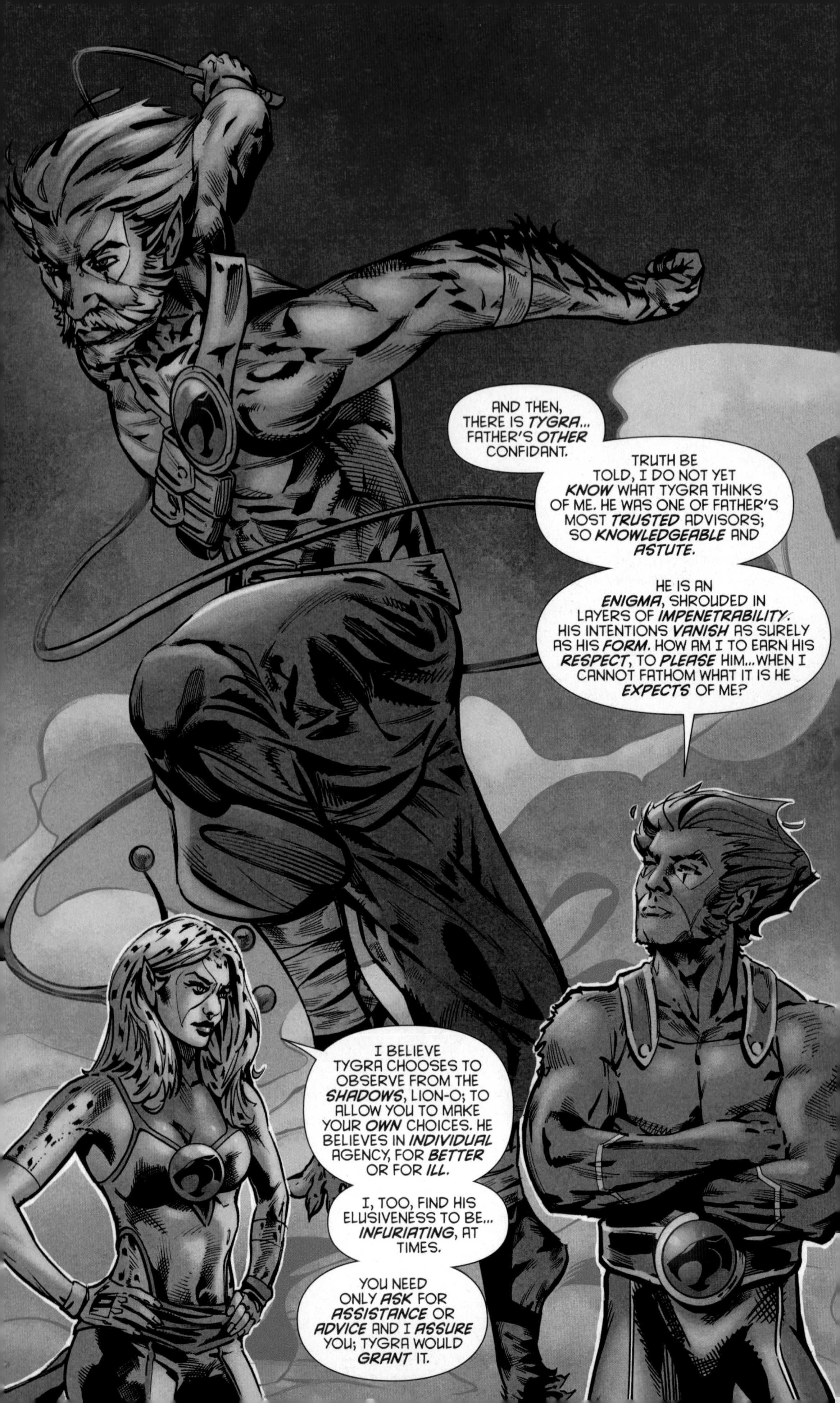
AND THEN, THERE IS TYGRA... FATHER'S OTHER CONFIDANT.
TRUTH BE TOLD, I DO NOT YET KNOW WHAT TYGRA THINKS OF ME. HE WAS ONE OF FATHER'S MOST TRUSTED ADVISORS; SO KNOWLEDGEABLE AND ASTUTE.
HE IS AN ENIGMA, SHROUDED IN LAYERS OF IMPENETRABILITY. HIS INTENTIONS VANISH AS SURELY AS HIS FORM. HOW AM I TO EARN HIS RESPECT, TO PLEASE HIM...WHEN I CANNOT FATHOM WHAT IT IS HE EXPECTS OF ME?
I BELIEVE TYGRA CHOOSES TO OBSERVE FROM THE SHADOWS, LION-O; TO ALLOW YOU TO MAKE YOUR OWN CHOICES. HE BELIEVES IN INDIVIDUAL AGENCY, FOR BETTER OR FOR ILL.
I, TOO, FIND HIS ELUSIVENESS TO BE... INFURIATING, AT TIMES.
YOU NEED ONLY ASK FOR ASSISTANCE OR ADVICE AND I ASSURE YOU; TYGRA WOULD GRANT IT.

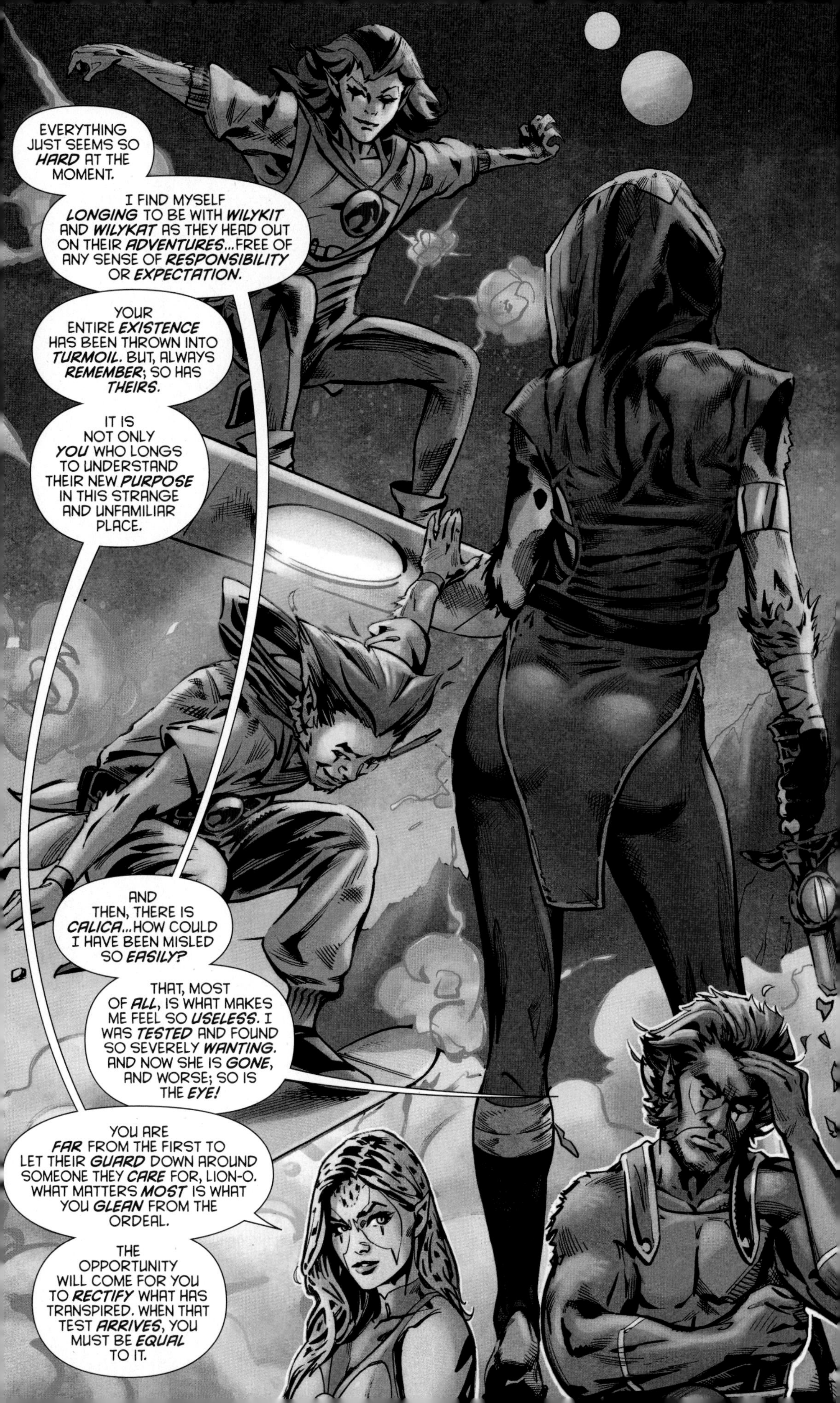
EVERYTHING JUST SEEMS SO HARD AT THE MOMENT.
I FIND MYSELF LONGING TO BE WITH WILYKIT AND WILYKAT AS THEY HEAD OUT ON THEIR ADVENTURES...FREE OF ANY SENSE OF RESPONSIBILITY OR EXPECTATION.
YOUR ENTIRE EXISTENCE HAS BEEN THROWN INTO TURMOIL. BUT, ALWAYS REMEMBER; SO HAS THEIRS.
IT IS NOT ONLY YOU WHO LONGS TO UNDERSTAND THEIR NEW PURPOSE IN THIS STRANGE AND UNFAMILIAR PLACE.
AND THEN, THERE IS CALICA...HOW COULD I HAVE BEEN MISLED SO EASILY?
THAT, MOST OF ALL, IS WHAT MAKES ME FEEL SO USELESS. I WAS TESTED AND FOUND SO SEVERELY WANTING. AND NOW SHE IS GONE, AND WORSE; SO IS THE EYE!
YOU ARE FAR FROM THE FIRST TO LET THEIR GUARD DOWN AROUND SOMEONE THEY CARE FOR, LION-O. WHAT MATTERS MOST IS WHAT YOU GLEAN FROM THE ORDEAL.
THE OPPORTUNITY WILL COME FOR YOU TO RECTIFY WHAT HAS TRANSPIRED. WHEN THAT TEST ARRIVES, YOU MUST BE EQUAL TO IT.

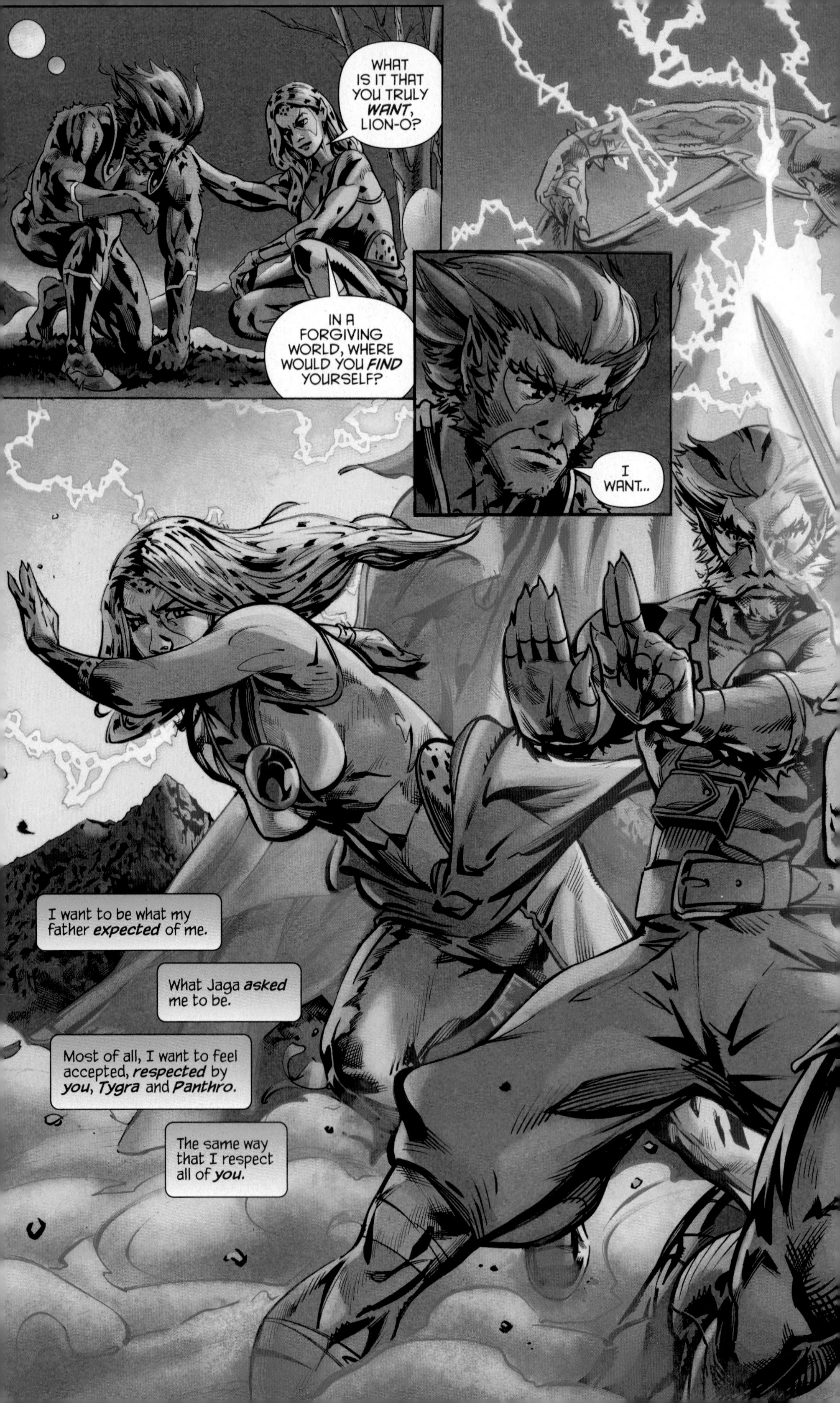
WHAT IS IT THAT YOU TRULY *WANT*, LION-O?
IN A FORGIVING WORLD, WHERE WOULD YOU *FIND* YOURSELF?
I WANT...
I want to be what my father *expected* of me.
What Jaga *asked* me to be.
Most of all, I want to feel accepted, *respected* by *you*, *Tygra* and *Panthro*.
The same way that I respect all of *you*.

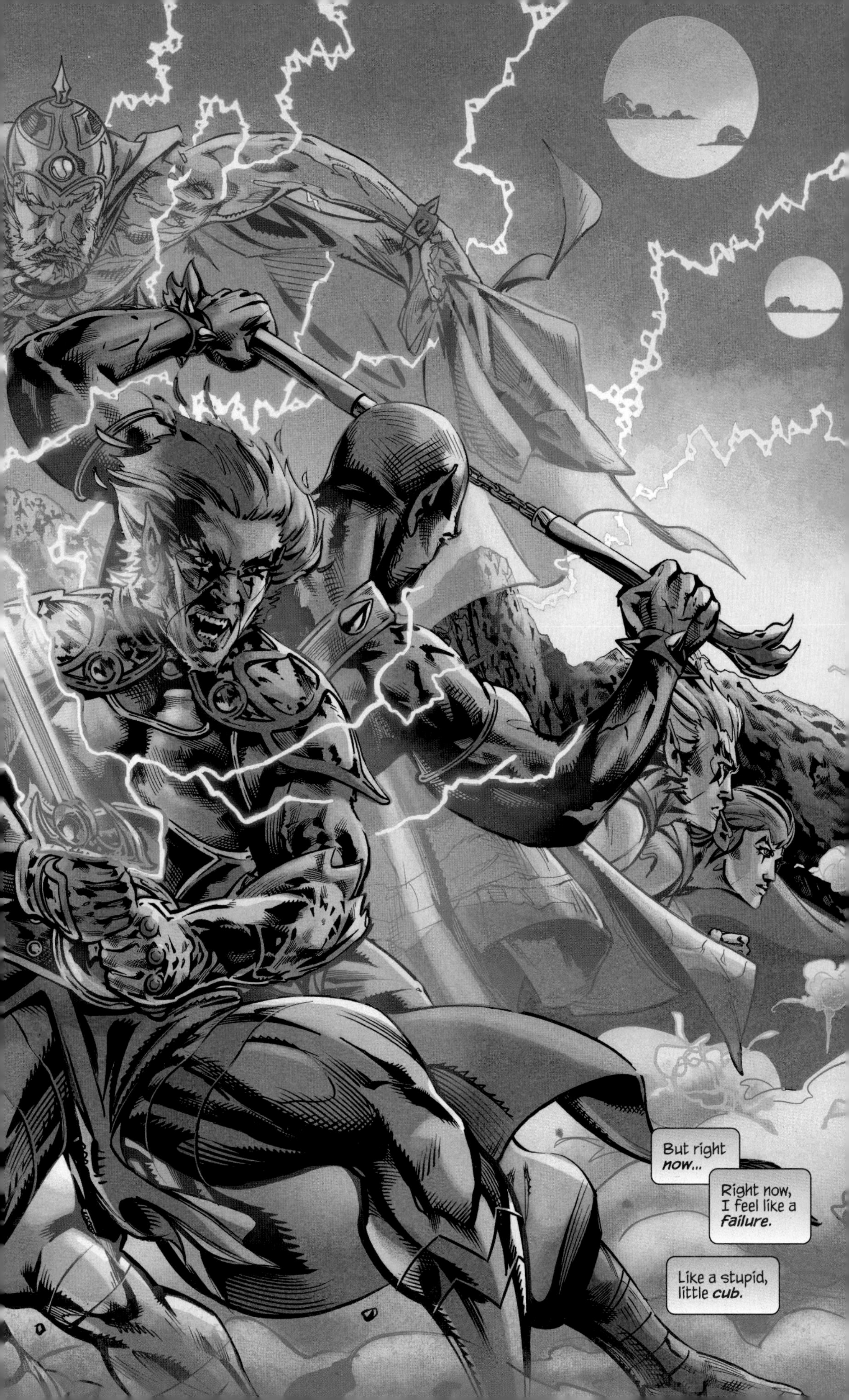

But right *now*...
Right now, I feel like a *failure*.
Like a stupid, little *cub*.

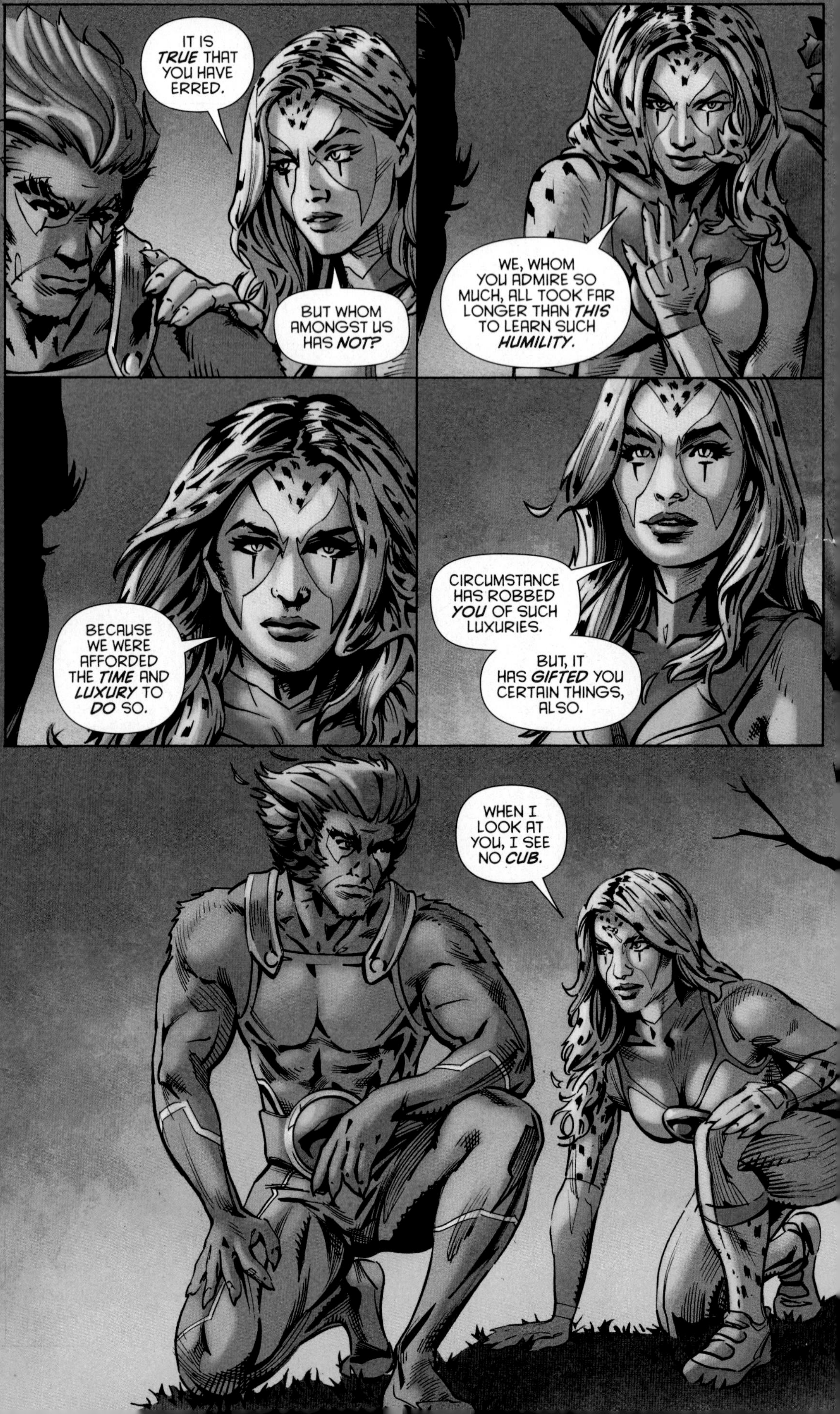

IT IS TRUE THAT YOU HAVE ERRED.
BUT WHOM AMONGST US HAS NOT?
WE, WHOM YOU ADMIRE SO MUCH, ALL TOOK FAR LONGER THAN THIS TO LEARN SUCH HUMILITY.
BECAUSE WE WERE AFFORDED THE TIME AND LUXURY TO DO SO.
CIRCUMSTANCE HAS ROBBED YOU OF SUCH LUXURIES.
BUT, IT HAS GIFTED YOU CERTAIN THINGS, ALSO.
WHEN I LOOK AT YOU, I SEE NO CUB.

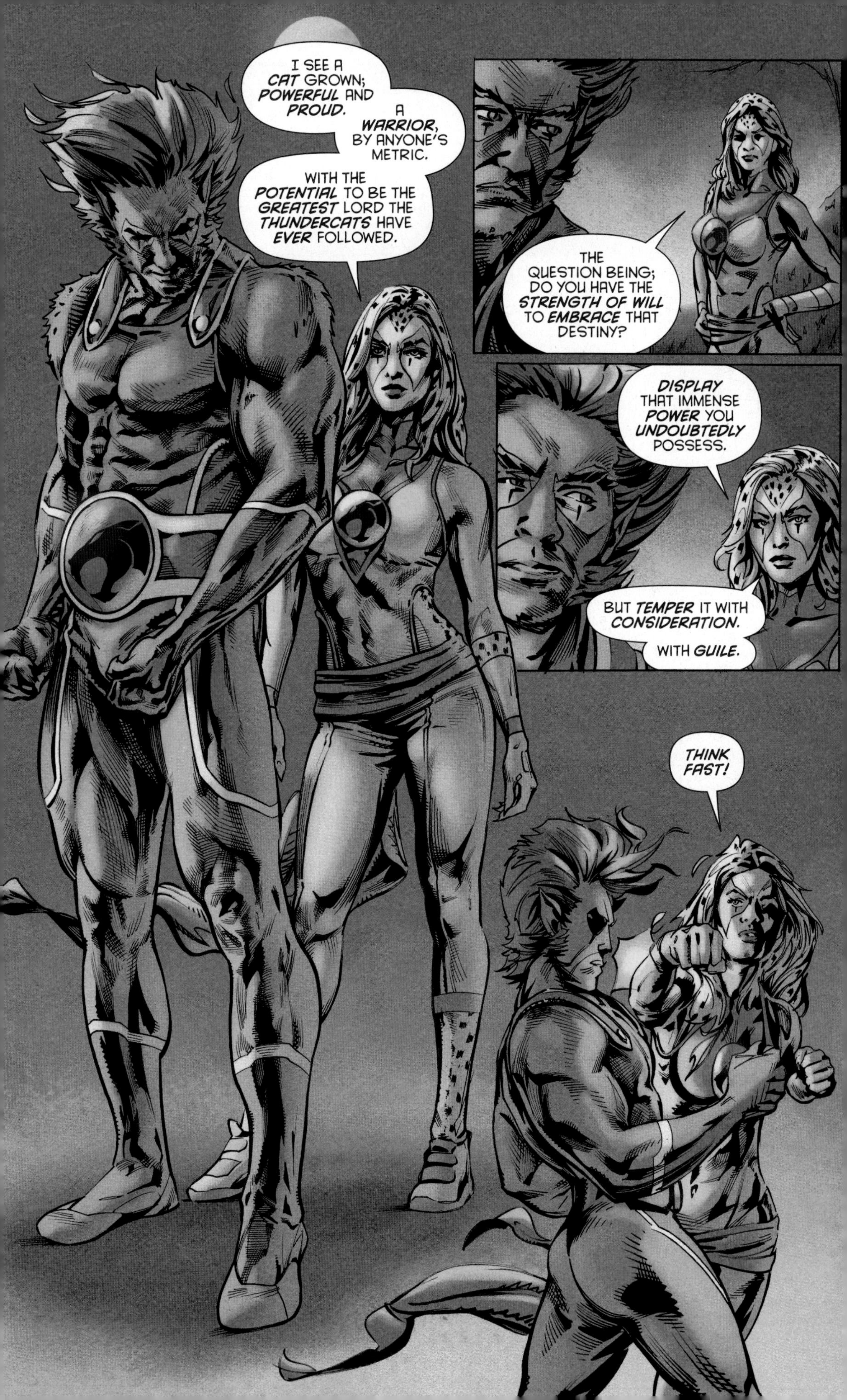
I SEE A CAT GROWN; POWERFUL AND PROUD.
A WARRIOR, BY ANYONE'S METRIC.
WITH THE POTENTIAL TO BE THE GREATEST LORD THE THUNDERCATS HAVE EVER FOLLOWED.
THE QUESTION BEING; DO YOU HAVE THE STRENGTH OF WILL TO EMBRACE THAT DESTINY?
DISPLAY THAT IMMENSE POWER YOU UNDOUBTEDLY POSSESS.
BUT TEMPER IT WITH CONSIDERATION.
WITH GUILE.
THINK FAST!

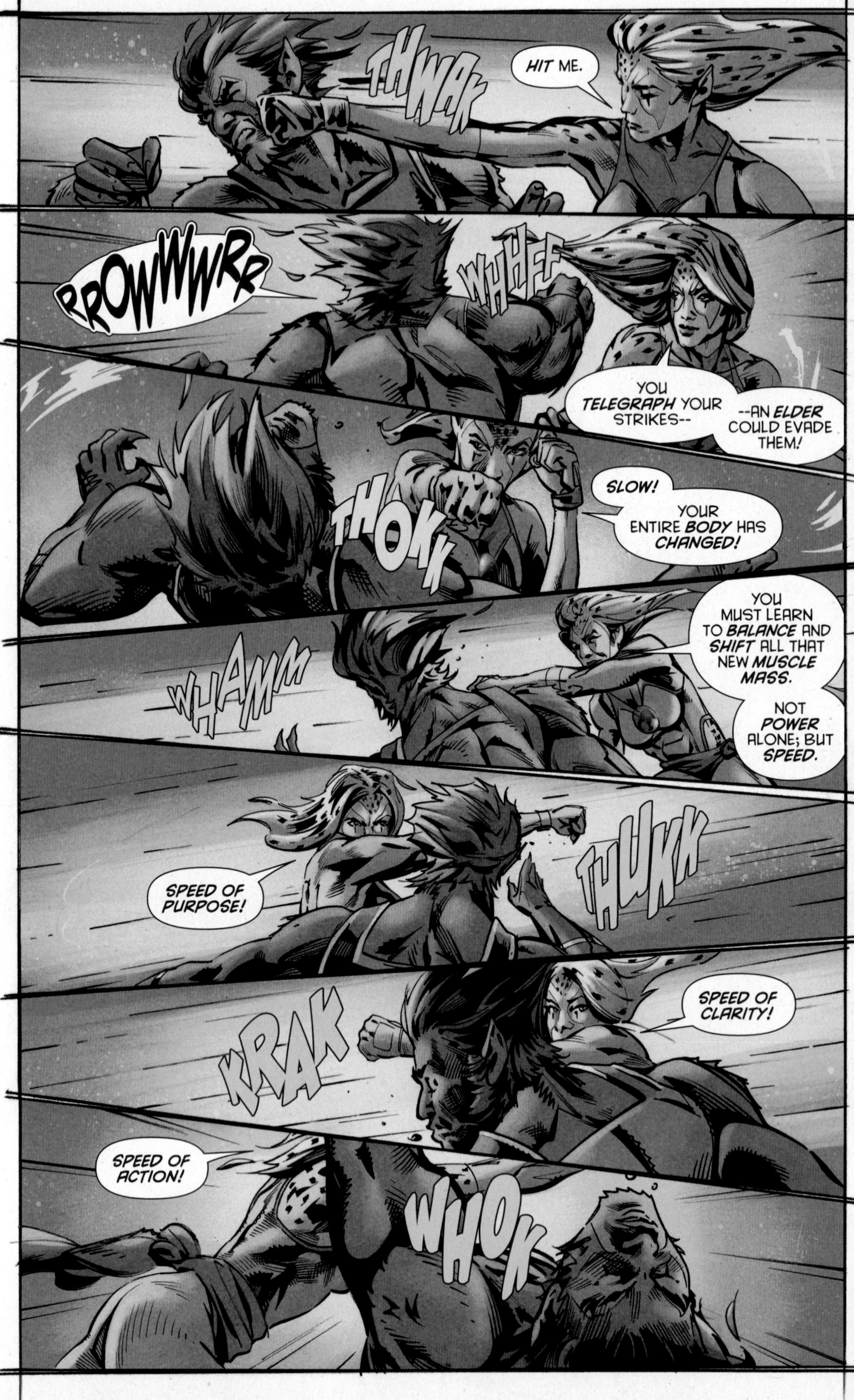
THWAK
HIT ME.
RROWWWRR
WHHFF
YOU TELEGRAPH YOUR STRIKES--
--AN ELDER COULD EVADE THEM!
THOKK
SLOW!
YOUR ENTIRE BODY HAS CHANGED!
WHAMM
YOU MUST LEARN TO BALANCE AND SHIFT ALL THAT NEW MUSCLE MASS.
NOT POWER ALONE; BUT SPEED.
SPEED OF PURPOSE!
THUKK
KRAK
SPEED OF CLARITY!
SPEED OF ACTION!
WHOK

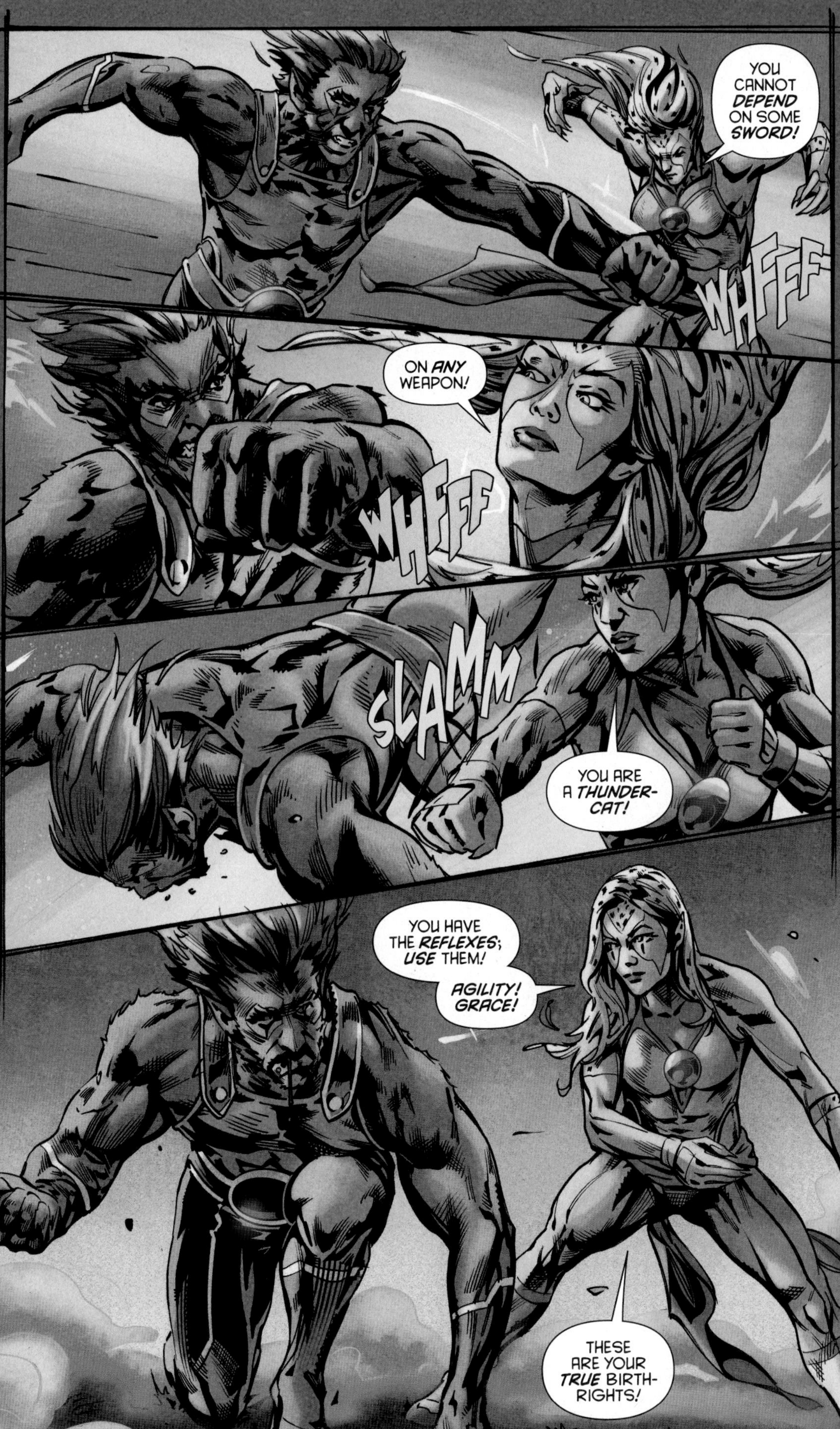
YOU CANNOT DEPEND ON SOME SWORD!
WHFFF
ON ANY WEAPON!
WHFFF
SLAMM
YOU ARE A THUNDER-CAT!
YOU HAVE THE REFLEXES; USE THEM!
AGILITY! GRACE!
THESE ARE YOUR TRUE BIRTH-RIGHTS!

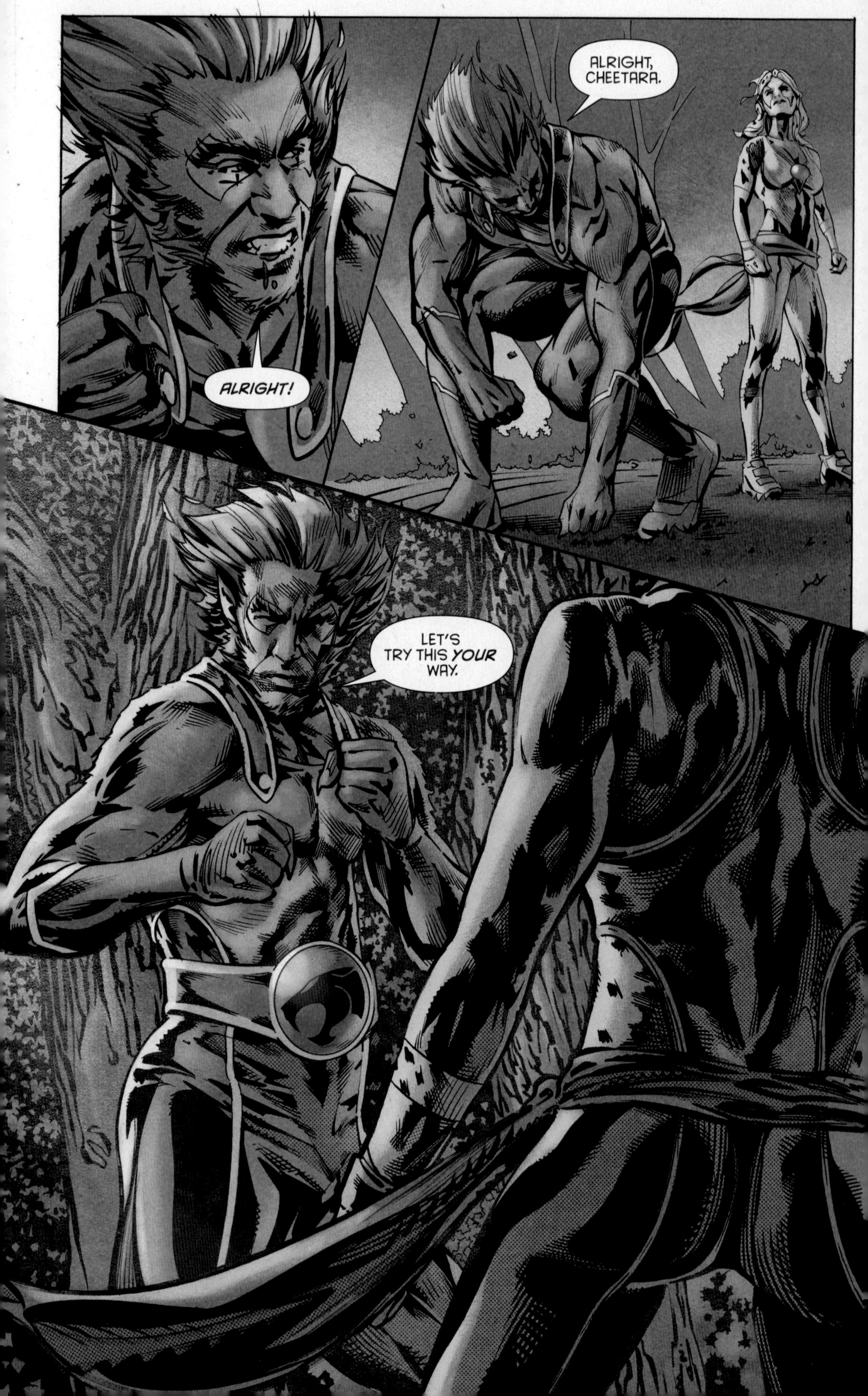
ALRIGHT!
ALRIGHT, CHEETARA.
LET'S TRY THIS *YOUR* WAY.

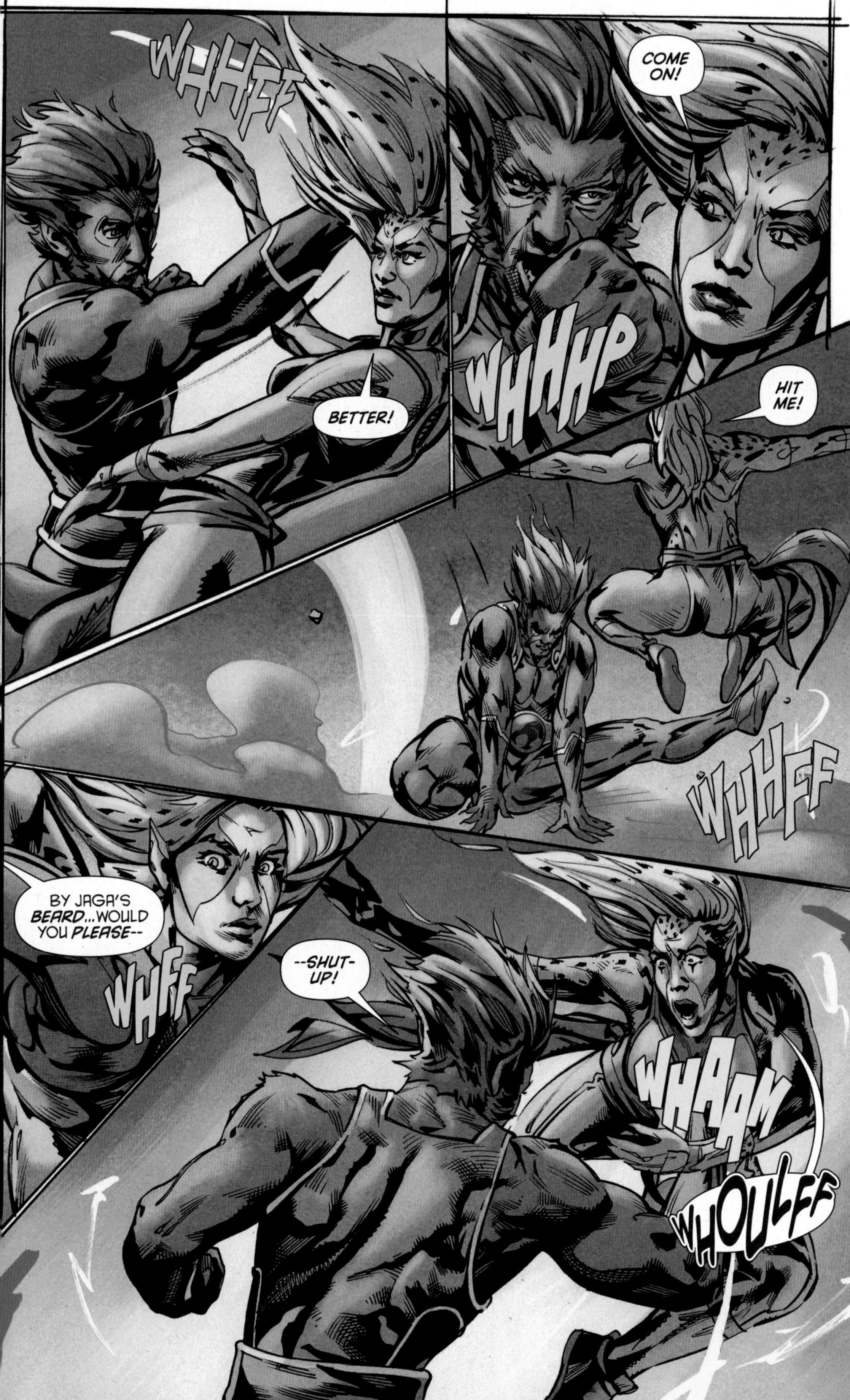
WHHFF
BETTER!
COME ON!
WHHHP
HIT ME!
WHHFF
BY JAGA'S BEARD...WOULD YOU PLEASE--
WHFF
--SHUT-UP!
WHAAM
WHOULFF

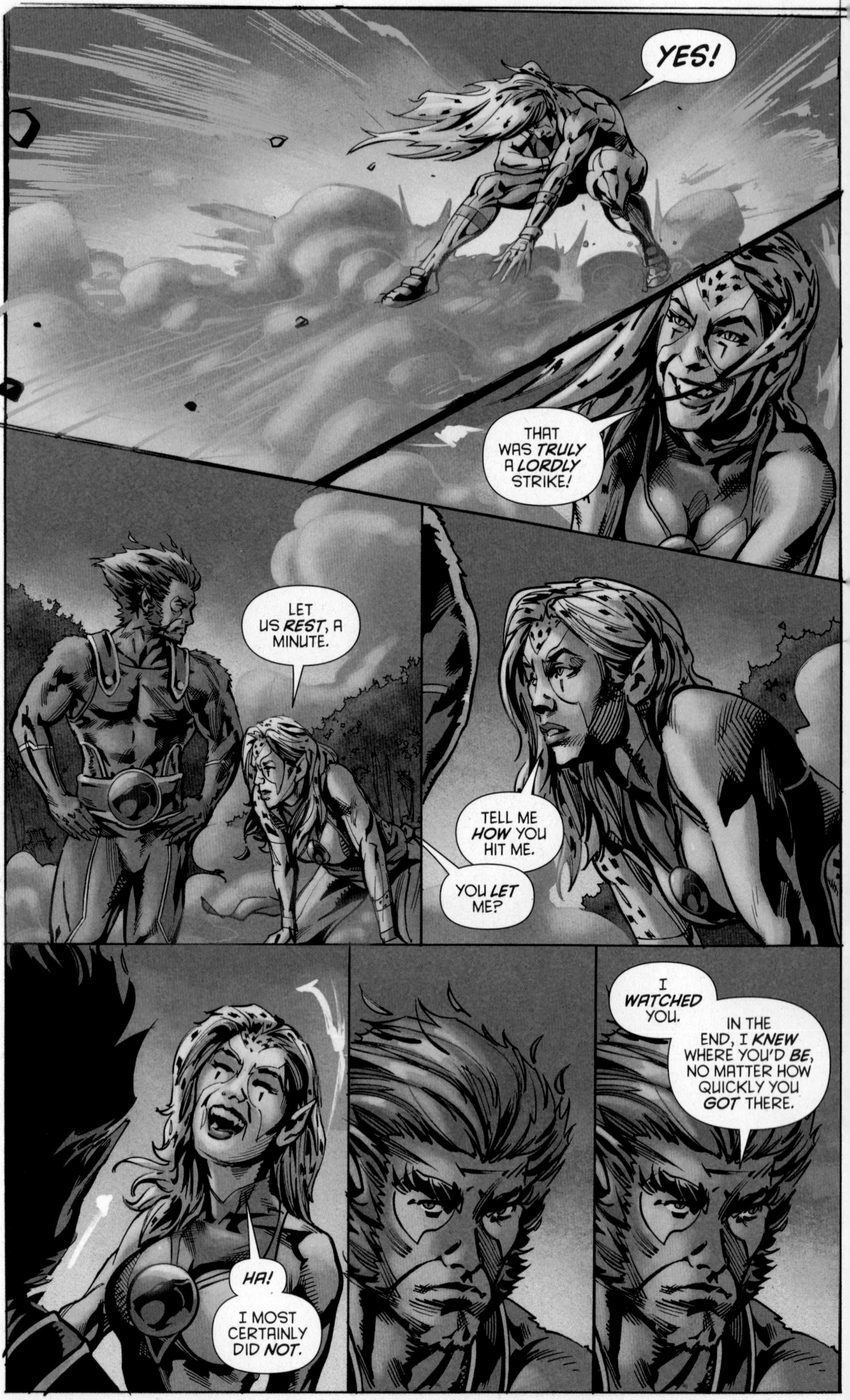
YES!
THAT WAS TRULY A LORDLY STRIKE!
LET US REST, A MINUTE.
TELL ME HOW YOU HIT ME.
YOU LET ME?
HA!
I MOST CERTAINLY DID NOT.
I WATCHED YOU.
IN THE END, I KNEW WHERE YOU'D BE, NO MATTER HOW QUICKLY YOU GOT THERE.

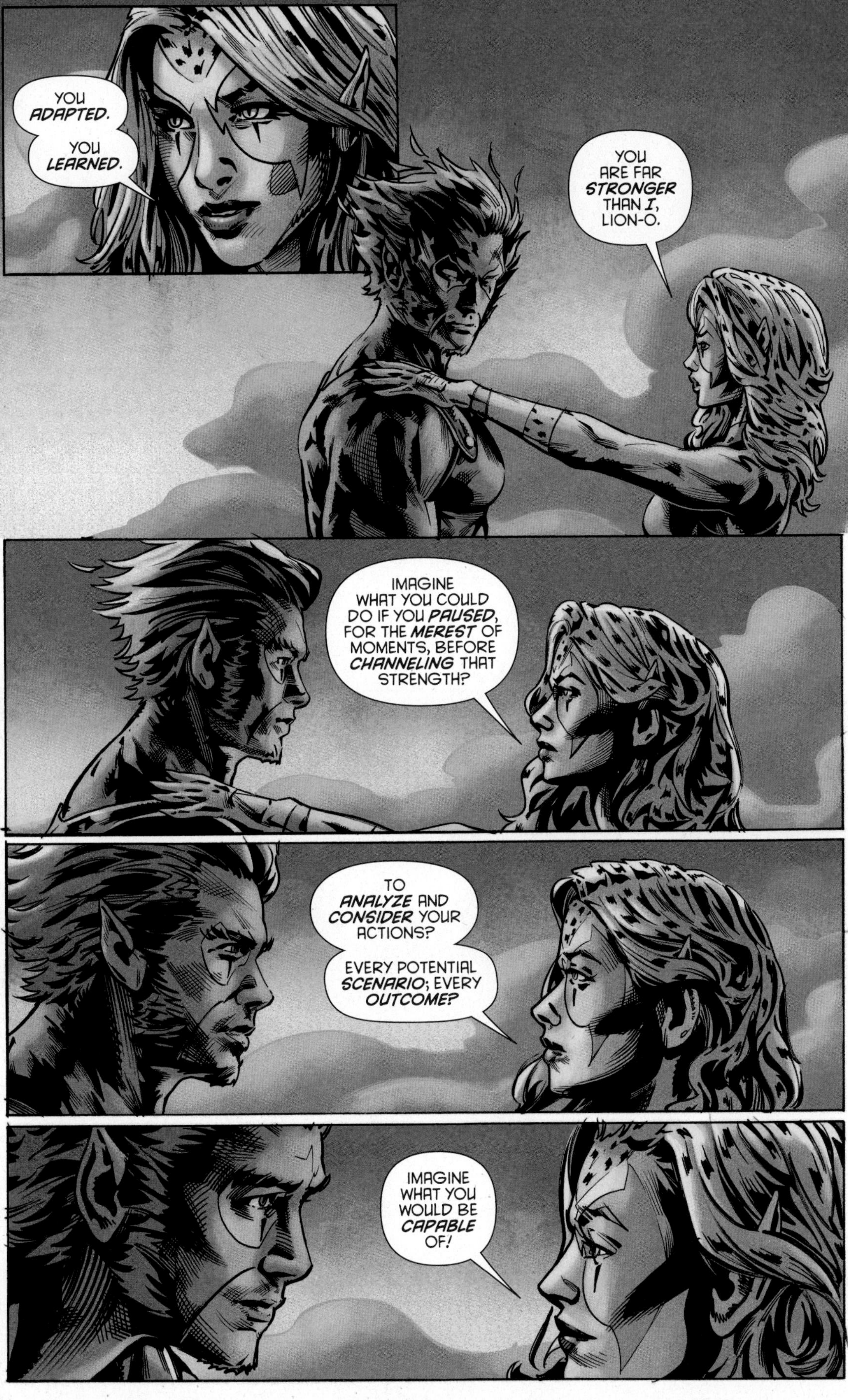
YOU ADAPTED.
YOU LEARNED.
YOU ARE FAR STRONGER THAN I, LION-O.
IMAGINE WHAT YOU COULD DO IF YOU PAUSED, FOR THE MEREST OF MOMENTS, BEFORE CHANNELING THAT STRENGTH?
TO ANALYZE AND CONSIDER YOUR ACTIONS?
EVERY POTENTIAL SCENARIO; EVERY OUTCOME?
IMAGINE WHAT YOU WOULD BE CAPABLE OF!

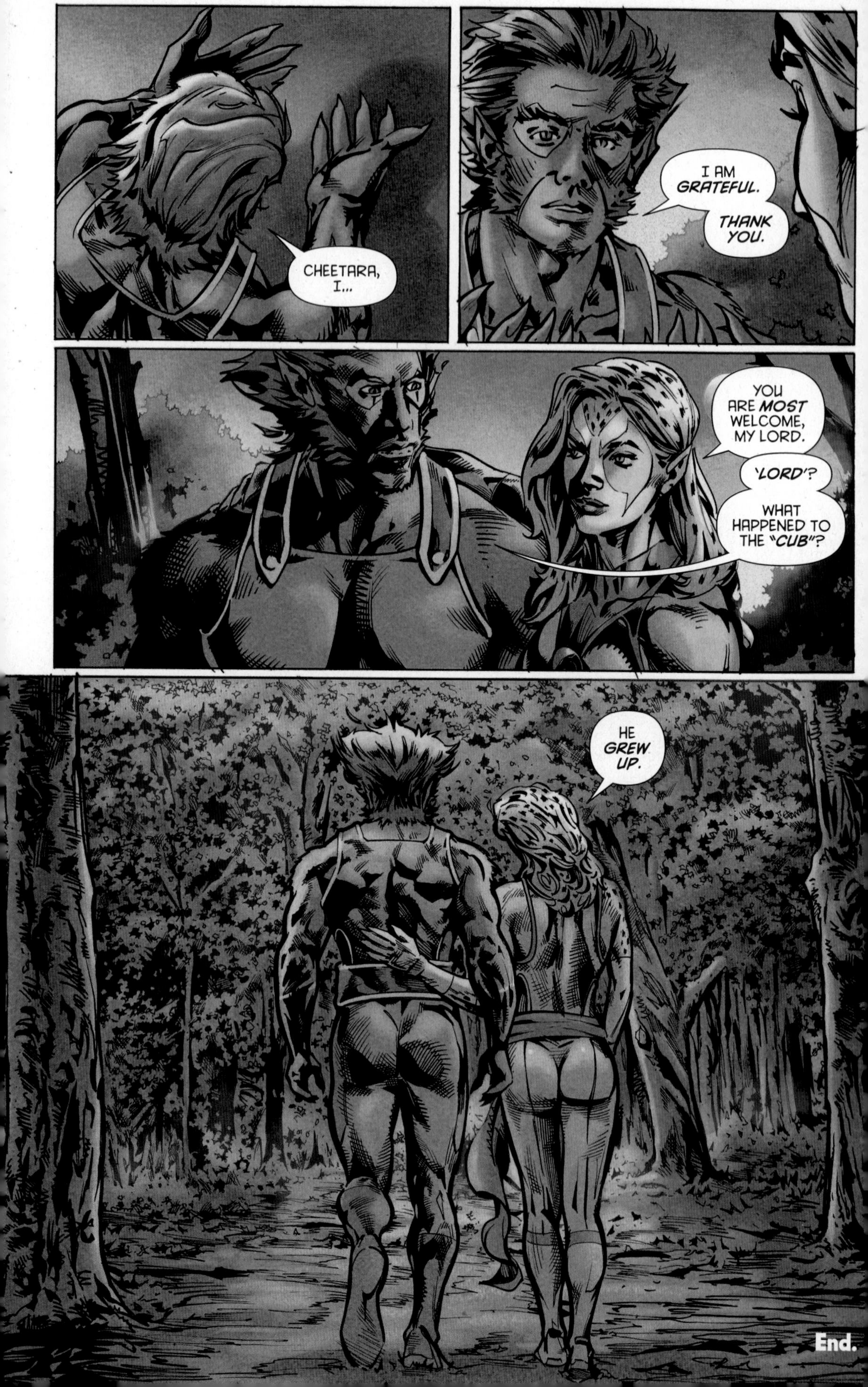
CHEETARA, I...
I AM GRATEFUL.
THANK YOU.
YOU ARE MOST WELCOME, MY LORD.
'LORD'?
WHAT HAPPENED TO THE "CUB"?
HE GREW UP.
End.

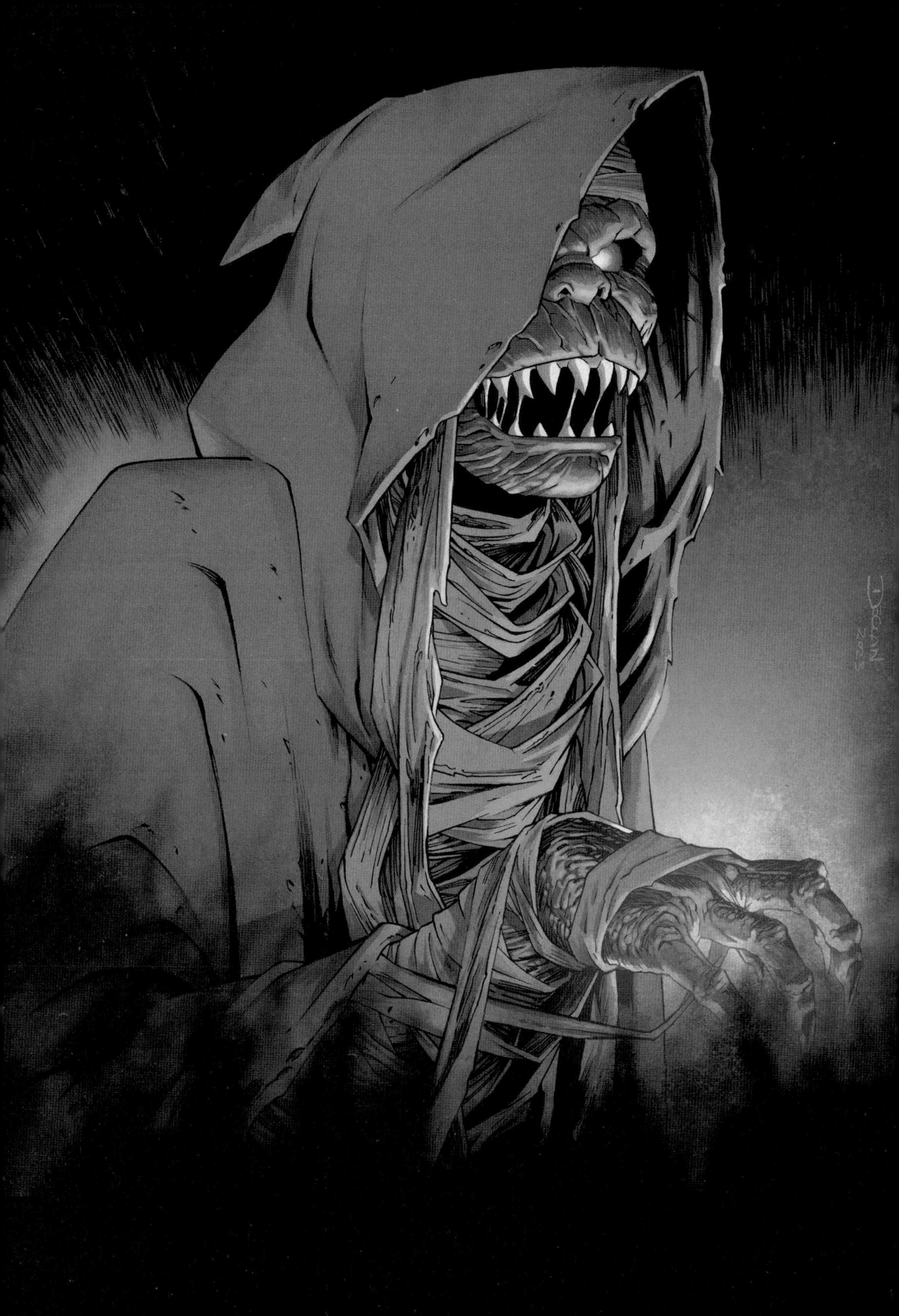
DECLAN
2023

COVER GALLERY

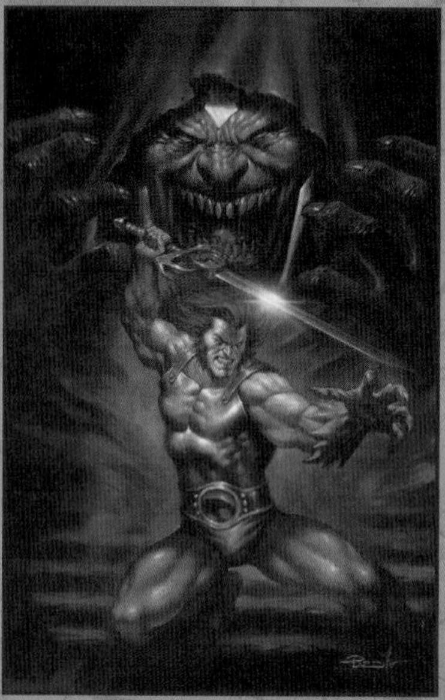

Issue #1 cover art by
LUCIO PARRILLO

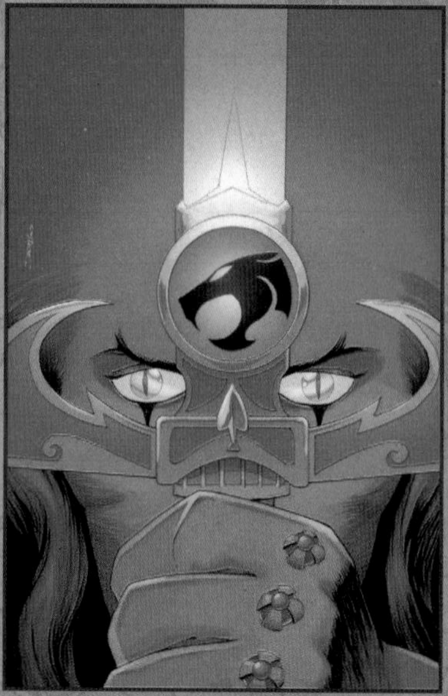

Issue #1 cover art by
DECLAN SHALVEY

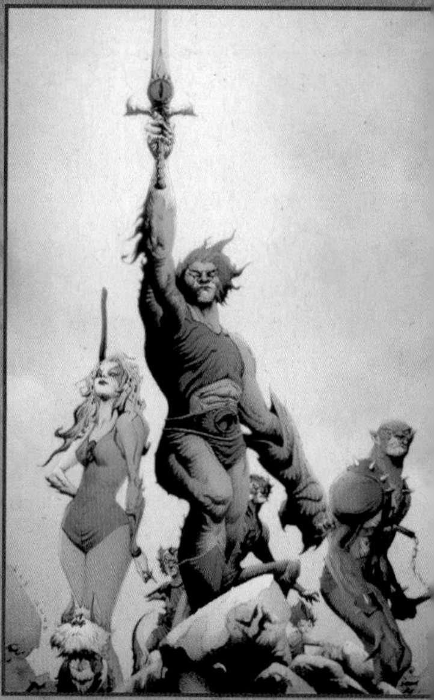

Issue #1 cover art by
JAE LEE & JUNE CHUNG

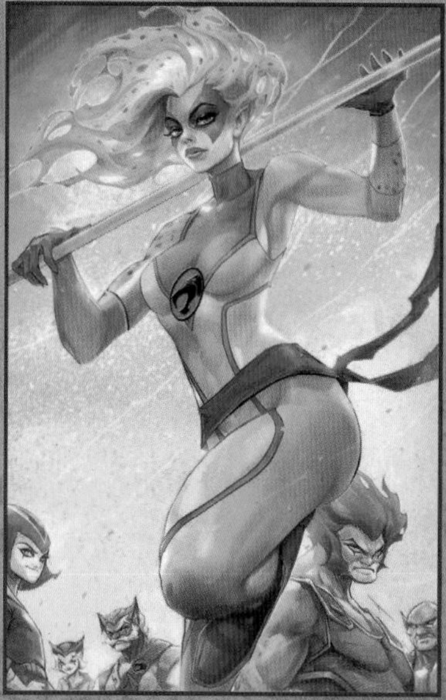

Issue #1 cover art by
IVAN TAO

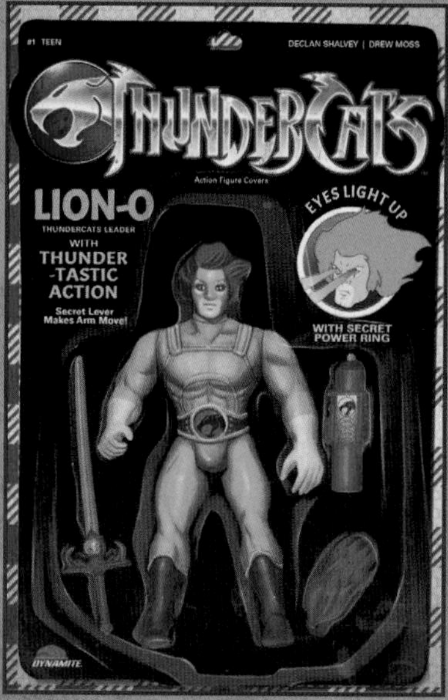
#1 TEEN
DECLAN SHALVEY | DREW MOSS
THUNDERCATS
Action Figure Covers
LION-O
THUNDERCATS LEADER
WITH
THUNDER
-TASTIC
ACTION
Secret Lever
Makes Arm Move!
EYES LIGHT UP
WITH SECRET
POWER RING
DYNAMITE

Issue #1 action figure cover
art by DREW MOSS

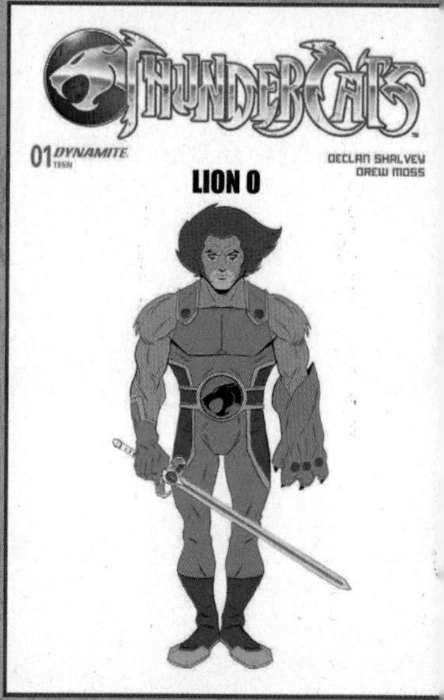
THUNDERCATS
01 DYNAMITE
TEEN
DECLAN SHALVEY
DREW MOSS
LION O

Issue #1 order incentive
character design cover
art by DREW MOSS

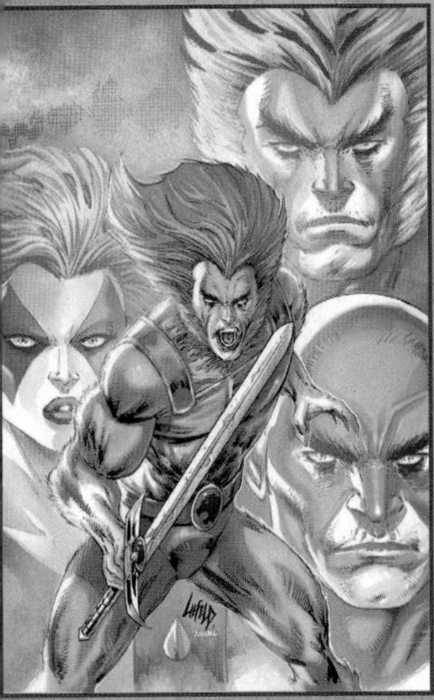

Issue #1 order incentive cover art by ROB LIEFELD

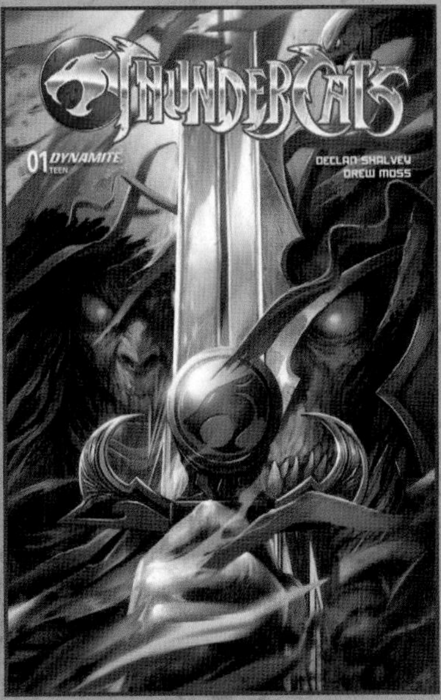
THUNDERCATS
01 DYNAMITE
TEEN
DECLAN SHALVEY
DREW MOSS

Issue #1 order incentive cover art by FRANCESCO MATTINA

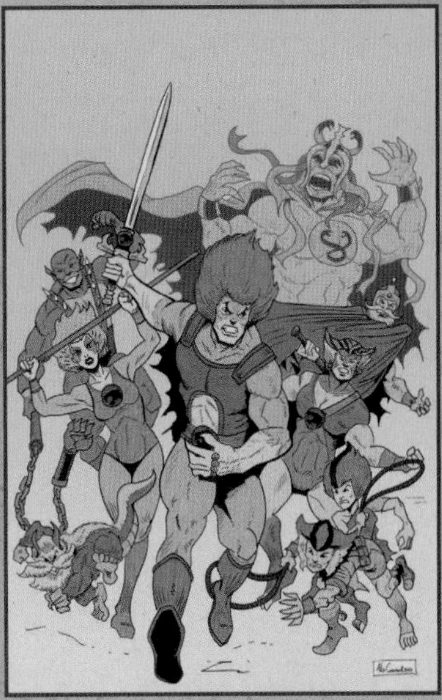

Issue #1 retailer exclusive cover art by ALEX CORMACK, KRS Comics krscomics.com

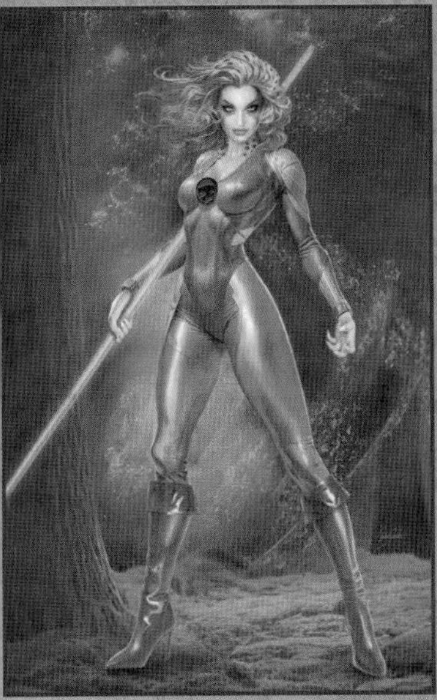

Issue #1 retailer exclusive cover art by NATALI SANDERS, KRS Comics krscomics.com

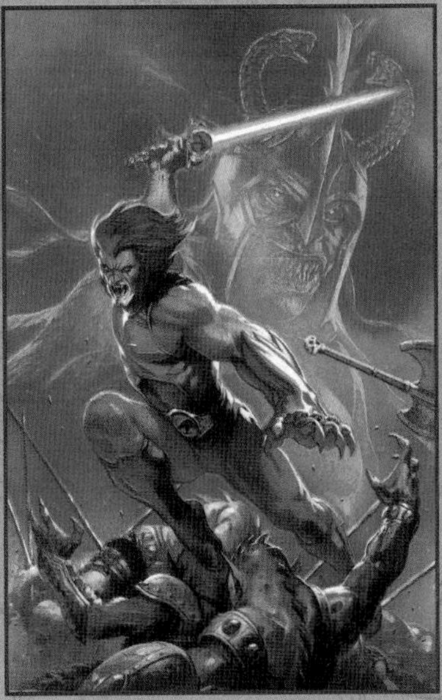

Issue #1 retailer exclusive cover art by GABRIELE DELL'OTTO, Spectral Comics spectral-comics.com

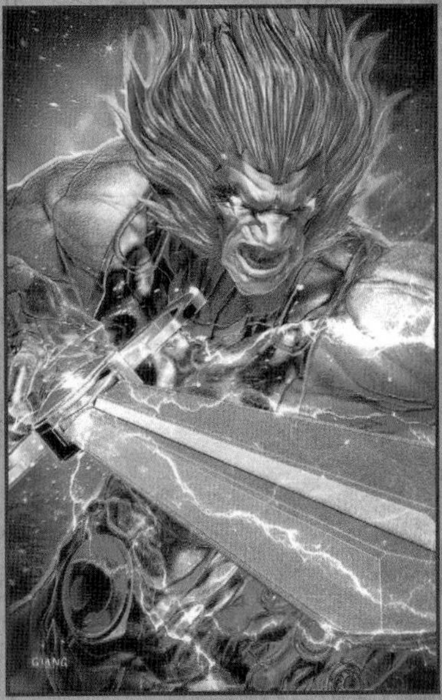
GIANG

Issue #1 retailer exclusive cover art by JOHN GIANG, East Side Comics eastsidecomics.com

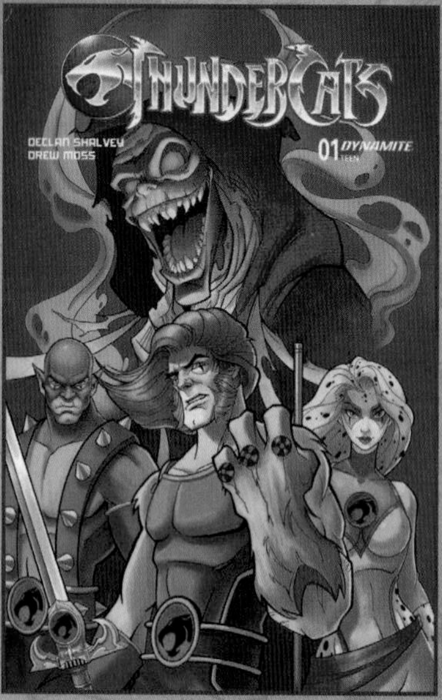
THUNDERCATS
DECLAN SHALVEY
DREW MOSS
01 DYNAMITE

Issue #1 retailer exclusive cover art by PETER SMITH, Krum's World krumscomics.com

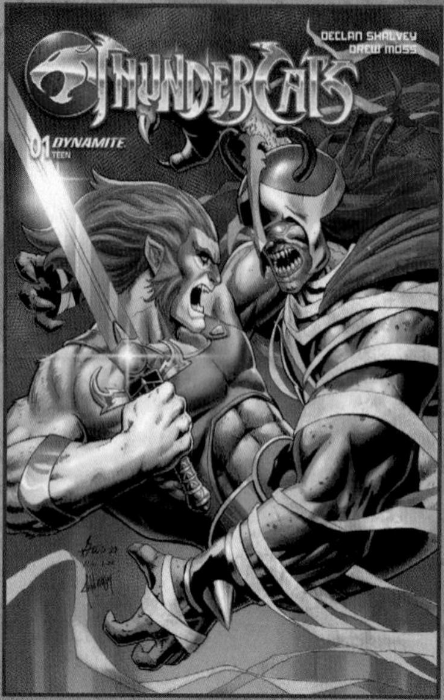
DECLAN SHALVEY
DREW MOSS
THUNDERCATS
01 DYNAMITE

Issue #1 retailer exclusive cover art by GUS MAUK, Nerdtopia nerdtopia.com

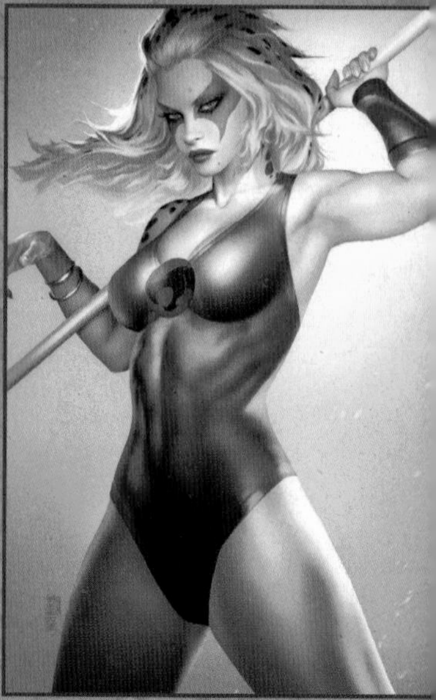

Issue #1 retailer exclusive cover art by JOSH BURNS, 616 Comics the616comics.com

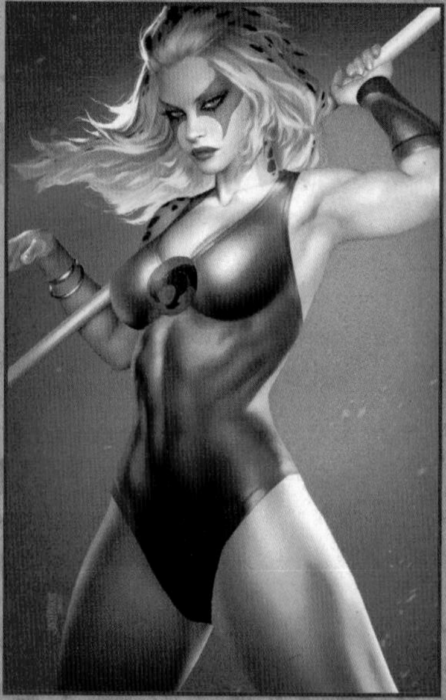

Issue #1 retailer exclusive cover art by JOSH BURNS, 616 Comics the616comics.com

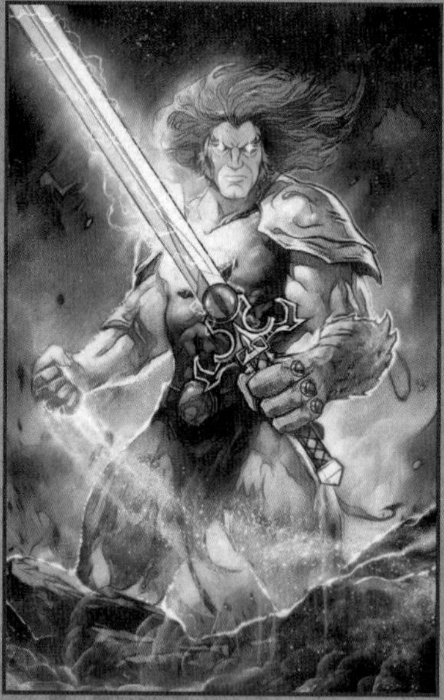

Issue #1 retailer exclusive cover art by CAMRON JOHNSON, Paladin's Gate instagram: /paladinsgatecomics

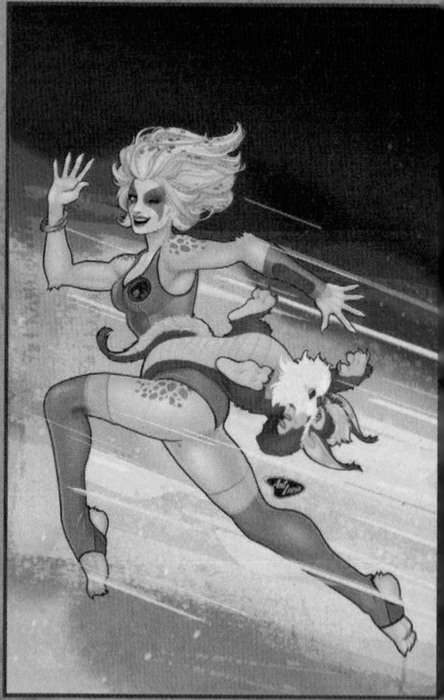

Issue #1 retailer exclusive cover art by ANT LUCIA, Buy Me Toys buymetoys.com

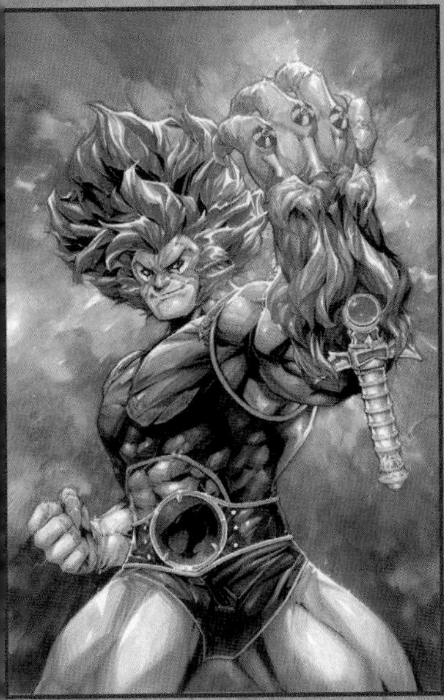

Issue #1 retailer exclusive cover art by LIPWEI CHANG, Comic Corner thecomiccornerstore.com

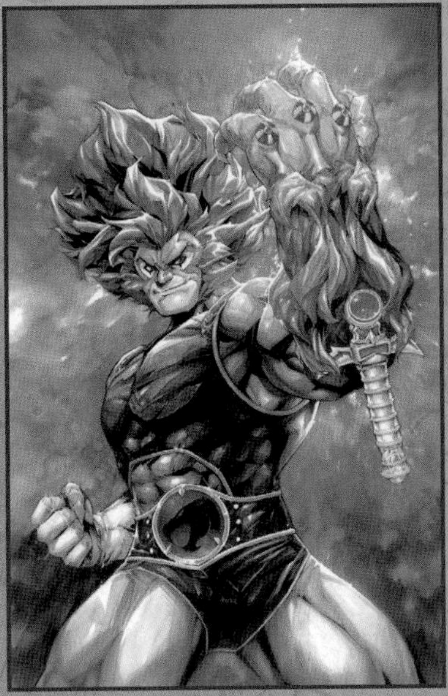

Issue #1 retailer exclusive cover art by LIPWEI CHANG, Comic Corner thecomiccornerstore.com

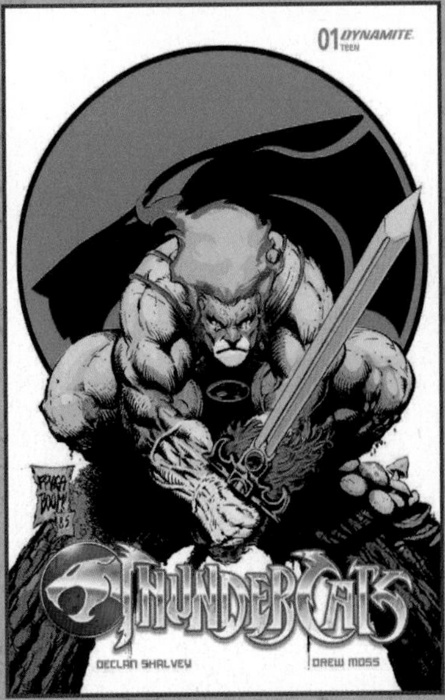
01 DYNAMITE
TEEN
THUNDERCATS
DECLAN SHALVEY
DREW MOSS

Issue #1 retailer exclusive cover art by DAN FRAGA, Borderlands borderlands.us

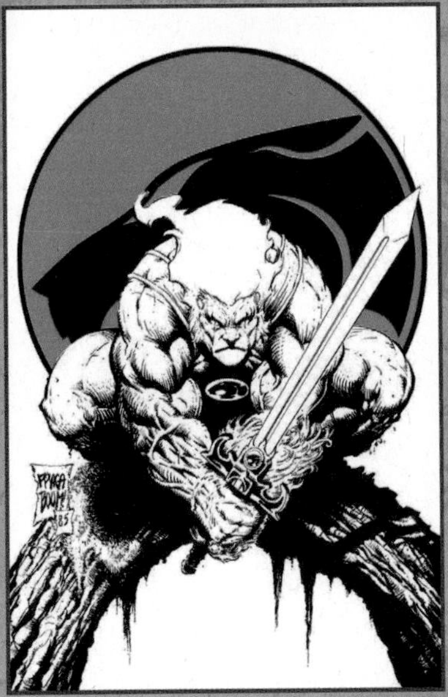

Issue #1 retailer exclusive cover art by DAN FRAGA, Borderlands borderlands.us

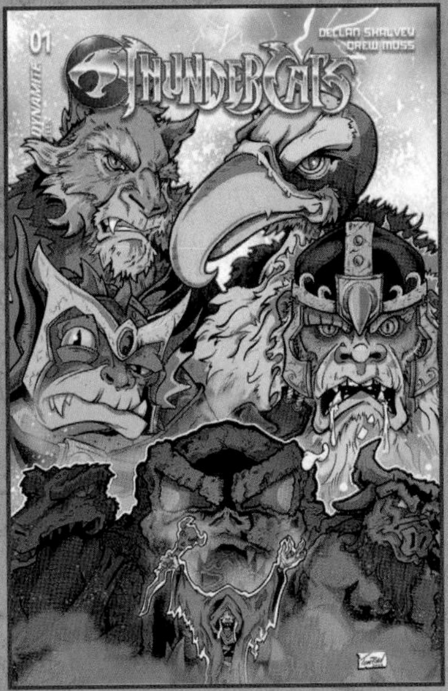
01
DYNAMITE
THUNDERCATS
DECLAN SHALVEY
DREW MOSS

Issue #1 retailer exclusive cover art by TOM RYAN, Alterniverse alterniverse.net

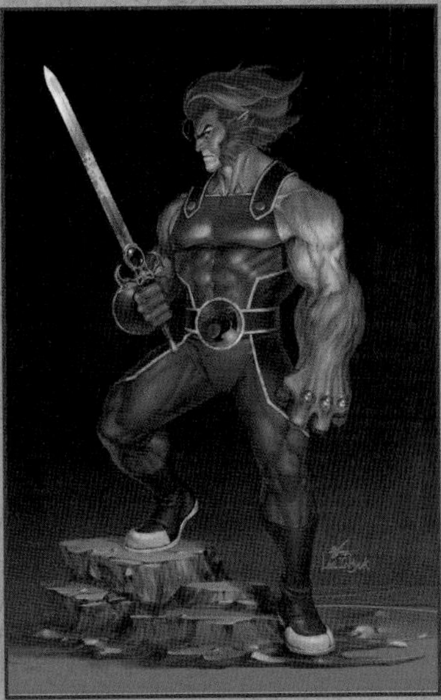

Issue #1 retailer exclusive cover art by INHYUK LEE, Final Order Comics finalordercomics.com

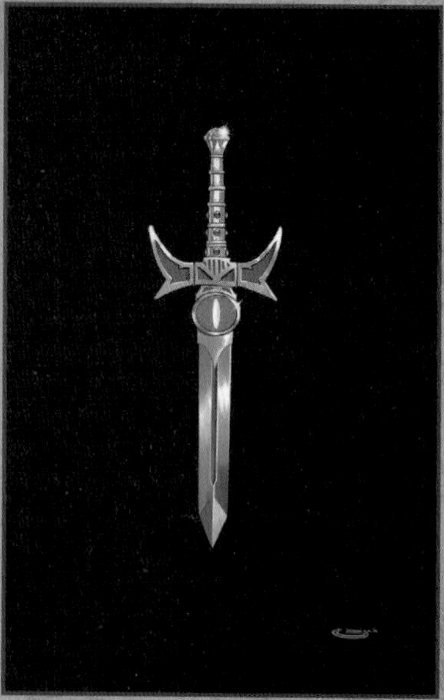

Issue #1 retailer exclusive
cover art by SAJAD SHAH,
Final Order Comics
finalordercomics.com

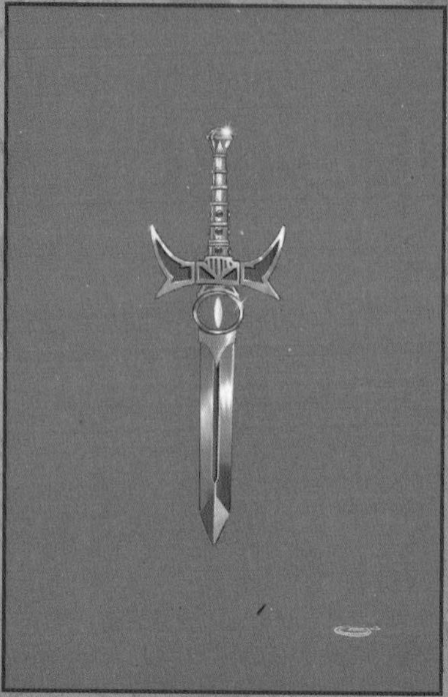

Issue #1 retailer exclusive
cover art by SAJAD SHAH,
Final Order Comics
finalordercomics.com

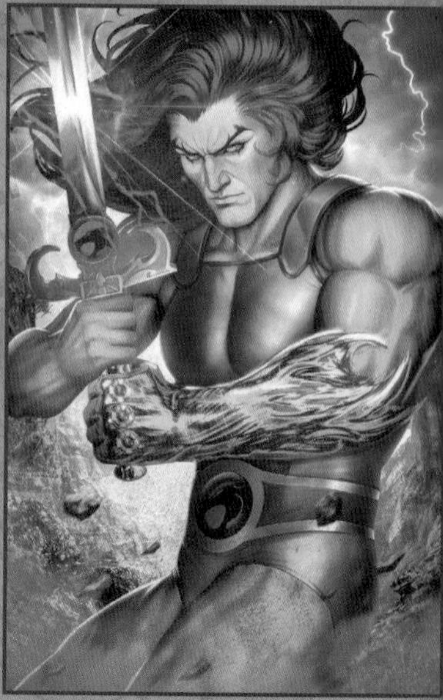

Issue #1 retailer exclusive
cover art by ARIEL DIAZ,
Nomass Comics
nomasscomics.com

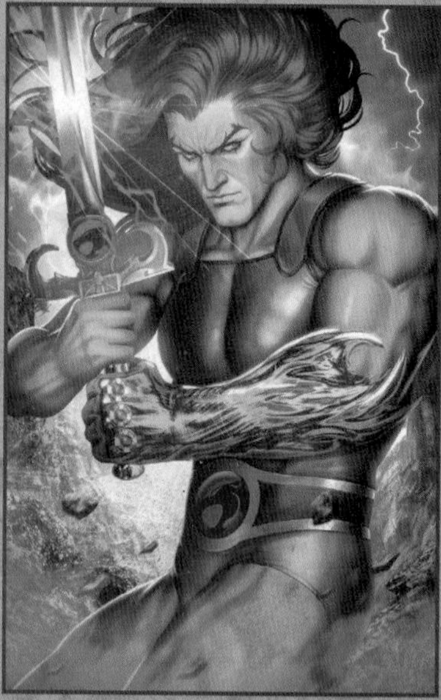

Issue #1 retailer exclusive
cover art by ARIEL DIAZ,
Nomass Comics
nomasscomics.com

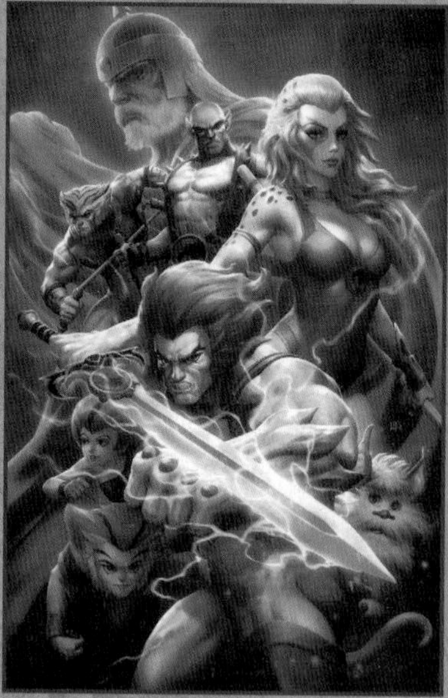

Issue #1 retailer exclusive
cover art by KENDRICK LIM,
Artgerm Collectibles
artgermcollectibles.com

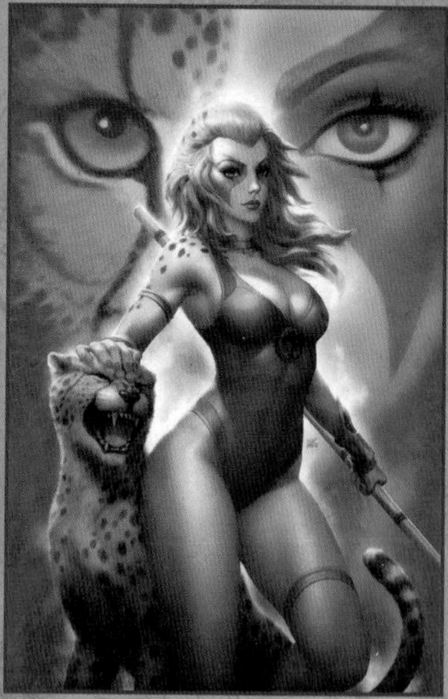

Issue #1 retailer exclusive
cover art by KENDRICK LIM,
Artgerm Collectibles
artgermcollectibles.com

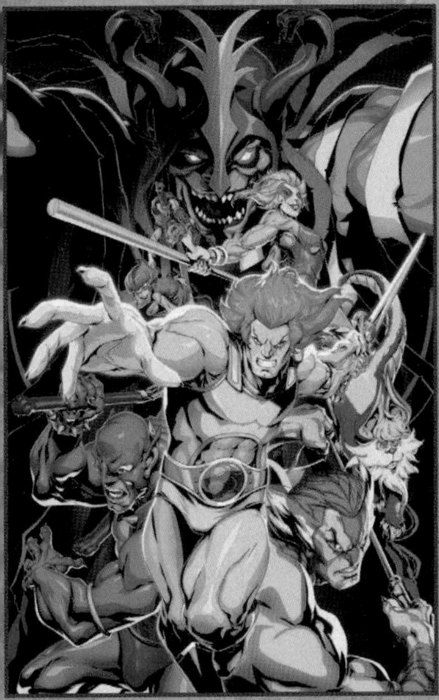

Issue #1 retailer exclusive cover art by CHAMBA, Udon Entertainment udonentertainment.com

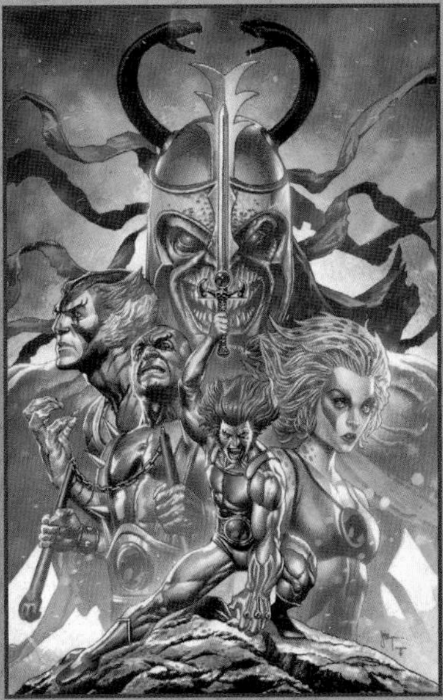

Issue #1 retailer exclusive cover art by MICO SUAYAN, Big Time Collectibles bigtimecollectibles.com

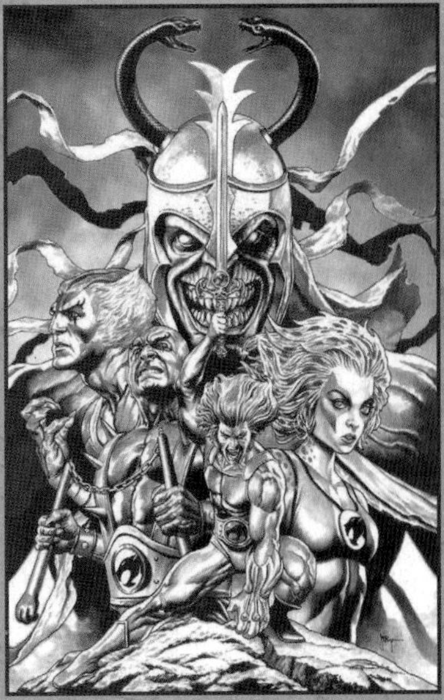

Issue #1 retailer exclusive cover art by MICO SUAYAN, Big Time Collectibles bigtimecollectibles.com

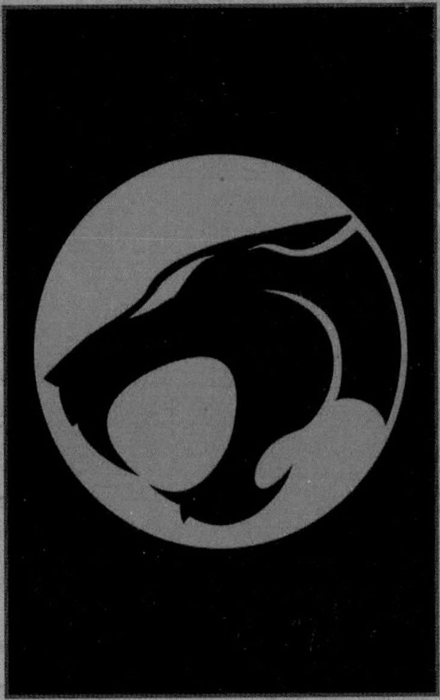

Issue #1 retailer exclusive Big Time Collectibles bigtimecollectibles.com

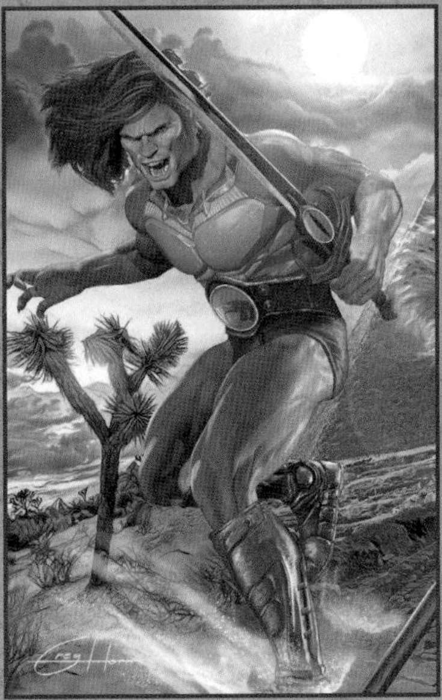

Issue #1 retailer exclusive cover art by GREG HORN, Comicxposure comicxposure.com

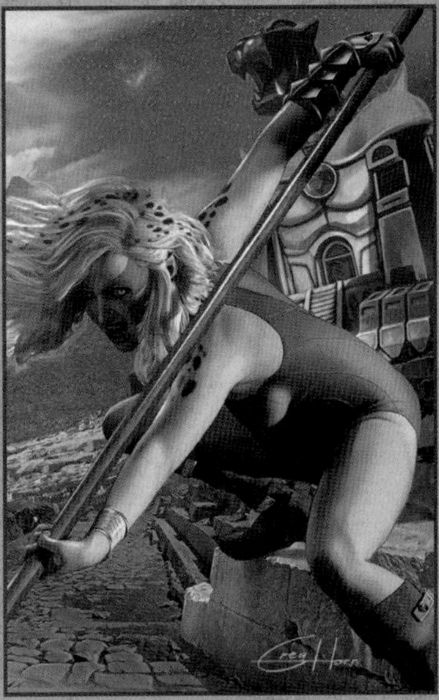

Issue #1 retailer exclusive cover art by GREG HORN, Comicxposure comicxposure.com

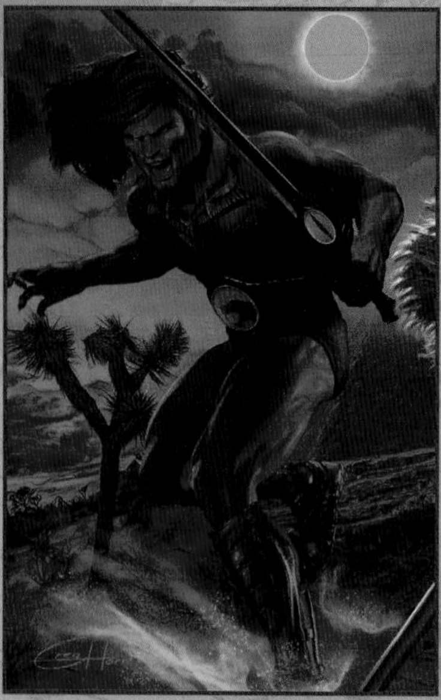

Issue #1 retailer exclusive
cover art by GREG HORN,
Comicxposure
comicxposure.com

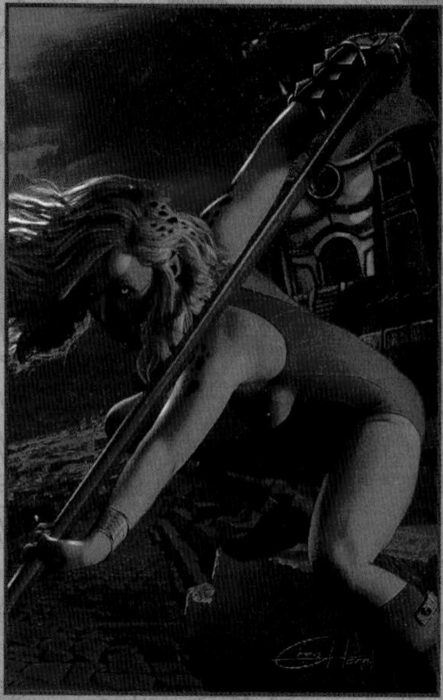

Issue #1 retailer exclusive
cover art by GREG HORN,
Comicxposure
comicxposure.com

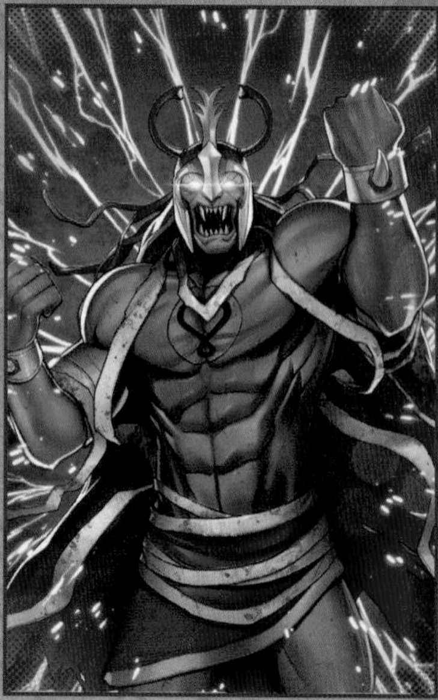

Issue #1 retailer exclusive
cover art by
NATE MELENDEZ,
Comicxposure
comicxposure.com

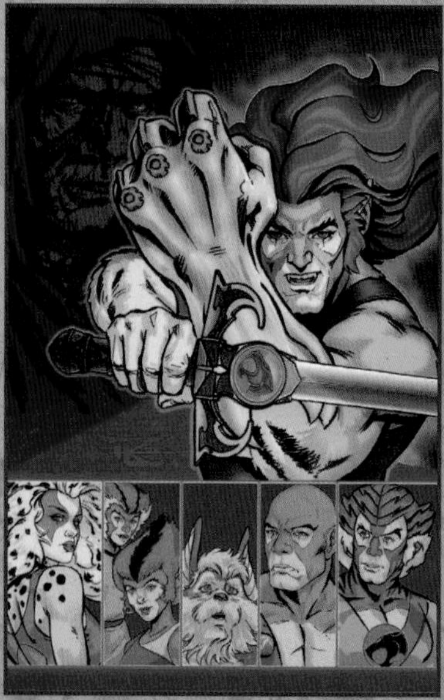

Issue #1 retailer exclusive
cover art by RON LEARY,
Comicxposure
comicxposure.com

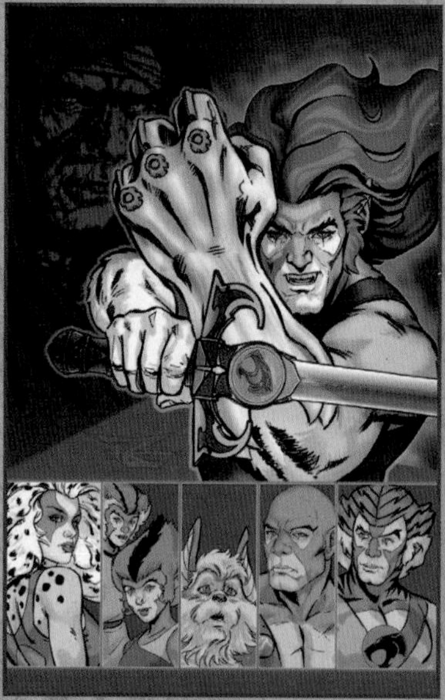

Issue #1 retailer exclusive
cover art by RON LEARY,
Comicxposure
comicxposure.com

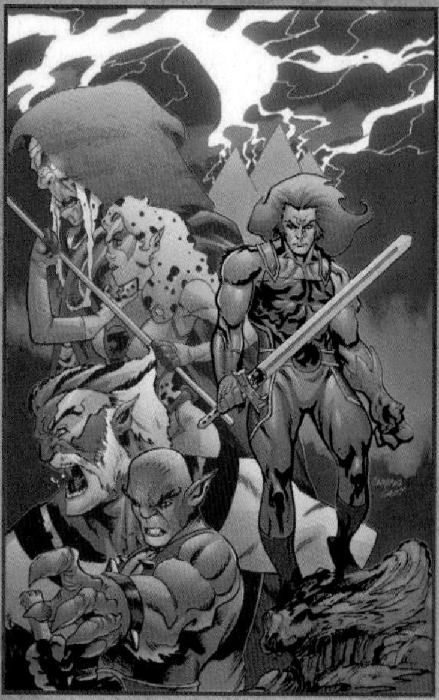

Issue #1 retailer exclusive
cover art by
CHRIS CAMPANA,
Very Gary Comics
verygarycomics.com

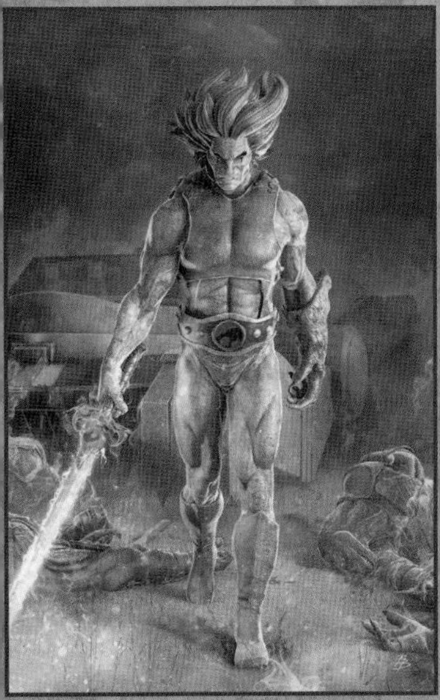

Issue #1 retailer exclusive cover art by BJORN BARENDS, Collector Cave collectorcave.shop

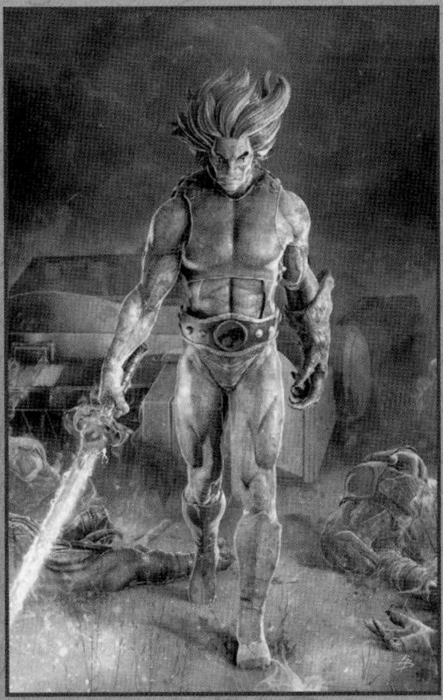

Issue #1 retailer exclusive cover art by BJORN BARENDS, Collector Cave collectorcave.shop

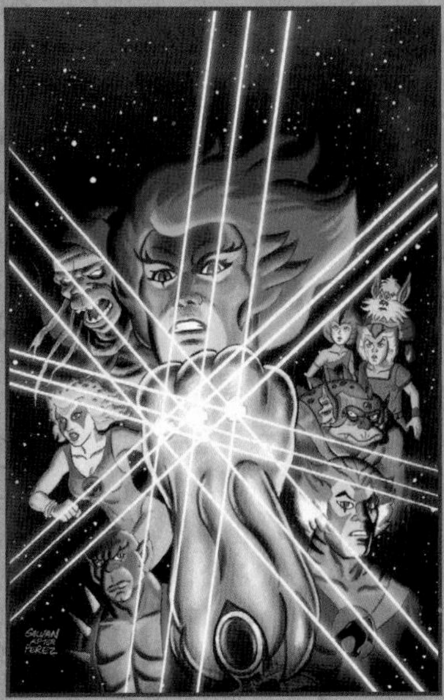

Issue #1 retailer exclusive cover art by BEN GALVAN, Whatnot

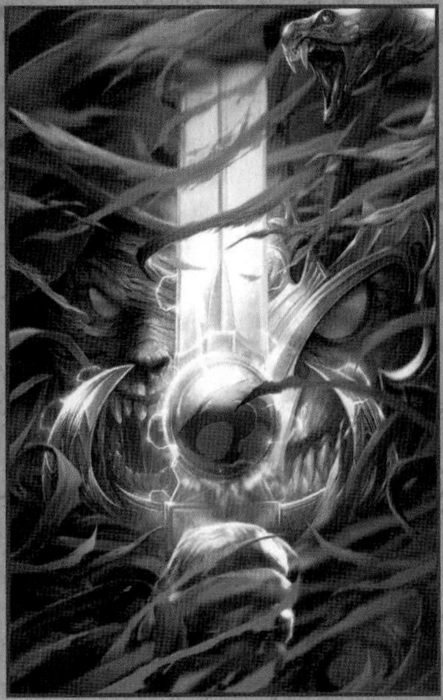

Issue #1 retailer exclusive cover art by FRANCESCO MATTINA, Scott's Collectibles scottscollectables-shop.co.uk

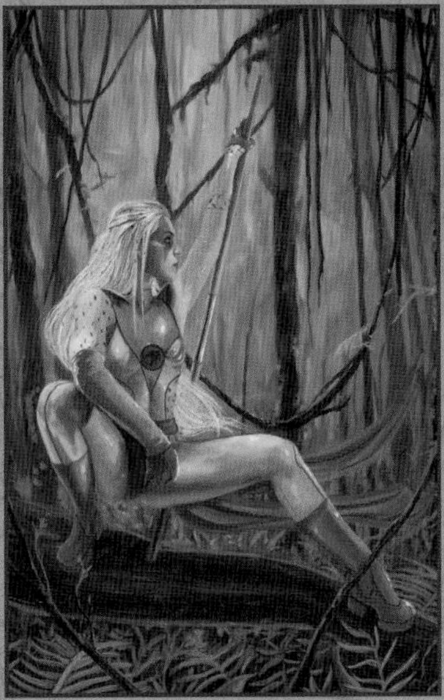

Issue #1 retailer exclusive cover art by INGRID GALA, Scott's Collectibles scottscollectables-shop.co.uk

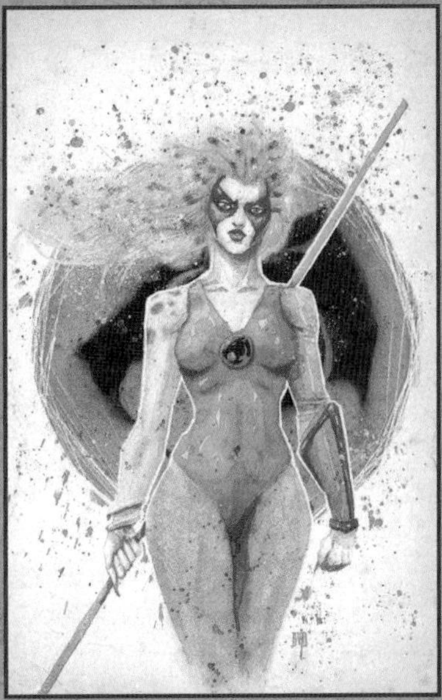

Issue #1 retailer exclusive cover art by BRAO, Scott's Collectibles scottscollectables-shop.co.uk

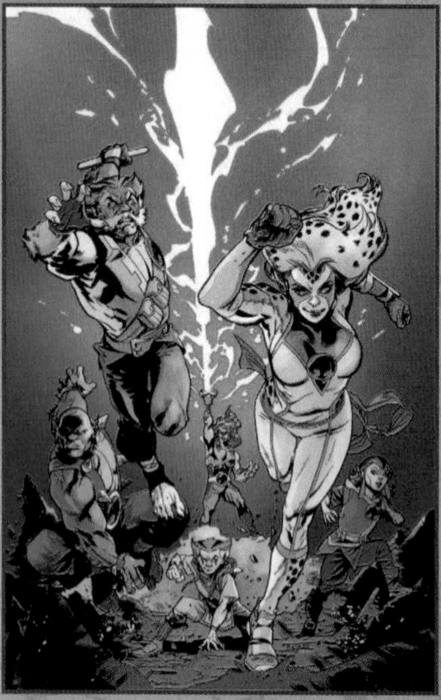

Issue #1 retailer exclusive cover art by MAHMUD ASRAR, Galaxycon galaxycon.com

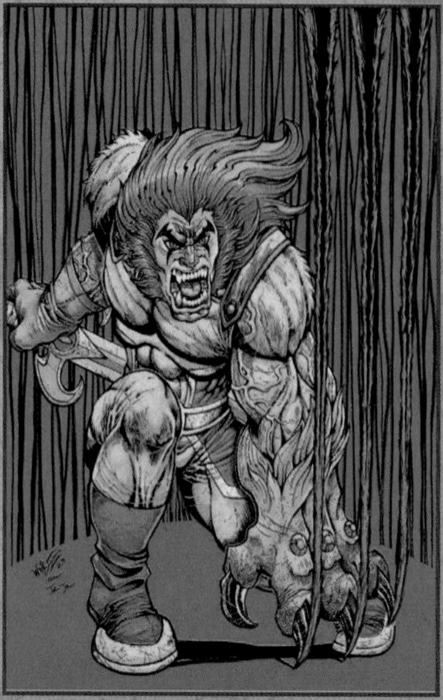

Issue #1 retailer exclusive cover art by MARIA WOLF, Rupp's Comics ruppworld.com

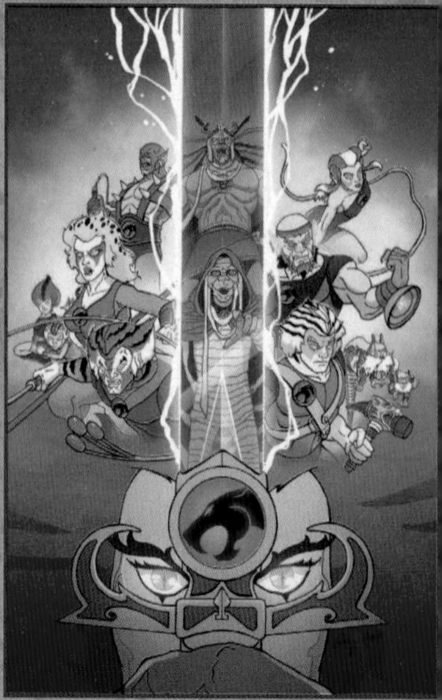

Issue #1 retailer exclusive cover art by STEVEN AHOLA, MB Artist mbartist.com

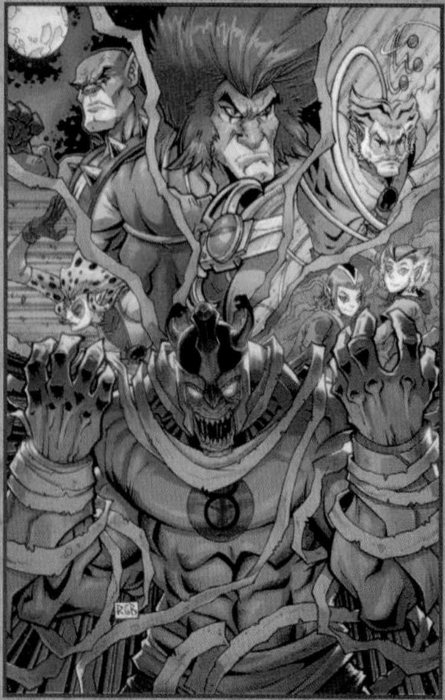

Issue #1 retailer exclusive cover art by RYAN G. BROWNE, Cavey Comix instagram: /caveycomix

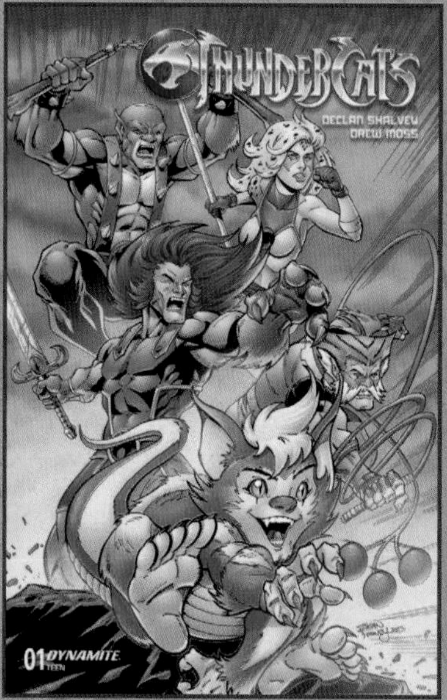
THUNDERCATS
DECLAN SHALVEY
DREW MOSS
01 DYNAMITE
TEEN

Issue #1 retailer exclusive cover art by SEAN FORNEY seanforney.com

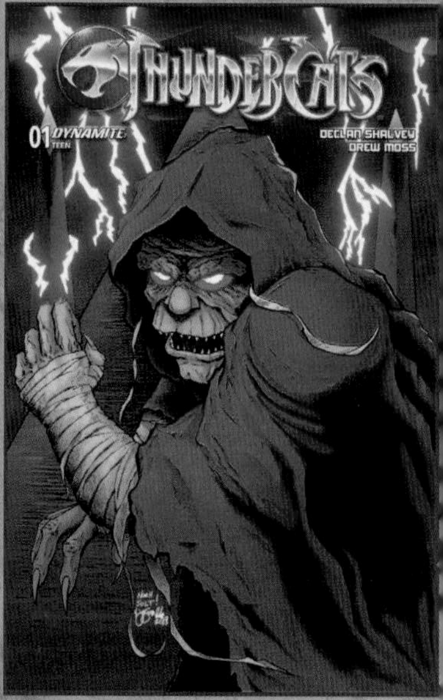
THUNDERCATS
01 DYNAMITE
TEEN
DECLAN SHALVEY
DREW MOSS

Issue #1 retailer exclusive cover art by NOAH SULT - Pencils, JASON MOORE - Inks, LUIS ANTONIO DELGADO - Colors Gorilla Warfare gorillawarfarecomics.com

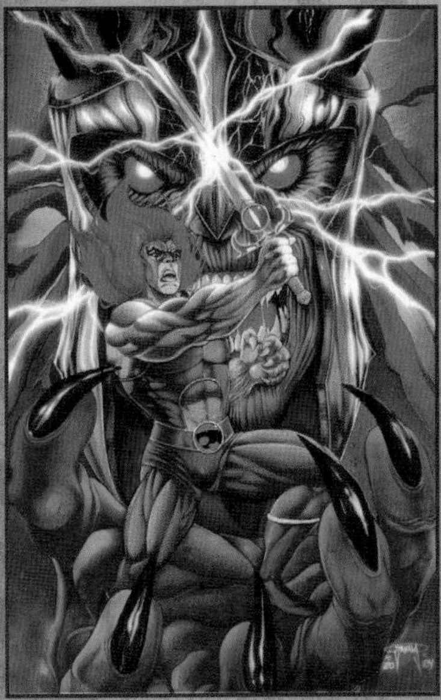

Issue #1 retailer exclusive cover by MARTIN ZAVALA, Altered Reality
alteredrealityentertainment.com

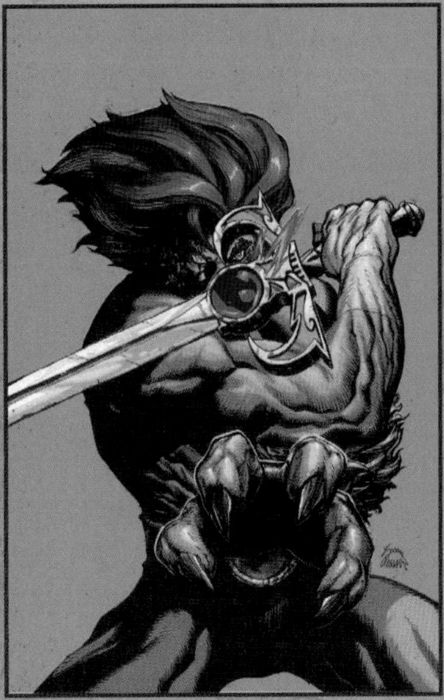

Issue #1 retailer exclusive cover art by RYAN STEGMAN, Comic Sketch Art
comicsketchart.com

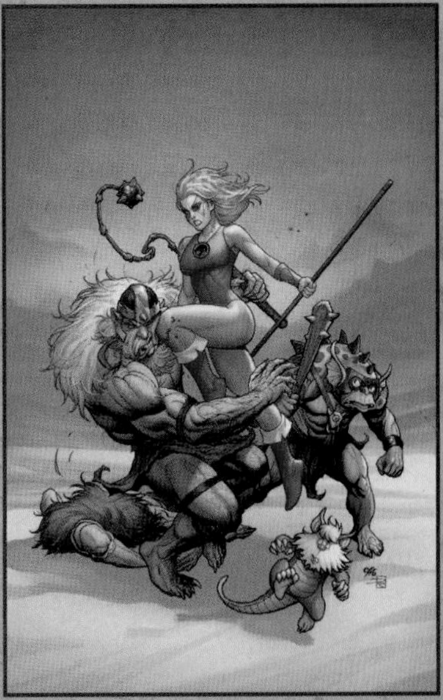

Issue #1 retailer exclusive cover art by FRANK CHO, Comic Sketch Art
comicsketchart.com

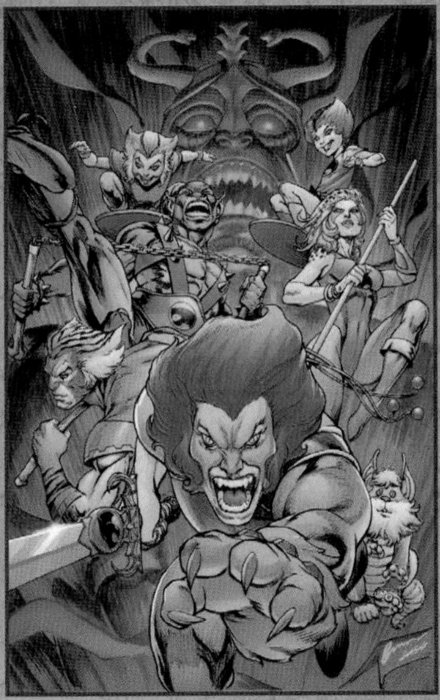

Issue #1 retailer exclusive cover art by BUZZ
justbuzzart.com

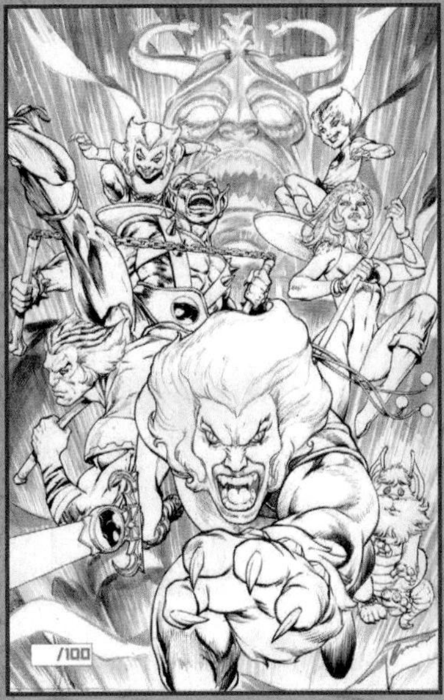
/100

Issue #1 retailer exclusive cover art by BUZZ
justbuzzart.com

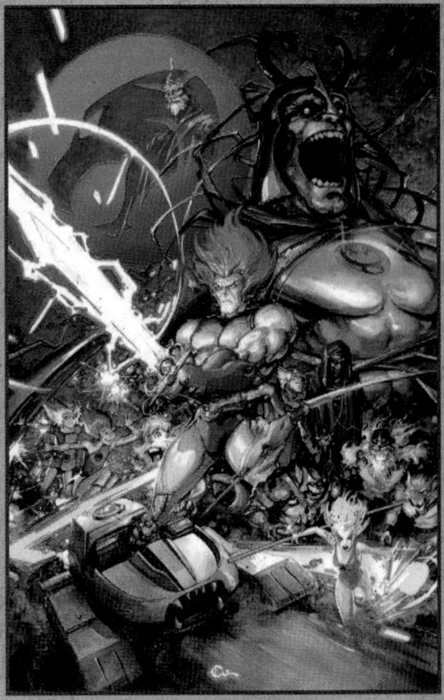

Issue #1 retailer exclusive cover art by CLAYTON CRAIN
claytoncrain.com

Issue #1 retailer exclusive
cover art by ROB LIEFELD,
Rob Liefeld Creations
robliefeldcreations.com

Issue #1 retailer exclusive
cover art by ROB LIEFELD,
Rob Liefeld Creations
robliefeldcreations.com

Issue #1 retailer exclusive cove
art by ROB LIEFELD,
Rob Liefeld Creations
robliefeldcreations.com

Issue #1 retailer exclusive cover art
by JAE LEE AND JUNE CHUNG,
Blowout Cards
blowoutcards.com

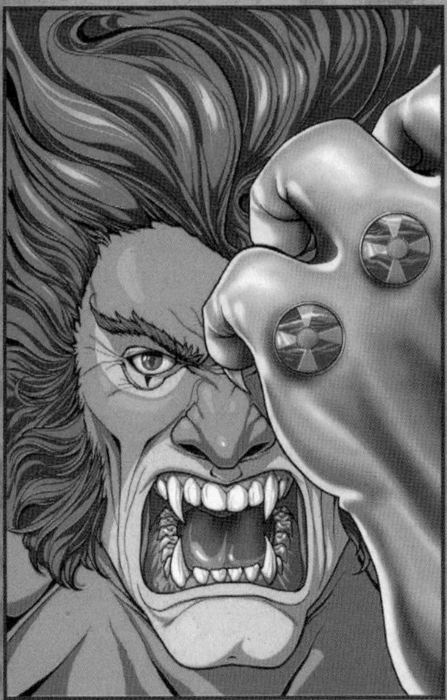

Issue #1 retailer exclusive cover art by JAMIE COKER, Epic Entertainment epicentertainmentus.com

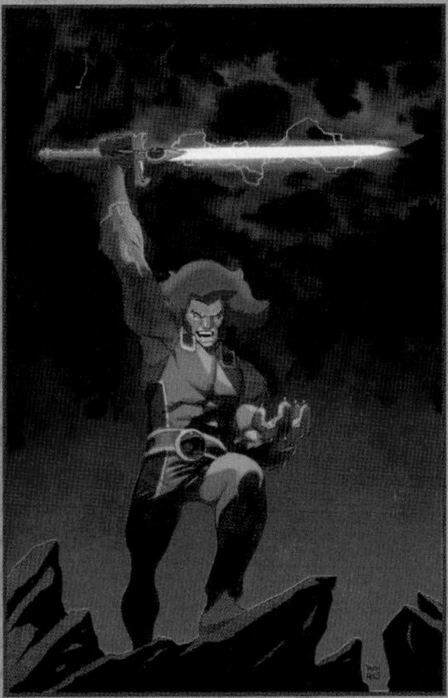

Issue #1 retailer exclusive cover art by DREW MOSS, Kwan Chang Art kwanchang.com

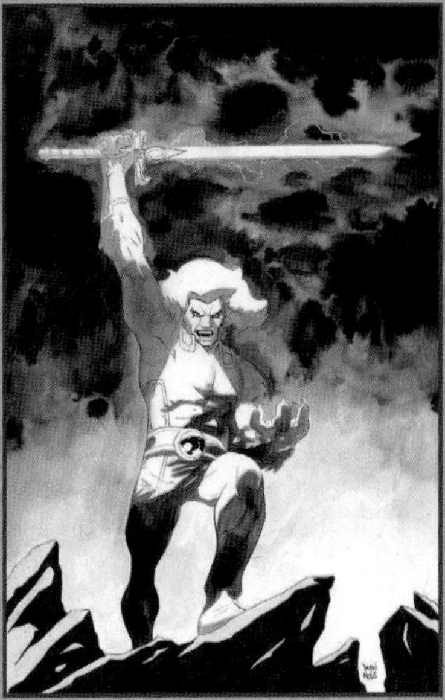

Issue #1 retailer exclusive cover art by DREW MOSS, Kwan Chang Art kwanchang.com

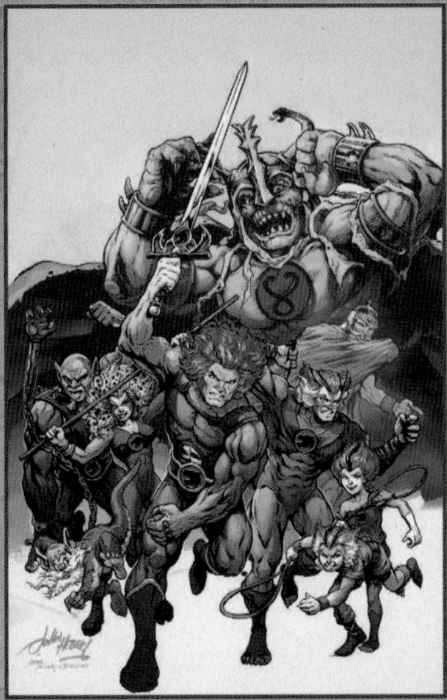

Issue #1 retailer exclusive cover art by JOHN HERBERT, MBArtist mbartist.com

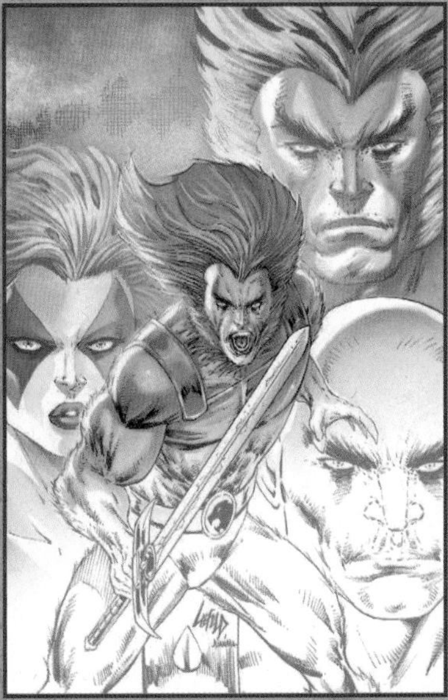

Issue #1 reprint cover art by ROB LIEFELD

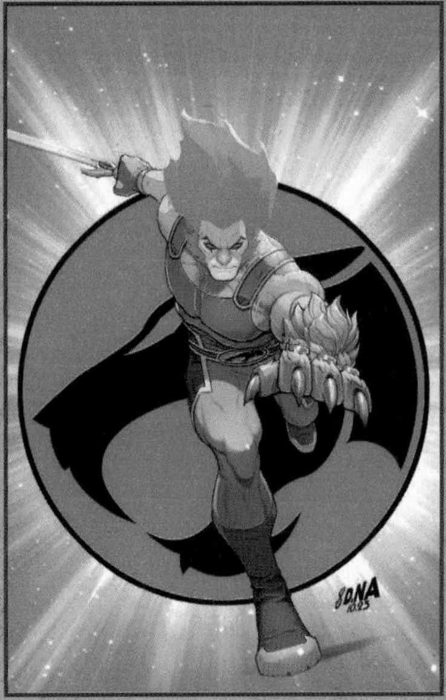

Issue #1 reprint cover art by DAVID NAKAYAMA

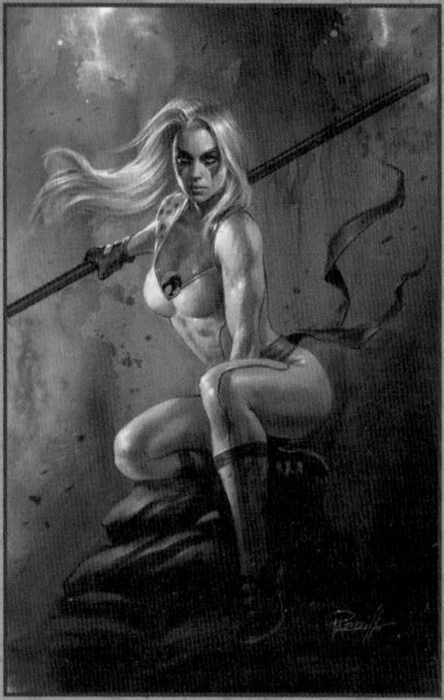

Issue #2 cover art by LUCIO PARRILLO

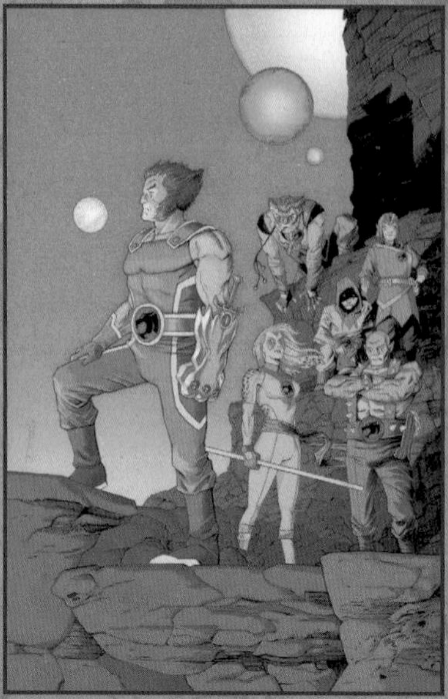

Issue #2 cover art by DECLAN SHALVEY

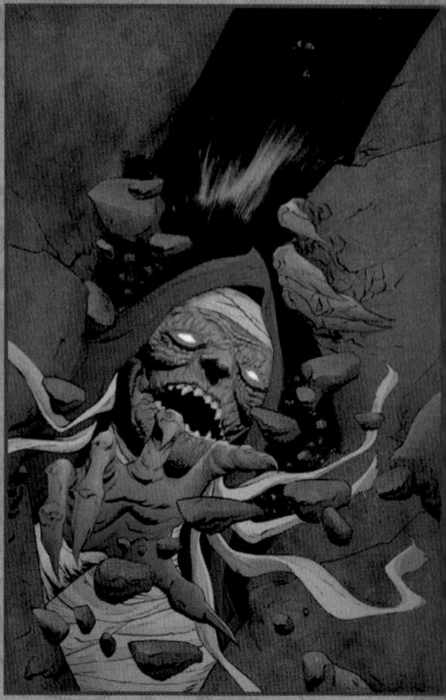

Issue #2 cover art by JAE LEE & JUNE CHUNG

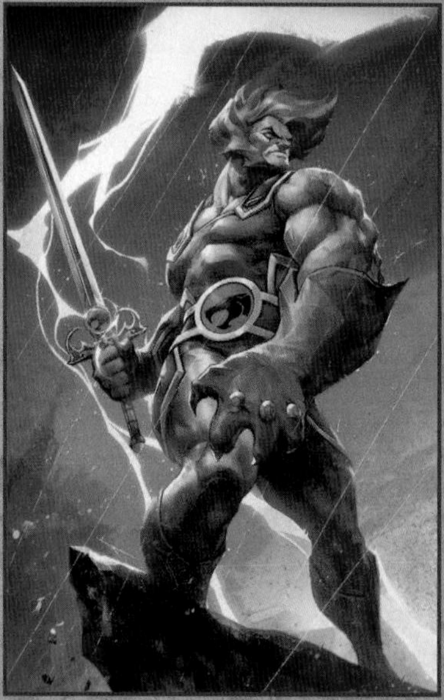

Issue #2 cover art by IVAN TAO

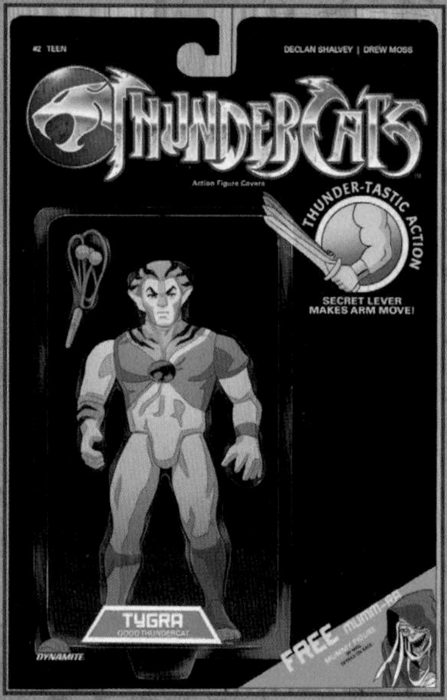
#2 TEEN
DECLAN SHALVEY | DREW MOSS
THUNDERCATS
Action Figure Covers
THUNDER-TASTIC ACTION
SECRET LEVER MAKES ARM MOVE!
TYGRA
GOOD THUNDERCAT
FREE
DYNAMITE

Issue #2 action figure cover art by DREW MOSS

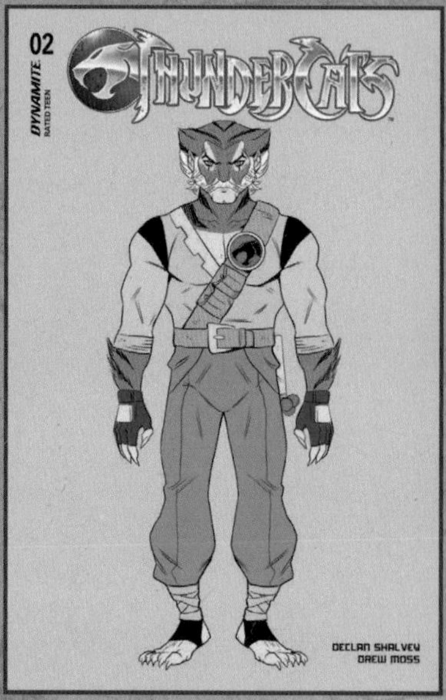
02
DYNAMITE
RATED TEEN
THUNDERCATS
DECLAN SHALVEY
DREW MOSS

Issue #2 order incentive character design cover art by DREW MOSS

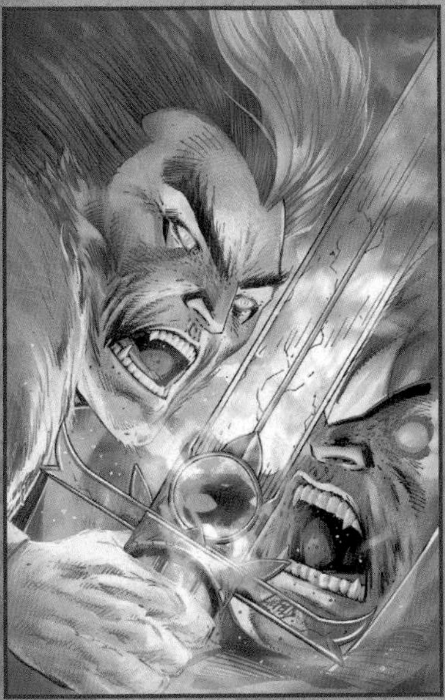

Issue #2 order incentive cover art by ROB LIEFELD

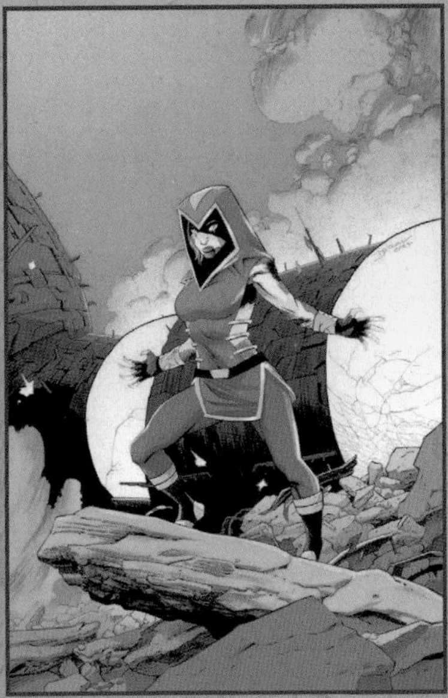

Issue #2 order incentive cover art by DECLAN SHALVEY

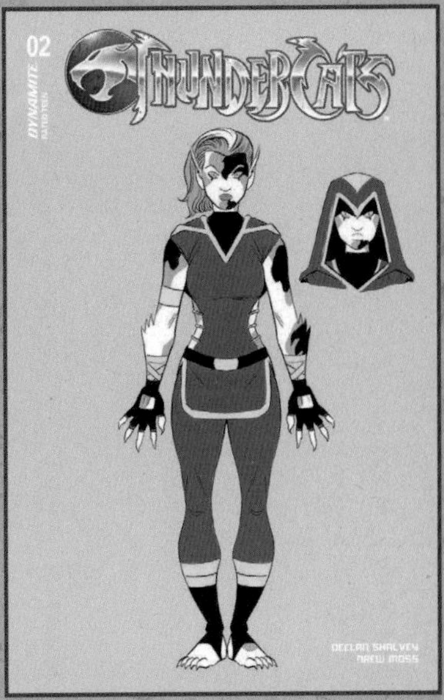
02
THUNDERCATS
DYNAMITE
DECLAN SHALVEY
DREW MOSS

Issue #2 order incentive character design cover art by DREW MOSS

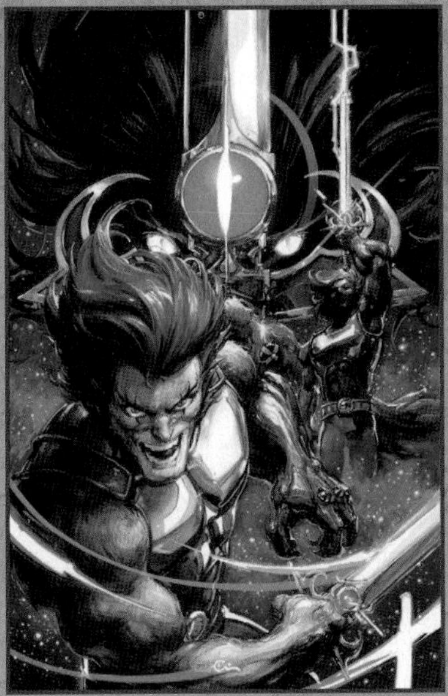

Issue #2 retailer exclusive cover art by CLAYTON CRAIN, claytoncrain.com

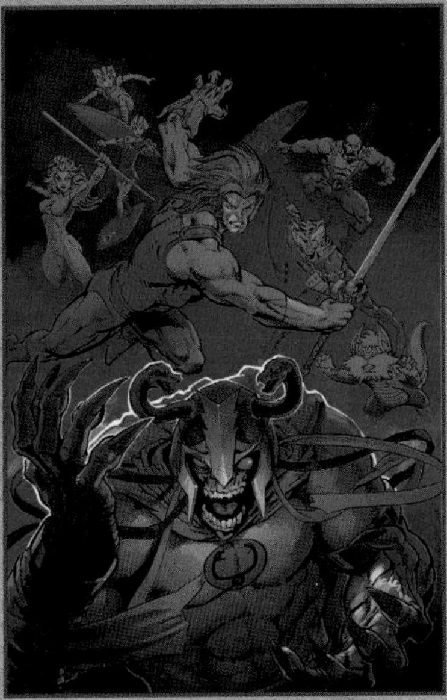

Issue #2 retailer exclusive cover art by JOSEF RUBENSTEIN, MB Artist mbartist.com

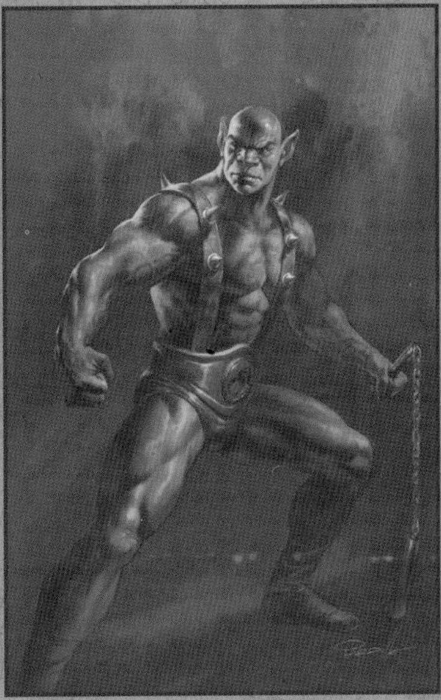

Issue #3 cover art by LUCIO PARRILLO

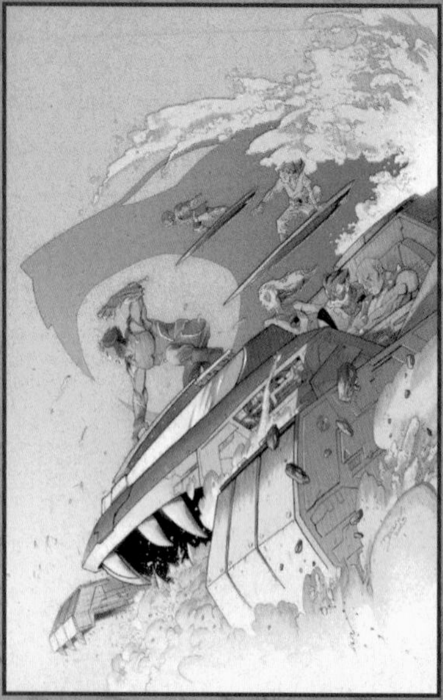

Issue #3 cover art by
DECLAN SHALVEY

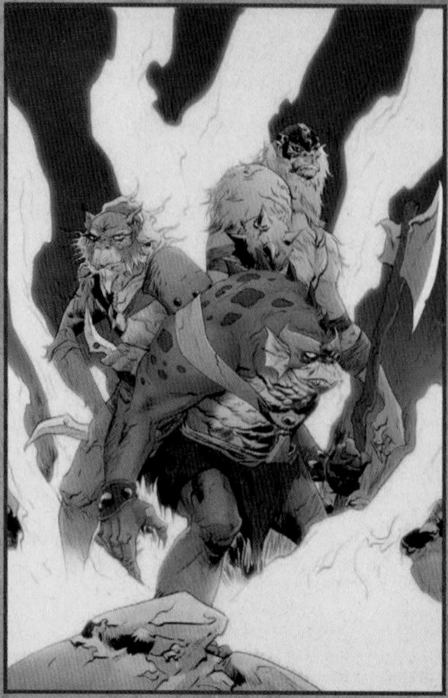

Issue #3 cover art by
JAE LEE & JUNE CHUNG

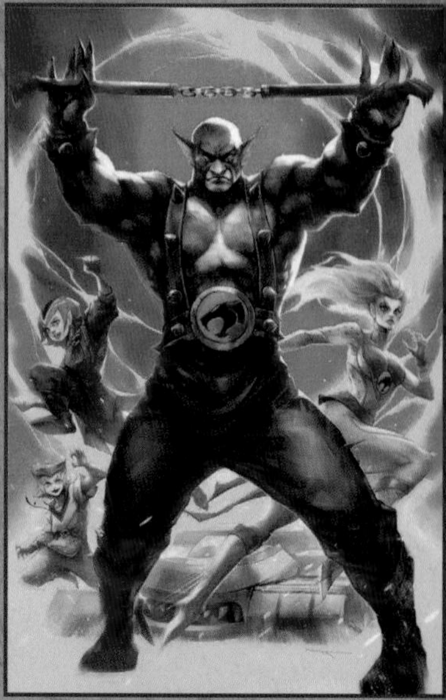

Issue #3 cover art by
IVAN TAO

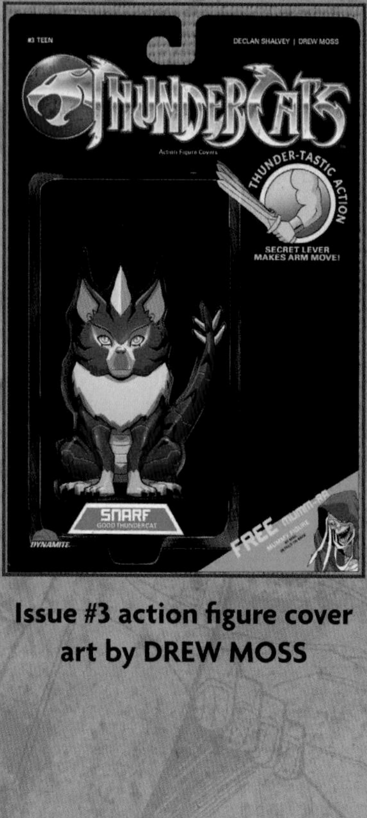
#3 TEEN
DECLAN SHALVEY | DREW MOSS
THUNDERCATS
Action Figure Covers
THUNDER-TASTIC ACTION
SECRET LEVER MAKES ARM MOVE!
SNARF
GOOD THUNDERCAT
FREE
DYNAMITE

Issue #3 action figure cover art by DREW MOSS

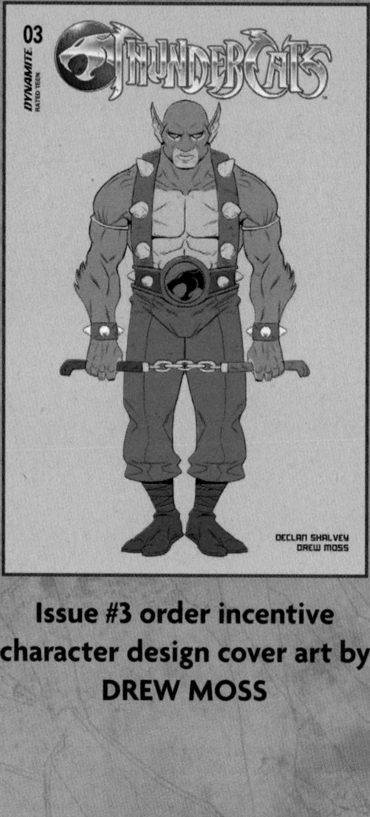
03
THUNDERCATS
DYNAMITE
RATED TEEN
DECLAN SHALVEY
DREW MOSS

Issue #3 order incentive character design cover art by DREW MOSS

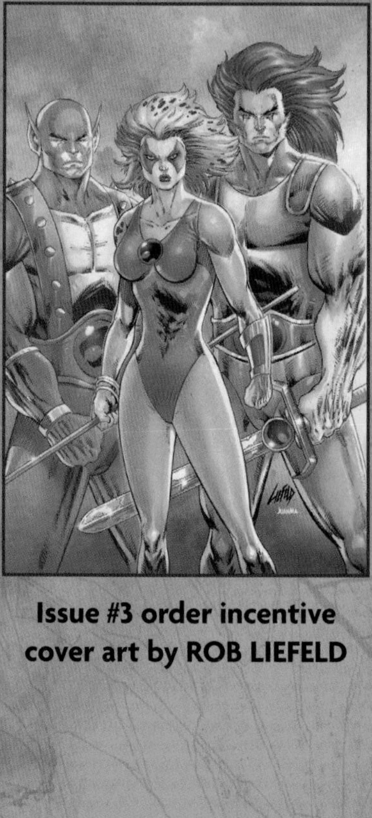

Issue #3 order incentive cover art by ROB LIEFELD

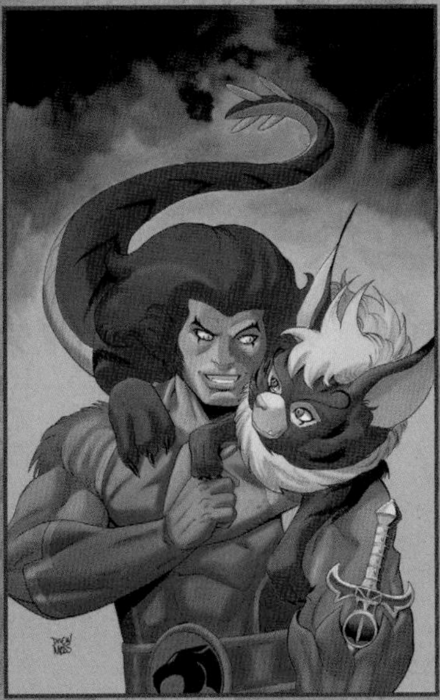

Issue #3 order incentive cover art by DREW MOSS

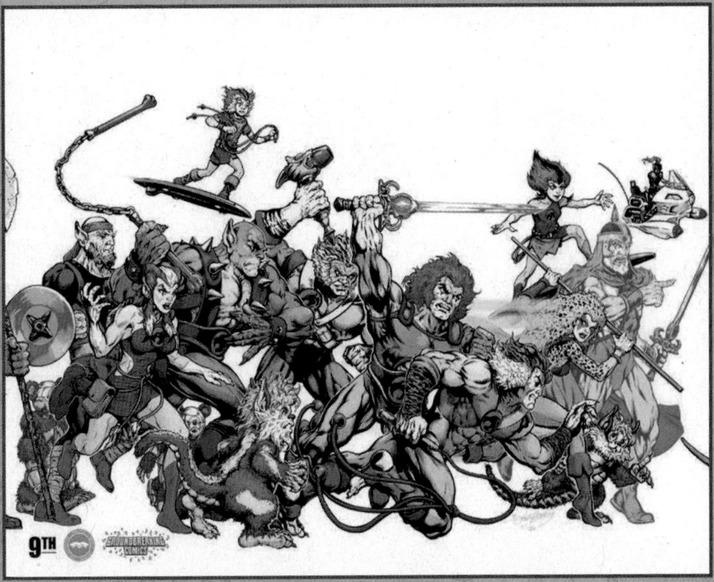

Issue #3 retailer exclusive cover art by JOHN HEBERT, MB Artist mbartist.com

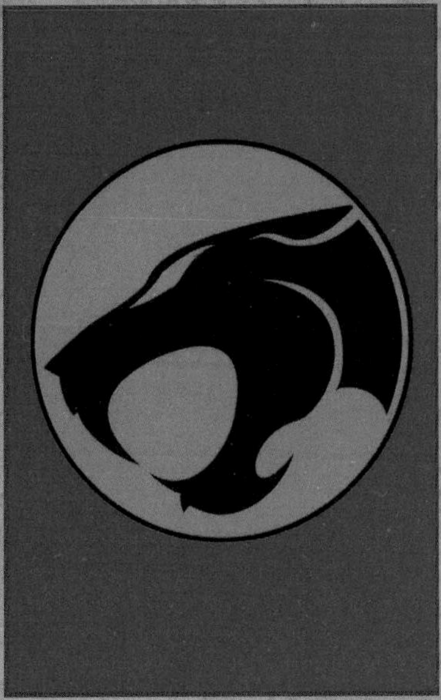

Issue #3 retailer exclusive No Masss Comics nomasscomics.com

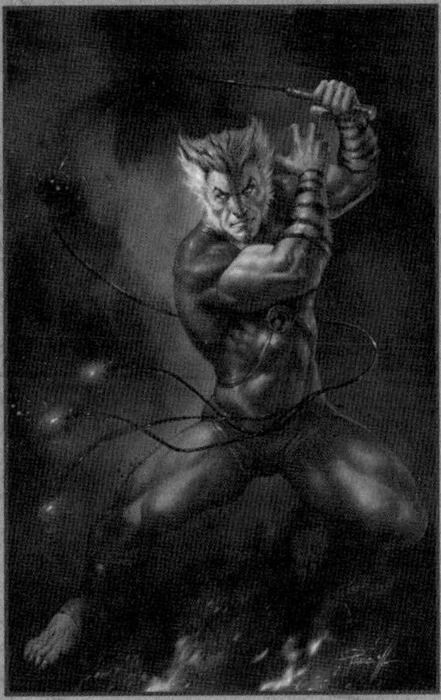

Issue #4 cover art by LUCIO PARRILLO

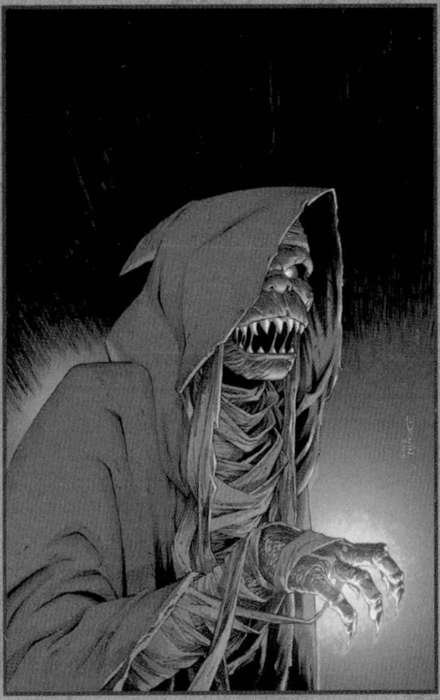

Issue #4 cover art by DECLAN SHALVEY

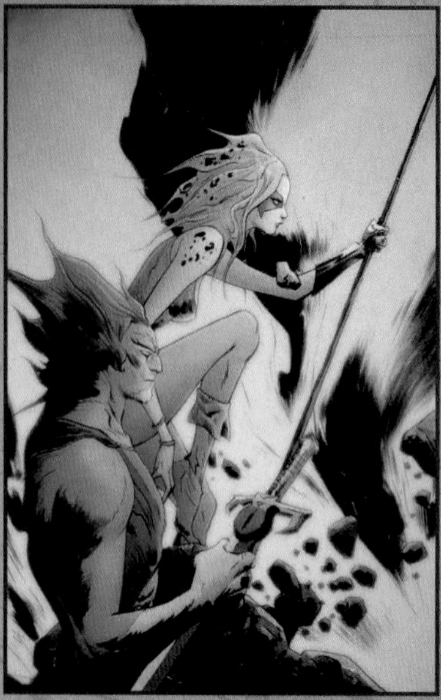

Issue #4 cover art by
JAE LEE & JUNE CHUNG

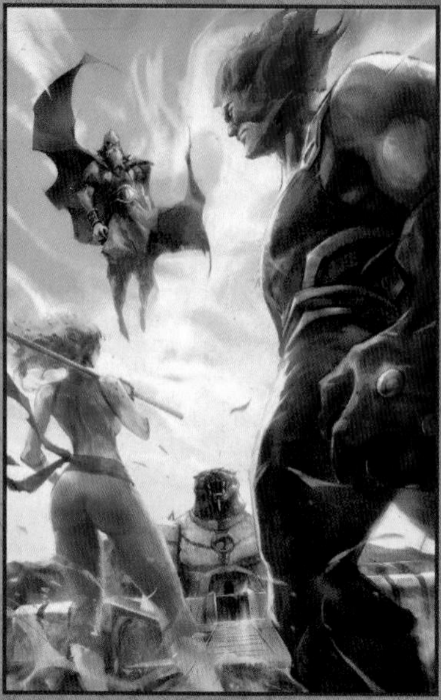

Issue #4 cover art by
IVAN TAO

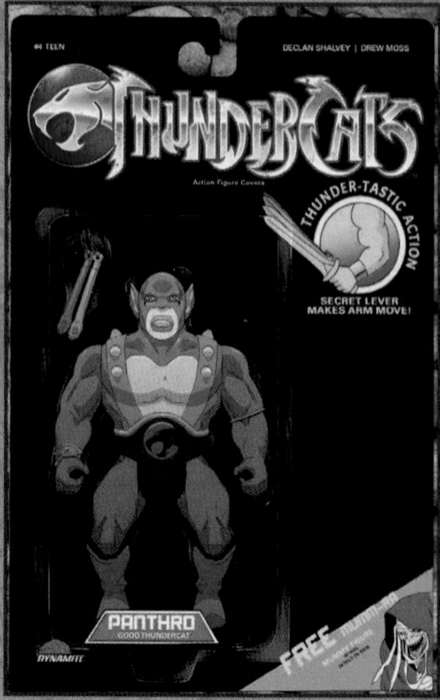
#4 TEEN
DECLAN SHALVEY | DREW MOSS
THUNDERCATS
Action Figure Covers
THUNDER-TASTIC ACTION
SECRET LEVER MAKES ARM MOVE!
PANTHRO
GOOD THUNDERCAT
DYNAMITE
FREE

Issue #4 action figure cover
art by DREW MOSS

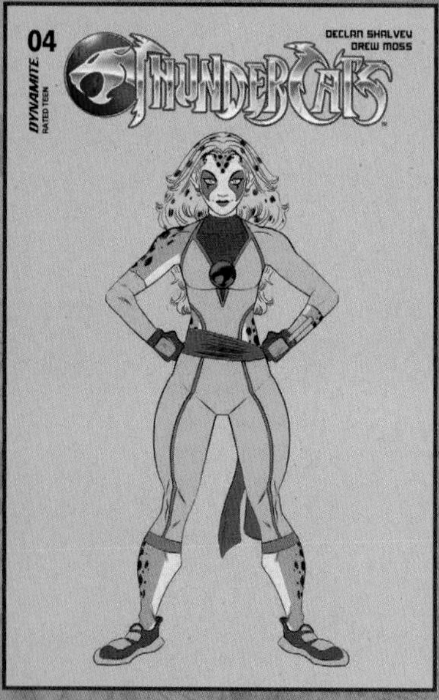
04
DECLAN SHALVEY
DREW MOSS
THUNDERCATS
DYNAMITE
RATED TEEN

Issue #4 order incentive
character design cover art
by DREW MOSS

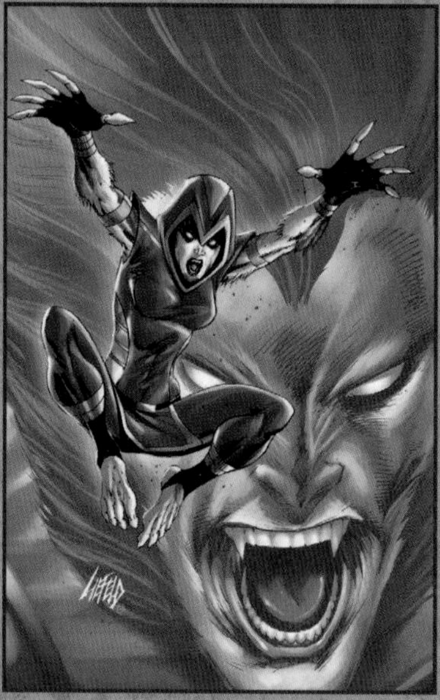

Issue #4 order incentive cover
art by ROB LIEFELD

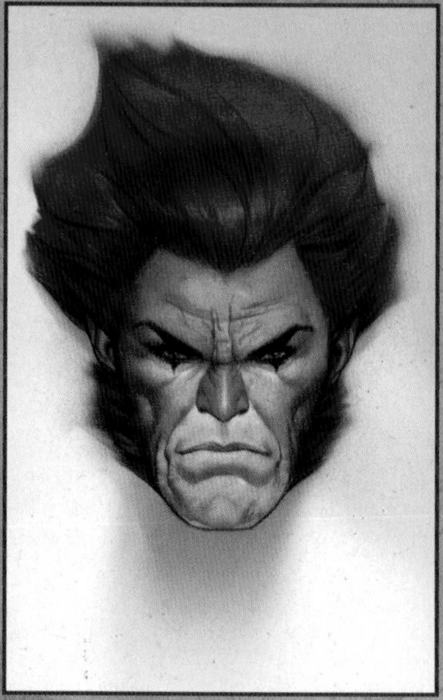

Issue #4 order incentive
cover art by BEN OLIVER

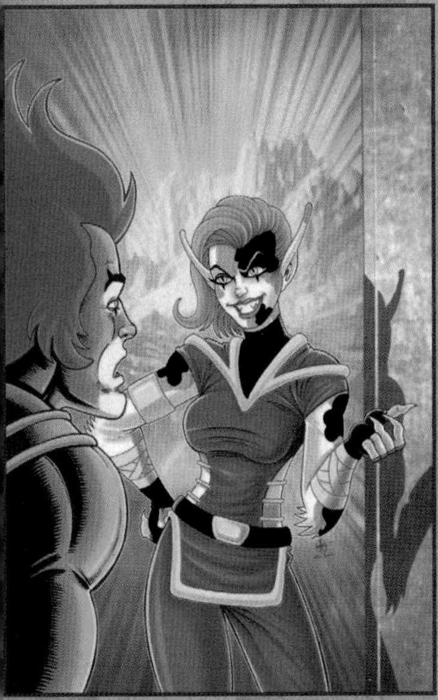

Issue #4 order incentive cover art by KEN HAESER

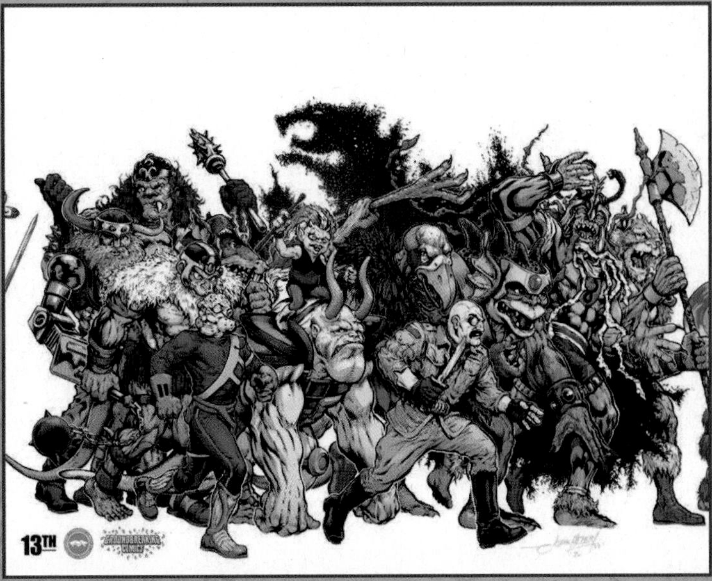
13TH

Issue #4 retailer exclusive cover art by JOHN HEBERT, MB Artist mbartist.com

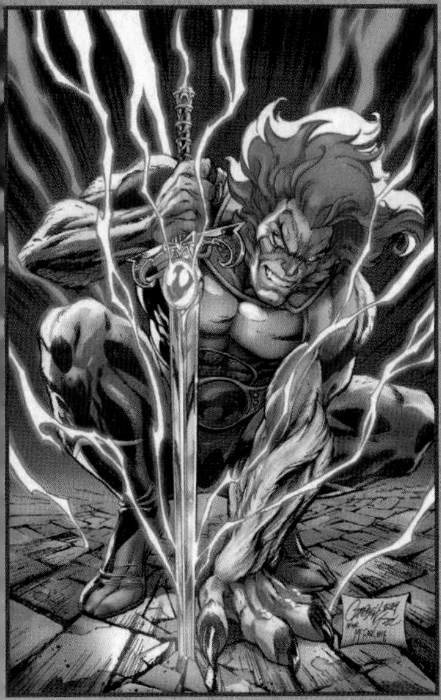

Issue #4 retailer exclusive cover art by J. SCOTT CAMPBELL, jscottcampbell.com

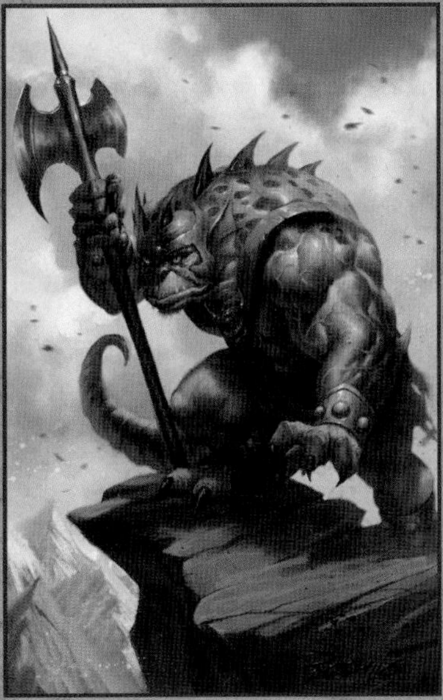

Issue #5 cover art by LUCIO PARRILLO

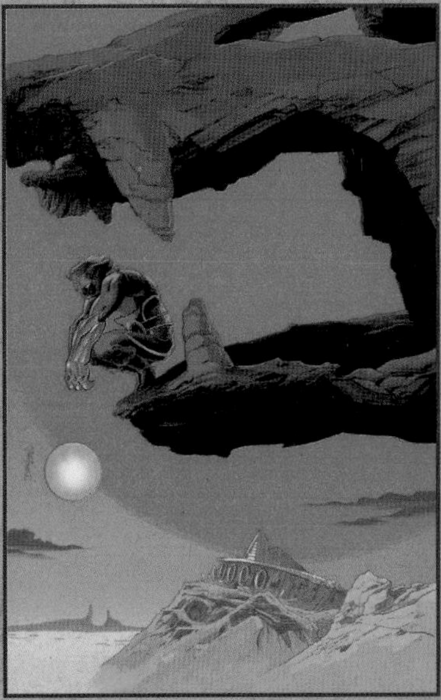

Issue #5 cover art by DECLAN SHALVEY

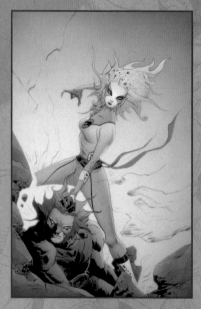

Issue #5 cover art by
JAE LEE & JUNE CHUNG

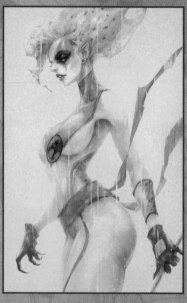

Issue #5 cover art by
IVAN TAO

#5 TEEN
DECLAN SHALVEY | STEPHEN MOONEY
THUNDERCATS
THUNDER-TASTIC ACTION
SECRET LEVER MAKES ARM MOVE!
CHEETARA
GOOD THUNDERCAT
DYNAMITE
FREE

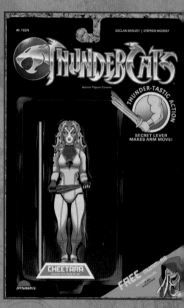

Issue #5 action figure cover
art by DREW MOSS

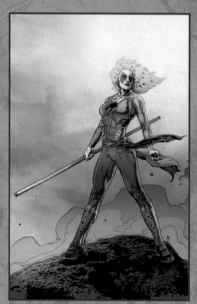

Issue #5 order incentive
cover art by
STEPHEN MOONEY

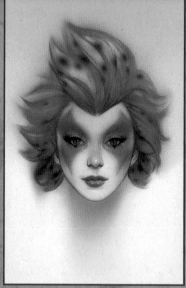

Issue #5 order incentive
cover art by BEN OLIVER

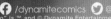

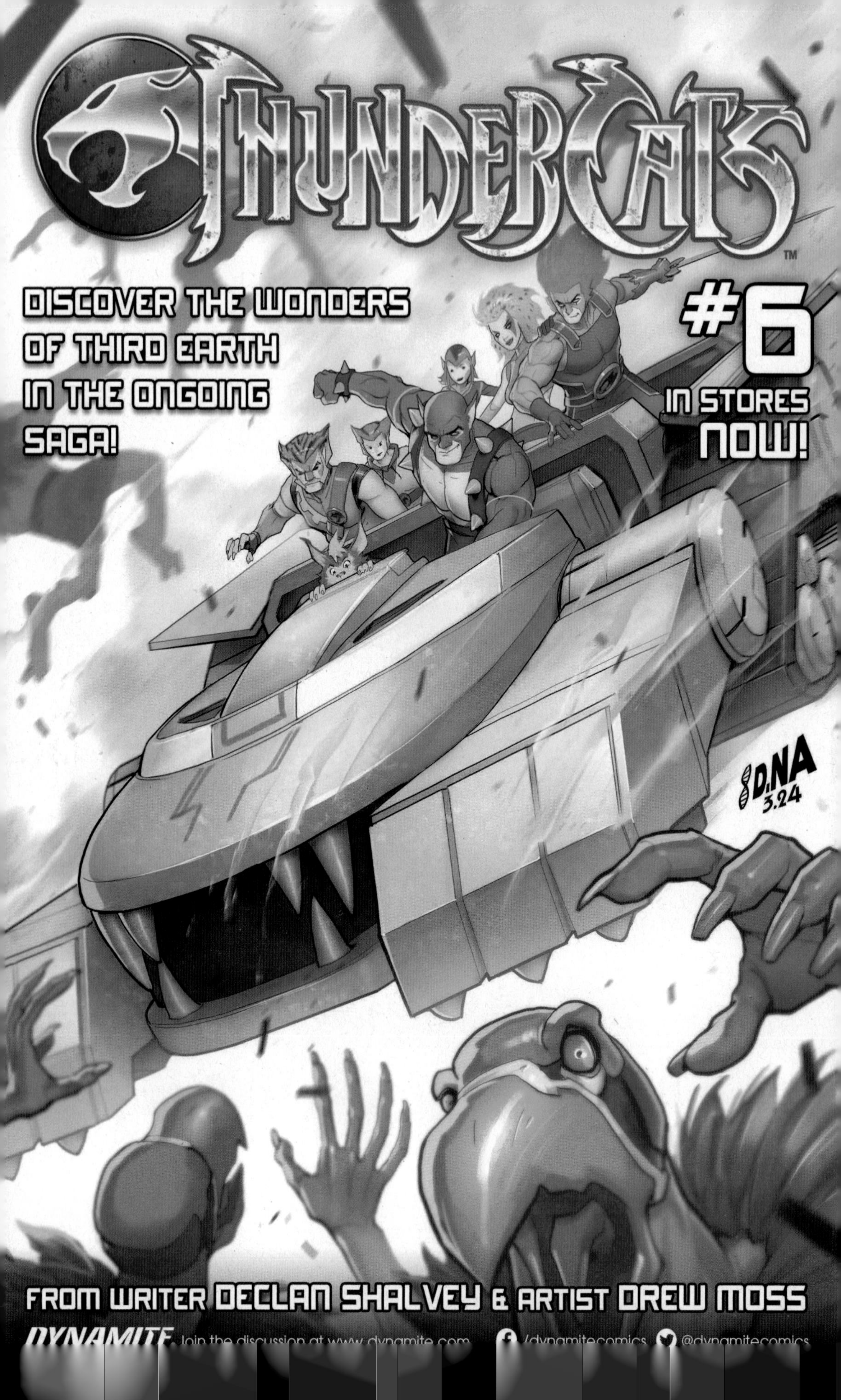
THUNDERCATS™
DISCOVER THE WONDERS OF THIRD EARTH IN THE ONGOING SAGA!
#6
IN STORES NOW!
D.NA 3.24
FROM WRITER DECLAN SHALVEY & ARTIST DREW MOSS
DYNAMITE Join the discussion at www.dynamite.com
/dynamitecomics
@dynamitecomics